Queens

Also by Ellen Freudenheim

Brooklyn! The Ultimate Guide to New York's Most Happening Borough
Looking Forward: An Optimist's Guide to Retirement
Healthspeak: A Complete Dictionary of America's Health Care System
The Executive Bride: A Ten-Week Wedding Planner

Queens

WHAT TO DO, WHERE TO GO
(AND HOW NOT TO GET LOST)
IN NEW YORK'S
UNDISCOVERED BOROUGH

Ellen Freudenheim

St. Martin's Griffin
New York

www.stmartins.com

Design by Phil Mazzone

Library of Congress Cataloging-in-Publication Data

Freudenheim, Ellen.
    Queens : what to do, where to go (and how not to get lost) in New York's undiscovered borough / Ellen Freudenheim.—1st ed.
      p. cm.
    Includes index.
    ISBN-13: 978-0-312-35818-1
    ISBN-10: 0-312-35818-0
    1. Queens (New York, N.Y.)—Guidebooks.   2. New York (N.Y.)—Guidebooks.
I. Title.

F128.68.Q4F74 2006
917.47'2430444—dc22

                                     2006046458

First Edition: November 2006

10 9 8 7 6 5 4 3 2 1

DEDICATED TO DANIEL P. WIENER,
MY LOVE AND LIFE COMPANION,
ON THE OCCASION OF (FINALLY!) TURNING 50
MARCH 7, 2006

Contents

Acknowledgments

I would like to say a special thank-you to many people, but first and foremost to those who took time out of their busy lives to write the short personal essays that flavor this book: Christine Alcalay, Irving Chipkin, Michael Cogswell, Jim Driscoll, Alanna Heiss, Stacy Kim, Max Lance, Morgan Meis, James L. Muyskens, and Stu Nitekman.

Thanks also to many people who shared their perspectives on Queens with me: the Honorable Helen Marshall, Queens Borough President, and Dan Andrews, Seth Bornstein, and Terri Osborne of the Queens Borough President's Office; Nancy Cataldi, Richmond Hill Historical Society; Colby Chamberlain, P.S. 1; Mary Ceruti and Katie Farrell, SculptureCenter; Stanley Cogan, historian; Andreia Davies, Queens Council on the Arts; Noah Dorsky, Dorsky Gallery Curatorial Programs; Jim Driscoll, Queens Historical Society; Tom Finkelpearl, Queens Museum of Art; Tom Gaynor, U.S. Post Office; Mary Howard, NY Designs; Andrew Jackson, Langston Hughes Community Library and Cultural Center; Daniel Karatzas, Jackson Heights historian; Theodore Levin, Dartmouth University; Alison McKay, Bayside Historical Society; Janel Patterson, New York City Economic Development Corp.; Elizabeth Roistacher and John Devereux, Queens College; Hal Rosenbluth and Elaine Ferranti, Kaufman Astoria Studio; Jeffrey Rosenstock, Queens Theater in the Park; Bob Singleton, Greater Astoria Historical Society; Rochelle Slovin, Museum of the Moving Image; Jennifer Ward Souder, Queens Botanical Gardens; David Strauss, Debra Wimpfheimer, and Blagovyesta Momchedjikova, Queens Museum of Art; Carol Sudhalter, musician; Dana Rubenstein and Gina Masullo of New York City Parks and Recreation; Maria Terrone at Queens College, and a bevy of PR and communications staff. The many shopkeepers, restaurateurs, fellow subway riders, and others I spoke briefly with were also very helpful and open, if bemused by the nature of my task. Thank you!

I'm grateful to my cadre of "Queens spies": Lesley Achitoff, Katherine Bendo, Linda Casper, Lauren Chung, Steve Feldheim, Alan B. Goldberg, Susan Gregg, Peter Lerangis, Linda Nasshan, Jordan Novet, Margaret Benczak Porter, Jenna

Sangostiano, Cindy Sherling, Marilyn Schorr, and Josh Weiss. To those who joined me for a meal or trek through Queens, thanks so much.

I'd like to express my appreciation for diligent fact-checking to Aileen Torres, Kristy Davis, and Marlene Naanes, and to Kathleen Kingsbury for fact-checking and reporting. It was fun to swap discoveries with John Roleke, online guide on About.com's Queens site, whose contributions on religious institutions and Jamaica enriched the book. I'd also like to acknowledge Mark Stonehill and my reliable bar spy, Seth Kennedy, for their respective contributions to the manuscript.

Hats off to Tom Mercer and the entire St. Martin's Press team, as well as mapmaker David Lindroth.

I learned a great deal from the Web sites and publications of the Queens Borough President, Queens historical societies, the Queens Chamber of Commerce, local Queens newspapers, along with major dailies and many institutional and neighborhood-specific Web sites, as well as the anecdote-rich www.chowhound .com and http://forgotten-ny.com and, of course, http://queensabout.com (see "Recommended Web Sites").

No doubt I have overlooked some individuals or sources; to those whose names I've omitted because of space constraints (or memory loss), a heartfelt thank-you as well.

Welcome to
Queens

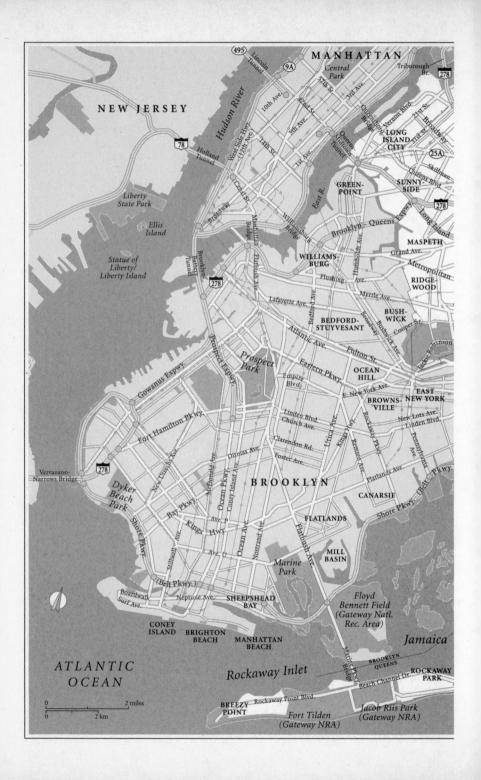

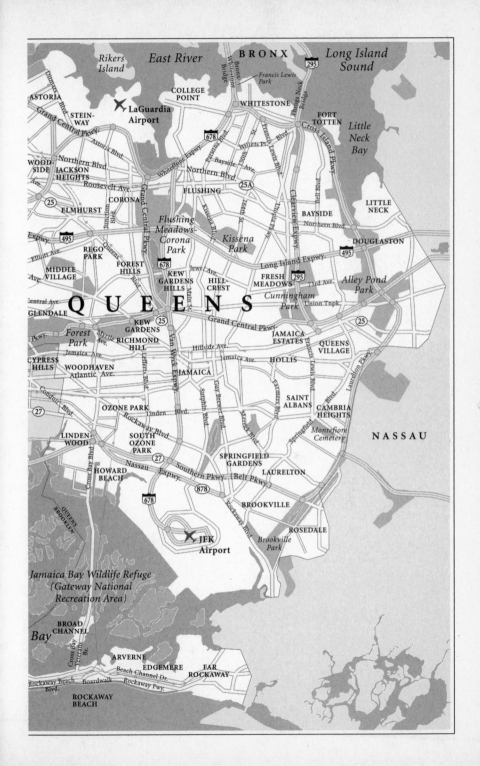

Introduction

QUEENS: ALL THIS . . .

Queens is New York's own terra incognita, a huge uncharted territory right here within our own urban enclave. Experiment for yourself. Ask any Manhattanite whether they ever go to Queens—or even know where it is. Many will vaguely wave a hand eastward. Others will say sure, they go to baseball games at Shea Stadium, or they will describe an urban "adventure" to an ethnic restaurant, usually the Jackson Diner. Business travelers might say that if going to JFK and LaGuardia airports counts, they go to Queens all the time.

Underrated and overlooked for too long, the truth is, there's a ton to see and do in Queens for other New Yorkers and tourists alike. You can find something new every time you go—whether you're poking around the Asian shops in Flushing, tracking down Mae West's drinking haunt in Richmond Hill, biking in Forest Park, or attending performances of Latin dance at the Thalia Theater. One measure of the value of a place as a destination is whether it gets more or less interesting the more you visit; in Queens you can keep peeling layer after layer. Admittedly, it can be frustrating to find your way around (and it's no big secret that everyone does get lost occasionally in Queens, which is why we've included a chapter called "Getting to and Around Queens"). But for people who want to see the real New York, Queens—understated, upside down, and quirky as hell—is a knockout.

Were it to secede from New York City today, Queens would be the fourth-largest city in America. It's a huge place full of interesting neighborhoods. About 120 languages are spoken in Queens; one of the top ten is a language few have even heard of: Tagalog, spoken in the Philippines. Queens officials claim that it is the most ethnically diverse county in the United States. Imagine if the pieces of a giant jigsaw puzzle of the world's cultures were tossed around in a bowl and randomly spilled out in a borough of New York—well, that's Queens.

Visitors can enjoy an amazing array of authentic ethnic food in both restaurants and groceries. It goes without saying that along with the Chinese, Korean,

Thai, Peruvian, Argentinean, Colombian, Romanian, Russian, Polish, and Filipino immigration, among others, there is excellent and cheap Chinese, Korean, Thai, Peruvian, Argentinean, Colombian, Romanian, Russian, Polish, and Filipino food, along with the usual New York standards of Italian, Irish, Jewish-style, and so on. And that's just for appetizers. . . .

There are major cultural institutions here, including several outstanding contemporary art museums, such as P.S. 1 and the Fisher Landau Center, which anchor a very interesting art scene in Long Island City. Queens has more parkland than any other borough, as well as miles of Atlantic Ocean beach and a National Wildlife Refuge in Jamaica Bay. You can drive along the waterfront under the Throgs Neck Bridge and feel light-years away from Manhattan. If you are shopping for unusual gold jewelry, saris, antique chandeliers, or the latest in Latino or Indian music, this is the place to go.

Idiosyncratic, jumbled-up Queens grabs at your heartstrings and even makes you laugh. It's a source of some mirth that there are more dead than living people in Queens. As anyone who's driven here knows, there are miles and miles of graves. More than 3 million souls are buried in about two dozen cemeteries. Graves are woven into the landscape; you see them along the highways, across from schools, and next to a gas station. Whether it's the constant reminder of mortality or some other factor, in general, Queens is a humble, not showy place, a middle- and working-class haven. It's a place where people are just living modest lives. Except, of course (there's always a *but* when generalizing about Queens), that Donald Trump grew up here, too.

It's that essential mixed-up-ness of Queens that's seductive. It's hard to pigeonhole or stereotype the borough. You can't even say, for instance, that "Flushing is an Asian neighborhood" without adding that it's mainly Chinese—both mainland and Taiwanese—but also Korean and Indian, plus some Jewish and Italian, and so on. Astoria has a reputation as a Greek community. It has recently drawn attention for an influx of young professionals and artists (always the canaries in the mine shaft of gentrification). But there are highly rated Italian restaurants there, too, and how about that marvelous little Middle Eastern strip of Steinway Street—with hookah shops, falafel joints, and a café straight out of Cairo? It's not surprising in Astoria that while walking to a Brazilian restaurant you pass a Bangladeshi mosque, a sari shop, and a spice market. Astoria also boasts an old German beer hall and one of the best classic movie theaters and film museums in the country. Sure, you could say Astoria is Greek—and then some. And so it goes in much of Queens.

In the nineteenth century, Queens was considered "the cornfields of New York." It was still largely a rural backwater with farms that helped feed a ravenously growing New York City. (Queens, like Brooklyn, joined up to create New York City as we know it in 1898.) As transportation from Manhattan became available—first trains, then in 1909 the Queensboro Bridge, and then more

subways—Queens' open spaces served as fodder for the dreams of utopian vi-
sionaries, urban planners, and entrepreneurial developers seeking to house the
city's burgeoning population. Queens residents still identify themselves not with
the larger municipal entity of the borough, but with their neighborhood, say
Forest Hills, Astoria, or Neponsit. (If you send a letter to someone in Queens, the
address lists the town name and zip code, as though it were some independent
village in Rockland County, not a part of the city.) It is one of many such Queens
ironies that plunked down in the middle of this small-townishness are two big
airports, one of which is the nation's largest international jet portal to the world:
JFK. Surprisingly, the borough is replete with experimental housing developments, some of which, like Tudor-besotted Kew Gardens and Forest Hills, are famous "garden communities in the city." Sunnyside Gardens, too, was built with
huge communal garden spaces as an alternative to cramped Manhattan apartments; Perry Como and Judy Holliday lived here. On the other side of the spectrum, the 1960s brought megadevelopment in the form of Lefrak City, billed as
"the largest apartment house in the world," and the low-income Queensbridge
Houses, where rough conditions gave rise to more than one hip-hop star. These
developments offer a kaleidoscopic historical view of ways to create community,
or at least affordable housing, in the megalopolis.

The past is present here in a way that will endear Queens to hobbyist (and
professional) historians. You can make a short foray to visit several historic
houses, including a Revolutionary War–era farmhouse on New York City's only
remaining working farm and museum, where children can harvest pumpkins in
the autumn. Rising from the flat parkland near LaGuardia Airport are vestiges of
the old world's fairs of the mid-twentieth century. Up close, the Unisphere (that
enormous metallic globe we've all seen from Grand Central Parkway en route to
LaGuardia or JFK airports) is eerily beautiful, an unsubtle reminder that we're
all in this world together. A stone's throw away from Shea Stadium is the world's
largest scale model, a 9,000-square-foot minicity of New York circa 1965, called
the Panorama. In a little museum near Rockaway Beach, you can see shards
from old Hog Island, a party place of the Tammany Hall set that was washed
away by a hurricane a century ago—and more.

A brief listing of famous Queens residents gives some hint of the borough's
creative and intellectual heft. Historically, Queens has been home to Ella Fitzgerald and Louis Armstrong, Jack Kerouac and Jimmy Breslin, Mae West and the
Marx Brothers, Helen Keller and Malcolm X, and Nobel Peace Prize recipient
Ralph Bunche. It's where Jerry Seinfeld, Donald Trump, and rap artists 50 Cent
and LL Cool J grew up. It's also where fictional characters Spiderman and Archie
Bunker lived.

Architecture buffs will find in Queens a rich smorgasbord of styles, from
beach bungalows in the Rockaways to factories adapted for reuse in Long Island
City. There's also an amazing amount of neo-Tudor architecture in Queens. The

borough has an extraordinary number of early-twentieth-century homes and institutional buildings, Tudor and otherwise, that would be considered landmarks were they located in Manhattan. Like some living urban archaeological site, there are layers and accretions in Queen. It's typical that at Kennedy Airport, JetBlue is building a big state-of-the-art terminal just about on top of the Terminal 5 TWA Flight Center, which is on the National Register of Historic Places. And the beat goes on today in the era of the so-called McMansion as older buildings (some historic) are torn down by newcomers who want bigger, brassier homes. The visual juxtapositions in the borough are so pervasive it seems fitting that artist Joseph Cornell, a surrealist collage artist who was a peer of Salvador Dalí, lived and worked in Queens.

Queens is on the upswing, but not in an all-shiny-and-new or corporate way. In Long Island City, old industrial buildings have been renovated into museums and art studios. A junk heap has been recycled into an award-winning waterfront sculpture park. A vast old public school building has become the internationally acclaimed P.S. 1 Contemporary Art Center. In Jamaica, a Pentecostal congregation uses an extravagant art deco theater as a church.

Queens is rich in opportunities for visitors and has good ethnic food, interesting history, art, and architecture. What more could a day tripper want?

AND THEN SOME . . .

In most guidebooks, this would be the end of the introduction, but Queens has something else special: Internationalism. Fully half of Queens residents were not born in the United States. The foreign-born men and women who flocked here (sometimes following family, friends, or faith communities) after the liberalization of U.S. immigration laws in 1965 have transformed entire neighborhoods. For example, Flushing was an Italian and Jewish neighborhood that went into decline in the post–World War II years. Today it's thriving as an Asian community, and the City of New York is pouring money into new buildings and parks.

Did you know that simply by hopping on a subway, you can go around the world? The #7 subway has been called the International Express, a national historic trail, because at every stop along its Queens route you land at another ethnic community as the train squeaks and screams its way along a rickety overhead track.

Making a living and surviving in a culture that speaks only English when you speak Chinese or Korean or Spanish isn't always easy, not to mention keeping one's home culture alive. Some immigrants work hours the average American would consider way too long, for far too little pay. It's a Darwinian myth that all immigrants are the "best and the brightest" who pull themselves up by their bootstraps in cheerful pursuit of the American dream; there's plenty of heartbreak, cross-cultural tension, and dysfunction, too. While personal dramas play out on an individual level, on a broader level the diverse foreign cultures here are kept alive through a borough-wide flowering of cultural institutions—language and music schools, cultural centers, and religious institutions such as mosques, Hindu and Buddhist temples—and in cultural celebrations such as the Pagbah Parade, Diwali festival, or Dragon Boat Festival in Flushing Meadows–Corona Park. Widespread immigration has brought world culture to the borough in a vibrant, tangible way.

The United Nations first convened in 1948 in that same Flushing Meadows–Corona Park in what today is the Queens Museum of Art while its headquarters building was under construction in Manhattan. Many things happened during the UN's brief outer-borough stint, including the divisions of Palestine and Korea. During those early years in Queens, the UN also adopted the UNESCO Universal Declaration on Cultural Diversity, which states:

> Cultural heritage in all its forms must be
> preserved, enhanced, and handed on to future
> generations as a record of human experience and
> aspirations, so as to foster creativity in all its
> diversity and to inspire genuine dialogue among cultures.

In a curious twist of history—for who knew then that a half century later Queens itself would become home to immigrants from all over the world?—that declaration seems to address both the richness and the challenges of contemporary Queens.

Queens has risen to the challenge of internationalism and embraced the newcomers. The Queens Public Library system is stocked with books in every language, and runs creative cultural programs. In Flushing Meadows–Corona Park you can see Latino immigrants playing soccer, Indian and Pakistani families out for a stroll, and cricket being played by South Asian and Caribbean men wearing proper whites, as though this were the British empire. Thousands show up for cultural festivals where Latin TV stars crack jokes and the music is from Buenos Aires. At Queens Theater in the Park, immigrant playwrights give voice to the ups and downs of the contemporary "melting pot" experience. The Queens Museum of Art mounts exhibits that open up the immigrant experience to the larger world, illuminating the richness of the cultures that foreign-born artists reflect. The director of that museum, musing on the remarkable lack of violent intercultural clashes in Queens, suggests that widespread diversity dilutes tension, that perhaps more diversity diminishes possible clashes of culture. Perhaps when so many cultures are present, the only logical way to survive is through tolerance. There are lessons to be learned from the Queens experience.

In a world that's globalizing faster than most of us can grasp, Queens is a living laboratory of internationalization. Beyond a tasty ethnic meal or art museum, historic site or Atlantic Ocean beach, Queens is also a place where you can get a glimpse of what a more diverse, internationalized, multilingual America may look like in the decades to come. If you want to see the face of globalization, you don't need a round-the-world airline ticket. You can see it for a two-dollar subway fare to Queens.

IS QUEENS "THE NEXT BROOKLYN"?

The buzz over the New York grapevine is that Queens is the "next Brooklyn," meaning that it is poised to undergo the same extraordinary gentrification that in the past decade has attracted young professionals and artists, boutiques and cafés that have transformed whole swaths of that other outer borough: Brooklyn. As the author of three editions of a popular guidebook to Brooklyn, I took a particular interest in this question.

Indeed, Queens has the three magic ingredients essential for greater visibility and the popularity that spark gentrification: good transportation, affordable housing, and urban livability. Queens boasts fast public transportation—less than 30 minutes from midtown Manhattan to neighborhoods such as Jackson Heights, Astoria, Long Island City, Sunnyside, and Woodside. Queens has a spectrum of housing options, too. It's true that Long Island City is being marketed as "Manhattan East" and half-million-dollar apartments are rising on its East River banks. However, Queens also has many interesting neighborhoods with affordable housing. On the livability front, Queens boasts great recreation and cultural life, including first-rate museums and parks, live music, movies, marinas, three public golf courses, horseback riding, circuses, outdoor performances of Shakespeare in the summer, not to mention Shea Stadium and the USTA Billie Jean King National Tennis Center.

And hey, it's closer to the Hamptons.

Like Brooklyn of the 1990s, the image of Queens today is on the uptick. If much of Queens still seems a quaint backwater—ethnically interesting, yet curiously undiscovered—well, it's just how Brooklyn looked, too, way back when.

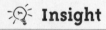 **Insight**

Why Is Queens Called Queens? Or, the Saga of the Queen Catherine of Braganza Statue

Why is Queens called Queens, anyway? For years, logically enough, people assumed that the borough was named after Queen Catherine of Braganza, the Portuguese-born bride of that fellow, King Charles of England, after whom Brooklyn

(Kings County) was named. In 1988 plans were made to celebrate the borough by erecting a sculpture of Queen Catherine at a prominent site in Astoria. A competition was announced, an artist chosen, work begun, but just before the completed thirty-five-foot statue was to be put in place, a royal brouhaha erupted over the queen. Some local historians asserted that there was no proof positive that "Queens" referred to that particular queen, noting that Catherine was unpopular in her day and, anyway, hadn't appeared in historical records until about two hundred years after her death. African-American leaders noted that Catherine had been involved in the slave trade. Irish residents had a beef with the idea of paying homage to a British queen (even if she was Portuguese), and so on. After much public airing of such laundry—to the glee of local newspapers—the Queen Catherine of Braganza statue was quietly exiled to upstate New York. Ever since, nobody's 100 percent sure why Queens is called Queens.

How to Use This Book

Chances are, you don't know much about Queens, even if you live there. Not many people do! There are several ways to get familiar with this fabulous place by using this guide.

You can read through the neighborhood chapters, which are organized alphabetically by neighborhood, see what interests you, and go exploring.

We've listed recommended itineraries and tours for all kinds of people, from nature enthusiasts to ethnic food fans to jazz buffs. (See pp. 299–302.)

Next time you find yourself going to JFK or LaGuardia Airport, build in a little extra time to explore one of the neighborhoods nearby (see "The Airports," p. 288).

Go to what's nearest and best known: Jackson Heights, Astoria, and Long Island City, to get your feet wet. Speaking of which, don't overlook the beach at the Rockaways!

Lastly, use the "Where to Find It" index at the back of the book to pinpoint what ethnic cuisine, cultural or historical site, or entertainment you're interested in. Then consider the surrounding neighborhood yours to explore. (See p. 305.)

WHAT'S INCLUDED IN THIS BOOK (AND WHAT'S NOT)

Queens is a huge, dynamic place—alas, we couldn't cover every neighborhood and every deli or landmark. We tried to include the most popular, most interesting, and most accessible sites and neighborhoods that hold something of interest to both curious New Yorkers and tourists.

Each listing had to meet one of the following criteria: be a point of cultural, culinary, retail, or ethnic interest; have some relationship to an interesting historical or cultural perspective; and seem likely to continue to be in existence for some time to come. Omitted were membership organizations, clubs, courses, schools, gyms, most movie theaters and religious institutions (unless there was a specific reason for their inclusion), and national franchises and chains, all of which you can find in a phone book. We've included several malls, but not many specific brand-name stores. Instead of listing every neighborhood restaurant, we listed a few good ones and hope that readers will explore others.

We also included some tips on how to make getting to and around Queens as easy as possible.

PHONE NUMBERS AND INTERNET URLS

Queens uses the 718 area code, as does Brooklyn, Staten Island, and the Bronx. Dial 1-718 before every telephone number listed in this book unless otherwise indicated. There's free Internet access in every New York City and Queens public library. There is also fee-based Internet access in many commercial stores throughout Queens.

APOLOGIES IN ADVANCE!

In trying to fit a big borough into a small book, we've run roughshod on some neighborhood boundaries, ignored whole residential communities, and lumped things together in ways that local residents might find odd. Our apologies if this causes confusion or upset. Also, while every effort has been made to ensure accuracy, in a work of this size there are bound to be errors, for which we also apologize (and hope to correct in future editions).

KEY TO SYMBOLS

☀ Insight—extra information of interest
🚶 self-guided walks you can take
🏷 actionable tips on how to get around or get a better bargain
✍ a short written piece contributed by someone who lives in or loves Queens
🏛 an official landmark either of the New York City Landmark Commission or listed on the National Register of Historic Places
☺ means a place is good for kids (only sites and parks, no restaurants included)

Eight Good Reasons to Go to Queens

1. Food, food, and more food! You can eat your way through world cuisine. Take your pick: Italian, Indian, Armenian, Greek, Colombian, Peruvian, Cuban, Argentinean, Egyptian, Korean, Chinese, and more.

2. Queens is closer than you think: The subway ride from midtown Manhattan to Long Island City takes less than five minutes. You can get to Forest Hills in sixteen minutes on the Long Island Railroad (LIRR). It's easy to get there.

3. Sports: Visit Shea Stadium and the USTA Billie Jean King National Tennis Center, or watch cricket, bike in the city's largest oak forest, and ride the surf.

4. Art and music: You can't beat P.S. 1 for innovative, international contemporary art. The Museum of the Moving Image rivals the Rock and Roll Hall of Fame for fun. You can learn about the history of hip-hop or take the Jazz Tour to see where Dizzie Gillespie and Louis Armstrong lived.

5. Sand and surf: The Rockaway beaches are spectacular. Period.

6. World culture: Queens is the most diverse county in America. Visit Little India and shop for saris and Indian condiments, hear Bukharan music in a Rego Park restaurant, or attend the Latin Festival.

7. History, architecture, and urban planning: There are dozens of destinations ranging from colonial-era sites to historic Bowne House to the WPA-era Astoria Pool to the garden community of Forest Hills Gardens to adaptive reuse of old warehouses in Long Island City.

8. You're going to be there anyway, so why not take advantage? When you arrive home from LaGuardia, stop in Jackson Heights for a meal. When you're headed to the Mets game, come and visit the Panorama at the Queens Museum of Art.

Queens Highlights

Something for Everyone

Queens has something for just about every kind of tourist or visitor, whether you're interested in food, art, or nature. Here are a dozen best bets, depending on your interests.

THE INTERNATIONAL TRAVELER

The #7 subway line is an official National Historic Trail! It's called "The International Express." The first stop: Long Island City, which has museums. Second stop: Sunnyside, where you can visit Korean or Turkish restaurants, and historic Sunnyside Gardens. Third stop: Woodside, where you can visit Divya Dam, a Hindu temple, or drink in an Irish pub. A few stops later, at 74th St., there's "Little India," with wonderful food and shops, menhdi tattoo salons, and also a large Latino community where you can find a fresh empanada or guava drink on every corner. A few stops farther at Junction Boulevard there's discount shopping galore. The last stop on the #7 is Flushing, a pan-Asian community, and nearby are Shea Stadium, the Queens Botanical Gardens, and more.

THE ART AFICIONADO

In Long Island City you can see world-class museums such as the Noguchi Museum and P.S. 1, the edgy affiliate of the Museum of Modern Art that helps define what's really "modern" today. See cutting-edge art at the SculptureCenter. Go on an art studio tour, see the huge, graffiti-covered building called 5 Pointz, and stop at the Fisher Landau Center for Art nearby.

HISTORY AND ARCHITECTURE BUFFS

If you love history or architecture, come to Queens for three days, not three hours. You can see the world's biggest scale model, called the Panorama of the City of New York. Take self-guided walking tours of historic garden communities of Sunnyside Gardens, Jackson Heights, and Forest Hills Gardens, all influenced by the British Garden Suburbs movement. See how nineteenth-century industrial buildings in Long Island City are being adapted for reuse in the new information economy as museums and art studios. Take a trip down memory lane at Flushing Meadows–Corona Park to see old World's Fair structures, including a huge globe and an original Buckminster Fuller geodesic dome.

Learn about an important stand taken for religious tolerance in the colonial-era Bowne House and Quaker Meeting House in Flushing. Visit King Manor, a colonial farmhouse in Jamaica. Also, take a guided tour of the historic Steinway Piano Factory.

THE JAZZ OR HIP-HOP MUSIC FAN

Many jazz musicians, from Ella Fitzgerald to Count Basie, lived in middle-class black neighborhoods such as Addesleigh Park and Hollis. Take the once-monthly, five-hour Jazz Tour and listen to some wonderful jazz concerts at Flushing Town Hall. Once a year, join the funky outdoor tribute at the Bix Beiderbecke Memorial. Hip-hop fans can learn how Marlon "Marley Marl," MC Shan, Roxanne Shanté, Nas, Mobb Deep, and Capone-N-Noreaga and many others got their start in Queens—and then shop for "bling" at the mall in Jamaica.

NOSHERS, NIBBLERS, AND ETHNIC FOOD FANS

Don't eat for about a month before embarking to Queens! If you want Middle Eastern or Greek, head to Astoria; for Mexican, Peruvian, Argentinean, or Indian food, make a beeline to Jackson Heights. Thai food lovers must make the pilgrimage to Sriprihani in Woodside. If it's East Asian food you like, take your pick of Korean, several kinds of Chinese, and various other fusion menus in Flushing. There are marvelous Italian restaurants and takeout delis, too, such as Trattoria l'Incontro and Mama's Latticeria. For Irish pubs, go to Woodside; for ethnic Russian nightclubs, check out Rego Park.

THE NATURE ENTHUSIAST

Spend a half day in Forest Park walking in the woods, or rent a horse and ride the trails. Bring your binoculars and enjoy the birds at Jamaica Bay National Park or nearby wildlife preserves. Book a boat tour of Jamaica Bay, or visit the

Queens County Farm Museum, the last working farm in the City of New York. Book a canoe with the LIC Community Boathouse for a boat ride with Manhattan skyline views you'll never forget. Environmentalists might want to visit the Queens Botanical Garden's new high-tech visitor center to see state-of-the-art environmentally green technologies.

THE SPORTS FAN

Tee off for a reasonable fee at Forest Park, Clearview Park, and Kissena Park public golf courses. Cyclist fans will enjoy watching the races at the Velodrome. You can rent Jet Skis and motorboats at the Bayside Marina. At Astoria Park, you can jog along the Queens waterfront and then do a few laps at the Olympic-sized Astoria Pool. If you like to watch sports, not do them, there's the world-class tennis facility at the Arthur Ashe Stadium at the USTA Billie Jean King National Tennis Center, where the U.S. Open tennis matches are held. Mets fans already know how, for sure, to get to Shea Stadium, soon to be rebuilt.

THE BEACH BUM

Stake out your spot on the beach at marvelous Riis Park. Explore Fort Tilden nearby, and if you're in the mood, go fishing there. Ride a curl or watch the surfers at the Surfers Beach. Walk along the boardwalk in Rockaway Park, then go to Plum Tomato for delicious fresh pizza.

THE FRUSTRATED AIR TRAVELER

For travelers stuck with long layovers at JFK or LaGuardia airports, there're tons of options for fun, relief from the airport, and exploring—without the hassle of going into Manhattan. We've included an entire chapter listing nearly fifty places to go and things to do between flights.

THE REAL ESTATE TREND SPOTTER

Visit the up-and-coming trendy neighborhoods of Jackson Heights, Astoria, Sunnyside, and Long Island City—and don't miss a trip to Ridgewood, either.

THE CEMETERY HAUNT

There are tons of famous people buried in Queens, including more than a dozen former New York City mayors, congressmen, and famous movie stars. After all, Queens is Cemetery Central in New York City. It's the borough where more people are dead than alive.

THE ROMANTIC

Kidnap your date for an adventure to Queens! You don't have to go farther than right across the East River, to Long Island City. Hop on the New York Water Taxi in Manhattan and have a picnic at the waterside Gantry Plaza State Park or Socrates Sculpture Park. Dine at French bistro Tournesol, just one subway stop from Bloomingdale's. Farther afield, you can take the LIRR to Bayside for a walk around Fort Totten and eat at a restaurant on the site of silent-film heartthrob Rudy Valentino's home. Or take the #7 subway to the end of the line, book a hotel room in Flushing, and enjoy a flightless trip to Asia.

5

Getting to and Around Queens

(Without Getting Too Lost)

Q ueens is incredibly accessible. You can get here by airplane, car, subway, Long Island Railroad, bus, or water taxi—by almost any means other than by camel. A driver's dream, it is crisscrossed by four major highways and a spiderweb of other multilane thoroughfares.

Getting to Queens by public transportation is as easy as getting on a subway or bus. From Manhattan, it is about five minutes and just one stop from Grand Central on the #7 to Long Island City. It takes twenty minutes to get from Penn Station to Forest Hills on the Long Island Railroad, and twenty minutes to get to Jackson Heights from midtown Manhattan by subway.

☼ Insight

Traveler's Advisory: Everybody Gets Lost in Queens

E ven people who live here get lost. As in Venice or the old parts of London, some streets start and stop, change names, curve around parks, go one way, and generally follow an illogic of their own. In places, Queens seems to have been laid out (or not) by a madman. However, there is at least some method to the madness. Queens evolved from farmland and villages, some dating back to the 1700s. It was only in the 1920s that a borough-wide street grid was imposed. Therefore, occasionally street numbers don't follow logically whatsoever, jumping capriciously, for instance, from 25th Ave. to 28th Ave. When that happens, or when you find terraces, drives, crescents, and roads in between streets all sporting the same name, do try to be understanding. These extra names were created, presumably, when the grid maker got in a pickle trying to square everything off neatly. Rest assured that when you find yourself at the intersection of 47th Street and 47th Avenue, uncertain which way to go, you will not be the first person standing there to mutter, "What the . . ." under your breath.

(continued)

This chapter offers basic information on getting to and around Queens. The best overall advice is this: Give yourself a little extra time and be patient. As with any learning curve, finding your way around Queens gets easier with practice. After a few visits, Queens actually begins to make sense. Is it worth the effort? Yes.

QUEENS SURVIVAL KIT

You don't need to pack C rations or grappling hooks when planning to visit Queens. After all, in population terms it is the fourth-largest urban center in the United States. So it's easy to find food, gasoline, ATMs, public transportation, public libraries with bathrooms, and Internet cafés here, and most people do speak English or some English. Still, a Queens Survival Kit is a good idea.

In addition to this book (of course!) your Queens Survival Kit might include: 1. a subway map; 2. a Queens map if you are driving or plan to explore by foot; 3. the addresses you're going to (because it's easy to forget whether your friend lives on 47th Ave. or 47th St.); 4. directions for getting from one neighborhood to another; and 5. a mobile phone because it's hard to find a working pay phone anywhere in New York. A compass wouldn't hurt, and a personal GPS system strapped to one's waist would be heavenly.

> ☛ **TIP: How to Get Good Directions.** Queens institutions such as museums or sports stadiums provide detailed directions on their Web sites (which are included in this book). The directions are usually tailored for people coming from Manhattan, Long Island, or Westchester (and sometimes from Brooklyn).
>
> If you want to visit more than one destination in Queens, however, you are on your own. For public transportation directions, we recommend www .hopstop.com or www.trips123.com. Unlike Manhattan, there is not a subway in or near every neighborhood in Queens, so be prepared to take a bus or car service. (Car services are listed in neighborhood chapters and also in the subject index, "Where to Find It," p. 305.)
>
> Note that some on-line map Web sites require that when searching for a location in Queens, the name of the neighborhood must be included, as if it were an independent town or city. That is, you must type "Jackson Heights, NY" after the street address, instead of "Queens, NY" or "NY, NY." If you don't know what neighborhood something is in, use the alphabetical index at the back of this book, or a service such as www.switchboard.com to find the neighborhood. Also, sometimes the map services require that you remove the hyphen in the street address. For instance "34-16 Broadway" becomes "3416 Broadway."

GETTING TO QUEENS FROM KENNEDY AND LAGUARDIA AIRPORTS

Mission accomplished. Queens is where you arrive when you land at either LaGuardia or Kennedy Airports. For places to visit, eat, and relax near the airports, and how to get there, see Chapter 19, "The Airports: JFK and LaGuardia."

GETTING TO QUEENS FROM MANHATTAN

You can get to Queens from Manhattan almost by closing your eyes, clicking your heels, and saying, "outer borough." You can get to Queens via the New York City subway, the Long Island Railroad (LIRR), and public local or express bus.

> ☛ **TIP: About New York City Mass Transit.** New York City Mass Transit runs the New York City subways and buses in all boroughs. Information on schedules, fares, and specials is available on-line at www.mta.info, at 330-1234, or by calling 311, New York's all-service information line. A single fare is $2 for adults, but various bargains can be obtained by buying multiple rides. One MetroCard fare entitles a rider to a subway or bus ride, plus one subway-to-bus, bus-to-subway, or bus-to-bus transfer free within two hours of the first ride. If you expect to explore three or more neighborhoods and get home by subway, it might pay to buy a 1-Day Fun Pass for $7, allowing unlimited rides on subways and buses. Out-of-town tourists should check out various multiday Metrocards; see www.mta.info. Note that all large packages and backpacks are subject to random police search by New York City transit police.

By Subway

The following subways run to Queens: the #7, A, C, E, F, G, J, L, R, M, V, and Z. Travel time from Manhattan can be as short as five minutes to Long Island City, or an hour or more to the beaches of Rockaway. Some subway stops in Manhattan at which you can catch a Queens-bound subway are 53rd St. and Lexington Ave. (E and V subways), 59th St. and Lexington Ave. (N, R, and W subways), 63rd and Lexington Ave. (F subway), and Grand Central (#7 subway).

If you plan on taking the subway on weekends, check the on-line MTA Service Advisory Postings for any changes in schedules before leaving home or call 330-1234.

☼ Insight

The #7 Subway Line = The International Express

The #7 subway line is called the International Express because it transverses so many ethnic neighborhoods. It's an easy, fun way to see different aspects of Queens, have a nibble of different ethnic foods, and see globalization up close. The #7 subway line was designated a National Historic Trail by the White House Millennium Council, the U.S. Department of Transportation, and the Rails-to-Trails Conservancy because it is representative of the American immigrant experience.

☞ **TIP:** Some of the stations along the #7 seem to have two names, such as 33rd St. (Rawston St.) or 46th St. (Bliss St.). That's a bit of nostalgia dating to the pre-grid system. Once upon a time, 33rd St. was called Rawston St. and 46th St. was called Bliss St. Don't look for these street names as they no longer exist aboveground, except in the names of the subway stops.

By Bus

Local and express buses that travel a Manhattan-Queens route are generally used by commuters but offer a transit option for tourists and visitors, too. For instance, the local Q101 runs from 2nd Ave. and E. 59th St. in Manhattan to Astoria, Queens; if you leave on Saturday at 10:00 a.m., you are scheduled to arrive in Astoria thirty-five minutes later, for the price of one MetroCard ride, or $2.

Express buses in Queens take commuters to areas where there's inadequate subway service. The QM2 express buses go to Bayside, for instance, where there's an LIRR stop but no subway. An express bus ride costs about $5 each way. Some express buses may run only on weekdays.

Any bus marked "QM" is an express that runs between Queens and Manhattan; buses marked "Q" mostly run only in Queens, although a few, like the Q101, is a local Queens bus that also goes to Manhattan. In 2005, all independent bus companies operating in Queens were taken over by the New York City transit system; call or check the MTA Web site for new schedules.

By Long Island Railroad (LIRR)

It can take just fifteen minutes from Pennsylvania Station to arrive in Queens. There are several different lines and more than a dozen Long Island Railroad stops in Queens. Most LIRR (not Amtrak) trains from Penn Station stop in Queens at LIRR stations in Woodside, Forest Hills, Kew Gardens, and Jamaica. There's less frequent service to Flushing, Murray Hill (Flushing), Auburndale, Bayside, Douglaston, Little Neck, Bellerose, Hollis, Floral Park, and St. Albans. The LIRR runs directly to Jamaica, where you can change for the AirTrain to JFK Airport.

Rail fares are distance-based. Buy your train tickets on-line or from a ticket machine at a LIRR station in advance; if you buy it on the train it costs almost double. Family fares during off-peak hours allow up to four children age five to eleven years old to ride for just 75 cents each when accompanied by a fare-paying adult. On weekends, the City Ticket for travel within the city (but not valid at Shea Stadium, Belmont, and Far Rockaway) must be purchased before you board the train, but costs only $3. To take a bicycle on the LIRR you need a $5 permit, which can be bought on the train or at a ticket window at any LIRR station. 558-8228, www.mta.info.

By Car
Coming from Manhattan, Queens is right across the East River, accessible via the Queensboro Bridge, Queens Midtown Tunnel, or the Triborough Bridge.

By Water Taxi (summer only)
You can take New York Water Taxi to Long Island City from Manhattan's 34th St. or Wall St. piers. (See p. 203 for details.)

By Foot or Bike from Brooklyn or Manhattan
You can walk to Queens across the Pulaski Bridge from Greenpoint, Brooklyn, or bike or walk across the Queensboro Bridge or Triborough Bridge from Manhattan.

GETTING TO QUEENS DIRECTLY FROM BROOKLYN
Queens and Brooklyn are connected at the proverbial hip. After all, the two boroughs are part of the same landmass and only divided for a short distance by a polluted spit of water called Newtown Creek.

By Public Transportation from Brooklyn
See Tip box, p. 21.

By Subway
Several subways connect Brooklyn and Queens directly without going via Manhattan (though the ride might not be especially fast). For example, the G train originates at Smith–9th Sts. in Carroll Gardens, Brooklyn, and runs through Fort Greene and Greenpoint, Brooklyn, to Long Island City in Queens, taking twenty-five minutes or less. The L train connects Williamsburg, Brooklyn, at Bedford Ave. to the Myrtle/Wyckoff Ave. stop in Ridgewood, Queens. The J train runs from Williamsburg to the Ozone Park area and eventually to Jamaica, Queens, and the M also goes from Williamsburg through Ridgewood to Middle Village. The A trains from various downtown Brooklyn stations run to Ozone

Park (where you can catch a Q10 bus to JFK Airport), Aqueduct Racetrack, and also to Howard Beach. There is regular but relatively infrequent A train service to Broad Channel, Jamaica Bay Wildlife Refuge, and the public Rockaway Park Beach at 116th St.

By LIRR

The Long Island Railroad line departing Brooklyn from Atlantic Avenue and Flatbush Ave. goes to Jamaica, Queens, and costs about $4 (you also can transfer to the AirTrain to JFK there). The LIRR that stops in Brooklyn does not go to Jackson Heights, Flushing, Bayside, or Douglaston. Except for destinations in and near Jamaica, going by subway via Manhattan may be cheaper and faster.

By Car

Obviously you can drive from Brooklyn to Queens via the Brooklyn-Queens Expressway (BQE). The Jackie Robinson Parkway is frequently a less hectic route that often does not show up on on-line map services.

By Water Taxi (summer only)

The New York Water Taxi runs from Fulton Ferry landing in DUMBO, Brooklyn, to Long Island City, Queens. (See p. 203.)

GETTING AROUND QUEENS (WITHOUT GETTING LOST)

On Foot or by Bike

Once you arrive in a given neighborhood in Queens, there are adjacent neighborhoods that you might want to explore. For instance, it's easy to visit both Astoria and Long Island City, or Sunnyside and Woodside. See each neighborhood chapter under the heading "What's Nearby."

Cyclists can follow bike trails in Forest Park, Kissena Park, and Flushing Meadows–Corona Park, or in Jamaica Bay, or travel the Rockaways or the Brooklyn-Queens Greenway. There's a lot of car traffic in Queens; cyclists are urged to be cautious when riding on city streets. For information on cycling, contact Transportation Alternatives, www.transalt.org.

By Subway and Bus

Stations where many subway lines intersect are Queens Plaza, Jackson Heights/Roosevelt Ave., Sutphin Blvd., and Jamaica. Don't overlook local bus service. For example, on the local Q66 bus, a trip from Flushing, Main St., to Long Island City takes about forty minutes (the buses run every twenty minutes during nonrush hours). The New York City subway map shows what buses you can pick up at subway stops.

By Cab or Car Service

Because Queens is an outer borough, you are more likely to end up in a livery car service, also known as "car service" or "radio cab," than to find a classic New York City yellow cab cruising the streets—despite the fact that many taxi drivers live in Queens. Car services are licensed by the Taxi and Limousine Service, and prices are set by a dispatcher instead of registering on a meter. The dispatcher should give you the price on the phone, or you can ask when you enter the cab. Expect to wait at least ten minutes for a car service. Car services are listed in neighborhood chapters and in "Subject Index: Where to Find It," p. 305.

☛ **TIP: Tips on Decoding Queens: Those Hyphenated Street Numbers.** What gives with street numbers like, say, 40-17 28th Ave.? In Queens, most addresses have a three- or four-digit number followed by a street or avenue name. (Sometimes the numbers are hyphenated, such as 40-17, and sometimes they are not.) The first two digits usually (but not always) refer to the cross street or avenue. The second digits refer to the number of the house or building on a given street. For example, 4017 28th Ave. is the same as 40-17 28th Ave. Glancing at the address, you know that you are going to 28th Ave. between 40th and 41st Streets, and that your destination is house 17 on the block. That said, it's Queens, so there are exceptions to every rule.

Decoding a Street Address in Queens
There *is* a system:

Address	Where it is	Between	House #
40-17 48th Ave.	48th Ave.	40-41 Sts.	17
40-12 Bell Blvd.	Bell Blvd.	40-41st Aves.	12

But it doesn't always apply:

135-18 Roosevelt Ave.	Roosevelt Ave.	Prince and Main	18

☛ **TIP: More Tips on Navigating Queens.** Getting around Queens can be positively baffling. Here's what you have to know for starters.

Logistically speaking, Queens is the opposite of Manhattan. In Manhattan, avenues run north-south, and streets go east-west, with 5th Ave. dividing east from west. In Queens, avenues run east-west, whereas streets run north-south. The smaller number avenues start at the northernmost tip, and get larger as you go south. (For instance, 3rd Ave. is in northern Queens near the Bronx-Whitestone Bridge; 165th Ave. is at the southern end near JFK Airport in Howard Beach.) Streets are numbered starting from the East River. (For instance, in Long Island City you will find 2nd St., and near the Queens-Nassau County boundary you will find 250th St.) Unlike 5th Ave. in Manhattan, which divides east from west, there are no official dividing lines in Queens.

By Car

The good news is that there are many routes to any given destination in Queens. Queens isn't Texas, so if you miss an exit, you don't have to drive one hundred miles until the next one. The bad news is that there are so many roads, newcomers can get confused. It helps to get acquainted with the major arteries and to have a sense of what roads run north-south or east-west.

There are four major highways in Queens, three of which run north-south. Queens Blvd. and Grand Central Parkway, however, both run east-west in some sections and north-south in other sections.

1. I-295 is the Clearview Expressway, which leads over the Throgs Neck Bridge to the Bronx.
2. I-678 is the Van Wyck Expressway, which leads over the Whitestone Bridge to the Bronx.
3. I-278 is the Brooklyn-Queens Expressway (BQE), which connects Brooklyn and Queens.
4. I-495 is the Long Island Expressway, which runs east-west from Queens into Long Island. Other major east-west routes are Northern Blvd. and Jackie Robinson–Grand Central Parkway.

Street Parking

Metered street parking is available in many neighborhoods. However, in certain busy areas such as Flushing, Kew Gardens, Forest Hills, and Jackson Heights, you may spend a lot of time searching for a parking spot or lot. Bring quarters, and be prompt because parking tickets are expensive.

Rush Hour

Rush hour is about 6:30 to 9:30 a.m. and 5:00 to 6:30 p.m., but there's often heavy car traffic in Queens.

 **Insight**

The Maze of Queens Is a Robert Moses Legacy

So it's a hot day in August and you are miserably stuck in traffic on a highway in Queens, wishing both for an aspirin and that your car could sprout wings. Hello, you're having a Robert Moses moment.

Love him or hate him, Robert Moses left a gargantuan footprint on the parks, roads, and overall layout of New York City. Holding a series of extraordinarily powerful positions in New York state and city government for forty-four years,

from 1924 until 1968, Moses was a master urban planner whose embrace of the automobile transformed New York. It was Robert Moses who conceived and built
most of the complex network of bridges and highways in Queens. Moses's vision
expressed a midtwentieth-century excitement over a more automated, and auto-
motive, future.

In Queens alone, Moses built the Triborough, Throgs Neck, and Bronx-
Whitestone bridges, the Grand Central and Interborough (later the Jackie Robinson) parkways, facilitating access among the boroughs and from the city to Long
Island and points north. The man was a force of nature, a workaholic before the
word was coined. Pursuing a vision of what he quaintly called a "motorized" society, Moses enhanced the commuter appeal of land-rich Queens. He introduced
high-speed routes for drivers, who could enjoy the city landscape while driving to
and from suburban communities, while avoiding the "riffraff" on the subway.

These blockbuster projects, however, came with high social costs. The publication of Robert Caro's critical biography, *The Power Broker,* documented the political machinations behind Moses's extraordinary influence. Many people harshly
criticized Moses as an elitist whose projects used public money to build monumental constructions and miles of paved roadways, whose low-income housing
developments were sterile, and whose highway projects cut heartlessly through
old neighborhoods, ripping apart the fabric of urban community life.

On the other hand, Moses also initiated construction of several fabulous parks
and recreation areas in Queens, including Flushing Meadows–Corona Park, Shea
Stadium, Astoria Park Pool, Jacob Riis Park, and countless playgrounds. Curiously,
one unanticipated Moses legacy was the rise of the urban preservation movement,
which places a high value on everything Robert Moses was not about: building local community, preserving historic structures, and fostering energy-efficient
mass transportation over reliance on cars.

History will judge the legacy of Robert Moses. Meanwhile, as you sit in traffic en
route to LaGuardia or JFK, ponder this urban irony: Robert Moses lived his entire
life in Manhattan, relied on chauffeurs, and never learned to drive.

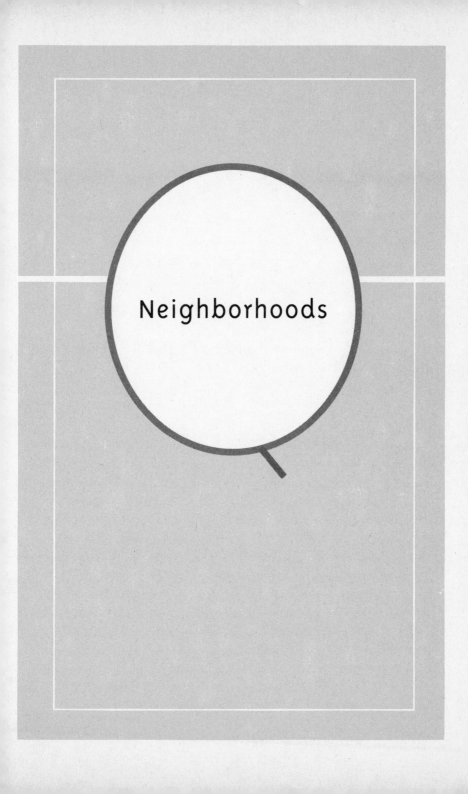

Neighborhoods

6

Astoria

WHERE IT IS: Northwestern Queens.
HOW TO GET THERE BY SUBWAY: N and W to Broadway, 30th Ave. (Grand Ave.), Astoria Blvd. (Hoyt Ave.), Ditmars Blvd./Astoria. Also G, R, and V to Steinway St., 46th St.
WHAT'S NEARBY: Jackson Heights to the east, Sunnyside and Woodside to the south, Triborough Bridge and East River to the north (and Manhattan to the west).
MAJOR SHOPPING/RESTAURANT STREETS: Steinway St., Broadway, Ditmars Blvd., and 30th Ave.
SPECIAL CHARACTERISTICS: Greek and Middle Eastern restaurants, and grape arbors in late summer.
ON NOT GETTING LOST: Astoria is well served by public transportation. Note that the N and W subways make several stops along 31st Ave., so know which stop you need. Also because it is an older part of Queens, sometimes things seem illogical (e.g., at Ditmars Blvd. bet. 35th and 45th Sts. you might expect to find 39th, 40th, and 44th Sts., but they don't exist). Orient yourself using 31st Ave., Broadway, and Steinway St.
CAR SERVICES: Lincoln 728-4946, Yes 539-7777, Hermes 274-1400.

A CULTURAL MOUSSAKA

Arguably the hippest neighborhood in Queens, Astoria is a crazy quilt of old-timers and newcomers, both American and foreign-born. Astoria has recently experienced a renaissance fueled by home buyers and renters from Manhattan and Brooklyn.

If Astoria were a culinary dish with layers, like lasagna or moussaka, the recipe would look something like this. For the base layer, there's a community of first-, second-, and third-generation Greek-American families who comprise nearly half of the area's population. In addition, both complementary but contrasting, are immigrants from other cultures: Egyptians and Italians, plus a

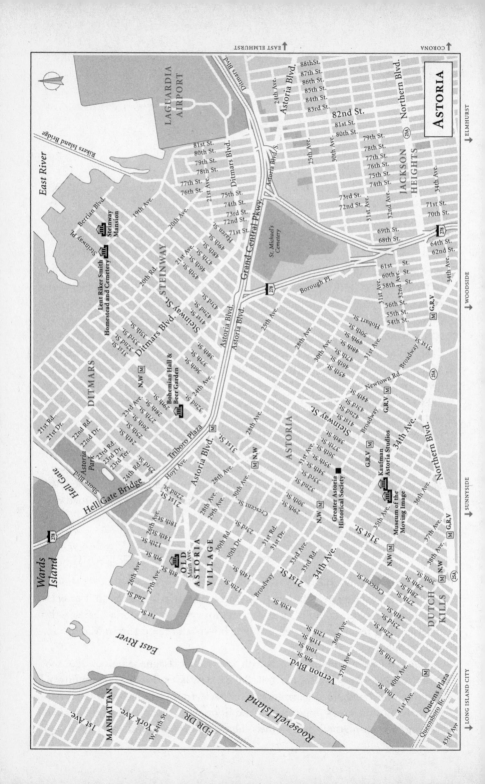

sprinkling of Bangladeshis and Bosnians. Infusing the dish is the salsa of more recent immigrants from Latin countries as disparate as Brazil and Colombia. Topping it off is a mishmash of artists, professionals, hipsters, and college grads for whom Astoria is just one more slice of the Big Apple. Astoria, like moussaka, is more than the sum of its parts.

THINGS TO SEE AND DO

Astoria is a food mecca, well known for its many Greek restaurants and Bohemian Park and Hall, which is one of the few remaining beer halls in New York City. In good weather, come people watch in the European-style Athens Cafe or Omonia Café. More than a dozen Greek tavernas specialize in traditional Greek and Cypriot foods, including memorable appetizers called meze, and fresh fish that's grilled in an open kitchen. For Middle Eastern flavors, head down Steinway Street to Sabry's for seafood or, for Egyptian food, to Mombar. And, there's Italian food here, too.

Astoria Park is large, with views, free summer weekend concerts, and the Olympic-sized Astoria Pool that's free and open to the public. You can have an interesting afternoon wandering around Steinway Street, and should you need one, you can pick up an authentic hookah at several Middle Eastern stores here. A lot of professional musicians live in and near Astoria. Midweek some can be found playing in cafés such as Sac's Place, where you can get excellent pizza, and for no cover, listen to live jazz. If you're interested in media, make a beeline to the Museum of the Moving Image, where you can spend a few hours behind the scenes in the world of cinema; it's also one of New York's leading art-flick theaters.

You may discover in Astoria something reminiscent of Greece or Italy that you don't often see on the streets of New York: ripe grapes hanging from arbors in late August and September. Their perfume is masked by city smells. At first you might not even notice it, but once you realize that locals have transplanted this beloved piece of the old country, it seems there are grapes growing everywhere: over the front porches of two- and three-story homes and trickling down from second-story decks to provide shade in a restaurant garden. It's this blend of old and new that spices up the moussaka of Astoria.

BITS OF HISTORY

Astoria was named after the wealthy fur trader John Jacob Astor in 1839. It was a political favor by his friend, fellow pelt trader, and "Father of Astoria," Stephen Halsey, who first built a village here and laid out streets. Astor neither lived nor built in the area, but it was prestigious to have a namesake town, and lore has it that Halsey was hoping Astor would contribute money toward a girls' school. A ferry installed by Halsey had made the area attractive to many wealthy New Yorkers seeking to escape Manhattan for the countryside, and you can get a sense of their lifestyle by viewing a few surviving mid-nineteenth-century homes in Old Astoria Village. A tale of a tougher life is told by the Irish Famine Cemetery, named after the Irish-born maids and gardeners who labored in the homes of the wealthy classes.

William Steinway, the son of a German immigrant piano maker, relocated his factory here in the 1870s from Manhattan as the city expanded rapidly and conditions became increasingly crowded. Steinway built the four-hundred-acre Steinway Village, complete with a post office, the Steinway Reformed Church, and housing for his workers' families. A factory here still turns out the acclaimed Steinway pianos, which are handcrafted as they were in the 1800s. You can also see the Steinway Mansion where William Steinway lived, walk the streets he named after his two sons, and see the Steinway Worker Housing (1877–79). Steinway's portrait hangs in the local public library, called, of course, the Steinway Branch.

In the early twentieth century, the movie industry came to Astoria when the Famous Players–Lasky Corporation opened a studio that subsequently became Paramount and is today the Kaufman Astoria Studios. In the 1920s, a large Greek-immigrant population settled here, followed by a second wave after the 1965 changes in immigration law, helping to create Astoria as it is today.

☺ PARKS, PUBLIC SPACES, AND PUBLIC WORKS

ASTORIA PARK. 21st St. and Hoyt Ave. at Ditmars Blvd. and the East River; extends from south of the Triborough Bridge to north of the Hell Gate Bridge, 626-8622 or New York City information line 311. www.nycgovparks.org. Daily dawn–10:00 p.m. Dogs: Off-leash hours (before 9:00 a.m.) at Astoria Park So.

Here are three reasons to visit Astoria Park. First there are panoramic views of Manhattan. Second, you can swim in one of the city's most spectacular Olympic-sized pools. Third, where else will you find a children's playground named after a Greek mythological monster?

Astoria Park is a sixty-five-acre public park with playgrounds, tennis courts, an athletic field, basketball courts, baseball diamonds, the renowned Astoria Pool (see below), a bandstand, comfort station, and walks throughout. You can enjoy free summer waterfront concerts and find a perch for watching the Fourth of July fireworks, too.

ASTORIA POOL. 19th St. and 23rd Dr., 626-8620. Memorial Day–Labor Day daily 11:00 a.m.–6:30 p.m. Free.

The pool in the park is bigger than a football field (330 × 165 feet), designed to accommodate 3,000 people. On hot days it's crowded with splashing families and exuberant teens. Opened July 4, 1936, the landmark Astoria Pool was built under Robert Moses as part of the WPA effort. Architecturally significant features include the art deco pavilion, with locker-room facilities built to accommodate more than 6,000 people, and underwater lighting, considered a "revolutionary development in recreation" in its day. If you're planning a swim, do check out the Parks Department rules and regs regarding sneakers, locks, and pool toys at www.nycgovparks.org.

☺ **CHARYBDIS PLAYGROUND.** At western edge of Astoria Park, corner Shore Blvd., 23rd Ave., 23rd Rd.

(So named because it is near to Hell Gate, a turbulent area in the East River) is a wonderful place for children to play. You can also teach them a little Greek mythology while pushing them on the swings. The playground is named after the monster Charybdis, daughter of the sea god Poseidon. As a young nymph she flooded lands to add to her father's kingdom until Zeus, the ruler of the gods, got fed up and turned her into a monster. (Rambunctious children can draw their own conclusions.)

If you're interested in New York City history, take a look at the 1926 granite Long Island War Memorial dedicated to "Long Island residents." Queens may have become a borough of New York City in 1898, but three decades later its heart still half belonged to Long Island.

ATHENS SQUARE PARK. 30th Ave. at 30th St. Call 311. www.nycgovparks.org.

Bringing a bit of Athens to Astoria, this park is charmingly evocative of Greece, with its three Doric columns and statues of a seated Socrates and a stately Athena. No matter that beyond the mini-amphitheater there's a basketball game going on. Old men sit on the benches and chat, families stroll by, teens hang out. The Athena statue, according to the sign in the park, was "A gift from the people of Athens, capital of Greece, to the people of the City of New York."

HELL GATE AND HELL GATE BRIDGE. Bet. the East River and Long Island Sound.

Hell Gate channel contains some of the deepest water in New York Harbor. Its rocky reefs have quaint names such as "Hen and Chickens," "Pot Rock," "Bread and Cheese," and "Bald-Headed Billy." On November 25, 1780, the frigate *Hussar* and its $5 million cargo in gold and silver for military paymasters sank to the bottom of Hell Gate, where the soggy treasure apparently remains. Attempts were made to remove the dangerous rocks of Hell Gate in the 1850s and 1870s. The latter effort shook windows as far away as Newark and, it's said, was the world's largest detonation. Today Amtrak trains running north, connecting New York City to New England, use the bright red Hell Gate Bridge that arches between Queens and Wards Island. When built in 1917, it was the longest steel arch bridge in the country.

POINTS OF CULTURAL AND HISTORICAL INTEREST

Astoria and the Entertainment Industry

FRANK SINATRA HIGH SCHOOL OF THE ARTS. 35th St. and 35th Ave., 361-9920.

Construction has begun on a new building on this spot, funded in part with support from Sinatra's friend, Astoria-born singer Tony Bennett. Admission criteria for this performing arts school, to open in 2008, include auditions in fields such as dance, music, singing, fine art, or drama.

KAUFMAN ASTORIA STUDIOS (KAS). 34-12 36th St. at 34th Ave., 392-5600. www.kaufmanastoria. com. No public tours. Landmark site at 35-11 35th Ave.

Astoria has been home to this major movie studio for nearly ninety years. These studios have been churning out major motion pictures, independent films, television shows, and commercials since World War I. Famous lines heard over the years include "Hoo ah!" spoken by Al Pacino in his Academy Award–winning *Scent of a Woman. Sesame Street* has been filmed at KAS for about fifteen years, and the nationally syndicated *Imus in the Morning* show is broadcast from a studio here. Well-known movies such as *Angels in America, The Pink Panther, The Manchurian Candidate, Glengarry Glen Ross,* and TV series such as *The Cosby Show* and *Law and Order* were filmed on sets on this site. Luminaries such as Paul Newman, Harrison Ford, and Meryl Streep worked here.

The Astoria studios were built in 1919–20 as part of the Famous Players–Lasky Corporation, which later morphed into Paramount Pictures, and is now owned by KAS. The empire that started with the huge 1919 landmarked building at 34-12 36th St. has grown to a twelve-acre complex, with its Studio Annex at 37-11 35th Ave., a new 18,000-square-foot stage, and a secure gated lot so stars can walk around outside protected from gawkers.

A full cast of talented ghosts haunts this building. Silent screen stars who filmed here include Gloria Swanson, Rudolf Valentino, and W. C. Fields. With the advent of talkies, from 1929 to 1941, a parade of theater giants found their way from the Broadway stage to the film studio in Queens: the Marx Brothers (Chico, Harpo, Groucho, Gummo, and Zeppo), Claudette Colbert, Edward G. Robinson, and Tallulah Bankhead. This site is also where the Paramount Newsreels ("the eyes and ears of the world") originated. After the movie industry moved to Los Angeles, the building was used by the federal government as the Signal Corps' Pictorial Center during World War II. After the studio fell into disuse for some time, it was rejuvenated in the 1980s by businessman George Kaufman and partners Alan King and the late Johnny Carson, among others. Billy Joel, Placido Domingo, Keith Richards, Tony Bennett, and Dizzy Gillespie, among others, have recorded in the KAS sound studios.

🏛 **MUSEUM OF THE MOVING IMAGE.** 36-01 35th Ave. bet. 36th and 37th Sts., 784-0077. www.ammi.org. W–Th 11:00 a.m.–5:00 p.m., F 11:00 a.m.–8:00 p.m., Sa–Su 11:00 a.m.–6:30 p.m. Admission is $10 for adults, $7.50 for seniors and students with college ID, $5 for children five to eighteen, free for children under five, and free for everyone Fridays after 4:00 p.m.

Come experience Hollywood—in Queens! The Museum of the Moving Image boasts the largest collection of motion pictures and television artifacts and memorabilia in the nation, and one of the largest in the world. There's nothing like it, even in California. Legions of foreign tourists visit annually from France, Italy, Japan, and Britain.

Kids and movie buffs of all ages will get a kick out of the interactive exhibits. You can record yourself on video and then turn the images into a souvenir flip-book. Using ADR, an automated dialogue replacement system, you can dub your own voice onto a famous scene. You can even insert yourself into the pictures on a high-tech green screen. Techies will enjoy demonstrations of professional equipment, for instance, of how animated film is made or how film editing is done.

This institution is also one of the city's premier art movie theaters in New York, showing film classics on weekends and hosting dozens of personal appearances annually by talents such as Martin Scorsese. (NOTE: Seating is limited and advance notice of programs goes to subscribers.) In summertime, they run weekend films in Socrates Sculpture Park (see p. 208).

An expansion project scheduled for completion in 2008 will add a hands-on filmmaking video game workshop, bigger theater, and outdoor space. There'll be more digital media in the new galleries, and a virtual environment to navigate. Meanwhile, come visit and log on to the on-line exhibitions. There's a great gift shop with tons of books and a café here, too.

The building in which the Museum of the Moving Image is housed was originally a Paramount Studio (1918), one of two in the area. More than a hundred feature silent films and, later, major sound films were made here, which is why this site, under the name Paramount Studio Complex, is listed on the National Register of Historic Places.

UA KAUFMAN ASTORIA CINEMA 14. 35-30 38th St. at 35th Ave., (800) 326-3264 x. 623 or 786-1722.

Take in a movie at this UA cinema, visit the Museum of the Moving Image next door, and try one of the local restaurants.

Arts and Live Performance

ASTORIA BIG BAND. 278-5331. www.sudhalter.com.

Astoria's had its very own "big band" for more than twenty years. Founded by Queens resident and baritone sax player Carol Sudhalter, the Astoria Big Band often plays swing classics at venues such as the Queens Botanical Garden, Kingsland Homestead, and the Flushing Cemetery Memorial Day jazz concert.

ASTORIA MUSIC SOCIETY. 38-11 Ditmars Blvd. #102, 204-9034. www.astoriamusic.org.

The Astoria Music Society plays chamber music and hosts the Astoria Symphony, an auditioned orchestra made up of professional and promising young musicians. The group presents four to eight programs of standard orchestral repertoire each season, at local venues. Season tickets cost about $10 per concert.

ASTORIA PERFORMING ARTS CENTER. 34-23 Steinway St. bet. 34th and 35th Aves., 393-7505. www.apacny.org.

This professional theater company, founded by actress Susan Scannell, produces musicals and dramas at reasonable prices in local parks, churches, and other performance venues.

BOHEMIAN HALL & BEER GARDEN CONCERTS. (See p. 49.)

MODERN ART FOUNDRY. 18-70 41st St. bet. 19th Ave. and Berrian Blvd., 728-2030. www.modern artfoundry.com. Not open to the public except for exhibits announced on Web site.

About 15,000 sculptures have been cast here—large and small—for artists like Lipchitz, Lachaise, Bourgeois, Miró, Archipenko, and Noguchi. The third-generation owner says this "is probably the oldest family-owned art foundry in the United States and offers artists and communities the opportunity to complete their work under one roof." The Modern Art Foundry uses a technique called wax casting, which is something of a lost art. You can get a sense of the skill involved in casting sculptures by viewing a bronze pour on the Web site.

OPERA COMPANY OF ASTORIA. 274-0399. www.operaastoria.org. Tickets are about $10 for adults and $7 for students and seniors, with free admission for youth and children under eighteen.

The Opera Company of Astoria was founded in June 2003 to "bring quality opera to Astoria in service to both the community and young professional opera singers." The programs are held at local churches.

Ethnic and Religious Diversity

Just walking around Astoria, you get a sense of the religious diversity in the area. For instance, stroll on Crescent St. near 30th Ave., near the Greek Orthodox St. Demetrios's Cathedral (see listing, p. 39), there's an Anglican Episcopal Church (30-14 Crescent St.) and the United Methodist Korean Church of Astoria (30-10 Crescent St.). The large Presbyterian Church of Astoria (at 31-40 33rd St.) is but a stone's throw away from the Astoria Islamic Center (21-27 27th St.), which in turn is a few minutes' walk from the Jewish Congregation of Beth Jacob (22-51 29th St.).

GREEK AMERICAN FOLKLORE SOCIETY. 21-80 Crescent St., 956-3544. M–F 9:00 a.m.–5:00 p.m.

This nonprofit organization offers instruction in folk dancing and hosts lectures, presentations, costume exhibitions, and festivals for the general public. Similarly, the **GREEK CULTURAL CENTER** (27-18 Hoyt Ave. So., bet. 27th and 29th Sts., 726-7329) supports a range of Greek cultural activities, including dances and book fairs. **THE HELLENIC CULTURAL CENTER** (27-09 Crescent St., 626-5293. www .hellenic.net/events.htm.), associated with the Greek Orthodox Archdiocese of America, hosts lectures and performances at Chapel of St. Kosmas, a two-hundred-seat cultural hall.

MASJID EL BER OF ASTORIA. 36-05 30th St., off 36th Ave., 784-0336.

You can hear the muezzin call several times a day from this mosque, the center of a small Bangladeshi enclave. Nearby are a handful of restaurants and shops serving the Bangladeshi community.

QUEENS RAINBOW COMMUNITY CENTER. 30-74 Steinway St. near 30th Ave., 429-2300. www.queenspride.com.

The main organization for gay life in Queens, this community center sponsors social events, public education campaigns, and celebrations such as the Queens Pride Parade in Jackson Heights.

ST. DEMETRIOS'S CATHEDRAL. 30-11 30th Dr. at 30th Ave. 728-1718.

St. Demetrios's Cathedral, a Greek Orthodox church, was erected in 1927 and today it represents one of the largest Hellenic-American communities in the United States.

ST. IRENE OF CHRYSOVALANTOU STAVROPIGIAL CATHEDRAL. 36-07 23rd Ave. bet. 36th and 37th Sts., 626-6225.

This church is home to many religious paintings and statues. Take a close look at the "miraculous weeping icon" of Saint Irene, the abbess of a ninth-century Greek monastery. The icon was painted in 1921 by an Orthodox monk on Mount Athos, a millennium-old, all-male monastic community of 1,500 people who spend their days in fasting and meditation. Believers claim that the icon of St. Irene still weeps.

PEOPLE, PLACES, AND THINGS OF HISTORICAL INTEREST

🏛 **BENJAMIN T. PIKE HOUSE.** 18-33 41st St. (See Steinway Mansion, p. 41.)

IRISH FAMINE CEMETERY. 21st St. and 26th Ave., south of Hoyt Ave.

Peek through the gate at this old cemetery. It was a burial ground for poor Irish immigrants from the 1840s to 1870s, an era when Irish workers lived on Emerald St. (now 21st St.) and worked in the homes of wealthy Americans, or in the greenhouses and silk factories in Astoria. It is called the Irish Famine Cemetery not necessarily because the interred died of starvation, but because many were born in Ireland, and were among the 2 million Irish who immigrated to the United States between 1845 and 1855 to escape starvation and epidemic disease at home caused by the potato famine.

🏛 **LAWRENCE FAMILY CEMETERY.** Southeast corner of 20th Rd. at 35th St. Visitors by permission only; private property.

Scattered throughout Queens are over a dozen historic family cemeteries. Dating from 1703, this tiny cemetery near the huge Con Edison site was a private burial ground for the prominent Lawrence family. The earliest of the eighty-nine graves is dated 1703. One family member, Cornelius Van Wyck Lawrence (1791–1861) was elected as a Democrat to the House of Representatives in 1832 and as Mayor of New York in 1834.

🏛 **LENT RIKER SMITH HOMESTEAD AND CEMETERY.** 78-03 19th Rd. at Steinway St., 721-0508. www.lentrikersmithhomestead.com.

Imagine Queens in the olden days: no trains, no bridges, no airports, no highways, no Seinfeld—just a lot of land, water, and a handful of settlers. This Dutch Colonial farmhouse was built a half century before the Revolutionary War, in 1729, and named after land owner Abraham Lent. Nearby is the 1810–1870 Riker/Rapalye/Lent Cemetery (78-03 19th Rd.), where some original settlers of the Lent and Riker families are buried. The Rikers were descendents of Abraham Rycken, who settled in Long Island in 1638 and whose family-owned Rikers Island is well known today as a jail facility.

🏛 **OLD ASTORIA VILLAGE. WEST OF 21ST ST. BET. BROADWAY AND ASTORIA PARK.**

There's not much left of the splendid old Astoria Village, founded in 1839 by Stephen A. Halsey, but if you take a walk around these streets you can get the feel of what the original Long Island village must have been like, with spacious homes, cottages, churches, and a cemetery. One of the best-known houses, 26-07 12 St., circa 1840s, belonged to a Dr. Baylies, who called it Tara. Others of this era on 12th St. are numbers 26-18; 26-22; 26-23; 26-25; 26-27; and 27-01. On 14th St. nearby, see numbers 26-05 and 26-26. And on nearby 14th Pl. and 26th Ave., there are three old houses on the same side of the street, numbers 14-01, 14-03, and 14-15. This area is not landmarked, so unfortunately these Civil War—era buildings can be legally torn down.

OLD NEW YORK CITY POLICE STATION. 3-16 30th Ave., 728-3585. No public tours.

This is a song of a building. It's a Romanesque revival structure erected in 1890 as a New York Police Station. Today it is used by a nonprofit social service agency.

☺ **QUEENS BOROUGH PUBLIC LIBRARY, ASTORIA BRANCH.** 14-01 Astoria Blvd. at the intersection of 14th St. and 28th Ave., 278-2220. www.queenslibrary.org. M 1:00–8:00 p.m., T 1:00–6:00 p.m., W 10:00 a.m.–6:00 p.m., Th 10:00 a.m.–6:00 p.m., F 1:00–6:00 p.m.

When Andrew Carnegie endowed libraries across the nation, his generosity extended to then still-rural Queens, too. Mr. Carnegie gave $240,000 to build three libraries in Queens. This was one. The original building dates to 1904.

STEINWAY FACTORY. 1 Steinway Pl. 38th St. and 19th Ave., 721-2600. www.steinway.com.

Steinway is a name associated worldwide with fine craftsmanship. The pianos made here are still individually crafted, as they were in 1872 when Steinway moved his factory to Queens. The Astoria Historical Society occasionally runs tours, and you can get a virtual factory tour on-line, too. Another factory, built in 1902, is at 45-02 Ditmars Blvd. bet. 45th and 46th Sts. In 2003, Steinway and Sons celebrated their one hundred and fiftieth anniversary.

🏛 **STEINWAY MANSION.** 18-33 41st St. bet. Berrian Blvd. and 19th Ave. (east side).

Entrepreneur William Steinway and his family lived in this large stone mansion, which was built by Benjamin Pike, Jr., an optician, in the 1850s.

🏛 **STEINWAY WORKER HOUSING.** 41-17 to 41-25, 40-12 to 41-20 20th (Winthrop) Ave. bet. Steinway, 41st (Albert) St. and 42nd (Theodore) St. Also 20-11 to 20-29 41st St. bet. 20th Ave. and 20th Rd.

These sturdy brick homes, still in use as residences, were built by Steinway between 1877 and 1879 as housing for his factory workers, who paid a modest rent. Two streets were originally named after Steinway's sons, Albert (now 41st St.) and Theodore (now 42nd St.).

ASTORIA'S GREEK SCENE: CAFÉS, RESTAURANTS, AND NIGHTLIFE

There are so many Greek cafés and restaurants in Astoria that you could have appetizers in one restaurant, an entrée in another, and save room for dessert in a local café.

Sidewalk Cafés

With scores of small tables packed onto the sidewalk and great people watching, you'll think you died and woke up in Syntagma Square, Athens.

ATHENS CAFE. 32-07 30th Ave. bet. 32nd and 33rd Sts., 626-2164. Daily 8:30 a.m.–3:00 p.m.

Athens Cafe is the biggest and busiest of numerous cafés in Astoria. Read the paper, check out the chicks and guys, relax, and plan your weekend.

AVENUE CAFÉ. 35-27 30th Ave. bet. 35th and 36th Sts., 278-6967. Daily 9:00 a.m.–midnight.

Popular among locals, you'll find a good neighborhood vibe here. They serve Greek foods such as spanakopita and strong coffee.

LEFKOS PIRGOS. 22-85 31st St. bet. 23rd Ave. and Ditmars Blvd., 932-4423. M–Th, Su 6:30 a.m.–1:00 a.m., F–Sa 6:30 a.m.–2:00 a.m.

At this large café you can enjoy the flavors of the Mediterranean—even if you're sitting right under the elevated subway line. Order the *galaktoboureko,* a lemony custard dessert, or various sticky wonders that are honey-phyllo-dough-and-nut variations on a theme.

OMONIA CAFE. 32-20 Broadway at 33rd St., 274-6650. Daily 24 hours.

Omonia Cafe made the wedding cake for the hit film *My Big Fat Greek Wedding*! So how can a person not stop in for a coffee and pastry? About nine hundred different kinds of cakes and cookies are on display. Omonia is bursting at its own seams at midnight on weekends with customers standing three- and four-deep in line.

Greek Restaurants

People often ask: Which Greek restaurant in Astoria is the best? That depends on your taste, the night you go—and whether you have a Greek-speaking friend dining with you, which, some say, mysteriously improves both the service and food. Most restaurants serve both fish and meat, and you can watch the chef at work grilling seafood—shrimp, octopus, and squid, whole porgy, sardines and red snapper—in the restaurant's front window, just as you can in a Greek taverna. Weekend nights are often busy, but what you may lose in slow service, you'll gain in local color as three-generation Greek families crowd around long tables for a family dinner.

> ☛ **TIP: Make a Meal of Meze.** You can make a meal of traditional Greek appetizers, called meze. These include *tirokafteri* (cheese dip), stuffed grape leaves, a garlic dip called *scordalia, melitzanosalada* (eggplant salad), *taramasalata* (red caviar with dressing), *spanakopita* (spinach and feta cheese wrapped in a light phyllo dough), beet salad, and, of course, feta cheese. Order meze, some bread and wine—it's heaven!

ANNA'S CORNER. 23-01 31st St. at 23rd Ave., 545-4000. M–Su 11:00 a.m.–11:00 p.m.

The perfect compromise for a carnivore dating a vegetarian! The veggie will purr over the spinach pie, zucchini croquettes, or grilled mushrooms. Meat eaters can growl contentedly over the lamb on the spit and *kontosouvli*, a marinated roast pork. A meal costs about $20 a person.

CHRISTOS HASAPO. 41-08 23rd Ave. at 41st St., 777-8400. M–Sa 3:00 p.m.–11:30 p.m., Su noon–midnight.

Christos Hasapo distinguishes itself from Astoria's sea of fish joints by serving up perfectly cooked, delicious aged steaks in comfortable surroundings with friendly service. The owners run a butcher shop, so you're assured of high quality. Dinner costs about $40 per person.

DEMETRIS. 32-11 Broadway near 41st Ave., 278-1877. Daily noon–midnight.

Judging from the weekend crowds, locals are voting Demetris one of the best Greek eateries in Astoria. The blue-and-white decor and live music are reminiscent of a vacation on the Greek isles. Try the porgies cooked whole, avgolemono chicken, and moussaka. Entrées range from $12 to $25.

ELIAS CORNER. 24-02 31st St. at 24th Ave., 932-1510. Daily 4:00 p.m.–midnight.

Expect an informal environment and service that's catch-as-catch can, but out-of-this-world wonderful fresh fish. Dinner runs about $30 a person, cash only.

STAMATIS. 29-12 23rd Ave. and 31 St., 932-8596. Daily noon–11:00 p.m.

One of the most highly regarded of the Greek eateries, Stamatis specializes in many fish dishes, and you also can't go wrong if you order the baby lamb with tomato sauce, stuffed cabbage, and pasticcio. There are two restaurants with the same name; at the Broadway Stamatis, make a meal of meze. 31-14 Broadway at 31st St., 204-8968. Daily noon–12:30 a.m.

TAVERNA KYCLADES. 33-07 Ditmars Blvd. bet. 33rd and 34th Sts., 545-8666. Daily noon–11:00 p.m.

Taverna Kyclades is known for especially excellent swordfish. Entrées run about $25 per person.

TELLY'S TAVERNA. 28-13 23rd Ave. at 28th St., 728-9194. M–F 3:00 p.m.–1:00 a.m., Sa 3:00 p.m.–1:00 a.m., Su 11:00 a.m.–midnight.

Telly's Greek owners serve up grilled octopus, giant shrimp, sardines, or whole porgy. For meze, thick fresh bread meets delicious cheese and grilled vegetables. Dinner runs about $30 a person.

UNCLE GEORGE'S. 33-19 Broadway at 34th St., 626-0593. Daily 24 hours.

Uncle George's serves up the opposite of haute cuisine, which is precisely why the film crews from nearby Kaufman Astoria Studios make a beeline here at 3:00 a.m. Sit family-style, chow down on big platefuls of standard Greek fare, and don't expect great decor. If you come for dinner, you can eat your fill for $20. It's a quintessential outer-borough experience.

ZENON TAVERNA. 34-10 31st Ave. at 34th St., 956-0133. M–F, Su 11:00 a.m.–11:00 p.m., Sa 11:00 a.m.–midnight.

Zenon welcomes guests with an ambience reminiscent of a summer in Cyprus. The menu is written in both English and Greek—a good sign. You can choose from a menu of delicious soups, pocket pita sandwiches, and a roster of daily dishes.

ZODIAC. 30-15 Newtown Ave., 726-3995. M–F, Su 11:00 a.m.–11:00 p.m., Sa 11:00 a.m.–midnight.

Zodiac is a particularly good place to go for the appetizer course of dips, cheeses, and stuffed grape leaves when you want to have a light, lingering dinner.

Greek Nightlife

CAVÓ. 42-18 31st Ave. bet. 42nd and 43rd Sts., 721-1001. M–Sa 5:00 p.m.–2:00 a.m., Su noon–4:00 a.m. (dinner stops at 2:00 a.m., dancing starts at 10:00 p.m.).

Cavó is a popular weekend destination for young locals looking for Manhattan exclusivity without having to cross the East River. You can dine and, after midnight, get a real hit of an outer-borough, Vegas-style club. TIP: Everyone is welcome early, for dinner—but after about 10:00 p.m., if you don't fit a certain look (being female helps) you might not get in. Dinner runs about $20 per person.

CENTRAL. 20-30 Steinway St. bet. 20th Ave. and 20th Rd., 726-1600. Tu–Su 9:00 p.m.–4:00 a.m.

A hot spot for the local, twenty-to-thirty-something Greek crowd, Central has a large, sunken lounge area, with couches, a fireplace, and a lofted DJ platform above. At a large square bar, $8–9 mixed drinks and $6 bottles of beer are served. There's rock on Tuesdays, hip-hop on Wednesdays, and techno on weekends. Late at night they put on traditional Greek tunes.

MIDDLE EASTERN RESTAURANTS

Most of the Middle Eastern eateries are found along Steinway St. around 25th Ave.

EASTERN NIGHTS. 35-25 Steinway St. bet. 35th and 36th Ave., 204-7608. Daily 1:00 p.m.–5:00 a.m.

If you are in a sultry Anthony-and-Cleopatra-at-the-pyramids mood, indulge yourself with a dinner of *molokhiyya*, a rich, chicken stock–based vegetable soup, stuffed pigeon (a Cairo specialty) or freshly stewed, roasted, or broiled lamb dishes. At a hookah bar in the back, local Egyptian-born immigrants (all men) meet to puff, discuss, and drink fresh mint-laden tea or thick sweet Turkish coffee.

EGYPTIAN COFFEE SHOP. 25-09 Steinway St. at 25th Ave., 777-5517. Daily 24 hours.

This is what's known as a hookah café (and there's a marvelous hookah store next door, too). It's not really a café, as they don't sell food, but you can sit in the back with a big ol' hookah and puff away just as if you were in Alexandria or Cairo. To conform to the city's laws, you must be eighteen years old to smoke, and what you're smoking is just a little tobacco mixed with a concoction based on fruit and molasses.

EL MANARA. 25-95 Steinway St. bet. 25th and 28th Ave., 267-9495. M–Sa 7:00 a.m.–2:00 a.m., Su 7:00 a.m.–midnight.

Try the spicy Armenian sausage, called *soujuk*, when you come here, along with a healthful meal of Middle Eastern hummus or baba ghanoush with freshly made pita. It's simple, good—and also inexpensive.

MOMBAR. 25-22 Steinway St. bet. 25th and 28th Ave., 726-2356. Tu–Su 5:00 p.m.–11:00 p.m.

The brightly colored facade at Mombar announces the fact that you've arrived at a place that values individuality. And that promise holds true, from the artsy decor inside to excellent clay-pot *tagine* dishes—stews made of lamb, beef, or chicken.

SABRY'S. 24-25 Steinway St. at Astoria Blvd. So., 721-9010. Daily noon–midnight.

For centuries, Egyptians have been hauling catfish, mullet, bolti, perch, and other *samak* (Arabic for "fish") to their kitchen from the nearby Nile. Tucked away in Little Egypt, Sabry's small airy restaurant has a reputation for serving only the freshest of fish (presumably not, therefore, from the East River!). For a Middle Eastern flavor, stick with the tasty *tagine,* a long-simmering stew made with either calamari or shrimp. A kids' menu offers chicken fingers and pizza.

OTHER INTERNATIONAL RESTAURANTS

BISTRO 33. 33-04 36th Ave. at 33rd St., 609-1367. Tu–Su 6:00 p.m.–10:00 p.m.

Tiny and intimate, Bistro 33 combines Japanese and French cuisine. Try the salmon with bok choy and wasabi dijon mayo, crawfish étouffée or baby New Zealand lamb. Entrées are in the $18 range. This is a nice quiet dinner place for a date, or after a day of looking around at Long Island City's art spaces, and is considered one of the best restaurants in Queens. Reservations on weekends.

BRICK CAFE. 30-95 33rd St. at 31st Ave., 267-2735. M–Th, Su 5:00 p.m.–11:00 p.m., F–Sa 11:00 a.m.–midnight.

Brick Cafe is a country-style restaurant serving both French and Italian dishes. The goat cheese salad and duck, lamb, chicken paillard, and pasta dishes are good. You can sit outside, too.

CAFÉ BAR. 32-90 36th St. at 34th Ave., 204-5273. Daily 10:00 a.m.–2:30 a.m., Sa–Su 10:00 a.m.–4:00 a.m. Cash only.

Refugees from Manhattan alongside local Greeks and Cypriots enjoy tasty Mediterranean-inspired food and an active bar scene at this hip restaurant. The place draws trendy twenty- and thirty-somethings with an appealing menu of sandwiches and salads, comfy couches, board games, and an eclectic vibe. In fine weather, outdoor seating is usually packed.

CEVABDZINICA SARAJEVO. 37-18 34th Ave., corner of 38th St., 752-9528. Daily 10:00 a.m.–10:00 p.m. Cash only.

You might do a double take when you see the word *Sarajevo* on the sign at this humble café. Given the incredible ethnic diversity in Queens, it's not surprising that there's a place to eat Bosnian-style sausage and *burekas,* too.

CHURRASCARIA GIRASSOL. 33-18 28th Ave. at 33rd St., 545-8250. Daily 11:30 a.m.–10:30 p.m.

This pleasant café is one of a number of good Brazilian restaurants in Queens. Try the *rodizio* (mixed grill) of barbecue chicken, pork, and beef tenderloin. Or order the *medalhao,* beef tenderloin in mushroom sauce, a *bandeja tropeiro,* western Brazilian beans with sliced beef, or a cheese *picanha* sandwich of sirloin steak with mozzarella. Wash it all down with mango juice, sangria, or a bottle of Schin Cariol, a Brazilian beer.

CUP. 35-01 36th St. at 35th Ave., 937-2322. M–Th, Su 7:00 a.m.–11:00 p.m., F–Sa 7:00 a.m.–1: 00 a.m.

A cool vibe usually bustling with area hipsters makes Cup the place to be, with its outdoor seating, free Wi-Fi, a bar, booths, good music, and TV. There are burgers, homemade quiches, tortellini primavera, and a wide range of sandwiches, reasonably priced.

KOLIBA. 31-11 23rd Ave. at 31st St., 626-0430. Tu–Sa 3:00 p.m.–1:00 a.m., Su noon–midnight.

The mood in tiny Koliba will remind you of your best moments sitting in a Prague café waiting for the astronomical clock to chime. The dumplings, pork, and schnitzel are ranked highly by Czech expats.

LA CASA DEL PAN. 33-20 30th Ave. at 34th St., 721-7991. Daily 24 hours.

Short on ambience but pocketbook-friendly, La Casa del Pan sells tasty rotisserie chicken, an empanada, and dessert—all for less than $6. You can also stuff your face with a workingman's brunch of steak, egg, rice, and beans, plus decent coffee, for about $7.50.

LE SANS SOUCI. 44-09 Broadway at 44th St., 728-2733. Tu–F noon–3:00 p.m. (lunch), 5:00 p.m.–10:00 p.m. (dinner). Sa–Su 11:00 a.m.–3:00 p.m. (brunch), 5:00 p.m.–10:00 p.m. (dinner).

Relax into good food and a rustic, inviting ambience reminiscent of the Brittany coast. At about $35 a person (less for the prix fixe) you can afford the cab ride back to the city with your date. Brunch is a good bargain and reservations are recommended.

MALAGUETA. 23-35 36th Ave. bet. Crescent and 28th Sts., 937-4821. Tu–F noon–10:00 p.m., Sa–Su 1:00 p.m.–10:00 p.m.

Tiny, white-tableclothed Malagueta, with its refined Brazilian cuisine prepared with a French twist, is one of the nicest Brazilian eateries in the borough. The *moqueca de camarao,* a shrimp stew made with palm oil, coconut milk, and cilantro, is satisfying. On Saturday try *feijoada,* the Brazilian national dish, a hearty bean-and-meat stew that will fuel you for hours. Reservations on weekends are recommended.

PICCOLA VENEZIA. 42-01 28th Ave. at 42nd St., 721-8470. M–F 11:30 a.m.–1:00 p.m., Sa 4:30 p.m.–midnight, Su 2:00 p.m.–10:30 p.m.

Piccola Venezia ("Little Venice") inspires such devotion that it's even been described as "the best restaurant in the world" by normally blasé TV producers who have eaten, quite literally, in restaurants around the world. The bruschetta and antipasto arrive unannounced, and the grilled octopus is the tenderest you've ever tasted. Try the signature pasta, homemade bows with parmigiana, cooked to al dente perfection. About $50 a person. Reservations recommended.

PONTICELLO. 46-11 Broadway bet. 46 and 47th Sts., 278-8470. M–Th, noon–10:00 p.m., F noon–11:30 p.m., Sa 4:30 p.m.–11:30 p.m., Su 1:00 p.m.–9:30 p.m.

Every big city in America has one of these kinds of restaurants: a big, comfortable, white-tableclothed Italian restaurant with good Northern Italian dishes, reasonably priced wines, and reliable service. Try the classics: mussels marinara, hot peppers and sausages, veal piccata, or eggplant parmigiana. You'll find an upscale ambience, contemporary decor, and attentive service. This is a nice place for a family occasion.

SAC'S PLACE. 25-41 Broadway bet. Crescent and 29th Sts., 204-5002. Su–Th 11:00 a.m.–11:00 p.m., F–Sa 11:00 a.m.–midnight.

Like good pizza with fresh mozzarella and fresh toppings, cooked in a coal oven to perrrrfection? Come to elegant, informal Sac's Place. There's live jazz on Mondays; no cover.

718 RESTAURANT. 35-01 Ditmars Blvd. at 35th St., 204-5553. M–Th, Su noon–midnight, F–Sa noon–2:00 a.m.

718 is an intimate bistro with an international palate combining the best of Spain and France. Named after the area code, it has an eclectic, international menu including tapas and traditional main courses, plus weekend entertainment such as belly dancing and Brazilian jazz.

TIERRAS COLOMBIANAS. 30-01 Broadway bet. 31st and 32nd Sts., 956-3012. Daily noon–11:00 p.m.

Tierras Colombianas pleases with cheap, plentiful food and a spanking-clean, dinerlike environment. It's perfect for families who like *arroz con frijoles* (rice 'n' beans) and grilled meats. Starving teens will appreciate the Sierra Madre–sized portions of *platos tipicos,* or typical dishes such as *carne asada* (grilled seasoned steak) and *bandeja montanera,* a "mountain plate with chopped beef, fried pork, rice and beans, *arepa,* plantains, egg, and avocado," both for under $13. Other location: 82-18 Roosevelt Ave. in Jackson Heights, 426-8868.

TRATTORIA L'INCONTRO. 21-76 31st St. bet. Ditmars Blvd. and 21st Ave., 721-3532. Tu–Th noon–10:00 p.m., F–Sa noon–11:00 p.m., Su 1:00 p.m.–10:00 p.m.

A mile-long string of daily specials gives this cozy restaurant that touch of the extraordinary. Beautifully presented food, lovingly prepared with fresh ingredients and imagination, is served in an intimate brick-walled, open-kitchen setting. Trattoria l'Incontro gets high marks for parmigianas and pastas, with a nod to regional favorites of Abruzzo, the owners' family home. About $40 a person for dinner. Reservations recommended.

UBOL'S KITCHEN. 24-42 Steinway St. at 25th Ave., 545-2874. Daily 4:00 p.m.–11:00 p.m.

Those who think that Astoria is just a Greek neighborhood might sample the fare at this excellent Thai restaurant. Be prepared for quite spicy food, absolutely no decor, and good prices. Try the "pork in the garden" dish.

OTHER CAFÉS, BARS, AND NIGHTLIFE

BOHEMIAN HALL & BEER GARDEN. 29-19 24th Ave. bet. 29th and 31st Aves., 274-4925. Bar: daily noon–4:00 a.m. Restaurant: M, W, Th 6:00 p.m.–midnight; F noon–midnight; Sa noon–midnight; Su noon–11:00 p.m.

The Bohemian Beer Garden is an Astoria must-see. In the summer, the big old leafy garden is packed with people—often hundreds of people—having a good time. Order a cold beer and a hot dog and relax with friends. Inside, the environment is homey with several booths and a thirty-foot-long bar. Downstairs there's another bar and a sit-down family-style restaurant, which serves Czech and Slovak dishes for a reasonable price (the back of the menu is completely in Czech). Don't miss the Memorial Day weekend Czech and Slovak Festival, with folk dancing and a brass band. There are events and concerts during the summer. (No cover or minimum when there's no entertainment.)

Now on the National Register of Historic Places, this old institution was built through the efforts of the Bohemian Citizens Benevolent Society (founded 1892). It opened its doors in 1910 not just as a bar, but as a social and cultural center, too, and was one of three beer halls in Astoria and eight hundred citywide. If you want to send your kids to after-school Czech classes, here's where you can do it.

BROADWAY STATION. 30-09 Broadway bet. 31st and 32nd Sts., 545-5869. M–Sa 9:30 a.m.–4:00 a.m., Su noon–4:00 a.m.

Two large flat-screen TVs (one for Mets/Jets, the other for Yankees/Giants) dominate the long bar, and a pool table in back makes this a great place to hang out with friends.

CASSIDY'S TAVERN AND SPORTS BAR. 34-16 Broadway at 34th St., 728-8680, www.cassidys tavern.com. Daily 12:30 p.m.–4:00 a.m. Cash only.

A local watering hole and tribute band venue (U2, Led Zeppelin, Van Halen, and Poison wannabes were some of those listed on their Web site's calendar), with nightly drink specials and karaoke every Friday. The interior is dark and drinks are cheap. In good weather, the youngish crowd heads out to the backyard patio for smokers and outdoor tippling. NFL Sunday Ticket during the football season, showing all games. Cover usually $5–10.

MCCAFFREY AND BURKE. 28-54 31st St. bet. 30th and Newtown Aves., 278-9751. Daily 11:00 a.m.–4:00 a.m.

McCaffrey and Burke has been in continuous operation since the 1960s, and as such has attracted a large group of regulars. Drinks are cheap, the atmosphere is friendly, and depending on the time of day or night, you'll either be surrounded by older patrons or a younger crowd returning from a night out in Manhattan. There's a pool table, darts, a couple of video games, and a jukebox with music ranging from jazz to country to rock and metal. There's usually a game on one of the nine television screens and they have the NFL Sunday Ticket during football season.

RAPTURE. 34-27 28th. Ave. bet. 34th and 35th Sts., 626-8044. Daily 5:00 p.m.–4:00 a.m.

It feels like Williamsburg, Brooklyn, circa 1995 here, with Independent Film Nights midweek showing the work of local filmmakers (currently free), all-night drink specials to lure the twenty-something clientele, and such fare as crêpes and guacamole. Fun for the growing youth cadre of hipsters and relaxed locals who want to chill out.

RITMOS '60S. 32-23 Steinway St. bet. 31st Ave. and Broadway, 204-1110. Daily 5:00 a.m.–4:00 a.m. Cash or credit.

Ritmo is Spanish for "rhythm," and anyone with a pulse that beats for Spanish romantic ballads would be happy here. The walls are decorated with drums, brass, and woodwind instruments; dim lighting accentuates the all-female staff's tight-fitting orange-and-white uniforms. You can sit at a table and order from a full menu of Latin-American standards, or get a bottle of hard liquor on ice with mixers on the side, and make your own cocktails. A mostly Spanish-speaking crowd of all ages makes for a lively evening. A must-see if you're in the area.

SPARROW. 24-01 29th St., corner of 24th Ave., 606-2260. Daily 8:00 p.m.–4:00 a.m. Cash only.

This former social club has been completely gutted and now has bare brick walls and a scuffed hardwood floor. Started up by veterans of the now-closed hipster hangout Tupelo, the Sparrow offers a no-frills drinking experience, an alternative to the European flavor of the beer garden across the street. It is mostly open floor space, but there is one long table and bar seating. Expect new wave and punk rock tunes from the late '70s and early '80s.

SHOPPING

Bakeries

ARTOPOLIS BAKERY. 23-18 31st St. (in Agora Plaza) bet. 22rd and 23nd Aves., 728-8484. M–F 7:30 a.m.–9:00 p.m., Sa 7:30 a.m.–9:00 p.m., Su 7:30 a.m.–8:00 p.m.

Get a taste of Greek pastries at this airy bakery, owned by bakers from Kefalonia and Ithaca, Greece. Take your pick: Greek village bread, Mediterranean olive oil flatbread, spinach pie, and *tsoureki,* a kind of Greek challah bread, *kaucouia Thessalonkis* (a donut-shaped, sesame seed–covered bread ring) and Mediterranean "savory cookies" flavored with grape syrup and other unusual tastes. Oh, and don't forget the baklava made with fig, chestnut, and chocolate fillings. You can order by mail (800) 553-2270.

LA GULI. 29-15 Ditmars Blvd. bet. 29th and 31st Sts., 728-5612. M–Sa 7:00 a.m.–7:00 p.m., Su 7:30 a.m.–7:00 p.m.

One of New York's great old-fashioned Italian bakeries, La Guli first opened its doors in 1937. That was a long time ago—the year cellophane tape was invented. La Guli sells a full range of delectables, from tiramisu to old-fashioned lemon ices. The tin ceilings and wood-paneled ambience suggest a sweet remembrance of things past.

LAZIZA SWEETS. 25-78 Steinway St. bet. 25th and 28th Aves., 777-7676. Daily 11:00 a.m.–midnight.

Honey, pistachio, almonds, pomegranate, dates, sesame, apricot, fig—these essential, delicious ingredients for a Middle Eastern bakery feast are used to perfection at Laziza Sweets. For parties, pick up a tantalizing pastry sampler with baklava, *burma* (a shredded dough filled with honey and nuts), cookies, and other treats.

ROSE AND JOE'S ITALIAN BAKERY. 22-40 31st St. bet. Ditmars Blvd. and 23rd Ave., 721-9422. M–Sa 6:00 a.m.–9:00 p.m., Su 6:00 a.m.–6:00 p.m.

If you ask a hungry teenager, he's likely to attest that this hole-in-the-wall bakery has the best Sicilian pizza in Astoria. There's not much elbow room, so don't plan on sitting around sipping an espresso while writing your first novel. It's a staple in an old neighborhood that was once predominantly Italian.

STE. HONORE PATISSERIE. 33-18 Ditmars Blvd. bet. 33rd and 35th Sts., 278-3558. M–F 7:00 a.m.–6:00 p.m., Sa–Su 7:00 a.m.–6:00 p.m.

This French-Italian bakery has been here for twenty-seven years. They turn out some of the freshest, fanciest, and most delicious pastries in food-rich Astoria.

Specialty and Ethnic Food Shops

BIP GROCERY. 29-18 36th Ave., 729-2566. M–Sa 10:00 a.m.–8:30 p.m.

This hole-in-the-wall Bangladeshi grocery sells enormous bags of herbs and spices (who could use that many bay leaves?) and twenty-pound sacks of rice. Lots of the imported products are labeled in Bangla, which is a language that resembles ancient Sanskrit.

CASSINELLI FOOD. 31-12 23rd Ave. bet. 31st and 32nd Sts., 274-4881. Tu–Su 7:30 a.m.–3:30 p.m.

Queens boasts a number of ethnic food stores that supply upscale eateries and shops in Manhattan. Come to Cassinelli for thirty-some splendid variations of fresh pasta from ravioli to manicotti to tortellini.

GRAND WINE AND LIQUOR. 30-05 31st St. at 30th Ave., 728-2520. www.grandwl.com. M–Th 9:00 a.m.–9:00 p.m., F–Sa 9:00 a.m.–10:00 p.m., Su noon–6:00 p.m.

Befitting a store located in one of the nation's most diverse communities, Grand Wine and Liquor says "Shop for wine from YOUR home country." Indeed, you can find wines, liquors, and spirits not just from Italy, France, and Argentina, but from Algeria, Armenia, Austria, Bulgaria, Croatia, Cyprus, Georgia, Greece, Hungary, Morocco, Portugal, Romania, Slovenia, Lebanon, Czech Republic, Israel, Denmark, and Poland. Prices are competitive.

GREENMARKET IN ASTORIA. 31st Ave. bet 12th and 14th Sts., (212) 788-7476. W 8:00 a.m.–5:00 p.m. (July–November).

Only regional growers may sell at this Greenmarket, which opened in 2005. You'll find fresh fruit, vegetables, fish, meat, eggs, dairy, honey, maple syrup, and sometimes plants. Greenmarket is a program of the New York City Council on the Environment.

MEDITERRANEAN FOODS. 23-18 31st St. bet. 23rd and 24th Aves., 721-0221. M–Sa 8:00 a.m.–9:00 p.m., Su 8:00 a.m.–7:00 p.m.

Q: Why come to Queens to shop for food?

A: Because your supermarket just doesn't have this stuff: fresh feta and imported Greek cheeses, imported olives, yogurts, Greek olive oil, honey, and stuffed grape leaves. There's another store at 30-12 34th St., 728-6166.

ROSARIO'S DELI. 22-55 31st St. bet. Ditmars Blvd. and 23rd Ave., 728-2920. M–Sa 8:00 a.m.–7:00 p.m.

Most of the time, you can walk into and out of this deli without hearing any English at all. You can get picnic fixings here: mozzarella balls, the freshest cold cuts, a small selection of prepared foods, and more imported Italian packaged goods than you've ever seen. Rosario's is a good place to look for hard-to-find European soft drinks and other specialty items.

TITAN FOODS. 25-56 31st St. bet. Astoria Blvd. and 30th Ave., 626-7771. www.titanfood.com. M–F 9:00 a.m.–9:00 p.m., Sa–Su 9:00 a.m.–8:00 p.m. Parking in rear.

This well-stocked food emporium is like Zabar's, but for the Greek set. You can get genuine Greek treats in the store or on-line, from imported chamomile teas to inexpensive sea salt to olives kept in big drum barrels to that incomparable fresh Greek yogurt. The folks at Titan understand that good ingredients are essential to good cooking.

Interesting Neighborhood Shops

LILLYTH. 31-90 37th St. off Broadway, 274-8376. M–Sa 11:00 a.m.–8:00 p.m., Su noon–7:00 p.m.

The hippest boutique in the borough of Queens, Lillyth isn't shy about sexy, colorful clothing for women. It's packed with fun gear from swinging skirts and peek-a-boo tops to high heels and high-fashion jewelry—all at surprisingly moderate prices. Imported gear from trendy Brazilian designers such as Schutz and CAOS appeal to the big expat Brazilian community in the area. There's another store at 130 Thompson St. in Manhattan.

SALVATION ARMY. 34-02 Steinway St. bet. 35th and 35th Aves., 472-2414. M–F 10:00 a.m.–7:30 p.m., Sa 10:00 a.m.–6:00 p.m.

This is one of the biggest thrift stores in the city, reportedly over 15,000 square feet filled with S*T*U*F*F. Whether you're looking for a Hawaiian shirt, props for the school play, an old goose-necked reading lamp, or objects for a collage, you will probably find it here.

SEABURN BOOKS. 33-18 Broadway bet. 33rd and 34th Sts., 267-7929. M–Sa 10:00 a.m.–9:00 p.m., Su noon–9:00 p.m.

Looking for an art book in Greek? A Spanish-language version of Shakespeare? Seaburn Books' eclectic selection includes African-American titles and books in multiple languages. The staff speaks English, Greek, and Spanish, among other languages.

SECOND BEST. 30-07 Astoria Blvd. at 31st St., 204-8844. Daily 10:00 a.m.–7:00 p.m.

An old-fashioned thrift store, you have to dig for surprises here, and you might find furniture, bric-a-brac, books, or clothing.

SONARGAON FABRICS. 29-03 36th Ave., 786-0422. Daily 10:00 a.m.–9:00 p.m.

A stunning palate of vibrant purples, greens, blues, oranges, reds, and yellows overwhelms you when you enter this store specializing in saris and *salwar kamiz* (the tunic-pant ensemble traditional to Indian, Pakistani, and Bangladeshi women). Saris start at $100 and salwar kamiz at $30. Both are made in cotton, silk, and polyester. Friendly service makes it easy to ask questions.

UNIQUE FASHION BOUTIQUE. 40-18 28th Ave. near 41st St., 545-6100. M–Sa 11:30 a.m.–8:00 p.m.

For that outer-borough *je ne sais quoi*, ladies with fashion flair should check out the hot, trendy outfits here: sassy skirts, skimpy tops, and a sexy style. Prices are moderate.

 ESSAY

THINGS YOU SAY REGULARLY IF YOU'RE A TWENTY-SOMETHING LIVING IN QUEENS

by Max Lance

Max Lance is a twenty-one-year-old stand-up comic who moved from Manhattan to Queens, mostly for the lower rents.

"You're sure you can't come back to my place?"

"I know a restaurant that'll make you feel like you're in Athens."

"It's exactly nineteen minutes and twenty-six seconds door-to-door to Times Square."

"Anyone going to Queens? No? Really?"

"Well, it's much quieter except for that subway next to my window."

"You're sure you can't come back to my place?"

"Yeah, I'm out of there as soon as the band gets signed."

"No, I have no idea which are the streets and which are the avenues."

"*The Cosby Show* was filmed at Kaufman Astoria Studios. Are you 100 percent positive you don't want to come back to my place?"

"Of course people buy Mets season tickets."

"I know where all the entrances to the Queensboro Bridge are."

"Queens is the largest borough in New York. How can you not be convinced about coming back to my apartment?"

"Ever see *The King of Queens*? A cousin of a friend of a friend totally knows that guy."

"At least I don't live on Staten Island."

"It's a great place to raise a family—if I could get a girl back to Queens."

7

Bayside, Douglaston, Whitestone, and Environs

ayside and nearby communities of northeast Queens are geographically far from Manhattan, and even more so in style and attitude. Malba and Whitestone are famously suburban. Far from the subway, they are accessible only by car or the Long Island Rail Road. Demographically, these communities are fairly uniformly middle- to upper-middle class; Douglaston, for instance, has the highest per capita income in Queens. People move to these far-flung corners of New York City precisely to get away from the congestion and mix of the urban center.

THINGS TO SEE AND DO

Inside-the-city suburbs may be great to live in, but would you really want to visit? Well, sure. There's golf and boating for the sporting enthusiast. The decommissioned Civil War–era Fort Totten will be of interest to any history buff, romantic couple, or urban explorer. Wonderful experiences await young families at Alley Pond Environmental Center and the Queens County Farm Museum. And, you can get an Italian meal at Il Toscano.

BITS OF HISTORY

Home to the Matinecock Indians, the area was settled as early as the mid-1650s by English colonizers. Wooded and rural, the northeastern swath of Queens was much less developed than other areas of New York until well after the Civil War. One good way to get a sense of Queens in the 1800s is to take a trip to the Queens County Farm Museum, where a landmarked farmhouse, fields, and live animals fuel the imagination enough to comprehend what Queens might have been like before highways, electricity, and subways.

In the 1830s, Wynant Van Zandt (whose 1819 mansion survives as a clubhouse for the Douglaston Yacht Club) sold some of his land to William Douglas, after whom contemporary Douglaston was named, in exchange for his allowing a rail sta-

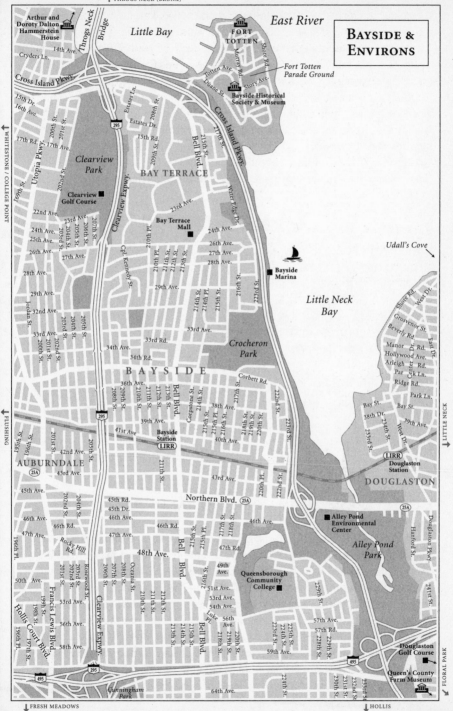

BAYSIDE & ENVIRONS

THROGS NECK (BRONX)

East River

Little Bay

Arthur and Doroty Dalton Hammerstein House

14th Ave.

Cryders Ln.

Cross Island Pkwy.

15th Dr.

16th Ave.

17th Rd. 17th Ave.

Utopia Pkwy.

Clearview Park

Clearview Golf Course

22nd Ave.

24th Ave.

25th Ave.

26th Ave.

28th Ave.

29th Ave.

32nd Ave.

Jordan St.

33rd Ave.

34th Ave.

BAYSIDE

36th Ave.

39th Ave.

41st Ave

Bayside Station LIRR

42nd Ave.

AUBURNDALE

43rd Ave.

45th Ave.

46th Ave.

47th Ave.

Rocky Hill Rd.

48th Ave.

50th Ave.

Francis Lewis Blvd.

Hollis Court Blvd.

53rd Ave.

56th Ave.

58th Ave.

Cunningham Park

FRESH MEADOWS

Throgs Neck

Throgs Neck Bridge

Estates Ln.

Estates Dr.

15th Rd.

BAY TERRACE

23rd Ave.

Bay Terrace Mall

24th Ave.

26th Ave.

27th Ave.

28th Ave.

29th Ave.

Cpl Kennedy St.

33rd Rd.

34th Rd.

33rd Ave.

Crocheron Park

Corbett Rd.

Bell Blvd.

Corporone St.

38th Ave.

40th Ave.

43rd Ave.

Northern Blvd.

45th Rd.

45th Dr.

46th Ave.

47th Ave.

46th Rd.

47th Rd.

49th Ave.

51st Ave.

53rd Ave.

54th Ave.

56th Ave.

59th Ave.

64th Ave.

FORT TOTTEN

Fort Totten Parade Ground

Bayside Historical Society & Museum

Cross Island Pkwy.

Shore Rd.

Murray Rd.

Totten Ave.

Duane St.

Story Ave.

Water Edge Dr.

Bayside Marina

Little Neck Bay

Udall's Cove

WHITESTONE / COLLEGE POINT

FLUSHING

Queensborough Community College

Alley Pond Environmental Center

Alley Pond Park

Douglaston Station LIRR

DOUGLASTON

Shore Rd.

West Dr.

Grosvenor St.

Beverly Rd.

Manor Rd.

Hollywood Ave.

Arleigh Rd.

Ridge Rd.

Park Ln.

Bay St.

38th Dr.

Bay St.

39th Ave.

East Dr.

Center Dr.

West Dr.

Douglaston Golf Course

Queen's County Farm Museum

Douglaston Pkwy.

Hanford St.

57th Ave.

57th Rd.

LITTLE NECK

FLORAL PARK

HOLLIS

tion to be built on his property. The high ground overlooking a strategic strait was the site where Fort Totten was built in the Civil War era, bringing a permanent military presence to the area. After the North Shore Railroad reached Bayside in 1866, making the area more accessible, it became a playground for the wealthy who built estates here, paving the way for the next generation of sportsmen and actors who, too, built extravagant homes. In turn, these estates were sold and the land subdivided for smaller, cheaper homes. During the mid-twentieth century, acquisition of land by the City for the construction nearby of first the Whitestone Bridge in 1939, the Clearview Expressway in 1955, and subsequently the Throgs Neck Bridge in 1961 changed the area again. In recent years, a sizable middle-class immigrant community has arrived in northeastern Queens, introducing greater ethnic diversity.

Bayside

WHERE IT IS: Northeastern Queens, on Little Neck Bay, including Bay Terrace.
HOW TO GET THERE: There's no subway; LIRR station at 213th St. and 41st Ave.
WHAT'S NEARBY: Alley Pond Park at the southeast and Cunningham Park to the southwest, Douglaston to the east, Flushing to the west, Little Neck Bay and Long Island to the east, and Throgs Neck Bridge to the north.
MAJOR SHOPPING/RESTAURANT STREETS: Bell Blvd.
SPECIAL CHARACTERISTICS: Old military base, boating, views of water and bridge.
ON NOT GETTING LOST: Orient yourself to Little Neck Bay and Long Island on the east, and Throgs Neck Bridge on the north. Note that three main roads run north-south: Clearview Expwy., Cross Island Expwy., and the local Bell Blvd. Northern Blvd. and the LIE run east-west.
CAR SERVICES: Kelly 229-6262, Century 465-1105 or 740-6600.

LIGHT-YEARS FROM MANHATTAN—AND THAT'S THE WAY THEY LIKE IT

Named after Little Neck Bay, the neighborhood of Bayside retains a villagey feel. The sense of cohesion is fostered, in part, by an old-fashioned main street, Bell Blvd., which is lined with little mom-and-pop stores. Many people know one another. For those who work in "the City"—that is, Manhattan—the all-important LIRR station is nearby. Realtors boast of the public golf course and picturesque views of the East River, Long Island Sound, and the Throgs Neck Bridge. Many streets are lined with two- and three-bedroom homes, each with private driveways and patches of green yards. With lots of space, a relaxed pace, and water views here, you feel far from Manhattan. That's precisely the point of Bayside, both a hundred years ago in its heyday and today.

⌖ Insight

A Prominent Past

In the early twentieth century movie stars lived here, some in large homes and mansions surrounded by land. Crocheron Park was once a huge private estate belonging to the prominent Crocheron family, and upscale Bayside Gables sprouted from the gardens and manicured grounds of elaborate, sprawling summer homes such as the Louis Harway House. The old private Bayside Yacht Club has been rehabbed into a Korean church for upwardly mobile immigrants. Plenty of old Bayside families have scrapbooks and long memories, and swap stories of local lore. It's not surprising for some guy fixing his car to point his wrench at a house down the block and say, "Yeah, that's where W. C. Fields's summer house used to be. My father knew him."

PARKS, PUBLIC SPACES, AND PUBLIC WORKS

☺ **BAYSIDE MARINA.** 28-05 Cross Island Pkwy. at Little Neck Bay off the Cross Island Expwy. at the foot of 28th Ave., near Northern Pkwy. and Bell Blvd., 229-0097. May 1–Oct. 31st 8 a.m.–8 p.m. or sundown; call for hours.

Boat owners rent slips and moorings at Bayside Marina for the season. Day-trippers can rent a motorboat, Jet Skis, or fishing equipment for a few hours of fun on Little Neck Bay. A sixteen-foot Carolina skiff with an eight-horsepower motor costs $35 for the first hour; bring a driver's license. Facilities include a snack bar, rod rentals, and bait and tackle. There's also a two-and-a-half-mile pathway for biking, Rollerblading, and running.

CLEARVIEW PARK AND GOLF COURSE. 202-12 Willets Point Blvd. entrance bet. Utopia Pkwy. and Clearview Expwy., 229-2570. www.nycteetimes.com, www.americangolf.com.

There's no public park, just a beginner-to-intermediate 18-hole golf course (3 to 5 par) here. Founded in 1925 as the Clearview Golf and Yacht Club, it was once an exclusive retreat. After the calamitous stock market crash of 1929, New York City purchased the land, renamed the golf course, and opened it to the public. It is located by Little Neck Bay and was named for its views; hole #17 is famous for its views of Long Island Sound and the Throgs Neck Bridge. Managed by the American Golf Corporation, its services include a pro shop, lessons, clubhouse, lounge/bar, etc.

☺ **CROCHERON PARK.** 215th Pl. and 33rd Rd. at Little Neck Bay. Call New York City information line 311. www.nycgovparks.org.

Facilities at the forty-five-acre Crocheron Park include a playground, tennis courts, a baseball diamond, picnic grounds, winding walks, and thousands of trees. The sledding is great.

The park is named after a prominent local family associated with the area for generations. The first Crocheron of note was a farmer John, whose will dates from 1695. One of his descendents, Joe, was the garrulous head of an establishment, the Bayside House, popularly known as "Crocheron House." Records show that politicians from Tammany Hall came to Crocheron House for picnics and clambakes; infamous pol William "Boss" Tweed (1823–78) fled there after escaping the Ludlow Street Jail in 1875. A 1907 fire destroyed the house, and it remained unused until it was transformed into the public park it is today. Crocheron Park was expanded after Broadway producer John Golden willed his thirty-acre estate to the City of New York for parkland in 1955.

☺ 🏛 **FORT TOTTEN AND FORT TOTTEN PARK.** Cross Island Pkwy., Totten Rd. to 15th Rd., 352-4793 ext.18. www.nycgovparks.org. No parking in Fort Totten; use lot across from entrance to the Fort. Not to be confused with Fort Tilden in the Rockaways.

Fort Totten was the fort that fizzled. It became functionally obsolete for defensive purposes almost as soon as it was built, starting in 1857. This 150-acre fort includes a boating dock, a Civil War–era battery, grassy expanses, a chapel, underground tunnels, old bunkers and torpedo rooms, a narrow five-hundred-foot underground arched tunnel, and those cool narrow windows in stone fortresses from which soldiers of yesteryear took aim. You will find extraordinary views, a calm quiet and, from time to time, a film crew here.

Fort Totten Park occupies a third of this property and was opened to the public in 2005. The public park includes the old battery, eleven historic buildings (several of which are official New York City landmarks), the thirteen-acre parade ground with soccer fields, and pathways with views of Long Island Sound. Visitors can attend Shakespeare performances, concerts, children's performances, and sports leagues here, and also use the Flushing YMCA's outdoor pool, which is open to adults, teams, and families several days a week. Urban Park Rangers offer weekend tours of the property's historic features. It's often quieter on summer weekends than better-known city parks.

Some buildings are used by nonprofit organizations. Fort Totten Mansion houses local chapters of professional organizations of engineers and registered architects. The 🏛 Officers Club, a gorgeous Gothic Revival castle, is occupied by the Bayside Historical Society (see listing, p. 64), and is open to the public. Outside the park, the land and buildings are used by the Coast Guard, the New York City Fire Department training academy, the Eastern Paralyzed Veterans Associations, and the U.S. Army Reserve.

Fort Totten was built with some 15,000 solid granite blocks and a quarter-mile concrete foundation and is considered an engineering feat in its own right. The stone rampart (1862–64) was built based on the plans of Captain Robert E. Lee. Located at the mouth of the Long Island Sound, across from its

Bronx counterpart Fort Schuyler, Fort Totten created a pinch point meant to protect the eastern approach to New York Harbor. Shortly after its completion, however, the fort became useless as a defensive structure, due to rapid advances made in artillery during the Civil War. Over the next century, it was used for hospital care, the Engineer School of Application, and Army School of Submarine Defense. Since 1969, it has been home to the U.S. Army Reserves 77th Command. It is one of several forts in the United States named for General Joseph Totten (1788–1864), who was killed in the Battle of the Wilderness in Virginia.

☛ **TIP: Bike trail: Brooklyn-Queens Greenway to Fort Totten.** Wouldn't it be nice to bike all the way from Brooklyn to Bayside on a greenway? The Brooklyn-Queens Greenway (BQG), a forty-mile on- and off-street trail, starts in Coney Island. A twenty-two-mile stretch in Queens goes from Highland Park (at the Brooklyn-Queens border) to Fort Totten (in northeastern Queens). Half of the trail is off-street. New bike paths are planned for Southern Queens, Laurelton, Cross Island Greenway, and a link from Cross Bay Blvd. to the Jamaica Bay Wildlife Refuge. Stay tuned. For an interactive map see www.nycgovparks.org/sub_things_to_do/facilities/af_bike_where_to_ride.html#top.

JOSEPH MICHAELS PATH AND BRIDGEWAY. Near the Bayside Marina at the foot of 28th Ave. Footbridge over the Cross Island Expwy.

This two-and-a-half-mile running path is named in memory of Joseph Michaels (1941–87), a Bayside resident. He played drums for Jay and the Americans, whose 1964 song "Come a Little Bit Closer" was a smash hit. At age twenty-eight he had the first of seven heart attacks. To combat his congenital heart disease, Michaels became a distance runner and inspiring advocate of cardiac fitness. He's a local hero.

THROGS NECK BRIDGE. From the Bronx: Cross Bronx Expwy. (I-95) or the Throgs Neck Expwy. (I-295) From Queens: Cross Island Pkwy., or the Clearview Expwy. www.mta.nyc.ny.us/bandt/html/throgs.

The Throgs Neck Bridge connects Queens and the Bronx, spanning the point where the East River and Long Island Sound meet. Built in 1961 to alleviate traffic congestion on the Bronx-Whitestone and Triborough Bridges, it was designed by Othmar H. Ammann, architect of both the George Washington and Bronx-Whitestone Bridges. Five-year-olds may call it Froggy Neck, but this bridge is named after John Throckmorton, who settled in the area in 1643. No path for bikers or walkers.

Also Nearby

☺ **CUNNINGHAM PARK.** Francis Lewis Blvd. and Union Tpke. bet. Long Island Expwy. and 199 to 210 Sts. in Fresh Meadows. Call New York City information line 311 or www.nycgovparks.org.

With its rolling hills and summertime performances, 360-acre Cunningham Park feels like Central Park or Prospect Park. Facilities include tennis courts, ball and soccer fields, and picnic seating. You can come for outdoor appearances by the New York Philharmonic, the Metropolitan Opera, and the Big Apple Circus. It's easy to combine a visit to the park with a shopping trip or meal in Bayside. Or, if you want to take a hike or bike ride, you can follow the 4.5-mile route starting at Cunningham Park to Flushing Meadows–Corona Park via Kissena Park and Alley Pond Park. Cyclists enjoy riding on the old Vanderbilt Motor Parkway here. Sections of Cunningham Park fall within the New York City Department of Parks Forever Wild Wildlife Preserve program.

POINTS OF CULTURAL INTEREST

BAYSIDE YACHT CLUB, NOW GRACE KOREAN CHURCH. At the foot of 28th Ave. at the Cross Island Expwy.

The old Bayside Yacht Club was built in the early 1900s, when prominent New Yorkers had homes here. Its history represents how the area has changed in a century. The Clearview Expressway now stands between the building and the area where sailboats were once moored. More recently the building has been renovated, the pool paved over, and new blue stained glass windows installed for the latest resident, a Korean Christian church.

MUSICA REGINAE. 33-19 210th St., 279-4842. www.musicareginae.org.

Musica Reginae means "Music of Queens." This professional nonprofit classical music ensemble performs at venues such as Flushing Town Hall. It was founded in the belief that "the people of Queens deserve to have first-rate classical and contemporary music available to them in their home communities and that they need not travel into Manhattan to find enriching experiences."

☺ **QUEENSBOROUGH COMMUNITY COLLEGE.** 222-05 56th Ave. bet. Springfield Blvd. and 223rd St., 631-6311.

Queensborough Community College, part of the City of New York (CUNY) system, is a two-year college built on the site of the old Oakland Country Club. Its 12,000 students are enrolled in associate degree or certificate programs, and another 10,000 students take continuing education classes.

Of particular interest to visitors are the theater programs and two small, admission-free museums. Performances for children and by touring musicians and dancers are held at **QUEENSBOROUGH PERFORMING ARTS CENTER.** (See schedules at www.qcc.cuny.edu/QPAC; buy tickets M–F 10:00 a.m.–4:00 p.m. at 631-6311 or at www.theatermania.com.) The **QCC ART GALLERY**—housed in a 1920s former clubhouse—features African art and works by contemporary Hispanic artists and American women artists. In the gallery library there's the Wyppensenwah collection of photographs of American Indians on Long Island (222-05 56th Ave., 631-6396, www.qccartgallery.org, Tu, F 10:00 a.m.–5:00 p.m., W–Th 10:00 a.m.–7:00 p.m., Sa–Su noon–5:00 p.m.). The **HOLOCAUST RESOURCE CENTER** sponsors exhibits, free lectures, and movies. (281-5770, www.qcc.cuny.edu/hrca, M–F 9:00 a.m.–5:00 p.m.) Twice yearly the college president holds public lectures on topical issues of the day.

SHIN KWANG CHURCH OF NEW YORK. 33-55 Bell Blvd. bet. 29th and 32nd Aves., 357-3355.

This picture-postcard traditional Christian church with its front-lawn sign now in Korean sits on the main street of Bayside. Like a testimony to the cultural kaleidoscope that Queens is today, churches all over the borough have more diverse congregations than in the past.

 **Insight**

McMansion-ization? Downzoning? Who's Right?

A raging debate is going on in Queens about what are derisively called McMansions. These big new homes—some with huge glass windows, others faced in pink marble—can be seen in almost every upscale residential neighborhood.

McMansions are built to maximize house size on small lots, which in Queens are usually 30 × 80 or 40 × 100 feet in size. Often they are bigger and taller than the homes around them. Sometimes their front gardens are paved over. Old-time residents frequently complain that the new homes are ugly and change the feel of a block. Insult is added to injury when a graceful older home is torn down by speculative developers who cram two or three new homes where there had been one. Most McMansions are legal. Zoning laws in the borough have historically been lax, and not many homes in Queens have been given landmark status, either. To grasp what the fuss is all about, take a drive around Bayside Gables, a tony residential community built in the roaring 1920s, where the differences in style are apparent. In another neighborhood, Fresh Meadows, you can see a block of 1960s-era ranch houses interrupted by much flashier new homes at 196th Place.

As we go to press, some of Bayside has been rezoned, and communities in College Point, Little Neck, and Flushing are lobbying for changes in zoning laws that would restrict house size.

PEOPLE, PLACES, AND THINGS OF HISTORICAL INTEREST

BAYSIDE HISTORICAL SOCIETY AND MUSEUM. Fort Totten Bldg. #208, 352-1548. Museum: Th–F 11:00 a.m.–4:00 p.m., Su noon–4:00 p.m. No parking in Fort Totten; use lot across from entrance to the Fort.

The Bayside Historical Society is housed in an old Officers Club at Fort Totten (see p. 60). The red Gothic Revival–style building resembles a castle, because it was built for the Army Corps of Engineers, whose insignia depicts a castle. This and other delightful historical trivia can be learned from a trip to the museum here. The Bayside Historical Society organizes lectures, walks, and educational programs, including tours of the Officers Club. By appointment, researchers can scour the archives. There's also a small gift shop.

JAMES J. CORBETT'S RESIDENCE. 221-04 Corbett Rd. bet. 221st and 222nd Sts. No tours, private.

Now a private home, this residence with water views was the home of "Gentleman Jim" (1866–1933), matinee idol and the world's heavyweight boxing champ from 1892–97. He was a local celebrity residing in Bayside from 1902 until his death. Note the plaque on the stone on the lawn.

HOUSE AT 35-34 BELL BOULEVARD. 35-34 Bell Blvd. at 35th Ave. No tours, private.

Take a moment to look at this old red-tiled-roof house and you'll notice something unusual: the walls are made of rugged, unevenly sized tan and gray cobblestones. Cobblestones were used to pave New York City streets but why use roughhewn rocks in the walls of a home? The New York City Landmarks Commission speculates, "Stone walls were frequently used to mark property boundaries and it is possible that cobblestones were chosen to evoke Bayside's fleeting agricultural past."

Built in 1906 as a residence, this was part of an upscale development called Bellcore, a project of the Rickert-Finlay Realty Company, which developed the last hundred acres of a large farm once owned by Abraham Bell. A Broadway actress, Maude Adams, is said to have resided here a century ago. Over time the building has been used as a boys' school, restaurant, apartment building, and today, a dentist's office.

LAWRENCE FAMILY BURIAL GROUND. 216th St. and 42nd Ave., 352-1548. Visitors by permission only.

One of several family cemeteries in Queens with landmark status, this one was used as a family burial site from 1832–1925 by the prominent Lawrence clan. A sign at the site informs visitors that "this plot of ground is the only part of Bayside that ties Bayside to its colonial past" because it dates back to the original patent granted by the Dutch governor in 1645. Among those buried here are Cornelius Van Wyck Lawrence (1791–1861), former New York City Mayor and member of U.S. Congress, and Mary Nicoll Lawrence (1822–96), second wife of

Andrew Mickle, also Mayor of New York. It's locked; contact the Bayside Historical Society for guided tours.

WHITE CASTLE. 213-17 Northern Blvd., corner Bell Ave. Daily 7:00 a.m.–9:00 p.m.

Alas, the interior of this 1930s White Castle has been modernized, but old photos show that the original restaurant had spiffy stainless-steel countertops with spinning stools. White Castle was one of the first fast food chains to open in New York City.

RESTAURANTS, CAFÉS, AND BARS

BEN'S KOSHER DELI OF BAYSIDE. 211-37 26th Ave. in Bay Terrace, 229-2367. www.bensdeli.net. Su–Th 11:00 a.m.–9:00 p.m., F–S 11:00 a.m.–10:30 p.m.

According to Ben Dragoon, owner of this popular deli, "To some, delicatessen is something you put between two slices of bread. To me, it's a calling." You can get Jewish comfort food here, such as overstuffed corned beef sandwiches, homemade knishes, chopped liver platter, and half-sour pickles. Don't miss the matzoh ball soup—or Ben's annual matzoh ball–eating competition. Check out kids' menus, promotions, and mail-order packages on the Web site. Ben's has locations in Manhattan's garment district and Boca Raton, Florida.

BOURBON ST. CAFÉ. 40-12 Bell Blvd. bet. 40th and 41st Aves., 224-2200. M–Th, Su 11:30 a.m.–10:00 p.m., F–Sa 11:30 a.m.–11:00 p.m. Live music: W 8:00 p.m., Su 11:00 p.m.

Soak up some youthful Bayside ambience at the Bourbon Street Café. The something-for-everyone menu includes cedar-planked salmon, New Orleans–style blackened chicken and gumbo, and such Italian favorites as pan-fried mozzarella. Entrées start at $20.

CAFFE ON THE GREEN. 201-10 Cross Island Pkwy. bet. Willis Point Blvd. and Utopia Pkwy., 423-7272. Tu–Th noon–10:00 p.m., F noon–11:00 p.m., Sa 5:00 p.m.–11:00 p.m., Su 2:00 p.m.–9:30 p.m.

Silent film heartthrob Rudolf Valentino's summer cottage looks like it was once a secluded spot near the waterfront, but the beachfront is gone and Rudy's old love shack is now marooned on the opposite side of a highway that cut off access to Little Neck Bay. Today there's a restaurant, and while you dine on light Italian fare, you can enjoy the views of a duck pond and the Throgs Neck Bridge.

ERAWAN 2. 42-31 Bell Blvd. bet. 43rd Ave. and Northern Blvd., 428-2112. M–Th noon–10:30 p.m., F–Sa noon–11:30 p.m., Su 3:00 p.m.–10:30 p.m.

When you're in Bayside and suddenly yen for pad thai, papaya salad, and other tasty Thai tidbits, come to Erawan. The standard dishes are well prepared and nicely presented. Typically hot Thai spicing has been toned down for American palates. Sometimes there's a wait on weekends.

OASIS CAFE & BAKERY. 196-30 Northern Blvd. bet. 196th and Francis Lewis Blvd., 357-4843. Daily 7:30 a.m.–2:00 a.m.

For Greek pastry that's arguably as good as what you'll find in Astoria, come to the Oasis. In the summer you can enjoy pastas or salad while sitting outside on a deck overlooking a burbling water fountain.

PAPAZZIO RESTAURANT. 39-38 Bell Blvd. at 40th Ave., 229-1962. Daily 11:00 a.m.–11:00 p.m.

This upscale, family-friendly Italian eatery serves Northern and Southern Italian fare. Share an appetizer platter, then indulge in some nicely turned-out pasta and grilled meat specials.

UNCLE JACK'S STEAKHOUSE. 39-40 Bell Blvd. bet. 39th and 40th Aves., 229-1100. M–F noon–4:00 p.m. (lunch), M–W 4:00 p.m.–11:00 p.m. (dinner), Tu–Sa 4:00 p.m.–midnight (dinner), Su 3:00 p.m.–10:00 p.m. (dinner).

Uncle Jack's has all the elements of an old-fashioned upscale steakhouse: USDA prime beef dry-aged for three weeks, dark wood decor, a cozy saloonlike bar, and cognacs and cigars to top off the evening. The melt-in-your-mouth filet mignon runs about $40. Uncle Jack's signature porterhouse steak is excellent, and costs over $80. You can also get Kobe beef here, a Japanese specialty. There's another Uncle Jack's near Penn Station in Manhattan.

SHOPPING

BAY TERRACE MALL. 26th Ave. and Bell Blvd. www.bayterrace.com.

"When guests come from out of town, they don't expect to find trees and lovely homes and gardens—and they really don't expect to *shop*. But that's what they do," exclaims one Bayside resident. Locals enjoy the not-so-jumbo Bay Terrace Mall with its suburban ambience and a mixture of chain and locally owned shops. You can go to the dentist or post office, get a facial, or go to the movies. Check the Web site to see if your favorite stores are there.

BELL FAMILY JEWELERS. 40-21 Bell Blvd. bet. 40th and 41st Aves., 279-3035. M–W, F 10:00 a.m.–6:00 p.m., Th 10:00 a.m.–7:00 p.m., Sa 10:00 a.m.–5:30 p.m.

Bring your watch to be repaired, or pearls to be restrung, or choose from a nice selection of watches, necklaces, bracelets, rings, and earrings at this full-service store. They also buy, sell, and will trade in your old jewelry. A saleswoman jokes, "We take the old jewelry—just not the ex-husbands and ex-boyfriends who gave it to you."

CHRISTIE & CO. SALON. Bay Terrace Shopping Center. 23-62/68 Bell Blvd. bet. 23rd and 24th Aves., 225-7766. M–W 10:00 a.m.–7:00 p.m., Th 10:00 a.m.–9:00 p.m., F 8:30 a.m.–9:00 p.m., Sa–Su 9:00 a.m.–6:00 p.m.

If you're buying yourself a "day of beauty" package at a salon, consider getting similar services, but for half the price of Manhattan salons, at Christie's. A day with full-body massage, facial, pedicure, manicure, haircut, and styling, makeup with lesson, and light lunch costs under $250.

HAZEL'S HOUSE OF SHOES. 35-16 Bell Blvd. bet. 35 and 36th Aves., 423-8666. M, W, F 10:00 a.m.–4:30 p.m., Tu, Th 10:00 a.m.–9:00 p.m., Sa 10:00 a.m.–5:00 p.m., Su noon–4:30 p.m. (hours may change).

Hazel's House of Shoes has been around for over twenty years. With a selection of designer shoes at discount prices, Hazel's is the place to go for everyday shoes, wedding shoes, or dyeables. The staff is friendly and if you have any questions, ask for Hazel herself! There's a bargain here: Buy ten, get one pair free.

PETER'S MARKET. 33-35 Francis Lewis Blvd. bet. 33rd and 34th Aves., 463-4141. M–F 9:00 a.m.–7:00 p.m., Sa 9:00 a.m.–6:30 p.m.

One-stop specialty shopping for fine foods makes Peter's a local favorite. Stop in for tasty take-out sandwiches for a picnic in Fort Totten Park. Don't miss the butcher counter.

✐ ESSAY

They Call Us Grandpa and Grandma

As told to the author by Irving Chipkin.

We moved here in August 1950. After World War II, with the discharge of many soldiers who were starting their own families, a lot of veterans bought homes in the area. It was all new, including a lot of the schools.

Bayside was just a great place to raise a family. Our street has about fourteen semidetached homes on each side. At one time we had as many as ninety kids playing in the street, all kinds of games: skip rope and Johnny on the pony and ringalevio. These are the games we played as kids, too; we passed it down.

There's been a big change in the past ten years. Most of the new homeowners are middle-class Chinese people. A lot of them have their own businesses not only as storekeepers but also in telecommunications and technology.

The children, now there aren't as many. You might see just a dozen playing on the street, and today they are Chinese. The school where most of our kids went, now is mostly filled with Chinese children. These kids speak perfect English. It's like in my generation; we were the first born in this country and our parents came

(continued)

from Europe and spoke Yiddish and also English. The children speak mostly English.

Our next-door neighbors are a Chinese family who moved in three years ago. Before that our friend had lived there since 1950. The new ones next door to us are a lovely family with a seven-year-old boy and an eleven-year-old girl.

We like them very much. The kids call us Grandpa Irving and Grandma Doris. They ring the bell and walk right in. If we are in the den, they sit with us. If we are busy in the kitchen, the little one will put his own TV program on. Twice I had extra tickets to a play out in Nassau County and took the kids. Most of the people at the theater were white seniors, and here we are with these two Chinese kids holding Doris's and my hands, calling us Grandma and Grandpa.

The children's grandparents, who are about seventy, come over sometimes to rake up, to help. In China they were professional people and just arrived here within the past three years. It is all very new to them, and of course they are shy. But if they see me working in the garden or snow, bingo, they come right on over. The man across the street, who works for the post office, also Chinese, he's very friendly, too.

I love to see changes. Some people might resent it. But I see these kids going to school in a modern school, they speak perfect English and have a deep appreciation of this country. I think it is great.

I am going to be eighty-six. Doris is going to be eighty-two this Monday.

Douglaston and Little Neck

It's hard to overestimate the impact on Douglaston (especially the historic district of Douglas Manor) and parts of Little Neck that their proximity to the large body of water known as Little Neck Bay has had. Sailing has long been associated with the area; late-nineteenth-century resident Willie Douglas competed in the America's Cup race, and a local street is even named Regatta Place. These communities are also on the border of Nassau County, and enjoy the quiet pleasures of the suburbs. The best way to see this predominantly residential area is to visit someone who lives here; otherwise, drive along Shore Road down to the tip of the peninsula at Bayviews Ave.

WHERE THEY ARE: Northwestern Queens.
WHAT'S NEARBY: Alley Pond Park, Bayside, Little Neck Bay (and Nassau County)

PARKS AND WATERFRONT

☺ **ALLEY POND PARK AND ALLEY POND ENVIRONMENTAL CENTER.** Union Tnpk. Little Neck Bay to Springfield Blvd., 217-6725. www.alleypond.com. Daily 10:00 a.m.–6:00 p.m.

Many New Yorkers don't even know this wonderful park exists. Relax and play in 625 acres with over a dozen tennis courts; ponds; baseball, soccer, and football fields; and wooded trails. You can practice your golf swing at **GOLDEN BEAR DRIVING RANGE** (enter at Northern Blvd. and 221st St., 225-9187, www .golfandsportsinfo.com); meanwhile, the kids can play miniature golf. Bike riders and runners enjoy a traffic-free Old Motor Parkway. Alley Pond Park has freshwater and saltwater wetlands, tidal flats, meadows, and forests, making for a diverse ecosystem and abundant bird life.

Whether you're eight or eighty, you can learn something new on a nature-trail walk or field trip at the **ALLEY POND ENVIRONMENTAL CENTER.** Where else in New York can you go for a guided hike during the full-moon tide to spy on horseshoe crabs as they indulge in their annual June mating ritual? Founded in 1972, the seven-hundred-acre facility has been designated a U.S. Park Service National Environmental Study Center for over twenty-five years. Come for one of their programs: spring bird-watching or autumn walks that show how animals adapt their habitats for the winter. Children enjoy fun seasonal projects like building scarecrows, Halloween haunted walks, and campfires. And for a rare treat, you, too, can go stargazing with their guides. (Enter at 228-06 Northern Blvd. at Cross Island Pkwy., 229-4000. M–Sa 9:00 a.m.–4:30 p.m., Su 9:30 a.m.–3:30 p.m., closed Su July–Aug.)

DOUGLASTON GOLF COURSE. 6320 Marathon Pkwy., 428-1617. www.golfnyc.com. Sunrise–sunset. Fee $30 on weekdays, after 1:00 p.m., $26, on weekends $36.50, after 1:00 p.m. $16.50.

This public 18-hole, par-67 beginner-to-intermediate golf course boasts a pro shop, lessons and clinics, putting green, clubhouse, men's locker room, restaurant, and a bar and lounge—and Manhattan skyline views on a clear day. Reservations required, call 224-6566.

UDALL'S COVE AND RAVINE. Marinette St. and Douglas Rd. (in Little Neck). Ravine: Cove Ravine, Northern Blvd. and 244–247 Sts.

Come visit this thirty-acre ravine and nature preserve and bring a tree guidebook with you to enjoy the huge variety of trees here, from white mulberry and black cherry to Norway maple, as well as rushes, giant reed grass, and salt marsh grass. Bring your binoculars, too; this is bird-watching heaven. The preserved wetland has become a local cause célèbre due to threats to the habitat from local pollution.

PEOPLE, PLACES, AND THINGS OF HISTORICAL INTEREST

🏛 **ALLEN-BEVILLE HOUSE.** 29 Center Dr., corner of Forest Rd. No tours, private residence.

This house, built in the antebellum period (1848–50), is on the National Register of Historic Places. Its significance is in its Italianate style—and the fact that it has survived for over 150 years! Note the white shingles and views of Little Neck Bay from the widow's walk above. As of late 2005, the owners (descendants of the Bevilles) were seeking a buyer who would finish restoring the five-bedroom house, on the market for $2.85 million.

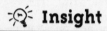 **Insight**

Black Oystermen of Little Neck Bay

The early history of Douglaston includes a short-lived colony of post–Civil War era black oyster fishermen who made a living off the shores of Little Neck Bay until pollution killed off the oyster trade here. Some of their homes can still be seen in the landmarked district.

🏛 **DOUGLASTON HISTORIC DISTRICTS.** Roughly bounded by Douglaston Pkwy., Northern Blvd., 244th St., 243rd St., and Long Island Railroad.

In 1997, New York City designated 600 homes as the Douglaston historic district, encompassing all of the section known as Douglas Manor and part of Douglaston. These areas capture a moment in time when Queens had been transformed from little villages, estates, and small farms to commuter suburbs. Douglaston Hill is a landmarked district, founded in 1853. Douglas Manor, started in 1906, is replete with large, historically interesting homes (and a catering facility called Douglaston Manor). Both are quintessential early-twentieth-century commuter suburbs, with a cornucopia of styles including Queen Anne, Colonial, Shingle, Arts and Crafts, and Tudor.

DOUGLASTON YACHT CLUB. 600 West Drive Manor Rd., 229-3900. www.douglaston.net. Private.

The Douglaston Yacht Club was founded in the 1880s, when the area was a rural retreat for wealthy New Yorkers. The rambling old clubhouse is still in use; it was once the residence of the founder of Douglaston.

ZION EPISCOPAL CHURCH AND CEMETERY. 243-01 Northern Blvd. bet. 44th Ave. and 244th St., 225-0466. www.mindspring.com/~zionchurch.

The white, clapboard-style Zion Episcopal Church could be on a lonely New England byway, but it happens to stand above busy Northern Blvd., just west of the Nassau County border. The church opened in 1830 on farmland donated by Wynant Van Zandt, of the prominent Van Wyck family. The historic churchyard holds the graves of the last Matinecock Indians, of Lewis Cornell, a Revolutionary War soldier, and of Civil War veterans.

RESTAURANTS

IL TOSCANO. 42-05 235th St. Dead end from Douglaston Pkwy., near the south side of the Douglaston LIRR station, 631-0300. Tu–S 5:00 p.m.–11:00 p.m.

Il Toscano—"The Tuscan"—stands out in a borough and a city known for its Italian food. The Northern Italian food and service are top-notch, rivaling Manhattan restaurants at a price that's expensive for Queens but a bargain for what you get. The rack of lamb is superb, and what they do with lasagna will make you wish the chef was your grandmother.

Specialty and Ethnic Food Shops

CERIELLO FINE FOODS. 44-35 Douglaston Pkwy. at Northern Blvd., 428-2494. www.ceriellofinefoods.com. M–F 10:00 a.m.–7:00 p.m., Sa 9:00 a.m.–6:00 p.m.

If you've been to the food court in Grand Central Station, you may already know Ceriello's. Their Douglaston store also offers a selection of fine steaks, roasts, and other meats, along with prepared foods.

MAZUR'S MARKET AND RESTAURANT. 254-51 Horace Harding Blvd. bet. 254th St. and Nassau Blvd., 897-4829. M–Th noon–11:00 p.m., Sa 7:30 p.m.–1:00 a.m., Su 12:30 p.m.–11:00 p.m.

Not just kosher, but glatt kosher! Mazur's Market, in business since 1960, sells a huge array of fine cuts of meat—which is why the white-tableclothed restaurant by the same name serves such fresh foods. Have some hot pastrami and fresh *tsimmis* for lunch. Then come back later for the broiled baby-rib lamb chops or Romanian tenderloin. Eat, darlink, eat.

Whitestone

Whitestone is largely suburban with a cute three-block downtown area around 150th St. that has several old-fashioned stores, including Stork Pastries. There are several marinas and lots of opportunities to enjoy gorgeous water views.

WHERE IT IS: Northwestern Queens.
WHAT'S NEARBY: Bayside, College Point, the East River, and Flushing.

PARKS, PUBLIC SPACES, AND PUBLIC WORKS

BRONX WHITESTONE BRIDGE. Via the Van Wyck Expressway or Whitestone Expressway (Route 678).

The Bronx-Whitestone Bridge is a six-lane bridge connecting the Bronx and Queens. It was opened on April 29th, the day before the 1939–40 World's Fair opened. According to the MTA, nearly 1.7 billion vehicles have crossed the bridge since that day. There's no bike or pedestrian paths. If the Whitestone is jammed up, try the Throgs Neck.

FRANCIS LEWIS PARK. Bounded by 3rd Ave., 147th St., the East River, and Parsons Blvd. www.nycgovparks.org.

With winding pathways and two overlooks with sunset views of the East River, Francis Lewis Park is one of the most romantic places in the city, yet most New Yorkers have never heard of this delicious little sixteen-acre hideaway.

POINTS OF CULTURAL INTEREST

🏛 **ARTHUR AND DOROTHY DALTON HAMMERSTEIN HOUSE.** 168-11 Powell's Cove Blvd. Privately owned, no tours.

This spacious, elegant, Tudor-style mansion is in Beechurst, the neighborhood directly east of Whitestone that served as a getaway for Broadway stars of the 1920s, who traveled from Manhattan via the LIRR to the Whitestone station nearby. This home was designed for Arthur Hammerstein, a successful Broadway producer who worked with George Gershwin and was an uncle of that Oscar Hammerstein who wrote *My Fair Lady*.

ST. NICHOLAS RUSSIAN ORTHODOX CHURCH OF WHITESTONE. 14-55 Clintonville St. and 14th Rd., 767-7292. www.stnicholasny.org. Services in English Sa evening and Su morning.

Founded in 1916 as a missionary Russian Orthodox parish by immigrants of Russian and Ukrainian heritage, today St. Nicholas parish tends to a primarily American congregation. Its Russian-style blue onion dome sits atop a contemporary church built in 1968, with white arches that are reminiscent of Orthodox architecture. Inside is traditional Orthodox iconography, and the church walls glow with images of saints painted by a Russian artist in the 1990s.

RESTAURANTS, CAFÉS, AND BARS

CHERRY VALLEY DELI AND GRILL. 12-29 150th St. at 12th Rd., 767-1937. Daily 24 hours.

Cherry Valley serves up rich deli food that's satisfying. Try the Beast, which combines a fried chicken cutlet, melted Swiss cheese, gravy, bacon, and onion rings in a roll or hero. Kids like the Waffle Couch Potato, which is waffle fries with melted mozzarella and gravy.

Specialty and Ethnic Food Shops

PANE D'ITALIA. 20-04 Utopia Parkway, 423-6260. W–M 7:00 a.m.–4:00 p.m.

Bread is the staff of life! And Pane d'Italia turns out some of the handsomest crusty loaves your hungry heart could desire, especially the traditional ciabatta.

STORK'S PASTRY. 12-42 150th St. bet. 12th and 13th Aves., 767-9220. M–Sa 7:00 a.m.–7:00 p.m., Su 6:30 a.m.–6:00 p.m.

You won't need a *Kochglossar* (culinary dictionary) to decipher what's what at this old-style German bakery, because the pastries, pies, and chocolates all seemed to be labeled with the same thing: Yummy! Stork's has been in business for more than a half century.

ALSO IN THE VICINITY

LIVING MUSEUM AT CREEDMOOR PSYCHIATRIC CENTER. Building 75, 80-45 Winchester Blvd., 264-3490. By appointment only.

The Living Museum is a huge 40,000-square-foot space filled with the artwork of people with mental illness. The idea for this museum was born in 1983 at this New York State psychiatric hospital not as "art therapy" but as an actual gallery and art studio for both inpatients and outpatients. It was the brainchild of the late Bolek Greczynski, and the current director, Austrian-born Dr. Janos Marton, who renovated an unused building into what the latter has described as a sheltered creative space. If the idea is powerful, so is some of the artwork. Living Museum pieces have been shown at the Queens Museum of Art and the Daborah Gallery in New York, and were the subject of a film by Oscar Award–winning Jessica Yu.

☺ 🏛 **QUEENS COUNTY FARM MUSEUM.** 73-50 Little Neck Pkwy. bet. Union Tnpk. and Northern Pkwy., 347-FARM (3276). www.queensfarm.org. M–F 9:00 a.m.–5:00 p.m., Sa–Su 10:00 a.m.–5:00 p.m. Admission is free, except for special events. Tours are available.

What city kid doesn't love a trip to the farm? The Queens County Farm, dating back to 1697, is New York City's only working historical farm and largest remaining tract of undisturbed farmland. There are lots of fun, hands-on experiences for children. The main house, the Cornell (Creedmoor) Farmhouse, is a national landmark that is maintained by the Restoration Society of Bellerose. On the forty-seven-acre site are historic farm buildings, greenhouses, livestock, farm vehicles and implements, planting fields, an orchard, and herb gardens.

Special events (with entrance fees in the $5–8 range) include seasonal Easter egg hunts, spring and autumn carnivals, a May farm festival featuring sheep-shearing demonstrations and Dutch crafts, a July three-day Thunderbird American Indian Powwow, a September corn maze (including a "maze by moonlight" for older kids), October pumpkin picking, and December holiday fairs. Adults might be interested in the pre-Thanksgiving eighteenth-century tavern nights, featuring traditional recipes prepared on an open hearth and served on period tableware ($60 per person; reservation required). There's a seasonal produce stand and both garden and museum shops.

Within a mile of the farm you can enjoy two Indian restaurants. **BANGLADESHI FIZA DINER** (259-07 Hillside Ave. bet. 259 and 260 Sts., 347-3100) is known for excellent kebabs and *haleem,* a spicy wheat-and-lentil combo. **SANTOOR** (257-05 Union Tnpk. at 257th St., 343-3939) is a good—and fiery—alternative to the Jackson Diner. Both are open for lunch and dinner.

8

Corona and Elmhurst

Corona and Elmhurst, two neighborhoods in northcentral Queens, are hardly top-of-mind tourist destinations. Yet together, these two diverse areas are rich in historical sites (including one museum and several national landmarks) and cheap, authentic ethnic food.

Corona

WHERE IT IS: Northwestern Queens, adjacent to Flushing Bay and Flushing Meadows-Corona Park.

HOW TO GET THERE BY SUBWAY: #7 to Junction Blvd., 103rd Street–Corona Plaza, 111th St.

SPECIAL CHARACTERISTICS: Corona has a high-population density, friendly ghosts (of famous jazz musicians), excellent fresh mozzarella, and a famous Italian ices shop.

WHAT'S NEARBY: Elmhurst to the southwest, Flushing Meadows–Corona Park to the east, Jackson Heights to the northwest, Rego Park to the south.

ON NOT GETTING LOST: Corona is easy to reach, if you happen to be at a Mets game or otherwise find yourself in Flushing Meadows–Corona Park. It's also a ten-minute cab ride from LaGuardia. The main north-south streets are 108th St. and Junction Blvd.; main east-west streets are the Long Island Expwy. and Roosevelt Ave. It's a small neighborhood, but the grid street system breaks down occasionally so you'll find lots of "40th Rd." and "40th Dr." streets here and many named streets that are just a block or two long. It's best to bring a map.

CAR SERVICES: Dominicana 507-1700, Santo Domingo 699-5959 or 899-5050.

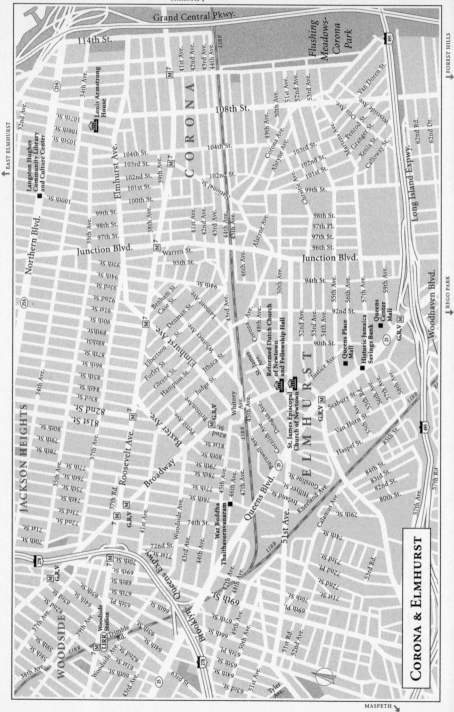

CORONA & ELMHURST

Close to Shea, Music, and Mozzarella

If you say, "Corona?" to someone from Queens, their knee-jerk reaction will probably be: "Lemon Ice King!" But say, "Corona?" to someone from Manhattan, and
they'll think you've just offered them a beer. Which is to say, working-class, Spanish-
speaking Corona's not exactly on most people's Top 10 Hot Tourist Destinations.

 Insight

The Should-I-Bother-Going-to-Corona? Quiz

If you answer "yes" to any one of the following three questions, you should absolutely, definitely plan a trip to Corona.

Do you love jazz?

When you go to Flushing Meadows—Corona Park for a Mets game or tennis
match, do you head straight home when it's over?

Do you consider yourself a connoisseur of fresh mozzarella?

The louder you say "yes," and the more "yeses" you have, the more reason to
discover Corona.

THINGS TO SEE AND DO

Unequivocally, the biggest tourist attraction in Corona is the Louis Armstrong
House. There's nothing like it in all of New York's marvelous wealth of museums.
There are some culinary attractions in this gritty setting, too. If you're going to
Shea Stadium or the USTA Billie Jean King National Tennis Center, consider carv-
ing out an extra twenty minutes to go get a big, fat, juicy sandwich from Mama's,
where the fresh mozzarella and heroes are good enough for New York's finest and
bravest, the cops and firemen who are regular customers. The Parkside Restaurant
is one of old New York's classic Italian eateries, and the Lemon King of Corona
serves up really regal ices.

 Insight

Reading the Colors

"Latino" is such a generalization that it's almost useless here. When in Corona,
think as the locals do: Ecuadorian, Dominican, Colombian, and Mexican. If you
are attuned, you can tell where a person is from by the Spanish he speaks, just as
any American can differentiate a Texan's drawl from a Bostonian's broad "a." And

(continued)

you can sometimes tell at a glance where someone comes from. For instance: Mexican storefronts are often decorated in red, white, and green, the colors of the Mexican flag. Similarly, Colombians decorate in yellow, blue, and red, and Dominicans use red, white, and blue.

BITS OF HISTORY

Corona was first settled by the Matinecock Indians, followed by colonial farmers. In the 1850s, this area was simply a rural part of the village of Newtown. During one brief decade or so in the eighteenth century the Fashion Race Course horse track was in operation nearby, and some roads were laid out. By 1872 the area had been named Corona (meaning crown, because, it's said, of its location on the top of a hill) by a developer. In 1893, a Tiffany Glass factory opened here and churned out popular decorative lamps until the 1930s.

The arrival of the #7 subway line in 1917, which made Manhattan accessible in a half hour, was described by Queens historian Vincent Seyfried as "the single most important event that has ever occurred in the history of Corona." (A less exciting but equally important improvement in the same era was that sewers were installed, facilitating further residential development.) The area boomed in the 1920s, thanks to the opening of several light industrial plants that made china, ceramics, and portable houses. In the early quarter of the twentieth century, the neighborhood had a mixed blue-collar population of Italians, Jews, Greeks, and a smattering of African-American residents. In the 1940s Louis Armstrong moved to Corona, and later, Dizzy Gillespie did, too. After World War II a large Puerto Rican population settled here, followed in the 1980s by Dominicans. Today the population is a U.N.-worthy mix of immigrants from Latin America, Korea, India, and Guyana. An Italian presence is still represented in cuisine; and a historic synagogue, now on the National Register of Historic Places, is a reminder of earlier immigrant communities.

PARKS, PUBLIC SPACES, AND PUBLIC WORKS

Flushing Meadows–Corona Park. (See p. 124.)

POINTS OF CULTURAL INTEREST

LANGSTON HUGHES COMMUNITY LIBRARY AND CULTURAL CENTER—QUEENS LIBRARY. 100-01 Northern Blvd. at 100th St., 651-1100. www.queenslibrary.org. M, F 10:00 a.m.–6:00 p.m., T 1:00 p.m.–6:00 p.m., W–Th 1:00 p.m.–8:00 p.m., Sa 10:00 a.m.–5:00 p.m.

This state-of-the-art library, opened in 1999, has the nation's largest circulating black heritage collection, with more than 45,000 volumes of print and nonprint materials related to African-American and African diasporic culture. This includes an on-line collection of twenty-six black newspapers, plus academic theses on black literature. Non-Queens residents can use library materials on-site. Special events are held upstairs in the 150-seat auditorium with stage and there's a community art gallery, too.

Founded by citizens in 1969 during the civil rights era, the Langston Hughes Community Library and Cultural Center was run for nearly two decades by the nonprofit Library Action Committee of Corona-Elmhurst. They sought to enable African-Americans to explore black culture through literature and art. Their beyond-the-book vision led to a creative expansion of library-based programs, including films, festivals, art shows, and performances. To attract people who might not normally visit a library, they innovated new ideas, for instance cobbling together collections of children's books featuring African-American heroes and heroines and using color codes instead of numbers to classify books. The Langston Hughes Community Library and Cultural Center was a pioneering collaboration between a large library system and grassroots activists seeking to address social issues. It joined the Queens library system in 1987.

Annual events include the Langston Hughes Celebration (second Sa in Feb.), Louis Armstrong Jazz Brunch (last Sa in June), and Kwanzaa (second Sa of Dec.). For film festivals, concerts, and exhibits, see Web site.

☺ 🏛 **LOUIS ARMSTRONG HOUSE.** 34-56 107th St., 478-8274. Tu–F 10:00 a.m.–5:00 p.m., Sa–Su noon–5:00 p.m. Fee: adults, $8; seniors, students, and children: $6. Hourly tours. For group reservations call 478-8274.

You'll feel like one of Louis Armstrong's best friends after taking the forty-minute tour of what he called "my little pad" that he lived in for nearly thirty years. Like Armstrong's jazz, his modest home is full of personality. As you tour, you hear tape recordings in each room of Satchmo yakking it up with friends and humming a tune. An indefatigable diarist who recorded his own personal conversations, Pops, as many called him, left over 650 reels of seven-inch tapes. In the dining room you hear Louis's voice, joking about red beans and rice, and whether the city of Brussels "sprouts."

The house is frozen in time, and fascinating personal memorabilia collected by Armstrong's pal, driver, and associate Jack Bradley, recently acquired by the museum, is on display—his suits, personal letters, and photos. There's even a piece of the banister from the New Orleans Home for Troubled Boys where Louis first played an instrument.

The father of American jazz, Satchmo was a huge star before the age of forty, but he put down roots in working-class Corona from 1943 until his death in 1971. Why did Armstrong stay in Queens? For one, his home was near the airport, and at the height of his career, he was on the road 300 days a year. (He is said to have played in every nation in the world except the USSR and China.) He was also comfortable here; snapshots capture Louis showing neighborhood children how to hold a trumpet.

A new visitors' center is planned for 2008. There's a gift shop with CDs and books, and an annual Jazzmobile concert around the Fourth of July, Armstrong's birthday. The Louis Armstrong Archives are at Queens College. (See pp. 106–7.)

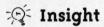 Insight

Illegal Conversions

Elmhurst and other areas of Queens suffer from what's known as the problem of "conversions." That refers to illegal residences being carved out of houses, where sometimes several dozen immigrants are living in substandard conditions, sometimes in basements that lack emergency exits and proper ventilation.

PEOPLE, PLACES, AND THINGS OF HISTORICAL INTEREST

CONGREGATION TIFERETH ISRAEL. 109-18 and 109-20 54th Ave., near 109th St.

For decades, there was a significant Jewish community in Corona. Founded in 1911 by Jewish immigrants, Congregation Tifereth Israel reflects the orthodox religious traditions of the era, with an upstairs section reserved for women, and the central prayer area downstairs, used exclusively by men. It is listed on the National Register of Historic Places as an exemplary building of its era.

CORONA THEATRE. 37-80 Junction Blvd., off 37th Ave.

The first known movie shown in Corona was in 1905, and the novelty cost ten cents for ladies, and a nickel for children. By 1910 there was an open-air "moving picture park" for silent films in Corona, called the National Airdrome. By the time the Corona Theater was built in the 1930s, talking movies were all the rage. Designed by architect Carl Boller in a luxurious Spanish Colonial Revival style, this building is a New York City landmark and is today used as a church.

DIZZIE GILLESPIE RESIDENCE. 34-68 106th St. Private; not open to the public.

Famous jazz musician Dizzy Gillespie (1917–93) lived here in the post–World War II era. Famous for his sunglasses, beret, and goatee, he helped create the fusion sound of Afro-Cuban music.

EDWARD E. SANFORD HOUSE. 102-45 47th Ave. at 102nd St. Private residence, not open to the public.

With carved trimmings on the porch and gable that bring to mind a child's gingerbread house, this late nineteenth-century landmark is a freestanding home originally built for Edward E. Sanford, about 1871. It is one of the few remains of the old community of Newtown that existed before Corona and Elmhurst were renamed by the Cord Meyer Company and developed for residential housing.

TIFFANY STUDIO. 44th Ave., 97th Pl. and 43rd Ave. Not open to the public.

In 1893, Louis Comfort Tiffany (1848–1933), the son of the highly successful owner of the luxury store Tiffany's, branched out and launched his own successful business making popular art nouveau–style glass lamps and windows. This old brick manufacturing building, now used by a clothing manufacturing company, was Tiffany Studios from 1893 to 1938. According to the Queens Museum of Art, which has a very large collection of Tiffany glass, "during the peak of production (1900–18) Tiffany glass furnaces turned out nearly 30,000 objects a year made of glass produced in 5,000 colors with a variety of thousands of patterns and textures."

 **Insight**

Lefrak City

Behemoth Lefrak City (off the Long Island Expressway at Junction Blvd., east of Queens Blvd.) has its own special place in New York City's urban lore. With a population of about 15,000, Lefrak City today is bigger than the entire town of Cherry Hill, New Jersey. Lefrak City was trumpeted in the 1960s as "the largest apartment house development in the world built with private, conventional financing and without some kind of government assistance." Covering forty acres, with twenty eighteen-story apartment buildings and self-contained shopping and transportation, it was designed for low-income and working-class families. Mostly Irish, German, and Italian families moved in. White flight followed a federal housing discrimination suit against the complex in 1970. Recently there's been an influx of Russian and Bukharan immigrants.

RESTAURANTS, CAFÉS (AND ICES)

CORONA PIZZA. 51-23 108th St. bet. 51st and 52nd Aves., 271-3736. M-Sa 10:30 a.m.–10:00 p.m., Su noon–8:00 p.m.

This pizza—especially the thin-sliced version with fresh mozzarella and tomatoes—is so good you could have it for breakfast. Afterward, walk across the street to watch the bocce game in Spaghetti Park or have an ice at Lemon Ice King.

LA ESPIGA BAKERY. 42-13 102nd St. bet. 42nd and 43rd Aves., 779-7898. Daily 10:00 a.m.–10:00 p.m.

Come in for an authentic Mexican taco, enchilada, or bakery sweets. The people are friendly, the prices are rock bottom, and the ambience, or total lack thereof, will remind you of a small village in Mexico. Other locations: 32-44 31st St., 777-1993, and 103-02 Roosevelt Ave., 533-1260.

☺ **LEMON ICE KING OF CORONA.** 52-02 108th St., at the corner of 52nd Ave., 699-5133. Daily 11:00 a.m.–7:00 p.m., later in summer.

As heard on the street in 2005: "The Ice King's a landmark, like the Empire State Building, but for Queens. Wanna know what it was like growing up Italian in New York? The Lemon Ice King is what it was like. It's nothin' fancy but it's got quality. You ain't been in Queens til you been to the Lemon Ice King."

The Lemon Ice King of Corona was established in 1941. You feel like you're in the back kitchen here, it's so simple. The flavors are good, but the scene is even better.

PARK SIDE RESTAURANT. 107-01 Corona Ave. bet. 51st and 52nd Aves., 271-9321. M–Sa noon–11:30 p.m., Su 1:00 p.m.–10:00 p.m.

Park Side is an old-fashioned, white-tableclothed, just-like-in-the-movies Italian restaurant with waiters dressed in dark suits. There's valet parking, and bocce games across the street in good weather. You can enjoy a $40 evening with excellent food that would cost $80 in Manhattan; reservations are recommended on weekends. The Lemon Ice King is a block away.

POLLADA DE LAURA. 102-03 Northern Blvd. at 102nd St., 426-7818. Su–Th, noon–11:00 p.m. F, Sa noon–1:00 a.m.

You will find some of the best ceviche in Queens here. This modest Peruvian eatery is another notable Queens restaurant that's still under the radar screen, so get there quick!

TONY'S PIZZERIA. 45-18 104th bet. 45th and 46th Aves., 779-1707. Daily 11:00 a.m.–11:00 p.m.

Beyond pizza (and the pizza is good) try any of the excellent pasta dishes, and don't miss the salad, which is ample and fresh. Tony's is not far from the Queens Museum of Art, N. Y. Hall of Science, and other attractions of Flushing Meadows–Corona Park.

SHOPPING

CORONA HEIGHTS PORK STORE. 107-04 Corona Ave., M–Sa 9:00 a.m.–7:00 p.m.

The homemade sausages and meats at Corona Heights Pork Store are phenomenal. The recipes, like the store name, harken back to a pre–fast food era. The secret ingredient at Corona Heights is "time." Proscuitto takes time to cure. Sausages, too. Aficionados say they make the best sandwich in the Big Apple.

JUNCTION BOULEVARD BARGAINS. 37th Ave. to Roosevelt Ave. and Junction Blvd.

Get off the #7 subway at Junction Blvd., and you're in a Spanish-language shoppers' heaven. There are bargains galore here, with stylish but inexpensive clothing, shoes, children's gear, and men's apparel, too. It's the perfect place to buy accessories to dress up for a special party, or pick up inexpensive gifts for friends. You'll save a bundle.

LEO'S LATTICINI (AKA "MAMA'S OF CORONA"). 46-02 104th St. bet. 46th and 47th Aves., 898-6069. Tu–W 10:00 a.m.–5:00 p.m., Th–F 10:00 a.m.–6:00 p.m., Sa 10:00 a.m.–5:00 p.m.

If there are angels in Queens, they're at Mama's. You walk in a stranger, you walk out part of the family. The magic ingredient isn't angel dust, it's mozzarella. Or love, because at Mama's there's love in that fresh mozzarella. How else could it be so warm, so squishy, and so incredibly good? New York's true gourmands—the cops, firemen, and sanitation crews—have been coming here since about the 1920s. If you can force yourself to look past the salumeria counter jammed with delicious cheeses, sausages, cold cuts, marinated mushrooms, sun-dried tomatoes, and fresh breads, you'll see a wall lined with signed photos of mayors and public officials.

The store's officially named Leo's Latticini, after her deceased husband, but everyone calls the place Mama's. Today her three fabulous daughters race around making big fat hero sandwiches (try the Original Mama Special, with pepper ham, Genoa salami, and fresh mozzarella), while Mama holds court from a table nearby.

Next door is **MAMA'S BACKYARD CAFÉ** (565-9104, Tu–Sa 7:00 a.m.–7:30 p.m., Su 7:00 a.m.–3:00 p.m.), a sit-down bakery-café where you can enjoy Napoleon pastry, torchetti, and wheelbarrows full of cookies, croissants, and turnovers in a backyard garden. Also part of the empire is **LEO'S RAVIOLI** (639-7211, Tu–Sa 9:00 a.m.–6:00 p.m., Su 9:00 a.m.–1:00 p.m.), selling fresh ravioli, sauces, and pasta dishes. The entire family lives upstairs and they all treat you like you've been there every day of your whole life.

SILVER BELL BAKERY. 43-04 Junction Blvd. at 43rd Ave., 779-5156. M–Sa 7:00 a.m.–8:00 p.m., Su 7:00 a.m.–7:00 p.m.

Try the old-fashioned rugalach and big loaves of European bread, the better to mop your soup up with. Don't confuse this bakery with Silvercup in Long Island City, which was once a bakery but today is a film production company.

✒ ESSAY

THE JAZZ GREATS: THEY ALL LIVED IN QUEENS

by Michael Cogswell, Director, Louis Armstrong House and Archives.
Michael Cogswell has preserved and cataloged Armstrong's vast collec-
tion of personal recordings and artifacts, and is widely considered a
leading expert on Satchmo's life.

Jazz is typically associated with Storyville in New Orleans, Beale Street in Memphis, Chicago's South Side, Kansas City's 18th and Vine, 52nd Street in Manhattan, Harlem, and Greenwich Village. Until recently, only insiders knew that one of the most significant communities in jazz history is the Borough of Queens. Why? Because more than fifty great jazz musicians made their homes in Queens.

Louis Armstrong lived for twenty-eight years on 107th Street, and today his house is a National Historic Landmark open to the public. Dizzy Gillespie moved one block away and used to drop by to swap jokes and news with Louis. In the nearby Dorie Miller apartment houses lived Clark Terry, Cannonball Adderley, and Nat Adderley, and Jimmy Heath resides there still. The Addisleigh Park neighborhood had perhaps the highest concentration of jazz musicians anywhere: Count Basie, Ella Fitzgerald, Lena Horne, Milt Hinton, Illinois Jacquet, Oliver Nelson, Mercer Ellington, Cootie Williams, and Wild Bill Davis all settled within a few blocks of one another. (Basie owned a huge swimming pool and his pool parties were legendary social events.) Also in Queens—at one time or another—were Benny Goodman, Tony Bennett, Jimmy Rushing, Billie Holiday, Milt Jackson, Glenn Miller, James P. Johnson, Ben Webster, Bix Beiderbecke, and a host of others.

Why did so many jazz greats reside in Queens? In part because Queens offered significant advantages to working musicians. The nightclubs, concert halls, and recording studios of Manhattan were just thirty minutes away, and the city's two major airports are both in Queens. Many musicians from the rural South preferred a full-sized house with a backyard to an apartment in Harlem. Although today we appropriately cherish these musicians as icons of American culture, we forget that, in the day-to-day life of the mid-twentieth century, many jazz musicians were striving for—and were elated to achieve—a comfortable, middle-class existence. Every jazz fan knows Billy Strayhorn/Duke Ellington's "Take the A Train." Perhaps it is time for a companion tune: "Take the E Train."

Elmhurst

WHERE IT IS: Northwestern Queens. Bounded to the north by Roosevelt Ave., to the east by Junction Ave., to the south by the LIRR, and to the west by railroad tracks.
HOW TO GET THERE BY SUBWAY: G, R, V to Woodhaven Blvd. /Queens Mall, Grand Ave./Newtown, and Elmhurst Ave.; or #7 to 90th Street/Elmhurst Ave.
WHAT'S NEARBY: Corona to the northeast, Jackson Heights to the north, the Long Island Expwy. and Rego Park to the southeast, Woodside to the west.
MAIN SHOPPING STREETS: Queens Blvd., Broadway, and Junction Blvd.; the Queens Center Mall contains more than seventy-five stores.
SPECIAL CHARACTERISTICS: High population density, ethnic diversity, and temples of different religious faiths.
ON NOT GETTING LOST: A few major roads intersect here, notably Broadway, Queens Blvd., Grand Ave., and 51st Ave. To avoid confusion when navigating the little streets on the eastern side of Elmhurst (adjacent to Corona), note that they are named alphabetically from Aske St. at Roosevelt Ave. to Macnish St. near Broadway. Orient yourself to Queens Blvd.
CAR SERVICES: Golden 429-7071, Flushing Express 961-2222 or 205-3341.

A KALEIDOSCOPIC EXPERIENCE

If you want to feel the pulse of the new immigrant scene, to see the melding of global cultures with American products and lifestyle, Elmhurst is as good a living laboratory as any. Elmhurst ranks as one of the most diverse of New York's neighborhoods, with a mix of Latino (Colombian, Dominican, Peruvian, and Ecuadorian), Asian (Korean, Chinese, Filipino), and South Asian (Indian, Pakistani, and Bangladeshi) residents. According to borough officials, residents today come from over one hundred different countries.

THINGS TO SEE AND DO

Because Elmhurst had a long colonial history, there are some architecturally significant buildings in the neighborhood, including two historic churches that look as though they could be on a typical New England Christmas card. On the same street, however, you may notice hair and nail salons galore, eyeglass shops, cell phone and electronics stores, all with signs in Chinese. If you don't mind simple decor, you can get some delicious ethnic meals in Elmhurst. If you're hungry enough to eat half a cow, you can find big portions of reasonably priced Argentinean beef dishes at La Fusta near Elmhurst Hospital. Or, take your pick of various Asian cuisines for instance at Penang (Malaysian), Ping's Seafood, and East Manor Buffet and Restaurant (Cantonese), or Incredible Pho Mini Mall

(Vietnamese). Terraza Cafe Art is wired and hip, an unusual place for this neighborhood that suggests a new wave of gentrification may begin.

> ☞ **TIP: Only in Queens Is North Called East.** In perhaps the single most confusing name twist in Queens, East Elmhurst is due north of Elmhurst. The moral of the story? Bring a map. For more on East Elmhurst, see page 92.

BITS OF HISTORY

Founded in 1683, the town known today as Elmhurst was an important municipal center for two hundred years. It was the hub of a larger area called Newtown by the original British settlers. The historic Cornell Family Cemetery and the historic St. James Episcopal Church of Newtown and Reformed Dutch Church of Newtown remain from that era. The precise boundaries of Newtown changed over the centuries but included parts of what today are Elmhurst and Corona.

This section of old Newtown was renamed Elmhurst in 1896 as real estate developers sought to differentiate marketable tracts of land from the highly polluted Newtown Creek nearby. From 1896 until 1910, Cord Meyer Development Company, which owned and developed large swaths of land in Queens, built expensive homes north of the railroad station. The opening of the Queensboro Bridge in 1909 and extension of rail lines a decade later subsequently led to a sustained burst in housing growth that lasted through the Great Depression of 1929.

Elmhurst was a quintessential upwardly mobile New York ethnic neighborhood (mostly Italian and Jewish) in the first half of the twentieth century. In the 1950s and 1960s the area was depleted as many residents moved to the suburbs. The construction of the first enclosed shopping mall in Queens in 1973 established a new commercial life for the neighborhood. By the 1980 census, the impact of liberalized 1965 immigration laws were seen in a new racial and ethnic diversity.

PUBLIC SPACES

ELMHURST GAS TANKS. 57th Ave., Grand Ave., 80th St. and the Long Island Expwy.

A new park is being carved out of the 6.5-acre former home of the big circular structures known as the "Elmhurst Tanks." The tanks were built in the early twentieth century, and were demolished in the 1990s after supplying gas to Queens residents for eighty years. In 2003, KeySpan sold the Elmhurst gas tanks site to the city for $1.

☺ **FISHER POOL.** 99th St. and 32nd Ave., 779-8356. Daily 11:00 a.m.–6:30 p.m., Memorial Day–Labor Day.

There are two pools here. The large pool measures 60 × 75 feet, and can hold 180 swimmers. There's a smaller wading pool for tots.

☀ Insight

"Avenue of Death": Queens Boulevard

Even New Yorkers who've never ventured into Queens (except to go to an airport) have heard of Queens Blvd. This eight-mile long, twelve-lane, two-hundred-foot-wide road is the widest and one of the busiest roads in the Big Apple. Tragically, it's also one of the most dangerous pedestrian crossings in the city, which explains why it was called "Boulevard of Broken Bones" by the *Queens Tribune* in 2000. More than 60,000 vehicles traverse its twelve traffic lanes daily, according to the Centers for Disease Control. After local newspapers raised a ruckus, changes were introduced to give pedestrians more time to cross, and there are fewer accidents today. Still, watch out as you're crossing the street.

POINTS OF CULTURAL INTEREST

ELMHURST HOSPITAL CENTER. 79-01 Broadway, off Baxter Ave., 334-4000.

Imagine walking into a hospital where the staff spoke only Mandarin Chinese, when all you speak is English. That's the kind of problem, in reverse, faced by many immigrants in Queens seeking health care services. Serving about 1 million people, public Elmhurst Hospital Center faces the challenge of providing health care for the most ethnically diverse community in the Big Apple. Further, one in three Queens residents between eighteen and sixty-five lacks health insurance. The hospital has grappled with the challenge in many ways, including providing interpreters in thirty languages.

GEETA TEMPLE. 92-09 Corona Ave. at 92nd St. 592-2925. www.geetatemple.net. Daily 6:15 a.m.–8:30 p.m.

Take a second look at this old A&P supermarket. Inside is one of the centers of Hindu cultural and religious life in New York. Visitors can peek inside to see the decorative temple, complete with carved statues. The temple is dedicated to the Bhagavad-Gita, a sacred Hindu text. Visitors are welcome but shoes off, please.

INSTITUTE OF BUDDHIST STUDIES AND CHAN MEDITATION CENTER. 90-56 Corona Ave. near 90th St. 592-6593.

The Institute of Buddhist Studies, located in a small storefront building, is devoted to Buddhist meditation and seeks to introduce Zen Buddhism to Westerners. Founded by Ven Sheng Yen in 1977, it offers beginner and intermediate meditation classes, one-day retreats, tai-chi classes, lectures, and chanting and meditation sessions in the evening and on weekends. The Center is also a small monastery where bhikshus and bhikshunis (fully ordained monks and nuns) "live and practice the traditional precepts including harmony, celibacy, and purity of mind."

WAT BUDDHA THAITHAVORNVANARAM. 76-16 46th Ave. near 76th St., 803-9881. Daily dawn–evening.

A gold-topped Thai Buddhist temple, Wat Buddha Thaithavornvanaram stands out on its quiet residential block of two-family homes and small apartment buildings. The Thai community flows in and out all day, whether in worship, classes, or just socializing. On the third floor, visitors can see the Emerald Buddha, a gift from the King of Thailand who came to Elmhurst for the temple's opening. The temple organizes the Royal Karin Day in November, a colorful Thai street festival.

TERRAZA CAFE ART. 40-19 Gleane St. bet. Baxter and Britton Aves., 803-9602. Daily noon–4:00 a.m.

Terraza Cafe Art combines all kinds of attractions that appeal to a young, hipster crowd. It's an Internet café and bar with a small gallery. There's an art film "cine club" that shows films regularly here, too, as well as workshops in drumming and Spanish.

PEOPLE, PLACES, AND THINGS OF HISTORICAL INTEREST
🏛 **CORNELL FAMILY CEMETERY.** Caffrey Ave. at New Haven Ave., adjacent to 1457 Gateway Blvd.

This tiny family cemetery, landmarked in 1970, holds more than two dozen graves dating from 1693 to 1820. Ezra Cornell, who founded Cornell University, was a descendent of the same family. Volunteer preservationists have worked on cleanup of the site for over a decade.

HISTORIC JAMAICA SAVINGS BANK. 89-01 Queens Blvd. at 56th Ave.

Take a look at this unusual building, which resembles a concrete *Jaws* shark with its triangular mouth gaping wide open. It was built next to Macy's in the go-go years of the 1960s when the 1964–65 World's Fair in nearby Flushing Meadows–Corona Park was replete with futuristic buildings. Locals described the building when it was first unveiled as "from outer space" or "a bird in flight or a butterfly." In 2005 it was denied New York City landmark status, which would have preserved its original structure.

🏛 **NEWTOWN HIGH SCHOOL.** 48-01 90th St., at 48th Ave. Not open to the public.

A public school has been standing on this site since 1866. The earliest building was a small, wooden schoolhouse. The New York City Landmark you see here today was built in 1917 in Flemish Renaissance style in a nod to Elmhurst's beginning as a Dutch settlement. After a population explosion in Queens following World War II, the school expanded in the late 1950s with an additional wing designed in International Style. The New York City Landmarks Commission calls it "one of Queen's most prominent buildings," and points out that the existence of a school here for more than 140 years is a "reminder of the long history of commitment and dedication to public education by the people of New York City." Today Newtown High School is one of the city's largest, serving 4,500 students.

🏛 REFORMED DUTCH CHURCH OF NEWTOWN AND FELLOWSHIP HALL. 85-15 Broadway corner of Corona Ave.

The simplicity of an earlier era is apparent in this one-story church, still a prominent feature of the local landscape. The white clapboard Greek Revival–style church (1831) and separate chapel called Fellowship Hall (1854) are landmarked. Located on an otherwise unremarkable shopping street directly across from the historic St. James Episcopal church, this is one of the few wood churches left in New York City. Features include a well-kept landmark cemetery in the side yards with 1830s tombstones and Victorian stained glass windows. An indication of the demographic changes in the area, today it serves a Chinese congregation, with services in Mandarin, Taiwanese, and English.

🏛 ST. JAMES EPISCOPAL CHURCH OF NEWTOWN. 84-07 Broadway at 51st Ave.

This historic church celebrated its three hundredth anniversary recently. The redbrick structure with a backyard cemetery is located directly across the street from the Reformed Dutch Church. Queens historians say that the list of early congregants "reads like a who's who of Queens colonial history: Moores, Sacketts, Alsops, Blackwells, Hazards, and Halletts." During the Revolutionary War, when the British occupied this area, the church held services attended by British troops. Due to collapse, renovation, and expansion, this building has changed greatly over the centuries. Today it serves a Latino congregation and holds services in Spanish and English.

SCOTT JOPLIN'S GRAVE. St. Michael's Cemetery, plot 5, row 2, grave 5. 72-02 Astoria Blvd. 278-3240. Office hours M–F 11:00 a.m.–4:30 p.m., Sa 10:00 a.m.–3:00 p.m., Su 10:00 a.m.–2:00 p.m.

Before jazz, there was ragtime. Scott Joplin, the African-American musician who was father of American ragtime and composer of "The Entertainer," "Maple Leaf Rag," and "Rose Time Rag," was born in about 1868 in Texarkana and died of syphilis in a mental institution in New York. He was buried in 1917 in this pauper's cemetery in an unmarked grave. A 1974 plaque presented by the American Society of Composers, Authors, and Publishers marks his grave. He was honored posthumously by the Pulitzer Committee in 1976 with an award for his contribution to American music. Joplin's music was incorporated into the 1973 Academy Award–winning movie *The Sting*.

RESTAURANTS

BOCA JUNIOR. 81-08 Queens Blvd. bet. St. James Ave. and Van Horn St., 429-2077. Daily noon–midnight.

Hungry? Come feast at this meat-lover's heaven, named after an Argentine soccer club, which serves typically large portions of grilled meats.

DAVID'S TAIWANESE GOURMET BAKERY. 84-02 Broadway, off St. James Ave., 429-4818. Daily 11:30 a.m.–2:00 a.m.

This is a Taiwanese restaurant but there's a Japanese simplicity to the decor. Food from Taiwan has more basil and different spicing than the Cantonese and Szechuan recipes most Americans associate with Chinese cuisine. Try the crabs or lobster, and if you're brave, go for the fabulously named stinky tofu. It's tofu marinated in a pungent concoction for several days, and then fried til it's tart on the outside and soft on the inside.

EAST MANOR BUFFET & RESTAURANT. 42-07 Main St. bet. Maple and Franklin Aves., 353-6333 (Flushing). 79-17 Albion Ave., 803-3952 (Elmhurst). Daily 11:30 a.m.–11:00 p.m.

Both East Manors—one in Flushing, one in Elmhurst—are enormous restaurants. Both serve a buffet with huge quantities of incredibly fresh Cantonese dishes and a terrific dim sum. Don't bother eating for about a day before or after coming here.

FAMOUS PIZZA. 83-07 Broadway, 271-3000. Daily 11:00 a.m.–10:00 p.m. (See listing in Jackson Heights, pp. 171–72.)

LA FUSTA. 80-32 Baxter Ave. at Layton St., 429-8222. Daily 11:00 a.m.–11:00 p.m.

La Fusta is one of the city's best-known meat restaurants, tucked neatly across the street from the Elmhurst hospital. It's Argentinean, which is to say, meat is viewed as one of the essentials of life, as in air, water, and meat. The portions are large. Try the mixed grill or a simple, beautifully prepared steak. Prices are moderate compared to Manhattan.

PENANG. 82-84 Broadway near Whitney Ave., 672-7380. Daily 6:30 p.m.–11:30 p.m.

Perhaps the best Malaysian restaurant in Queens, Penang is an upscale family-run chain. They have noodle soups (try ginger duck lo mee), and house specials such as beef rendang (beef stewed with coconut milk, chilies, and spices) or green curry.

PING'S SEAFOOD. 83-02 Queens Blvd. bet. Goldsmith and Van Loon Sts., 396-1238. M–Th 10:00 a.m.–midnight, F–Sa 10:00 a.m.–2:00 a.m., Su 9:00 a.m.–midnight.

This is a terrific seafood restaurant, specializing in Hong Kong–style Cantonese food. Try crispy fried loofah or prawns the size of that proverbial fish you once caught when nobody was looking.

TANGRA MASALA. 87-09 Grand Ave. bet. Queens Blvd. and Seabury St., 803-2298. Su–Th noon–9:30 p.m., F–Sa noon–10:30 p.m.

Indian Chinese halal? Well, in an era of fusion food, why not? The menu includes such dishes as beef or chicken *masala* fried rice, or vegetable *masala* chow mein, and crisp, fried lollipop chicken. Try the corn soup. Beware the highly spiced dishes unless you truly like it hot; the emphasis is on Indian more than Chinese flavoring. Sometimes there's a wait on weekends. There's another Tangra Masala in Sunnyside.

THE INCREDIBLE PHO MINI MALL. 82-90 Broadway near Whitney Ave. Daily 10:00 a.m.–9:30 p.m.

It must be Elmhurst if you see, cheek-by-jowl, two Vietnamese restaurants named Pho in one otherwise boring minimall. (Pho is a hot noodle soup with bits of meat or fish and vegetables.) Red-roofed Pho Bang (205-1500) is popular for its light, flavorful fish and seafood dishes. Your taste buds will enjoy the garlic and basil, mint and coriander flavors and fresh raw veggies. Pho Bac (263-9000) is highly also regarded. TIP: If you dislike strong flavors, avoid *belachan*, the fermented shrimp paste. (In Flushing, Pho Bang is at 41-07 Kissena Blvd.)

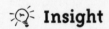 Insight

What's missing from this picture? Bars.

Noticeably absent in Asian communities in Queens are bars. Instead, there's the occasional teashop and quite a number of bakeries, which sell both traditional Chinese sweets and also European-style pastries and coffee.

SHOPPING

CUEVAS BICYCLES. 30-57 90 St. bet. 30th and 31st Aves., 396-0546. M–Sa 10:00 a.m.–7:00 p.m.

The son of Fernando Cuevas, a legendary Spanish racing-bike frame maker, runs Cuevas Bikes. Expert cyclists are likely to say things in admiring tones like, "His tandem frames are a sight to behold." In case you aren't aware, custom bikes are expensive, costing upwards of several thousand dollars.

HONG KONG SUPERMARKET. 82-02 45th Ave. bet. 82nd and 83rd Sts., 651-3838. Daily 9:00 am–9:30 p.m.

What a fantastic plethora of Asian food products! The perfect place to shop for Chinese foods, both fresh and packaged, Hong Kong Supermarket sells soup-to-nuts for a snack or banquet meal. It's boggling, but fun, to walk the aisles of dried mushrooms, Asian vegetables, canned, salted, pressed, and vinegary ingredients, not to mention what seems to be a quarter mile's worth of bottled sauces. Busy, crowded, brash, and commercial—like Hong Kong itself—don't miss it.

QUEENS CENTER MALL. 9015 Queens Blvd. (north side) and Woodhaven Blvd., off the LIE. 592-3900. www.shopqueenscenter.com. M–Sa 10:00 a.m.–9:30 p.m., Su 11:00 a.m.–8:00 p.m.

Stuck at LaGuardia with a five-hour flight delay? Go shopping! Just a three-mile cab ride away the seventy-store Queens Center Mall has a new food court and a wing anchored by JCPenney and Macy's, as well as a number of other popular chains. Check the Web site for free events and phone numbers of livery cabs for LaGuardia travelers. Moms: you can rent strollers here.

QUEENS PLACE MALL. 88-01 Queens Blvd. (north side) and Woodhaven Blvd., just off the LIE. M–Sa 10:00 a.m.–9:00 p.m., Su 11:00 a.m.–8:00 p.m.

Not to be confused with the larger Queens Center Mall nearby, at this smaller mall you will find the anchor stores Best Buy, Target, and Rockaway Bedding.

AND A WORD ON EAST ELMHURST

As you're driving from Long Island along Grand Central Pkwy., with LaGuardia to the north, racially and socio-economically diverse East Elmhurst is to the south. East Elmhurst abuts Astoria and Jackson Heights (although not Elmhurst). Many Queens' dignitaries live in the beautiful homes tucked away here and along such side streets as Butler, Ericsson, and Humphreys. If you have some time to kill, take a drive on Ditmars Avenue along the blocks with street numbers from the low nineties into the low hundreds to view this lovely residential area. East Elmhurst is also known for airport hotels, the Vaughn College of Aeronautics and Technology, and the historic Bulova Corporate Center, described on page 93.

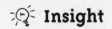 **Insight**

Malcolm X and One Room Schoolhouse Park

American history buffs will be interested in two tidbits. On Valentine's Day 1965, a week before he was murdered in Washington Heights, there was a firebomb attack on **BLACK NATIONALIST LEADER MALCOLM X'S HOME** (23-11 97th St.), and 97th St. is now called Malcolm X Place. On a happier note, **ONE ROOM SCHOOL-HOUSE PARK** (Astoria Blvd. and 90th St.) commemorates the last single-room school in Queens, built in 1879.

BULOVA CORPORATE CENTER. 75-20 Astoria Blvd., 899-0700. M–F 7:00 a.m.–5:00 p.m., Sa 10:00 a.m.–4:00 p.m.

You've seen that gorgeous art deco Bulova sign as you pass by on the way to LaGuardia. Bulova, founded in 1875, remains one of the world's most recognized timekeeping brands and has been in Queens for decades. The Bulova Accutron, chosen as one of the most innovative inventions of the mid-twentieth century, was included in a time capsule buried at New York's 1964–65 World's Fair in Flushing Meadows–Corona Park. A small atrium has displays of art on loan from the Queens Museum of Art (M–F 9:00 a.m.–5:00 p.m.). This building is a corporate office today; Bulova has moved around the corner.

 ESSAY

THE MANICURE BUSINESS

by Stacy Kim

Stacy Kim emigrated from Seoul, Korea, when she was twenty-four in the 1980s with a four-year college degree and a middle-class background. She lives in Elmhurst and since 1989 has run a successful nail salon in Brooklyn, employing a dozen Korean women.

When I came to America. I didn't expect my life would be like this. I didn't expect anything too fancy but not this. The good thing was that I was making my own money and I didn't have to ask for money from my mother; I was independent. But the job I had to do was labor. I thought, Oh, my god, but what else can I do?

I got into the manicure business because a friend of mine had a fruit store here. I worked for her for a couple years as a cashier. That was really hard. I spoke no English at that time. It was so frustrating and embarrassing. People ignore

(continued)

you because you can't speak English. People treated me very badly, and looked down on me because I had no English and also was Asian.

In Korea I had gone to school and never worked. I wasn't too studious, I was into being pretty, and shopping and boyfriends and ohlalala, you know, having a good time. When I came here it was a totally different life. My father said, "Come back. Why are you suffering and you have no family there." But I didn't want to. I wanted to succeed by myself. So I had to stay here.

The cashier job was very hard. I had to stand up long hours, working twelve-hour days with no break except lunch. I worked six days a week for under $200. I was miserable. I looked at the Korean paper and went to interview at manicure salons in Manhattan. The owners said, "You look too fancy for this kind of job." I said no, I work hard. "But you look fancy," they said. I was all dressed up. Finally one lady said okay, so I started as a trainee and learned little by little. I worked at nails for three and a half years from 9:30 a.m. to 7:00 p.m., five days a week for about $300 a week. When my son was six months old, I borrowed money from home to start my own manicure business. I got through some difficult situations with it. I have become very strong and satisfied with myself, I can say, I did it. In Korea women don't have work, and it is hard to find a job. But here even doing this kind of work you make money.

And now people treat me okay. I never took an English class, but I've had a big improvement in speaking English as I listen all the time. I also meditate, I read philosophy. I am a Buddhist, I just let it go, I don't care now. Before it hurt.

9

Greater Flushing

WHERE IT IS: Northeastern to northcentral Queens. Bounded to the west by Flushing Meadows Park, to the east by the Clearview Expwy., to the north by Bayside Ave., to the south by the LIE.

HOW TO GET THERE BY SUBWAY: #7 subway to Main St., Flushing. Also LIRR station at Main St. and 41st Ave.

WHAT'S NEARBY: Bayside to the northeast, College Point to the northwest, Flushing Meadows–Corona Park to the southwest, Kissena Park to the southeast, and La-Guardia to the west.

MAJOR SHOPPING/RESTAURANT STREETS: Main St., Northern Blvd., Union St.

SPECIAL CHARACTERISTICS: Asian immigrants. Asian retail shops, Asian restaurants, Asian businesses.

ON NOT GETTING LOST: Flushing is one of the oldest towns in Queens and so the street grid isn't consistent. There are many short streets, so a map is helpful. In the area near the Queens Botanical Garden, streets named after trees and plants follow an alphabetical sequence. For most of the listings in this chapter, it will suffice to orient yourself to Main St., Roosevelt Ave., and Northern Blvd.

CAR SERVICES: Flushing Express 961-2222 or 205-3341, Imperial 939-6666, Jewel 875-1212.

THE EAST COAST'S BIGGEST CHINATOWN

The street vendors in Flushing sell hot dumplings, not hot dogs. You're in New York, but it feels a bit like Hong Kong. Flushing has the biggest concentrated Asian community in the United States outside of California. Flushing residents come from Shanghai, Beijing, Taiwan, South Korea, and to a lesser extent, Japan—as well as India and South Asia. If you grew up in Queens and haven't been back for a few decades, you're in for a big surprise. The old Flushing—with its deeply entrenched Jewish and Italian community—has almost completely vanished.

You can walk for about three miles and see more storefront signs in Chinese

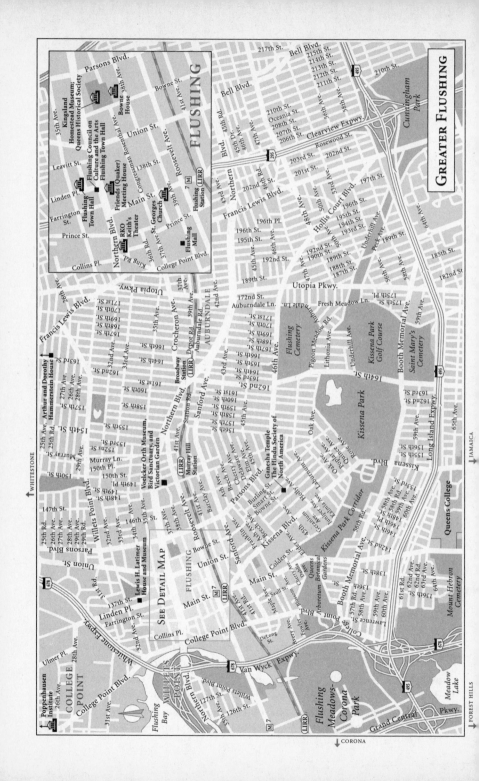

GREATER FLUSHING

FLUSHING

Detail map labels:
Parsons Blvd.
Kingsland Homestead Museum; Queens Historical Society
Bowne St.
Bowne House
41st Ave.
35th Ave.
Union St.
Leavitt St.
Flushing Council on Culture and the Arts
Flushing Town Hall
138th St.
Linden Pl.
Friends (Quaker) Meeting House
Congressman Rosenthal Ave.
Roosevelt Ave.
7 M LIRR
Flushing Station
Flushing Town Hall
Main St.
St. Georges Church
39th Ave.
Farrington St.
RKO Keith's Theater
Prince St.
36th Rd.
37th Ave.
Prince St.
Flushing Mall
Collins Pl.
Northern Blvd.
King Rd.
College Point Blvd.

Main map labels:
Bell Blvd.
217th St.
215th St.
214th St.
213th St.
212th St.
211th St.
210th St.
Cunningham Park
Clearview Expwy.
Rosewood Dr.
210th St.
Oceania St.
208th St.
207th St.
206th St.
203rd St.
202nd St.
Bell Blvd.
45th Rd.
45th Dr.
46th Ave.
47th Ave.
Northern Blvd.
201st St.
Hollis Court Blvd.
197th St.
196th St.
195th St.
194th St.
193rd St.
Underhill Ave.
189th St.
185th St.
182nd St.
Francis Lewis Blvd.
43rd Ave.
202nd St.
46th Rd.
53rd Ave.
196th Pl.
196th St.
195th St.
192nd St.
192nd St.
190th St.
189th St.
188th St.
187th St.
48th Ave.
47th Ave.
50th Ave.
Utopia Pkwy.
172nd St.
Auburndale Ln.
Fresh Meadow Ln.
175th St.
175th Pl.
37th Ave.
Crocheron Ave.
39th Ave.
42nd Ave.
Depot Rd.
Auburndale Rd.
Broadway Station LIRR
181st St.
171st St.
170th St.
169th St.
168th St.
166th St.
165th St.
164th St.
162nd St.
46th Ave.
Auburndale Ln.
Pigeon Meadow Rd.
Lithonia Ave.
Underhill Ave.
Flushing Cemetery
Kissena Park Golf Course
Saint Mary's Cemetery
Booth Memorial Ave.
162nd St.
163rd St.
65th Ave.
AUBURNDALE
Francis Lewis Blvd.
25th Ave.
26th Ave.
171st St.
170th St.
169th St.
168th St.
167th St.
Arthur and Dorothy Hammerstein House
163rd St.
27th Ave.
26th Ave.
28th Ave.
157th St.
162nd St.
33rd St.
35th St.
166th St.
164th St.
161st St.
160th St.
158th St.
Northern Blvd.
Station Rd.
Sanford Ave.
Murray Hill Station LIRR
41st Ave.
43rd Ave.
45th Ave.
159th St.
158th St.
157th St.
156th St.
162nd St.
Kissena Park
Oak Ave.
Underhill Ave.
Kissena Blvd.
WHITESTONE
154th St.
153rd St.
155th St.
Murray St.
29th Ave.
Murray Ln.
150th Pl.
150th St.
149th Pl.
149th St.
148th St.
Voelcker Orth Museum, Bird Sanctuary, and Victorian Garden
Beech Ave.
Cherry Ave.
Ash Ave.
Barclay Ave.
Parsons Blvd.
Burling St.
Smart St.
Bowne St.
Elm Ave.
Delaware Ave.
Ganesha Temple The Hindu Society of North America
Holly Ave.
Laburnum Ave.
Geranium Ave.
Juniper Ave.
Kalmia Ave.
45th Ave.
Quince Ave.
Rose Ave.
Poplar Ave.
Oak Ave.
Kissena Park Corridor
Kissena Blvd.
Booth Memorial Ave.
Queens College
150th St.
147th St.
Willets Point Blvd.
25th Rd.
26th Ave.
27th Ave.
28th Ave.
29th Ave.
29th Rd.
32nd Ave.
33rd Ave.
146th St.
35th Ave.
58th Ave.
Roosevelt Ave.
Bowne St.
Sanford Ave.
Franklin Ave.
Beech Ave.
Kissena Blvd.
Colden St.
Queens Botanical Gardens
Maple Ave.
Holly Ave.
Elder Ave.
Lawrence St.
Booth Memorial Ave.
61st Rd.
62nd Ave.
62nd Rd.
63rd Ave.
64th Ave.
Mount Hebron Cemetery
138th St.
140th St.
141st Pl.
138th St.
59th Ave.
60th Ave.
142nd St.
678
COLLEGE POINT
Poppenhausen Institute
Ulmer Pl.
26th Ave.
Whitestone Expwy.
31st Ave.
28th Ave.
Union St.
137th St.
Lewis H. Latimer House and Museum
Linden Pl.
Farrington St.
Parsons Blvd.
25th Rd.
Parsons Blvd.
SEE DETAIL MAP
FLUSHING
Bowne St.
Union St.
Main St.
Main St. M 7 LIRR
41st Rd.
41st Ave.
Sanford Ave.
Collins Pl.
College Point Blvd.
Collins Pl.
Avery Ave.
Fowler Ave.
Blossom Ave.
Colden St.
Delong St.
College Point Blvd.
Lawrence St.
57th Ave.
58th Ave.
136th St.
59th Ave.
60th Ave.
61st Rd.
JAMAICA
Long Island Expwy.
495
Kissena Blvd.
Booth Memorial Ave.
678
Van Wyck Expwy.
WILLETS POINT
Northern Blvd.
Willets Point Blvd.
35th Ave.
127th Pl.
126th St.
M 7
Flushing Meadows-Corona Park
LIRR
Grand Central Pkwy.
495
Meadow Lake
FOREST HILLS
Flushing Bay
CORONA

and Korean than in English. In the place of pizzerias and burger joints there are noodle shops. You will see big bookstores with not one single English volume, jewelers with rich displays of jade, electronics stores selling Chinese and Korean brands, Japanese Shisheido cosmetics boutiques, tea emporiums, an unusual number of music schools, herbal pharmacies, wedding stores that rent gowns, and cavernous supermarkets with tanks of live fish and aisles of unfamiliar, imported foods. What isn't visible are the import-export and information service businesses based here, though Merrill Lynch and foreign banks, and investment companies occupy prominent storefronts.

Flushing today is a multilingual, technology-savvy Asian and Asian-American center that's thriving locally at precisely a moment in history when China is flexing its economic muscle internationally. It's no accident that the city and private sector are investing in what promises to be an important international small business hub in New York City. (See Major New Developments, p. 112.) If you are curious about the Asia-ascendant world economy toward which we are hurtling, you may get a glimpse of the future right here in humble Flushing.

 **Insight**

Not to Be Impolite, but Why Is It Called "Flushing"?

The name *Flushing* is derived from the Dutch *Vlissingen,* a port in Holland.

THINGS TO SEE AND DO

Do visit the Hong Kong Supermarket, a football field worth of food products you've likely never dreamed existed, or the Korean Han Ah Reum Market. Shun An Tong Health Herbal Co. is the oldest herbal pharmacy in Flushing. Shoppers will find unusual items and inexpensive household goods at the Flushing Mall. The largest Hindu temple in America, the colorful Ganesha Temple, attracts worshipers from all over the tristate area.

For dinner, you can have fun cooking your own meal tableside in a hotpot at Minni's Shabu Shabu and Hibachi. If you think you can take the heat, try a Chinese meal at Spicy and Tasty. Seafood lovers will enjoy the cuisine from the Yangtze River area, and meat lovers can find excellent Korean barbecue at Kum Gang San Korean Restaurant. Gum Fung is one of many favorite dim sum restaurants, and vegetarians rave about Buddha Bodai. For a snack, try a dumpling and bubble tea at any bakery.

You can attend terrific performances at Flushing Town Hall and the Colden

Center for the Performing Arts. Don't miss the historic Bowne House Museum, associated with religious freedom, or the colonial era Kingsland Homestead Museum. Both are included in our Self-Guided Tour. Flushing Meadows–Corona Park and Shea Stadium, the U.S. Open, Queens Botanical Garden, Queens Museum of Art and Panorama of the City of New York, and the New York Hall of Science are fabulous (see p. 128).

> ☛ **TIP: Exotic Getaway.** For an airfare-free Asian adventure, spend a night in Queens. You can shop, have lunch at a bubble tea café, and dine at a Korean or Chinese restaurant. The Sheraton LaGuardia East has an Asian motif and lower-than-Manhattan rates (135-20 39th Ave., 460-6666, www.starwoodhotels.com/sheraton; rates vary). Even cheaper is the Flushing YMCA, where singles start at $50 (138-46 Northern Blvd. bet. Union and Bowne Sts. 961-6880 ext. 133, www.ymcanyc.org/flushing).

BITS OF HISTORY

A theme of religious and racial tolerance runs throughout Flushing's history. Flushing was established by English settlers in 1654 as one of the original independent towns in what is now Queens. It was where a 350-year-old document hailed as the precursor to the Bill of Rights, called the Flushing Remonstrance, was issued. The colonial Quaker Meeting House still stands today, as does the John Bowne House. Some free blacks, including inventor Lewis Latimer, settled in the area.

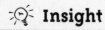 **Insight**

George Washington Shopped (Not Chopped) Here for Trees

A 1789 entry in George Washington's journal reads, "I set off from New York in my barge to visit Mr. Prince's fruit gardens and shrubberies in Flushing." In the mid-1700s William Prince Nurseries was one of the first in the United States. The colonies were agrarian and even military leaders appreciated the value of importing European species that weren't indigenous to North America; in 1777 General Howe ordered a guard to protect the Flushing nursery. Another famous nursery was begun by Quaker Samuel Parsons in 1838. He imported over one hundred varieties of exotic trees, and introduced Japanese maples and propagated rhododendron in the United States. Frederick Olmsted purchased trees from Parsons for plantings in Central and Prospect Parks.

Flushing became part of New York City in 1898, and residential development was spurred by the opening of the Queensboro Bridge in 1909 and the #7 subway in 1917. Huge waves of Irish, Jews, and Italians in the 1880s through 1920s brought new residents to Greater Flushing. A post–World War II decline was reversed starting in the 1960s, when Asian immigrants began to revitalize the area.

PARKS, PUBLIC SPACES, AND PUBLIC WORKS

Flushing Meadows–Corona Park. (See p. 124.)

☺ **KISSENA PARK.** Bounded by Oak Ave., Hemstead Tnpk., Kissena Blvd., and Fresh Meadow Lane, 352-4793, or call New York City information line 311. www.nycgovparks.org. Year-round dawn–9:00 p.m.

There's a lot that 235-acre Kissena Park has to offer: a boathouse, bike trails, community garden, tennis, bocce, and handball courts, playing fields, playgrounds, and parkland. Plus, it's one of New York's romantic places, with weeping willows around Kissena Lake, rare trees, and beautiful birds. Once paved over by WPA workers (earning it the nickname "bathtub lake"), Kissena Lake supports a wide variety of plant and animal life, including snapping turtles, ducks, herons, egrets, and gallinules. The Charles Emerson Wildlife Garden and Nature Grove is a treat; some species date to the colonial era when Flushing was a center for nurseries.

You can also play golf at **KISSENA GOLF COURSE**, a year-round, par-64 public course (164-15 Booth Memorial Ave., 939-4594). Or, watch the bike racers zoom around **KISSENA PARK VELODROME**. (Booth Memorial Ave. and 150th St., 783-8642, www.kissenavelodrome.com or www.bikecult.com/works/kissena track.html.)

If you want to hike through Queens' greenway, check out the one-hundred-acre Kissena Corridor Park (bet. Flushing Meadows–Corona Park and Cunningham Park), which links Kissena Park to Flushing Meadows–Corona Park and Cunningham Park.

✏ **ESSAY**

FLYING LIKE THE WIND

As told to the author by Stu Nitekman.

A track bike is a bicycle without gears—or brakes—and a velodrome is a racetrack on which you can fly like the wind. Imagine thirty cyclists on a small track going thirty-five miles an hour, bunched together, leaning into each other against banked curves, yet not going down. Come see for yourself on a Wednesday evening between May and September. It's free to watch. Track-bike racers converge here, a diverse crowd linked by a shared passion. You'll see bike

(continued)

messengers (who travel from work in Manhattan's office districts on the same bikes they then race), middle-class white teenagers and their parents arriving in SUVs with bike racks, buff bikers from Latin America, and fifty-year-old cycling enthusiasts who won't give it up. Some races last twenty seconds, others twenty minutes. The competition is friendly but intense. Among the onlookers are men and women who themselves once competed at this velodrome.

Track-bike racing was a huge sport in early-twentieth-century New York. Six-day bike races were held at Madison Square Garden in the 1920s. The velodrome at Coney Island (built for both bike and motorcycle racing) held 15,000 spectators. The sport officially arrived in Queens when Robert Moses built the 400-meter Kissena Velodrome for the 1964 U.S. Olympic Team Trials. It was subsequently the training ground for many world-class cyclists. As part of New York City's bid for the 2012 Olympics, Kissena Velodrome was refurbished after years of neglect.

POINTS OF CULTURAL INTEREST

Cultural Centers

Immigrants converging from many different cultures and religions often try to maintain contact with their own traditions, languages, and religions through cultural centers, and their children not infrequently attend classes in their parents' native tongue as well. The cultural centers listed below are a sampling of the numerous such organizations throughout Queens. Those listed have events or programs that are open to the public, some of which are free. (If you call for information you may not always find someone on hand who is fluent in English, but most Web sites have an English option.)

CHINESE CULTURAL CENTER. 41-61 Kissena Blvd. bet. Barclay and Sanford Aves., 886-7770. Tu–F 10:00 a.m.–6:00 p.m., Sa–Su 9:00 a.m.–9:00 p.m.

The Chinese Cultural Center holds language classes, organizes cultural events, and provides services for the Chinese community in Flushing. Visitors might be interested in a small exhibit of Chinese masks and instruments and the library of Chinese books.

FREE SYNAGOGUE OF FLUSHING. 41-60 Kissena Blvd., 961-0030. www.freesynagogue.org. M–Th 9:00 a.m.–5:00 p.m., F 9:00 a.m.–2:00 p.m.

This prominent synagogue hosts a range of cultural activities including concerts (from klezmer to doo-wop music), a film series, and guest speakers on topics of concern to Jewish audiences. The neo-classical building dates to 1926, an era when an enormous population explosion was triggered by the opening of the Queensboro Bridge and subway extension into Queens.

GANESHA TEMPLE (AKA THE HINDU TEMPLE SOCIETY OF NORTH AMERICA). 45-57 Bowne St. bet. Holly and 45th Aves., 460-8484. www.nyganeshtemple.org. Daily 9:00 a.m.–9:00 p.m.

Ganesha Temple is one of the largest Hindu temples in the United States. The Hindu Temple Society of North America was the first of its kind when it opened in North America in 1977. If you come by in the early evening hours after work, you'll see a steady stream of people of all ethnicities headed into the gates at this remarkable Hindu temple, tucked away on an unassuming residential side street. Open to the public, the Ganesha Temple's pastala, or school, holds a full schedule of classes in Sanskrit, philosophy, meditation, and traditional arts such as classical Indian dance.

Built in 1977 in the style of ancient temple design, the building features carvings, shrines, and architectural detail made of black granite stones imported from India. The stairs are flanked by ornamental elephants. Inside, worshipers meditate sitting on a red carpet in front of colorful, flower-strewn altars with carved statues of the Hindu gods Shiva, Krishna, and Ganesh. Smaller idols adorn the side walls. Ceremonies are held in Sanskrit. Visitors are welcome but are asked to be respectful; no shoes are worn in the temple.

The Ganesha Temple Canteen, which serves very cheap, spicy food cafeteria-style in the basement, is also open to the public.

INTERNATIONAL BUDDHIST PROGRESS SOCIETY. 154-37 Barclay Ave., 939-8318. www.ibps.org. By appointment only.

If you're a serious student of Chinese Buddhism, Buddhist philosophy, meditation and related practices, check out this humanist organization that combines traditional Buddhist religious practice with social activism. The International Buddhist Progress Society, founded in 1991, has nongovernmental (NGO) status with the United Nation's Economic and Social Council, and temples in Los Angeles, San Diego, Boston, Denver, Austin, and in sixty nations. Volunteer activities include relief programs for victims of natural disasters and projects to build cross-cultural understanding.

☺ **INTERNATIONAL RESOURCE CENTER AND GALLERY AT FLUSHING PUBLIC LIBRARY.** 41-17 Main St. at Kissena Blvd., 358-8899. www.queenslibrary.org. M, W 10:00 a.m.–8:00 p.m., T 1:00 p.m.–8:00 p.m., Th–F 10:00 a.m.–6:00 p.m., Sa 10:00 a.m.–5:00 p.m., Su noon–5:00 p.m.

The Flushing branch of the Queens Public Library holds free special events such as the celebration of Korean Day or the Indian Diwali Festival. The gallery has an international focus, as does the multilingual collection of books. Incidentally, this library was built on the site of one of the original three Queens libraries funded a hundred years ago by Andrew Carnegie.

KOREAN CALLIGRAPHY CENTER. 35-14 Farrington Street, 2nd floor, 279-4577.

You can take lessons here in calligraphy and learn to paint on long strips of cloth.

KOREAN CULTURE SOCIETY OF EASTERN USA. 42-40 Bowne Street, 358-5010.

There are periodic exhibits held here as well as classes in flower arranging.

SHIKSHAYATAN CULTURAL CENTER. 146-29 Wawthorn Ave., 461-4065.

Opened in 1990, this Hindu community arts organization presents classical and folk traditions of Indian art, music, and dance.

TAIWAN CENTER. 137-44 Northern Blvd. bet. Main and Linden Sts., 445-7007. www.nytaiwancenter.us. Hours based on program.

In operation for a decade, the Taiwan Center runs a range of social and educational programs for Chinese immigrants. Classes in traditional Chinese arts, music, and dance are open to the public. Special events promote Taiwanese and Taiwanese-American cultures, with performances by outstanding musicians (some of whom use the Steinway piano on the premises). Interestingly, the Taiwan Center is also a site for poll-worker training and voter registration with Chinese speakers available to help.

Four House Museums

The Queens Botanical Garden, Queens Museum of Art, and New York Hall of Science are located in Flushing Meadows–Corona Park, and are listed in chapter 10 (see pp. 128–30). The four small historical museums listed below are well worth a visit, too.

☺ 🏛 **BOWNE HOUSE.** 37-01 Bowne St., 359-0528. www.bownehouse.org. Tu, Sa, Su 2:30 p.m.–4:00 p.m.

It's hard to believe that this rambling house, with "1661" stenciled under the dormer window, was the scene of roaring political passions and courageous moral stands taken in the name of liberty—but so it was. The sign outside the Bowne House simply reads, "A National Shrine to Religious Freedom." The museum's collection of more than 5,000 objects is a fascinating window onto early American history. This quiet house under a leafy maple tree is well worth a visit; the kitchen wing is the oldest structure in Queens.

John Bowne built this home on land sold to him by the Matinecock Indians for eight strings of wampum. During this era, the Dutch administrator Peter Stuyvesant prohibited the practice of any religions other than the Dutch Reformed Church. Stuyvesant called on citizens to "not receive or entertain" any of those people called Quakers. A town meeting in Flushing defiantly issued a letter called the Flushing Remonstrance (1657). Bowne, who was from a prominent family, opened his new home for Quaker meetings. He was arrested, imprisoned, and fined in 1662 for harboring Quakers. He was deported to Holland where he appealed and was released in 1664. The political pressure created by Bowne's case caused Stuyvesant's proprietor, the Dutch East India Company, to order the persecution of religious dissenters to cease.

Look for a stone marker honoring George Fox Stone, a leader of the Religious Society of Friends in England. He preached here in 1672 under two large oak trees subsequently named "The Fox Oaks." The Bowne House may also have been a stopover on the Underground Railroad in the years before the Civil War.

☺ 🏛 **KINGSLAND HOMESTEAD MUSEUM, WEEPING BEECH TREE PARK.** 143-35 37th Ave. bet. Parsons Blvd. and Bowne St., 939-0647. Museum hours: Tu, Sa–Su 2:30 p.m.–4:30 p.m.; adults $3, seniors $2, members free. (Don't confuse this with King Manor.)

Charles Doughty, the son of a Quaker, built this homestead (circa 1785) in heady times, just a few years after the Paris Peace Treaty formalized the end of the American Revolutionary War. The building, saved twice from development by being relocated, is noted for such elements as its gambrel roof and a crescent-shaped window. Whet your historical imagination with the on-site museum displays of Victorian memorabilia and special exhibits. The Queens Historical Society, located on the premises, maintains the house. There's a good bookshop with plenty to interest Queensophiles, and outside, the Weeping Beech Tree Park.

Odd as it may seem, the Weeping Beech Tree (which died in 1998) was an official New York City landmark. It grew on 37th Ave. west of Parsons Blvd. Samuel Bowne Parsons, owner of one of the prominent Flushing nurseries, had planted the tree in 1847 (see Insight box, p. 98). As the story goes, it grew from a shoot acquired by Parsons while he was in Belgium in 1847, and was the first of its species in the United States.

☺ **LEWIS H. LATIMER HOUSE AND MUSEUM.** 34-41 137th St. bet. 34th Ave. and Leavitt St., 961-8585. www.latimerhousemuseum.org. Tu and Th 1:00 p.m.–3:00 p.m. Otherwise by appointment.

Visit this old home and learn about the famous African-American inventor Lewis H. Latimer, who lived here from 1902 until his death a quarter-century later. A close associate of Thomas Edison and Alexander Graham Bell, Latimer's name will be forever linked with inventions that changed how we live: the incandescent electric lightbulb and the telephone. He was born in 1848 in Boston as the son of Virginia runaway slaves and self-educated. His genius for precise mechanical drawing, electrical engineering, and mastery of the competitive patent process led to his success. The only African-American in the original group of Edison Pioneers (a kind of early think tank) he is known for his 1890 book *Incandescent Electric Lighting: A Practical Description of the Edison System.* The Queens Borough Public Library holds a collection of Latimer's papers and artifacts.

☺ **VOELKER ORTH MUSEUM, BIRD SANCTUARY, AND VICTORIAN GARDEN.** 149-19 38th Ave., 359-6227. www.voelkerorthmuseum.org. W, Sa–Su 1:00 p.m.–4:00 p.m.

This Victorian garden and home-turned-museum gives a sense of how our American ancestors lived. The carriage house, garden, and bird sanctuary have particular appeal. Inside the 1880 home, note the formality of the proper Victorian tea party setting. Renovated as a museum in 2002, the mission of the Voelker Orth Museum is to preserve the history of Long Island and Queens. Visitors can join on neighborhood walks (free) and Sunday teas and lectures. There are snacks and a gift shop.

Music, Drama, Performances, and Galleries

It's surprising how much music is being made in Queens. There are several music institutes, a highly regarded college music department, a community-based conservatory, two major performance venues, a symphony orchestra, and a choral society in Flushing alone. Queens has a long musical history, and the recent influx of Russian and Asian immigrants, who value music and bring their own rich heritage, has helped create a robust musical environment. Visitors will find high-quality performances at reasonable ticket prices at various Queens venues.

AARON COPLAND SCHOOL OF MUSIC. (See listing under Queens College, p. 106.)

THE AMERASIA BANK ART GALLERY. 41-04 Main St. bet. Union St. and College Point Blvd., 380-6414. M–F 9:00 a.m.–5:00 p.m.; exhibits vary and are ongoing.

This local bank offers as a community service a space for the display of local artwork, which often reflects traditional Chinese styles or Chinese immigrant themes. The gallery hosts the annual Flushing Art League of Queens juried art show.

BROOKLYN-QUEENS CONSERVATORY OF MUSIC. 42-76 Main St. at Blossom Ave., 461-8910. www.bqcm.org. M–F 9:00 a.m.–8:00 p.m., Sa 9:30 a.m.–4:00 p.m.

The Brooklyn-Queens Conservatory of Music offers a range of classes from preschool programs to advanced certificates in jazz and classical music. There are occasional concerts, too. The Find a Musician referral service is a resource for parties and special events. The sister conservatory is in Park Slope, Brooklyn.

CRYSTAL FOUNDATION ART GALLERY. 31-10 Whitestone Expwy., 961-7300.

Sponsored by a private company, the Crystal Window and Door Systems, this 2,200-square-foot exhibition space hosts shows by artists.

COLDEN CENTER AT QUEENS COLLEGE. (See listing under Queens College, p. 106.)

☺ 🏛 **FLUSHING TOWN HALL (FLUSHING COUNCIL ON CULTURE AND THE ARTS).**
137-35 Northern Blvd. at Linden Place, 463-7700. www.flushingtownhall.org. M–F 9:00 a.m.–5:00 p.m., Sa–Su
noon–5:00 p.m. Free performance parking.

Whoa! The Smithsonian Institution—in Queens? You bet! You could literally
count on one hand the number of organizations in New York City who can boast
being a member of the Smithsonian's national network of affiliates. The Flushing Council on Culture and the Arts, which holds events at Flushing Town Hall,
is one of them.

Flushing Town Hall is a cultural hub for the borough. For a fraction of Manhattan prices, you can enjoy family-oriented shows and award-winning performances of jazz, opera, theater, dance, and classical music. Live jazz has featured
Jon Hendricks and other living legends. Composer and pianist Bright Sheng is
currently Flushing Town Hall's resident composer and director of a series of
classical concerts.

Film festivals include the well-established American-Asian International Film
Festival in June. Top-notch special exhibits of painting, sculpture, and photography are mounted here, too. For instance, an exhibition "With or Without
Strings" in the fall of 2005 explored two centuries of puppetry from around the
world. Other shows explored the demographic diversity of New York, the cultural forces transforming twenty-first-century urban America, and the social
and musical history of jazz in Queens.

The **QUEENS JAZZ TRAIL TOUR** is organized by the Flushing Council on the
Arts (first Sa. of every month except Jan. and Feb.). This five-hour bus and walk-
ing tour includes nearby Corona (where Dizzie Gillespie and Louis Armstrong
lived), Satchmo's home, the Louis Armstrong Archives at Queens College, and
Addisleigh Park, the middle-class neighborhood where Ella Fitzgerald and Billie
Holiday lived. It wraps up with a soul food meal and concert back at Flushing
Town Hall.

The building itself is a landmark. Built by a local carpenter in 1862 in Romanesque revival style, this landmark sits like a memory of yesteryear on the
heavily trafficked six-lane Northern Blvd. Notable for its arched doors and
windows, it was almost demolished in 1976 but survived as a restaurant and
theater. It is located near the other historic Flushing buildings such as the
Quaker Meeting House and pre–Revolutionary War–era Bowne House. Nestled behind it on Carleton Place (corner Linden Pl.) is a row of fourteen
Depression-era cottage homes. As a note, don't confuse Flushing Town Hall
with a functioning town hall, as there are no longer any municipal services
here, except an annual swearing-in ceremony for new citizens. There's a gift
shop on the premises.

KOREAN TRADITIONAL MUSIC INSTITUTE. 137-45 Northern Blvd. bet. Linden Pl. and Leavitt St., 961-9255. Call for schedule.

You can learn (or listen to) traditional Korean music here, with an emphasis on drumming and zithers. This is one of many institutions in Queens with one foot in two worlds: contemporary American culture, which is hard to escape, and traditional Korean culture, which is sustained in churches, language, family life, and music institutes like this.

ORATORIO SOCIETY OF QUEENS. 25-33 154th St., 460-0726. www.queensoratorio.org.

The oldest performing arts organization in Queens, this community chorus was founded in 1917 and it's still thriving today under the direction of maestro David Close. Their repertoire includes choral classics such as Verdi's *Requiem* and Beethoven's Ninth Symphony. Tickets are about $20. If you'd like to sing, you can arrange for a "listening" (no scary auditions here).

☺ **QUEENS COLLEGE.** 65-30 Kissena Blvd., corner of the Long Island Expwy. (exit 24), 997-5000.

Queens College has cultural opportunities for visitors. The excellent **EVE-NING READING SERIES** attracts top-notch speakers, recently featuring Salman Rushdie, Frank McCourt, and Mary Gordon (997-4646, www.qc.edu/readings). The **COLDEN CENTER** features an active schedule of performances that include family shows, classical music, and pop stars. Among those who have performed here are the Dance Theatre of Harlem, the New York Philharmonic, Dionne Warwick, and Billy Joel. (Tickets and information at www.coldencenter.org, or box office 793-8080.) **THE AARON COPLAND SCHOOL OF MUSIC,** one of the most distinguished departments at Queens College, also has public concerts and recitals. These are usually held in the Music Building, in the professional-quality **SAMUEL J. AND ETHEL LEFRAK CONCERT HALL** (997-5411), which is considered one of the acoustically finest in New York. It also has a very beautiful 1991 Bedient Pipe Organ.

As for art, the **GODWIN-TERNBACH MUSEUM** displays selections from a collection that spans from antiquities to Rembrandt to Warhol (Klapper Hall 405, 997-4747, http://qcpages.qc.cuny.edu/art/gtmus.html, M–Th 11:00 a.m.–7:00 p.m., Sa 11:00 a.m.–5:00 p.m.). The petite **QUEENS COLLEGE ART CENTER** in the Benjamin S. Rosenthal Library (997-3770) has community exhibitions. The **LOUIS ARMSTRONG ARCHIVES** are located in the library, too; what started as seventy-two shipping cartons of Satchmo's personal artifacts is today a lovingly archived collection (by appointment only, 997-3670). Queens College administers the Louis Armstrong House as well (see pp. 79–80). A small **WALT WHITMAN GARDEN,** commemorating the 150th publication anniversary of *Leaves of Grass,* honors the poet who taught in a one-room schoolhouse that stood on this spot in 1839.

With a large, grassy quad, newly renovated buildings, and all this art and culture, the Queens College campus exudes vigor. Part of the City University of New York, it offers over 115 undergraduate and graduate majors in arts and humanities; education; mathematics and the natural sciences; social sciences; and business administration. An all-commuter student body of 17,600 students represent 140 nationalities, with a preponderance of Asian and white students. Since almost half of the students study only part-time because many have family or work commitments, Queens College offers satellite classes in Manhattan, on-site day care, credit for life achievement, and weekend classes for older learners. Tuition is $4,000 per year for undergraduates. Queens College accepts students citywide, from New York State and out of state. Jerry Seinfeld and Paul Simon are two well-known alumni.

☺ **QUEENS SYMPHONY ORCHESTRA.** 786-8880. www.queenssymphony.org.

The only professional orchestra in Queens, QSO performs in schools, city parks, and at Queens College's Colden Center. The orchestra also produces young people's concerts.

PEOPLE, PLACES, AND THINGS OF HISTORICAL INTEREST
BOWNE PARK. Bounded by 29th and 32nd Aves. and 155th and 159th Sts.

The early history of Queens is peppered with the names of prominent families who appear repeatedly over the course of several generations. In this corner of Flushing resides the landmarked home (1661) of John Bowne, whose defense of religious tolerance earned him a stellar place in American history. Adjacent to his house, this park is named in honor of Walter Bowne (1770–1846), of the same family, who served as Mayor of New York City. Walter is remembered for trying to stem a cholera epidemic by imposing a ban on travel in and out of the city. He was ignorant of the fact that water and food, not human contact, are the source of transmission. Hundreds of New Yorkers died of cholera on his watch anyway in 1832.

JOSEPH CORNELL RESIDENCE. 3708 Utopia Pkwy. No tours; not open to the public.

Parrots, a button, bits of old photos are the materials used by artist Joseph Cornell (1903–72). Cornell won acclaim for his surrealist collages of found objects set under glass in little shadow boxes and lived and worked for much of his life in this home, which he shared with his mother and sickly brother. Cornell's work was introduced to the general public at the Museum of Modern Art's 1936 exhibition Fantastic Art, Dada, and Surrealism. Cornell's idiosyncratic oeuvre seems all the more surprising when set in the context of the modest, conventional Queens home where, for forty years, he created avant-garde art in the basement.

FITZGERALD-GINSBERG HOUSE. 145-15 Bayside Ave. bet. 145th St. and 145th Pl. Private residence, not open to the public.

This picturesque 1920s home is one of Flushing's last surviving early-twentieth-century mansions. With its rustic look, fieldstone walls, a multicolored slate roof, leaded glass windows, and overall wishful neo-Tudor Britishness, it's a hint of what Flushing looked like a century ago, before the opening of the Queensboro Bridge.

🏛 **FLUSHING ARMORY.** (See Self-Guided Tour, p. 110.)

🏛 **FLUSHING HIGH SCHOOL.** (See Self-Guided Tour, p. 110.)

FLUSHING CEMETERY. 163-06 46th Ave. near 163rd St., 359-0100.

This is the final resting place of jazz greats Louis Armstrong, Johnny Hodges, and Dizzy Gillespie. In death they joined a number of nineteenth-century public officials, including U.S. Representatives William Valk (1806–79) and Thomas Jackson (1797–1881), who are buried here. Come to the Memorial Day Tribute Concert to Jazz Musicians.

FLUSHING REMONSTRANCE (1657).

This document, written by the freeholders of the town of Flushing, defied Governor Peter Stuyvesant's persecution of Quakers. It is widely cited as a precursor to the Bill of Rights, written more than a century later. The freeholders who signed the document wrote, "We are bounded by the law of God and man to doe good unto all men and evil to noe man." They set forth an argument "not to judge least we be judged, neither to condemn least we be condemned, but rather let every man stand and fall to his own Master." In 2007, the anniversary of the Flushing Remonstrance will be celebrated.

See Bowne House, pp. 102–3.

🏛 **FLUSHING TOWN HALL.** (See p. 105.)

🏛 **KINGSLAND HOMESTEAD MUSEUM, WEEPING BEECH PARK.** (See listing, p. 103.)

🏛 **POPPENHUSEN INSTITUTE.** 114-04 14th Rd., 358-0067. www.poppenhuseninstitute.org. M–T 9:00 a.m.–8:00 p.m., W 9:00 a.m.–5:00 p.m., F noon–7:00 p.m., Th closed; open on weekends only for special events.

Come see how a wealthy industrialist "gave back" to his community a century or more ago. Tucked away in College Point, Poppenhusen Institute is one of those curious places you expect to stumble on in, say, Cincinnati: a relic of individual philanthropy from the industrial era. While here, you can sit in a teepee, visit a tiny historic jail cell, and walk around an interesting old building and grounds.

After the Civil War, German immigrant Conrad Poppenhusen, a manufacturer of whalebone items such as buttons and dress stays, obtained a license to manufacture and sell items made of the promising new material developed by Charles Goodyear. To house his new plant and workers, he purchased large tracts of land in what is today College Point. Like Steinway in Astoria (see p. 34), Poppenhusen built schools and houses, carved out neighborhoods and streets, and built this community educational center. He specified that the Poppenhusen Institute be open to all, irrespective of race, creed, or religion. In its early days, the Institute was a kind of one-stop civic center for the area, housing the kindergarten, free educational programs for the local workers, the sheriff's office, as well as the court and Justice of the Peace. It was also the first home of the College Point Savings Bank, German Singing Societies, and the area's first library. Today you can rent out this 1868 landmark for a special occasion.

☺ 🏛 **FRIENDS (QUAKER) MEETING HOUSE.** 137-16 Northern Blvd. bet. Main and Union Sts., 358-9636. Su services 11:00 a.m.–noon; tours: noon–12:30 p.m. or by appointment.

Peacefulness exudes from this old Quaker Meeting House, the only surviving example in New York of a typical early-seventeenth-century ecclesiastical frame building. Construction began in 1694. It has been in use continuously as a meetinghouse since 1696, except for time during the American Revolution when the British used it as a prison and hospital. In the pre–Civil War era, Quakers, including Samuel Parsons (see p. 98 and p. 103) and his sons, served as "conductors" on the Underground Railroad. Note the small colonial-era graveyard. Only several dozen people are active members of this Quaker congregation today.

🏛 **QUEENS HISTORICAL SOCIETY.** 143-35 37th Ave. bet. Parsons Blvd. and Bowne St., 939-0647. www.queenshistoricalsociety.org. M–F 9:30 a.m.–5:00 p.m.; Museum: Tu, Sa–Su 2:30 p.m.–4:40 p.m.

The Queens Historical Society is the repository of archives and records documenting three hundred years of local history. Check their Web site for tours, lectures, and special exhibits. The library and archive of primary and secondary source material is available only by appointment. It's housed in the Kingsland Homestead Museum. (See p. 103.)

🏛 **RKO KEITH'S THEATER.** 135-29 Northern Blvd. (See listing, p. 113.)

ST. GEORGE'S EPISCOPAL CHURCH. 38-02 Main St., near 38th Ave., 359-1171.

Founded in 1702, St. George's Church was granted a royal charter in 1761 by King George III of England, who would surely "flip his Whig" if he witnessed the multinational congregation here today. Worship services are conducted in English, Chinese, and Spanish. The church was only the second religious organization to be founded in Flushing. Tiffany-glass lovers will enjoy the two stained glass panels on the church's north wall. Note the plaques dedicated to Francis Lewis, a signer of the Declaration of Independence, juxtaposed with church bulletins printed in Chinese, for a sense of Flushing's unusual history.

 ## SELF-GUIDED TOUR: TWO HUNDRED YEARS OF HISTORY IN UNDER TWO MILES

The following is a self-guided walking tour of landmarks from 1661 to 1866, or pre—Revolutionary War to post—Civil War era, based in part on a route outlined by the Queens Historical Society. The total distance covered is less than two miles. Bring a map! You can obtain a "Flushing Freedom Mile" brochure from the Queens Historical Society at 939-0647. Or, get "The Insider's Guide to Queens" map from the Queens Borough President's Office at 268-3300.

Start at the 1. 🏛 1661 Bowne House (37-01 Bowne St. pp. 102–3), the oldest house in Queens. Walk west on 32nd Ave. and turn south on Union St. for five blocks to 2. 🏛 Flushing High School (35-01 Union St.), a Gothic structure built in 1912–15 that, complete with gargoyles and a grassy campus, resembles Cambridge or Oxford. Proceed to Northern Blvd. to see the 3. 🏛 Kingsland Homestead and Weeping Beech Tree Park (143-35 37th Ave. p. 103), go two blocks east to Parsons Blvd., then south a half block to 37th Ave. Or, to shorten the trip, from the junction of Union and Northern Blvd., head west on Northern Blvd. You'll pass the 4. 🏛 Armory (137-58 Northern Blvd.) built in 1906 and now home to the Queens North Police Force. The Flushing Remonstrance (p. 108) was signed in a home belonging to Michael Milner, which stood on or near this site, in 1657. Passing 5. two war memorials (1866 for the Civil War and 1920 for World War I), you will see, on the right, 6. 🏛 Flushing Town Hall (137-35 Northern Blvd. p. 105), an early Romanesque revival building dating to 1862. Three years after it was built, African-American abolitionist Frederick Douglass spoke here. Across the street is 7. 🏛 Friends Meeting House, 1694–96 (137-16 Northern Blvd. p. 109), also a landmark and stop on the Underground Railroad. Turn left (south) on Main St. one block to 8. 🏛 St. George's Episcopal Church (35-32 38th Ave.), founded in colonial times. Backtrack going north on Union near Congressman Rosenthal Plaza to see the Macedonia A.M.E. Church (37-22 Union St) where in 1811 the 9. African Methodist Society was founded as the third religious organization in Flushing and was an Underground Railroad station.

OTHER POINTS OF CULTURAL INTEREST

AMERICAN NAIL SCHOOL. 37-08 Main St., near 37th Ave., 661-2700.

Nail salons dot every few blocks in New York's middle- and upper-middle-class neighborhoods. Nobody ever wonders how it is that they all provide almost identical cutting, buffing, polishing, and nail-painting services. This is one of several nail schools in Flushing where the manicurists learn their trade. The estimated thirty-five hundred such small businesses are run almost exclusively by Korean women, many with limited English skills.

☼ Insight

There's No College in College Point.

College Point is the name of a neighborhood near Flushing that sounds as though it is home to an institution of higher education but is not. Its founder had hopes that one might be established. St. Paul's College survived here for nine years, closing in 1848. Locals thought the name sounded good, and so kept it anyway. But there is not a college in College Point.

KOREAN CHANNEL. 137-77 Northern Blvd. near Union St., 353-8970. By appointment only.

Most Americans just click past the foreign language channels, but they're like lifelines for many immigrants who rely on cable TV for news from their country, English lessons, and tips on adjusting to life in the United States. In Queens you often see cable TV programs in different languages (Korean, Chinese, Arabic, Tagalog, Spanish, Portuguese, you name it) in ethnic cafés and shops. As the name suggests, the Korean Channel broadcasts cable TV shows in Korean.

NY ARM WRESTLING ASSOCIATION. 7230 Kissena Blvd. bet. 71st and 73rd Aves., 544-4592. www.nycarms.com. M–F 9:00 a.m.–5:00 p.m.

Headquartered in Flushing, the New York Arm Wrestling Association organizes matches citywide and in Queens on Rockaway Beach, for both men and women. Heavyweight, lightweight, men, women, masters, left-handed and right-handed—they've got them all. For some amusing photos, see the Web site.

TOWNSEND HARRIS HIGH SCHOOL. 149-11 Melbourne St., 793-0441. Not open to visitors without appointment.

This public high school may be one of the best-kept secrets in academically competitive New York City. Its 1,000 ethnically diverse students, including many whose parents are foreign-born, attend school in a building on the Queens College campus. With a program as rigorous as any in the nation, and with stellar college acceptances, Townsend Harris ranks up there with Stuyvesant and Bronx Science.

Miscellaneous Things to Do in Flushing

☺ **BIG APPLE ARCHERY LANES.** 170-20 39th Ave., 461-1756. www.archery-nyc.com. Tu—Th 5:00 p.m.—11:00 p.m., F 6:00 p.m.—11:00 p.m., Sa—Su 11:00 a.m.—5:00 p.m.

For a change of pace, take your date to Big Apple Archery. You can rent equipment and get lessons. At $16 an hour it's cheaper than a movie, soda, and popcorn. You get a free lesson with your first rental.

COLLEGE POINT MULTIPLEX CINEMAS. 28-55 Ulmer St., 886-4900.

Not in Flushing proper, but in nearby Whitestone, this is a comfy, modern movie theater. It's about three-quarters of a mile from the nearest subway, the #7 at Main St., Flushing.

☺ **NEW YORK TABLE TENNIS CENTER.** 35-26 Prince St. bet. 32nd and 35th Aves., 359-3272. Tu—F 2:30 p.m.—11:30 p.m., Sa—Su 1:00 p.m.—11:00 p.m. Rates per player: $8 for half hour, $14 for one hour, $20 for one and a half hours.

Want to see some table tennis action? It's a big sport in this community. Come upstairs to the second-floor table tennis center. Lessons cost $40 per hour. You can also play at the Flushing YMCA, 138-46 Northern Blvd., 961-6880.

POLYKING DANCING KARAOKE. 133-36 39th Ave. bet. College Pt. Blvd. and Prince St., 353-1068. Call for schedule.

Believe it or not, there's ballroom dancing here midweek, to both Chinese and English live music. Add karaoke in English and Chinese to the mix for weekend fun. Also, ask about free ballroom dance lessons on weekends. This is another example of how Asian and Western cultures are mixing it up in Queens.

MAJOR NEW DEVELOPMENTS

A number of private and public sector projects are underway that promise to continue to change Flushing and make it an increasingly vital outer-borough center. Investors are attracted by the fact that Flushing is centrally located to major sports and cultural institutions in Flushing Meadows–Corona Park, as well as to major roads, an airport, and the subway into Manhattan.

COLLEGE POINT PARK. College Point Blvd.

The city is constructing a $40 million public parks facility that will include indoor and outdoor sports and recreation fields and facilities, as well as space to accommodate a computer room, day care, and after-school programs.

FLUSHING COMMONS. Municipal Parking Lot #1, bounded by 7th and 39th Aves, Union St. and 138th St.

An old parking lot located smack-dab in the middle of downtown Flushing is being transformed into a new commercial center, scheduled for completion by 2008. Flushing Commons, as it's called, will include a town square, a 50,000-square-foot recreational center with a swimming pool, a business-class hotel, about 500 apartments, underground parking, plus a shopping area designed for major national retailers, restaurants, and a multiscreen cinema.

FLUSHING RIVER CLEANUP.

Finally, the city has initiated plans to clean up the highly polluted Flushing River and restore its tidal wetlands. A proposed waterfront promenade, to be built in conjunction with private development and new community open space might eventually increase public access to the waterfront. In the future, a pedestrian bridge may eventually connect downtown Flushing to a redeveloped Willets Point.

FLUSHING TOWN CENTER. Site of old Con Ed plant, at College Point Blvd. and Roosevelt Ave., adjacent to Flushing River and the Van Wyck Expwy.

A $600 million retail and residential center is being built on a fourteen-acre brownfield site near Main St. When finished it will add 750,000 square feet of retail space, some 1,000 residential units, and a parking lot. The shops are slated to open in late 2007. There'll also be a new fifty-five-foot-wide waterfront esplanade along Flushing River and a connection to 40th Road.

🏛 **RKO KEITH'S THEATER.** 135-29 Northern Blvd. (Don't confuse this with RKO Keith's in Richmond Hill.)

Opened on Christmas 1928, with great fanfare, the 2,500-seat, Mexican baroque extravaganza was designed by Thomas Lamb. Stars Jack Benny, Bob Hope, Milton Berle, Roy Rogers, and Burns and Allen performed here. The ticket lobby and grand foyer are landmarked. In 2005 plans were approved for commercial development of the site into an eighteen-story condo complex with ground-level shops and a fully restored lobby, to be completed in 2007.

WILLETS POINT. Also known as the Iron Triangle. 127th St. at Roosevelt Ave. bet. Corona and Flushing.

What an eyesore this is—a forty-acre dump of used car parts east of Shea Stadium. The local Chamber of Commerce has promoted the idea of an exposition/conference center and hotel facility like the Javits Center. Stay tuned.

NEW DEVELOPMENTS, TEAHOUSES, AND RESTAURANTS

Most Flushing restaurants cater to a local Asian clientele, not tourists. That means three things: 1. You can be pretty sure you're getting authentic regional cuisine; 2. restaurants often fall short on decor and explanations in English; 3. the best places are often busy late, because the local business environment is competitive and people work long hours. Take your pick of cuisines: Beijing, Cantonese, Szechuan, Shanghai, Korean, Vietnamese, and (in nearby neighborhoods) Indian-Chinese, Caribbean-Chinese, and kosher Chinese.

Dumplings and Tea

☺ **DUMPLING STALL.** 40-52 Main St. at 41st St., 353-6265, 7:00 a.m.–2:00 a.m.

Come and get 'em, dumplings fresh and delicious, from a street stall. You'll pay about $2 for four dumplings from Chu Kee Dumpling.

FLUSHING MALL. 133-31 39th Ave. bet. College Point Blvd. and Prince St., 762-9000. M–Th 11:00 a.m.–9:00 p.m., F 11:00 a.m.–10:00 p.m., Sa–Su 10:00 a.m.–10:00 p.m.

You can find several stalls where Chinese noodles are freshly made, such as **HAND-DRAWN NOODLE** (stall #C26, 886-6996). **CHINESE NOODLES AND DUMPLING** (stall #M38, 886-6996) serves exotica such as "stinky tofu," a dish that is to the Taiwanese what a ripe Roquefort is to the French.

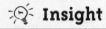

Insight

☺The Bubble Tea Phenomenon.

Bubble tea originated in Taiwan and in the past decade has become a favorite Chinese treat. Imagine a spoonful of pea-sized round tapioca "pearls" mixed with tea, milk, or juice in many delicious combinations. Some tapioca pearls are black, and are made of brown sugar and sweet potato. Others are white, made of chamomile root extract and starch. When you stir, the floating tapioca pearls move slowly like a lava lamp. The drinks are served with a fat straw. When you suck on it, both the drink and squishy pearls roll around in your mouth. It's hilarious, weird, and wonderful. Bubble tea is sold at most Chinese bakeries and cafés. Kids and teens love this whimsical drink.

SAGO TEA CAFE. 39-02 Main St. bet. 39th and Roosevelt Aves., 353-2899. Daily 11:30 a.m.–midnight.

There's a world of choice on the menu at Sago Tea: flavored black and green teas (try #20, ginger, or #9, sesame milk tea), special milkshakes (try #27, mung bean), Sago's healthy beverages (try #31, green barley with lemon juice and honey), *matcha* agar drink (try #44, *matcha aulait* with *matcha* agar), and special frostees (try #69, dark plum). Or play it safe and order pearl tapioca tea, sweet and delicious. You can't beat the $3 dumplings (#99). Sago is a convenient rendezvous location if you're meeting a friend.

Restaurants

BUDDHA BODAI. 42-96 Main St. at Cherry Ave., 939-1188. M–Sa 11:00 a.m.–10:30 p.m., Su 10:30 a.m.–10:30 p.m.

Buddha Bodai serves a meatless Cantonese cuisine with vegan options. Your food comes spiced with a sense of humor, too; some of the dishes made of mushrooms, veggies, or tofu are cleverly made to look like a duck, pig, cow, or fish.

CHOOPAN KABAB. 43-27 Main St. near Dahlia Ave., 539-3180. Daily 11:30 a.m.–11:30 p.m.

For a meal in Flushing, try going to this great Afghani restaurant that serves kebabs, breads, and rice dishes. It's conveniently located across from the Queens Botanical Garden.

DOSA HUTT. 45-63 Bowne St. off Holly Ave., 961-5897. M and W–Sa 9:00 a.m.–9:00 p.m., Tu 11:00 a.m.–9:00 p.m., Su 8:00 a.m.–9:00 p.m.

Dosa Hutt concocts very fresh, delicious, spicy, South Indian, all-vegetarian treats. Come when you're feeling wishy-washy because you won't have many decisions to make here. You have a choice of just two basic categories: *dosa* or *utpappam*. The *dosa* are eight-inch-long paper-thin crêpes made with rice and lentil flower, or wheat and rice, filled with spiced potato-based mixtures. Try the special butter masala dosa, or mysore masala dosa. *Utpappam,* a soft, freshly made flat bread that's sort of an Indian pizza with neither cheese nor tomato, is topped with combinations of vegetables. As for decor, it's bare-bones basic.

EAST LAKE RESTAURANT. 42-33 Main St., 539-8532. Daily 9:00 a.m.–2:00 a.m.

A dim sum favorite; patrons rave about the superb on choi (Chinese water spinach) and great snow pea shoots here. If they're too crowded, try **OCEAN JEWEL SEAFOOD** (across from Flushing Mall at 133-30 39th Ave., 359-8603).

See also: **EAST MANOR BUFFET AND RESTAURANT.** (See p. 90.)

GANESHA TEMPLE CANTEEN. (See listing for the Hindu Temple Society of North America, p. 101.)

GUM FUNG. 136-28 39th Ave. bet. 138th and Main Sts., 762-8821. Daily 9:00 a.m.–midnight.

It's a great dim sum destination: The dishes of tasty dumplings, crabs, shrimp, pork, and more fly by so fast you barely know what you are eating. Come with your ten best friends—the better for sharing.

HAPPY BUDDHA VEGETARIAN RESTAURANT. 135-37 37th Ave. bet. Main and Prince Sts., 358-0079. Su–Th 10:00 a.m.–10:00 p.m., F–Sa 10:00 a.m.–11:00 p.m.

Artful, delicious Asian vegetarian cuisine is served here. Start with simple edamame or veggie chicken fingers for appetizers. Then you can progress onto stir-fried chowfoon with carrots, baby corns, mushrooms, pea pods, Chinese broccoli, and bamboo shoots. Entrées of this healthy fare cost well under $10.

JOE'S SHANGHAI. 136-21 37th Ave. bet. Main and Union Sts., 539-3838. Su–Th 11:00 a.m.–11:00 p.m., F–Sa 11:00 a.m.–midnight.

Joe's Shanghai specializes in Chinese cuisine characteristic of the Yangtze River area. There's an especially varied menu of seafood dishes. Try such specialties as dragon buns ("long bao"), chicken wrapped in lotus leaves, and "drunken" fish and chicken that have been cooked in rice wine, also known as "yellow wine." Joe's Shanghai has multiple locations in Manhattan. Cash only, and sometimes there's a line.

KUM GANG SAN KOREAN RESTAURANT. 138-28 Northern Blvd. bet. Union and Bowne Sts., 461-0909. Daily 24 hours.

You know you have insider information when your Korean manicurist swears that this is the best Korean restaurant in town, and it's where she takes her mother. Try the scallion pancakes (*pa jon*), *galbi, and bulgogi*, various fish or meat dishes cooked at your tableside in traditional Korean BBQ style (*gui*) over a charcoal fire after being marinated in a complex-tasting soy-garlic-ginger sauce. There's ambience galore: a waterfall and live music played on the kayakum, a stringed instrument. For a restaurant that cooks with oak, try **SULRAK GARDEN** (154-01 Northern Blvd., 888-1850).

LITTLE LAMB HAPPY FAMILY RESTAURANT. 35-35 Main St. bet. 35th and Roosevelt Aves., 358-6667. Daily 11:00 a.m.–midnight.

Come to Little Lamb Happy Family Restaurant for a classic hot pot soup, sort of a Chinese version of fondue, in which you dip bits of meat, fish, and vegetables into a large communal pot of boiling hot soup—literally a hot pot—until they're cooked. It's great fun and delicious.

MINNI'S SHABU SHABU AND HIBACHI. 136-17 38th Ave. off 138th St., 762-6277. Daily 11:00 a.m.–midnight.

The more the merrier when you're eating shabu shabu, so bring a few friends. Like fondue, you cook your own meal here on the table. You get a large pot of boiling hot, flavorful broth and with little skewers cook your own beef, pork, lamb, fresh lobster, or combination as the main course, with sides of fish balls, bean curd, *udon,* and egg dumplings. It's busy on weekends.

RESTAURANT ROW. Near Sheraton LaGuardia East Hotel and 39th Ave.

There are a half dozen or more good restaurants on a one-block strip across from the hotel, each specializing in a different kind of Asian cuisine. **SPICY AND**

TASTY (see below) is known for hot Szechuan cuisine. **SENTOSA** next door serves Malaysian (39-07 Prince St., 866-6331); plus there's a Japanese restaurant, and **KING NOODLE HOUSE.**

SPICY AND TASTY. 39-07 Prince St., off 39th Ave., 359-1601. Daily 11:00 a.m.–11:30 p.m.

Put this on your list if you like it hot, hot, hot. Szechuan food is the specialty at this aptly named restaurant, which serves variations on a theme: meats, seafood, garlic, and ginger, all turned up as high as a Bunsen burner with tongue-searing pepper concoctions. If you come with more than five you can sit upstairs; order the communal lamb hot pot if you can, as it's fun to cook at your table. English is spoken so you can ask about dishes. Entrées under $10.

SWEET-N-TART. 136-11 38th Ave. bet. 138th and Main Sts., 661-3380. Daily 9:00 a.m.–midnight.

This brightly lit café just one block from the #7 subway station specializes in Chinese *tong shui*—hot/sweet desserts with medicinal qualities. (Ask the waiters to suggest something for that cold or aching back.) If you're healthy as a horse but just crave Cantonese fried shrimp balls or steam dumplings, you can get them, too. Main courses cost from $3.25 to $13.75.

SZECHUAN GOURMET. 135-15 37th Ave. bet. Main and Prince Sts., 888-9388. Daily noon–9:15 p.m.

You can get very good Szechuan-style food here in a more subdued environment than some of Flushing's more chaotic eateries. It's cheap, at about $10 per person for a filling meal of fiery beef, veggies, and chicken. Fire extinguishers recommended.

UDON NOODLE. 137-80 Northern Blvd. bet. Union and Leavitt Sts., 359-2324. Daily 11:00 a.m.–11:00 p.m.

In a McDonald's-like setting you can get a fast-food fusion of Indian and Chinese cuisines. Try the *karaage* curry (fried chicken curry), *katsu don* (pork cutlet egg bowl), or *niku* (marinated beef). All dishes cost about $7 or less. This fast-food chain is one of the largest in Japan.

YANG TZE RIVER. 135-21 40th Rd. at Main St., 353-8500. Daily 11:00 a.m.–10:00 p.m.

Yang Tze is a Shanghai Chinese restaurant, perfect if you love seafood and rice dishes served with lots of vegetables. Don't miss the delectable juicy dumplings, or *xiao long bao,* filled with meat.

SHOPPING

Food Shops

DURSO'S PASTA. 189-01 Crocheron Ave. near Utopia Parkway, 358-1311. Tu–F 8:30 a.m.–7:00 p.m., Sa 8:30 a.m.–6 p.m., Su 8:30 a.m.–2:00 p.m.

Surprise! Italian food! This popular, high-quality gourmet Italian specialty food shop sells a huge range of prepared foods, as well as high-quality Italian foods such as pastas, fresh sausages, and bakery goods.

☺ **FLUSHING MALL.** 133-31 39th Ave. bet. College Point Blvd. and Prince St., 762-9000. www.888flushing mall.com. M–Th 11:00 a.m.–9:00 p.m., F 11:00 a.m.–10:00 p.m., Sa–Su 10:00 a.m.–10:00 p.m.

Flushing Mall may be one of the most unusual malls you're likely to visit in the United States. Imagine a small supermarket-sized space carved into about fifty small shops and stalls with signs mostly in Chinese. Each stall is jam-packed with trinkets, food, electronics, and other stuff, some of which is imported from Asia and would be hard to find elsewhere. Both the quantity and quality of jade is likely better than what you'll see elsewhere. You can find Chinese cosmetics and food brands, especially in candies, that are rare in the United States. Some Chinese electronics are cheaper than American brands. There is also clothing by brands such as Uniqlo, which is hard to find in the United States. Typically stalls have names such as Ginseng & Herbs, Two-Way Jade & Jewelry, Happy Travel & Tours, and True Love Wedding Center.

☺ **HAN AH REUM MARKET.** 141-40 Northern Blvd. at Roosevelt Ave. bet. 59th and 60th Sts., 358-0700. Daily 24 hours.

Wander the aisles at this fascinating Korean grocery. What's life without toasted, roasted, seasoned seaweed snacks? Or hot pepper paste? Sure, you'll see nori wrappers for make-it-yourself sushi, fresh veggies, teas, meats, the freshest of artisanal tofu, and various sauces. You can spice up your life—and dinner table conversation, too—with exotic sliced cabbage kimchi, seasoned and fried soybean curd, green tea *naengmyun* noodle, cheese *kamaboko* sausage, medium hot golden curry, or hot Chinese Mao tofu sauce. You can buy an Enure Fuzzy rice cooker made by the Japanese brand Zojirushi with settings for white/sushi rice; brown rice; semibrown, mixed, and sweet rice; and porridge. Even the ready-to-eat-meals such as chicken and vegetable skewers (*taksanjok*), red-hot soft bean curd stew (*sundubu jigae*), or grilled red snapper (*domi gui*) appeal.

See also:

HONG KONG SUPERMARKET. 37-11 Main St., 539-6868. 9:00 a.m.–9:30 p.m. (See p. 92.)

PATEL BROS. 42-79C Main St. and also 42-92 Main St., both bet. Blossom and Cherry Aves., 321-9847. www.patelbrothersusa.com. M–Sa 9:30 a.m.–9:00 p.m., Su 9:30 a.m.–8:30 p.m. See listing, p. 180.

TAI PAN BAKERY. 42-05 Main St. bet. Maple and Franklin Aves., 460-8787. Daily 7:30 a.m.–8:00 p.m.

Well known for its delicious pork buns, Tai Pan also sells moon cakes. Try double yolk with white lotus seed snowy moon cake. Or green tea with bean paste snowy moon cake. If you prefer to stay with Western-style pastries there are ample choices: strawberry shortcake and fruit tarts, and sandwiches, too. Also in Chinatown in Manhattan. Inexpensive, cash only.

TEN REN TEA. 135-18 Roosevelt Ave. bet. Prince and Main Sts., 461-9305. www.tenren.com. Su–Th 11:00 a.m.–11:00 p.m., F–Sa 11:00 a.m.–midnight.

Natural herbs have been used in China for thousands of years. Decide for yourself if they really improve sexual deficiencies, decrease blood fat and cholesterol, and cure migraines. In business for over forty years, this tea-and-ginseng international marketing consortium has worldwide locations. It's as homey as a duty-free shop, but you can find jasmine, oolong, green, and herbal teas, tea equipment, and special event products such as moon cakes, a traditional Chinese dessert for the autumn Moon Festival. Plus you can watch a traditional tea ceremony demonstration for free. On-line ordering.

Other Interesting Neighborhood Shops

FASHION IMAGE TOWN. 36-33 Main St., 359-4364. Daily 10:00–7:00 p.m.

Fashion Image Town is one of several Korean futon shops specializing in imported decorative items for the home: large bolster pillows, gorgeous linens, and comforters in popular Asian patterns and styles. They're not cheaper than American brands, but are high-quality.

GOLDEN OLDIES, LTD. 13-29 33rd Ave. bet. College Pt. Blvd. and Downing St., 445-4400. M–Sa, 9:00 a.m.–6:00 p.m. Su 11:00 a.m.–6:00 p.m. Complimentary car service to and from Manhattan.

A family business for over thirty years, the Golden Oldies warehouse store takes up an entire city block in Flushing. They carry more than 600 armoires, chandeliers, chairs, tables, and tasteful bric-a-brac, with prices ranging from several hundred dollars into the thousands. The owners travel the world hunting down good pieces, with a particular focus on antique European home furnishings. Among their customers they count Billy Joel, Star Jones, and Bryant Gumbel. Services include restoration and customization.

HOMEPLUS. 31-85 Whitestone Expwy., 445-4772. M–Sa 10:00 a.m.–8:30 p.m., Su 10:00 a.m.–7:30 p.m.

Think Target, but with a Korean twist. This department store sells household goods: kitchenware, linens, and home-decorating items geared to the Korean market. It's an offshoot of Tesco, the United Kingdom's biggest supermarket chain, which has over forty Homeplus stores in South Korea.

JIE-LI. 37-10 Main St., at the corner of 37th Ave., 445-8928. Daily 10:00 a.m.–7:00 p.m.

Check out the Hong Kong look: skimpy, pretty, and flirty. Flushing is filled with boutiques like this, specializing in Asian trendy clothing for women. The prices are low and the styles are perfect for teenagers or twenty-somethings.

☺ **PICA PICA.** 136-53 Roosevelt Ave., 321-1422. Daily 10:00 a.m.–8:30 p.m.

This unpretentious Japanese import store specializes in high-quality Asian-style tchotchkes. Pick up cute chopsticks, inexpensive tea sets, Japanese toiletries, sushi-sized plastic food storage units, and stationery items. This is one of a small chain of shops in the United States, including others in Queens and one in Manhattan. A similar operation is run by Samurai next door.

☺ **SAMURAI.** 136-41 Roosevelt Ave. bet. Main and Union Sts., 321-1283. Daily 10:00 a.m.–8:00 p.m.

Like an old-fashioned five-and-dime store, but Japanese-style, Samurai is a great place for Christmas stocking stuffers and kids' gifts. This franchise sells cups and bowls, home organizing and bath items, toys, and more. Everywhere you look there are smiley faces—on pencils, stationery, towels, towel hangers. You just may find yourself dying to buy things you never quite knew you needed: chopsticks with cats on them.

SHISEIDO COSMETICS. 24825 Northern Blvd. bet. 248th and 249 Sts., 224-5678. M–Sa 10:00 a.m.–7:00 p.m., Su noon–5:00 p.m.

This cosmetics chain store is often found in malls, but it's almost ubiquitous in the Asian neighborhoods of Queens. There are four such shops in downtown Flushing alone. Prices are the same as you'll find in department stores.

SHUN AN TONG HEALTH HERBAL CO. 135-24 Roosevelt Ave., 445-2252. Daily 9:00 a.m.–9:00 p.m.

Said to be the oldest Chinese herbal emporium in Flushing, there's an *amazing* amount of stuff here. It is a walk-in pharmacy, and if you are with someone who speaks Chinese, you can walk in with an ailment and walk out with a traditional Chinese remedy.

SSANG BANG WOOL AKA VENUS UNDERWEAR. 36-42 Union St. bet. Northern Blvd. and 37th Ave., 359-1801. M–Sa 8:00 a.m.–10:00 p.m.

The plunging necklines of the past decade have presented challenges of a very personal sort to the small-chested among us. Shoppers can find gorgeous imported-from-Korea (and padded) bras sized to fit petite, slender women. Bras in delicate sorbet colors and lots of lace run about $35; matching panties cost $25. As a point of cross-cultural interest, note the adult women's sleepwear in baby-doll styles and cheery juvenile patterns, guaranteed to gall Western feminists.

STAR CD. 40-09 Prince St. near Roosevelt Ave., 353-6896. Daily 9:00 a.m.–9:00 p.m.

What's the latest in Chinese pop music? Star CD is where the local kids go to find out—and you can, too.

SUN MI HANBOK KOREAN TRADITIONAL DRESS. 37-13 Union St., 338-0804. Daily 10:30 a.m.–8:00 p.m.

Beautiful traditional Korean robes, called *hanbok,* are custom-made on the premises from vibrantly colored bolts of fabric you can see on display. There are rows of infant-sized robes lining the back wall. These traditional costumes, for both men and women, are worn at life-cycle celebrations such as births, Sweet Sixteen parties, weddings, and New Year parties. This isn't a tourist shop, so please be respectful of the owner's time. Be prepared to slip off your shoes and wear little slippers when you come in. Other *hanbok* stores nearby are **SONG JUNG HANBOK** (36-25 Union St. #1C, 321-2413), **SUSAEK HANBOK** (36-25 Union St. #6F, 961-0445), and **NAKWON HANBOK** 42-30 Union St. #102, 961-6835).

WEDDING BOX PHOTOGRAPHY. 36-53 Main St. bet. Northern Blvd. and 37th Ave., 359-4477. Daily 9:30 a.m.–7:30 p.m.

Asian brides often don't buy their dresses when they get married. Instead, they rent. Wedding Box has tons of fancy made-in-Taiwan dresses, mostly in small sizes (2, 4, and 6) designed for the Asian market. Gown rentals start at $250 and up for three days. While you're here they'll also snap your wedding photo. There are several large wedding rental stores in downtown Flushing.

WORLD JOURNAL BOOKSTORE. 136-19 38 Ave. off Main St., 445-2661. M–F 9:00 a.m.–7:00 p.m., Sa 9:00 a.m.–6:00 p.m., Su 10:00 a.m.–6:00 p.m.

Absolutely everything in this bookstore is written in Chinese. Spend a few minutes and you'll experience a bit of what new immigrants face, trying to get along in the United States without being able to read English.

✒ ESSAY

RELIGIOUS DIVERSITY IN QUEENS

by James L. Muyskens, President, Queens College
James L. Muyskens, who holds a Ph.D. in Philosophy from the University
of Michigan, has been president of Queens College since 2002.

Walk the streets of Flushing on a busy day and take in the ever-changing sea of faces and the dozens of languages on the signs and shop windows. At such a time it is possible to believe that the final thing the builders of the Tower of Babel agreed upon before God scattered them to the four corners of the earth was that they would hold a reunion six thousand years later in Queens. Since God sent them all off speaking different languages, they would return the favor by coming back worshiping different gods.

Without a doubt, the Borough of Queens has the most extraordinary mix of religions in the world. In Flushing alone there are more than 200 places of worship within a space of two and a half miles, many offering services in five or six languages. Brooklyn may be called the city of churches, but Queens is the city of temples, synagogues, mosques, and gurdwaras, as well as hundreds of Korean and other churches.

Queens has a long history of religious tolerance. In 1657 a group of its citizens wrote one of the New World's first defenses of religious freedom. Known as the Flushing Remonstrance, this document defended the right of Quakers to worship as their conscience dictated. A remarkable thing about the authors of the Flushing Remonstrance is that not one of them was a Quaker. (The house of John Bowne, where the Quakers often met, has been declared "a national shrine to religious freedom." It is fitting that it now shares Bowne Street with about a dozen houses of worship.)

A more recent impetus for the influx of religions to the borough is the Immigration Act of 1965. This did away with the quota-by-nation system in favor of one based on a person's skills and profession. As a borough with two major airports—and pockets of exceptionally liberal zoning laws—it is no wonder so many immigrants settled in Queens.

The new diversity in the borough led to an explosion of new businesses and a blooming of ethnic and language studies at Flushing's own institute of higher education, Queens College. We now have programs, centers, and institutes that study the rich histories of Asians, Jews, Italians, Greeks, Latinos, African-Americans, the Irish, and others, and offer a thriving English as a Second Language program. Our New Immigrants and Old Americans project has published six books on the effects of this new wave of immigration. Our professors can often be found giving their students tours of the community laboratory that is Flushing, and even leading groups of people from outside the borough who are eager to learn more about us.

Early in my career I lived in Flushing for seventeen years. When I left in the 1980s to take a position at the University of Kansas, there was much tension between blacks and whites in the borough. One of the things I have noticed since returning is the lack of tension between groups. At first I found this puzzling. After all, the number of ethnic groups in Flushing had grown dramatically in the years I had been away. Perhaps just as a little learning can be a dangerous thing, a little diversity is dangerous also. But when you are overwhelmed with diversity, differences no longer count for much, and you look for the things that unite rather than divide.

The Flushing Remonstrance ends: "[I]f any of these said persons [Quakers] come in love unto us, we cannot in conscience lay violent hands upon them, but give them free ingresse and regresse unto our town, and houses, as God shall persuade our consciences." And, to a great extent, this is what the people of Queens still do.

10

Flushing Meadows–Corona Park

WHERE IT IS: Northcentral Queens.

HOW TO GET THERE: #7 subway to Willets Point/Shea Stadium, Flushing or LIRR station to Main St. and 41st Ave.

WHAT'S NEARBY: Corona, East Elmhurst, Flushing, Forest Hills, Kew Gardens, LaGuardia Airport.

SPECIAL CHARACTERISTICS: Major sports stadiums, major cultural institutions, and memorabilia from two World's Fairs.

Contact Info. www.nycgovparks.org., www.queensbp.org/content_web/depts/parks/parks.html. Or call New York City information line 311, or Flushing Meadows–Corona Park administration 760-6565.

ON NOT GETTING LOST: The park is large but fairly well marked thanks to the many cultural institutions here. Each provides detailed directions on their Web sites. See p. 125 for information on a free trolley and park map.

CAR SERVICES: Fairway 592-3333, Caprice 424-4410, Community 846-4500, Deborah 956-4007 or 803-1920.

A WORLD CULTURE PARK: INTERNATIONAL SPORTS, MUSEUMS, AND FESTIVALS

Every child in New York should be given a free subway pass to Flushing Meadows–Corona Park. The second-largest park in New York City, Flushing Meadows–Corona Park crams a lot into its 1,255 acres: two sports stadiums, the world's largest scale model, two space rockets, time capsules buried for 5,000 years, a zoo with an aviary in a geodesic dome, an air-conditioned theater, an immense globe showing all the continents of the world, *plus* great urban park amenities: tennis courts, playing fields, bike paths, two lakes with rental boats and a marina, bird-watching, model-plane flying, open spaces to romp in, free summer festivals, and seven playgrounds. Now, how cool is that?

↑ COLLEGE POINT

Northern Blvd.

World's Fair Marina

Flushing Bay

34th Ave.
35th Ave.
Elmhurst Ave.
Roosevelt Ave.

104th St. 104th St. 104th St.
111th St. 111th St.
110th St.
109th St.
112th St.
114th St.

25A

Northern Blvd.

32nd Ave.

College Point Blvd.

Prince St.
Farrington St.
Linden Pl.

25A

678

37th Ave.

Main St.

35th Ave.
36th Ave.

127th Ave.

Willets Point Blvd.

126th St.

Shea Stadium

7

Roosevelt Ave.

LIRR
Flushing Station

41st Rd.
41st Rd.

Sanford Ave.
FLUSHING

108th St.

38th Ave.
39th Ave.

41st Ave.
42nd Ave.
43rd Ave.
44th Ave.
46th Ave.
45th Ave.

CORONA

41st Ave.

National St.
102nd St.

7

M

99th St.
100th St.
101st St.
102nd St.
103rd St.
104th St.

Shea Stadium Station
LIRR

U.S.T.A. National Tennis Center; Arthur Ashe & Louis Armstrong Stadiums

Maple Ave.
Saull St.
Franklin Ave.

Avery Ave.
Fowler Ave.

Blossom Ave.

Cherry Ave.
Dahlia Ave.

Colden St.
Elder Ave.

New York Hall of Science

Queens Museum of Art;
Panorama of the City of New York
Queens Museum

Unisphere

Arboretum

Queens Botanical Garden

49th Ave.
Corona Ave.
Alstyne Ave.
50th Ave.
51st Ave.
52nd Ave.
53rd Ave.

Queens Zoo

Ice Skating Rink

Christie Ave.
99th St.
101st St.
102nd St.
103rd St.

Martens Ave.
Penrod St.
Otis Ave.
Granger St.
Van Cleef St.
Xenia St.
Van Doren St.
Calloway St.
Westside Ave.

Antique Carousel

Queens Theatre in the Park

495

57th Ave.
57th Rd.
58th Ave.
58th Rd.
59th Ave.
60th Ave.

Lawrence St.
136th St.

Kissena Park Corridor

50th Rd.

College Point Blvd.
Booth Memorial Ave.

Main St.

58th St.
142nd St.
146th St.
148th St.
138th St.
59th Rd.
60th St.

495

62nd Ave.
62nd Dr.
63rd Ave.

108th St.

62nd Ave.

Flushing Meadows-Corona Park

Meadow Lake

61st Rd.

Long Island Expwy.

Van Wyck Expwy.

61st Rd.
62nd Rd.
62nd Rd.
63rd Ave.
64th Ave.

63rd Rd.
63rd Dr.
64th Ave.
64th Rd.
65th Ave.

65th Rd.
66th Ave.
66th Rd.

67th Ave.
67th Rd.
67th Dr.
68th
Ave.
68th Rd.
68th Dr.

69th Ave.

G,R,V
M

110th St.

112th St.

Grand Central Pkwy.

Peartree Ave.

Mount Hebron Cemetery

Queens College C.U.N.Y.

Melbourne Ave.

140th St.

69th Ave.
69th Rd.

140th St.
153rd Rd.
150th St.
Kissena Blvd.

Yellowstone Blvd.
69th Rd.
69th Rd.

69th Rd.
Jewel Ave.
70th Ave.
70th Rd.
71st Rd.
72nd Ave.
72nd Rd.
72nd Dr.

E,F,G,R,V
M

71st Ave.
LIRR
Forest Hills Station
Greenway Ter.

113th St.

Jewel
Ave.

Willow Lake

678

Park Dr. E. Ave.

KEW GARDENS HILLS

71st Rd.

72nd Ave.
73rd Ter.

141st St.
137th St.
136th St.

70th Ave.
70th Rd.

Vleigh Pl.
147th St.

71st Ave.

72nd Rd.
72nd Dr.
73rd Rd.

70th Ave.
FOREST HILLS

Continental Ave.
Queens Blvd.
Austin St.
Burns St.

E,F
M

113th Pl.

Park Dr. E.

75th Rd.
75th Rd.
76th Ave.
76th Rd.
77th Ave.
77th Rd.

2nd Ave.
72nd Ave.

FOREST HILLS GARDENS

Ascan Ave.
74th Ave.
75th Ave.

76th Rd.
77th Ave.
77th Rd.

25

78th Ave.

E,F
M

78th
Ave.

Van Wyck Expwy.

138th St.
137th St.
136th St.

77th Ave.
77th Ave.

78th Dr.

Jackie Robinson Pkwy.

80th Rd.

Union Tnpk.

FLUSHING MEADOWS-CORONA PARK

← ELMHURST
← REGO PARK

↓ KEW GARDENS   ↓ JAMAICA

THINGS TO SEE AND DO

Most New Yorkers know that they can go to a Mets game at Shea Stadium, and watch the U.S. Open or take tennis lessons from the pros at Arthur Ashe Tennis Stadium. But few realize they can take the kids to New York's only science museum, the New York Hall of Science, or the Queens Zoo, and also attend ethnic cultural festivals, catch a performance at the Queens Theatre in the Park, find their own apartment in the huge scale model called the Panorama of the City of New York, or learn about green technologies at the Queens Botanical Garden. It's a remarkable and well-kept secret that all these attractions, and more, are centered in one large park.

BITS OF HISTORY

The area known as Flushing Meadows–Corona Park started out as a dump for industrial ash generated by manufacturing plants. In 1925, F. Scott Fitzgerald described it in *The Great Gatsby* as "a fantastic farm where ashes grow like wheat into ridges and hills and grotesque gardens." Robert Moses looked at the same "desolate area of land" and, instead, saw a site for a World's Fair in 1939. This flat, man-made park has since had an unusual history as the site of two World's Fairs, temporary headquarters of the United Nations, and, since 1978, home to the nation's most important tennis match, the U.S. Open.

In recent decades, the hub of cultural institutions located in the park have grown in stature and appeal. The range of experiences here—from world-class tennis to that small moment when a bilingual, bicultural child learns about gravity at the New York Hall of Science—is as richly varied as any park in the world could offer.

> ☛ **TIP: Free Map.** Call 750-6561 to request a map of Flushing Meadows–Corona Park, complete with lists of vendors, a brief park history, and other information.

> ☛ **TIP: Free weekend Culture Trolley.** 592-9700 ext. 306. Sa–Su noon–5:00 p.m. This free trolley makes three loops daily on the weekends, stopping at the Queens Museum of Art, Queens Botanical Garden, Queens Theatre in the Park, Queens Zoo, and the New York Hall of Science. It also goes to the Louis Armstrong House, Northern Blvd. restaurants, historic Jackson Heights, and the LaGuardia Marriott. Arrive at least ten minutes before scheduled departure times.

SPORTS STADIUMS

☺ **THE METS AT SHEA STADIUM.** 123-01 Roosevelt Ave., 507-6387, www.mets.com. Open 2½ hours before home games and for other stadium events. No tours. New stadium to open in 2009.

In a city with two baseball franchises, the Mets may still play second fiddle, but they're most definitely a team on the rise. The Mets have become more competitive of late, and with plans to open a world-class stadium in 2009, the team's popularity and attendance could begin to rival that of the Yankees.

Shea Stadium opened in April 1964, along with the World's Fair extravaganza (see pp. 131–32). It played host to both the Mets and the New York Jets football team in its early years, and it was a popular spot for major '60s and '70s concerts, including the legendary Beatles show in August 1965 that kicked off their American tour. After the terrorist attacks of September 11, 2001, the stadium served as a relief center and staging area for rescue and recovery crews.

Shea, known for its massive concrete grandstands, an open outfield, a scoreboard looming in right centerfield, and the "big apple" that rises out of the black top hat in centerfield whenever a Met hits a home run, is slated for demolition. A cozier, more fan-friendly "Mets Ballpark," to open in 2009, will change things. Expect to see a façade reminiscent of the Brooklyn Dodgers' Ebbets Field, and improved amenities, including a picnic area, concessions, and a "Fan Fest" entertainment area. One thing that won't change is the roar of the airplanes from nearby LaGuardia that fly in over the stadium like clockwork, adding decibels (and distraction) to the Mets experience.

On the field, the Mets have become more competitive in recent seasons, and also more international. General manager Omar Minaya has signed a number of high-profile Latino stars like Pedro Martinez, Carlos Beltran, and Carlos Delgado, and the team has become known as "Los Mets." How fitting indeed that the team from Queens is widely regarded as an up-and-comer with a melting-pot roster.

☺ **USTA BILLIE JEAN KING NATIONAL TENNIS CENTER.** 760-6200, ext. 6213. www.usta.org. Open daily, except during the U.S. Open in Aug.–Sept.

The enormous tennis complex in Flushing Meadows–Corona Park is the largest public tennis facility *in the world*. Renamed the USTA Billie Jean King National Tennis Center in 2006 to honor the tennis legend and trailblazer widely recognized for spearheading the women's movement in tennis by fighting for equal rights in the sport, it comprises 22,000-seat Arthur Ashe Stadium and the 10,000-seat Louis Armstrong Tennis Stadium, plus other indoor and outdoor courts. A new state-of-the-art tennis center with twelve courts, an expanded fitness center, and a full-service pro shop is scheduled to open in 2007. An American Tennis Hall of Fame is in the planning phases.

The U.S. Open, held the week before and after Labor Day, is one of the largest sporting events in the world. Tickets are expensive, but both the tennis and people-watching are great fun. In between matches, you can eat at any number of on-site restaurants, or explore nearby neighborhoods such as Jackson Heights, Corona, and Flushing. (See chapters on each in this book.)

The U.S. Tennis Association (www.usta.com.), which runs the U.S. Open tournament, is a nonprofit organization with more than 665,000 members that is also the governing body for tennis in the United States. It also hosts other tournaments here, including the U.S.T.A. NTC Women's College Tennis Invitational and the Turn Back the Clock (wooden racquets only) tournament, as well as some at the West Side Tennis Club in Forest Hills. (See pp. 145–46.)

CULTURAL INSTITUTIONS

☺ **NEW YORK HALL OF SCIENCE.** 47-01 111th St., 699-0005. www.nyhallsci.org. M–Th 9:30 a.m.–2:00 p.m., F 9:30 a.m.–5:00 p.m., Sa–Su 10:00 a.m.–6:00 p.m. Adults $11. Ages two to seventeen and senior citizens, $8. Science Playground–only fee: $3 per person. Free for public on F 2:00 p.m.–5:00 p.m., and Su 10:00 a.m.–11:00 a.m., Labor Day–Memorial Day. Free for members.

The New York Hall of Science is New York City's only museum dedicated to hands-on, interactive science and technology exhibitions and education. It's called the "Hall of Science," not "museum," because it was originally built for the 1964 World's Fair. An award-winning $92-million upgrade completed in 2004 expanded the museum's focus to five key areas: earth and space environments, the concept of networks, the science behind sports, mathematics, and the relationship between art and technology. Four hundred interactive exhibits entice visitors to explore everything from biology, chemistry, and physics to outer space. Strategically placed throughout the museum are entertaining demonstrations, conducted by bright interns whose genuine excitement about science is contagious. Visitors can hunker down for in-depth experiments in one of the two excellent Discovery Labs, which are hands-on classroomlike spaces set up with individual desks and friendly guides.

Preschool Place has many buttons to push, bubbles to blow, things to pour, and also a safe area for babies. Kids from tots to teens can romp in the Science Playground, 30,000 square feet of educational physical fun where they can steer, yank, and crank, and use their own weight, reflexes, and imagination to explore how things work in the physical and mechanized world.

Outside, Rocket Park is not to be missed. You may blink in disbelief at the sight of two rockets, noses pointed skyward, looking for all the world like it's countdown time. These are the Atlas and Titan rockets, a hit display at the 1964–65 New York World's Fair. You can see two replica capsules, too. One is of Mercury 1, the first U.S. spacecraft used for an unmanned, nonspace-testing mission in 1960. The other is of the two-man Gemini capsule, which conveyed the first American to "walk" in space. Kids love the interactive "climb-in" replica of the Friendship 7 Mercury capsule, which carried John Glenn, the first American astronaut orbiting the earth.

There's a good café and a gift shop with educational toys and games for children. The museum rents out space for birthday parties and "science sleepovers" for organized groups.

☺ **QUEENS BOTANICAL GARDEN.** 43-50 Main St. bet. Peck and Dahlia Aves., 886-3800. www.queens botanical.org. Mar.–Oct., Tu–F 8:00 a.m.–7:00 p.m., Sa–Su 8:00 a.m.–7:00 p.m; Nov.–Mar. Daily 8:00 a.m.–4:30 p.m. Free.

The Queens Botanical Garden is embracing the future—the renewable-energy and sustainable-resources future. Yes, it's got a rose garden, children's garden, and senior garden, as well as paths through countless varieties of herbs, flowers, bushes, and a peaceful twenty-one-acre arboretum. There's also an herb garden, bee garden, woodland garden, backyard gardens (where people can get inspiration for planting small urban spaces), and more.

That said, the new and spectacular $12 million environmental demonstration project is what places the Queens Botanical Garden squarely on the "must see" list. When fully completed in 2007, the new visitor center will combine energy efficiency, sustainable design, and resource recycling in a vast and glorious ecosystem. It will have a green roof and use electricity-producing photovoltaic cells that will provide about 20 percent of the building's total electricity needs. Rainwater and gray water (recycled water) are moved through man-made wetlands that serve as a natural filter. (Speaking of the latter, the gray water is reused to flush toilets in the building.) For those who want to see what geothermal heat exchangers are all about, the Queens Botanical Garden will have those, too. Visitors can see the wind speed, temperature, amount of sunlight and current, and cumulative power generation of the rooftop system on an interactive display. If you can, visit when it rains! From the Visitor Center you can watch the rainwater cascade in front of your nose and flow from the terrace roof into what, for lack of better lingo, they call the "water feature." It's a fountain with a meander channel and cleansing biotope through which the rainwater circulates. It's cool and environmentally advanced, as well as fun and educational. See the Web site for the schedule of gardening demonstrations and lectures.

QUEENS MUSEUM OF ART. Across from the Unisphere, about a block from an entrance to the USTA Billie Jean King National Tennis Center, 592-9700. www.queensmuseum.org. June–Sept, W–Su noon–6:00 p.m., F noon–8:00 p.m.; Sept.–June, W–F 10:00 a.m.–5:00 p.m., Sa–Su noon–5:00 p.m. Adults $5, seniors and children $2.50, members free.

The Queens Museum of Art has a flair for quirky, intelligent exhibits, the kind of small-show-with-big-idea combo that tickles New Yorkers. There are strong holdings of photography and Tiffany glass here, too, and work by local and international artists is shown in the Queens International showcases.

It also boasts the world's largest scale architectural model, called the Panorama of the City of New York. The Panorama isn't a cute "model" like a toy Christmas village. It's huge. Set in a large hall, it's a detailed, scale model of New York, complete with buildings and bridges, roads and rivers.

It takes up 9,335 square feet, which is space enough to park thirty yellow school buses, fit a tennis court, or build eight average-sized Manhattan apartments. In an instant it conveys the vastness and complexity of New York.

The Panorama literally lays New York City at your feet. As you enter the display hall, walking on a wide, elevated viewer's ramp, the city stretches out below you on a sunken floor. From above you can see the five boroughs, the East and Hudson Rivers, the Brooklyn Bridge, George Washington Bridge, and others. Manhattan is jammed with skyscrapers, and every street is lined with little miniature buildings. The Statue of Liberty rises from New York Harbor. You can see how Central Park cuts a green swath through Manhattan, and where Kennedy and La-Guardia Airports are situated at opposite ends of a huge and sprawling Queens. Block by endless block, the Panorama reveals the intimate details of the city.

You can't walk in, on, or through the model, only hike around its perimeters. Even so, you get a better overview of New York than from anywhere, even from the observation decks atop the Empire State Building or the old World Trade Center towers (which, for the moment, remain on the model). Overhead lights simulate day and night. Oddly, the Panorama depicts the city without people.

The Panorama was a hit attraction in the 1964–65 World's Fair. The building it is in, which is the Queens Museum of Art today, was built to house the Panorama exhibit. Visitors would ride little rail cars in an eight-minute loop around the perimeter of the simulated city, listening to a narration by Lowell Thomas. A small airplane once flew over the city but it suffered mechanical failure in 2001 and has not been replaced. Designed by Lester and Associates, the Panorama was the brainchild of Robert Moses, chief architect of much of New York's highway and park infrastructure, and head of the 1964–65 World's Fair. Some critics say the Panorama was Moses's monument to himself, and, if you look carefully, you will see that some of Moses's projects, like the Triborough Bridge, are disproportionately large.

Summer visitors should check out **PASSPORT FRIDAYS** for free movies and international outdoor film, dance, and music. The Queens Museum of Art is undergoing an expansion as we go to press.

☺ **QUEENS THEATRE IN THE PARK (QTIP).** Off the Grand Central Parkway in Flushing Meadows–Corona Park. Adjacent to the Queens Museum of Art and Unisphere, 760-0064. www.queenstheatre.org. Some events are free, subscriptions and discounts available. Free shuttle to and from subway, before and after shows.

One of the most beloved of all Queens' cultural venues, this year-round indoor theater hosts a rich feast of performances. For instance, in the 2005–06 season, the theater held five world premieres, seven dance programs by professional companies, and a roster of children's and family programming. Stars ranged from comedian Jackie Mason to Tony Award–winning Shakespearean actors. Special events and concerts capture the exciting multiculturalism of the New York audience. Check out their new Asian Cultural Initiative, the Black Cultural Arts Series, and the innovative Immigrant Voices New Play Development project for local playwrights.

Get tickets well in advance for the two-week-long annual summer Latino Cultural Festival (www.latinofestival.org). Every year, leading musicians are flown in from hot music scenes in the Spanish-speaking world. Recent shows featured Lima-based Peru Negro, Dominican merengue king Joseito Mateo, oc-togenarian Afro-Cuban percussionist Ivan Acosta, and icons of the Latin rock scene. It's a multicultural fiesta, complete with open mike, art exhibit, film, dance, free kids' shows, and food stalls.

You might think, from its name, that the Queens Theatre in the Park is an out-door venue, like Shakespeare in the Park. However, all performances are held in modern air-conditioned theaters: the 464-seat Claire Shulman Theatre and ninety-nine-seat Studio Theatre. A seventy-five-seat café/cabaret is scheduled to open in 2006–07. In general, tickets cost about half the price you'll pay for Broadway shows or concerts in Manhattan.

☺ **QUEENS ZOO AND CAROUSEL (AKA QUEENS WILDLIFE CENTER).** 53-51 111th St. at 53rd Ave., 271-1500. www.queenszoo.org. Daily, winter 10:00 a.m.–4:30 p.m.; summer 10:00 a.m.–5:00 p.m. Adults $5, seniors $1.25, children three to twelve $1, under three, free.

The bite-sized eleven-acre Queens Zoo, run by the Wildlife Conservation Fund, has more than two hundred indigenous North American animals like bison, sea li-ons, and American bald eagles. Meet Wynton and Marsh Alice (trumpeting ducks) and Simon and Garfunkel (Nubian goat kids). You can watch birds zoom around an aviary in a geodesic dome designed by Buckminster Fuller for the 1964–65 World's Fair. The kids can "do" the zoo in about an hour. Afterward, wander over to the New York Hall of Science, or kick a ball around in the park. For a calendar of fun seasonal events such as the Halloween Boo at the Zoo, see the Web site. Kids love the **FELTMAN CAROUSEL** located near the zoo (760-9583, daily 10:00 a.m.–7:00 p.m., $1 per ride). This rare classic wood carousel dates to 1908. In anticipa-tion of the 1964–65 World's Fair, the carousel was expanded to include forty-seven animals from an original Staubbman carousel in Coney Island, plus nearly two dozen original Feltman horses. You can book private birthday parties here.

THE WORLD'S FAIRS 1939—40 AND 1964—65

It's impossible to separate this park from its early association with the World's Fairs. Some interesting (but not all) of the remnants of the World's Fairs are described in this chapter. In addition to the listings below, see the New York Hall of Science (pp. 128–29), the Panorama of the City of New York (see pp. 129–30), and the World's Fair Marina (see p. 136). Note that some of the World's Fair sites have fallen into disrepair, such as the large area called Fountain of the Planets. To get oriented, check out the Queens Museum of Art displays and bookstore and gift shop, which is chockablock with World's Fair information and memorabilia (pp. 129–30).

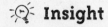 **Insight**

When the Global Community Came to Queens

Two World's Fairs were held in this park in the mid-twentieth century. Both were huge, exciting, multimillion dollar events attended by upward of 40 million visitors. Dozens of nations and companies hosted pavilions with exhibits ranging from food to technology. The theme of the 1939–40 World's Fair was The World of Tomorrow. The theme of the 1964–65 World's Fair was Peace Through Understanding. Akin to the Olympics and the United Nations in their internationalism, the World's Fairs were an opportunity for average people to experience the culture, products, and perspectives of other nations. For photos of the 1964–65 World's Fair see http://naid.sppsr.ucla.edu/ny64fair/, for info on contemporary events http://expomuseum.com.

☛ **TIP: Traveler's Advisory: Tell the Cabbie "El Mundo."** Some New York cabbies may not know their way around this park. If you want to go to the Queens Museum of Art or the zoo, which are near the Unisphere, try directing them to "el mundo" (meaning "world" in Spanish), or just "the big world" in Flushing Meadows—Corona Park. Many New York City cabbies live in Queens, and chances are they've been to this park with their own families. Nobody outside of officialdom calls it "the Unisphere."

Sculpture and Monuments

Scattered throughout the park are some outdoor sculptures created for the 1964–65 World's Fair. By the LIRR station, see if you can find the *Rocket Thrower* by Donald Delue. Other favorites include the *Freedom of the Human Spirit*, a twenty-eight-foot-tall bronze sculpture by Marshal M. Fredericks, and an aluminum-and-steel forty-foot-long abstract piece by Theodore Roszak called *Forms in Transit*.

TERRACE ON THE PARK. 52-11 111 St., bet. 52nd and 53rd Aves., 592-5000. Daily noon–9:00 p.m.

They call it the "Big T in the sky" because this large, popular catering facility dating from the World's Fair looks like a large *T* from the Long Island Expressway and Grand Central Parkway.

☺ **TIME CAPSULES.** Mosaics in the sidewalk in front of the Passerelle Building, near the #7 subway stop to the U.S.T.A. Billie Jean King National Tennis Center and Shea Stadium.

What would you put in a time capsule to be buried for 5,000 years? Look for the four discs in the floor of the plaza at the entrance to the park. Inscribed on the 1965 Time Capsule disc is the following: "Buried alongside the 1938 capsule this container holds an additional 50,000 microfilm pages, tranquilizers, one checkered bikini, credit cards, a fifty-star American flag, detergent, tektite, a Beatles record, "A Hard Day's Night," birth control pills, plastic wrap, material from the Echo II satellite, Kent filter cigarettes, freeze-dried foods, irradiated seeds, a plastic heart valve, an electric toothbrush, and desalted Pacific Ocean water."

Among other things included in the time capsule buried on October 16, 1965, were a Polaroid camera, transistor radio, fuel cells, a Bulova electronic watch, antibiotics, contact lenses, ceramic magnet, a rechargeable flashlight, synthetic fibers, a heat shield from Aurora 7, a film history of the USS *Nautilus*, a computer memory unit, a pocket radiation monitor, graphite from the first nuclear reactor, a Vanguard satellite container for carbon-14, and more.

Newspaper records of the 1939 Time Capsule, constructed by Westinghouse, indicate that it held thirty-five items, including a slide rule, a woman's hat, fountain pens, alphabet blocks, bits of common fabrics, metals, and plastics, seeds, and 10 million words on microfilm of art, literature, and news events. There were also messages to the future from Albert Einstein and Thomas Mann.

The actual time capsules are buried near the Theatre in the Park, in a mound called Time Capsule Hill.

☺ 🏛 **THE UNISPHERE.** Across from the Queens Museum of Art.

The Unisphere is that big globe you see as you're speeding down the Grand Central Parkway or flying into or out of LaGuardia Airport. If you saw the Tommy Lee Jones movie *Men in Black,* you also saw it explode. The Unisphere is a 140-foot-high stainless steel globe—and up close, it's stunning. On it the world's continents and mountain ranges are inscribed in relief. During the 1964–65 Fair, over forty years ago, the world's major cities—Paris, London, and Rome—sparkled with flashing lights. Orbiting around the globe are three rings representing the first satellite ventures into space.

It sits in a skating rink–like circle that in nice weather is often, and surrealistically, used by skateboarders. Designed by Gilmore D. Clarke, who also designed the layout of Flushing Meadows–Corona Park for both the 1939–40 and 1964–65 World's Fairs, the Unisphere was donated by U.S. Steel Corporation. The Unisphere is monumental and is guaranteed to give you goose bumps.

⌨ Insight

The United Nations in Queens

Unbeknown to many New Yorkers, the United Nations operated in part from Queens during its infancy. From 1946 to 1950, U.N. sessions were temporarily held in Flushing Meadows—Corona Park. This came about because when the U.N. was created after World War II and New York was selected as its home base, there was no appropriate building for the world body. While the U.N. complex in Manhattan was being built, the young organization sought temporary housing. One available spot was the site of the then-recent 1939–40 World's Fair. The New York State Building (now the Queens Museum of Art) was suitable for conversion into a hall big enough to accommodate delegates from around the world.

A lot happened during the years that the United Nation operated from Queens. President Truman addressed the first Special Session of the U.N. General Assembly. The United Nations oversaw the partition of Palestine and Korea. Nobel Peace Prize winner (and Queens resident) Dr. Ralph Bunche (see p. 157) negotiated an armistice between Israel and its Arab neighbors.

The Universal Declaration of Human Rights was adopted when the United Nations was in session in Queens. Part of it reads, "Whereas disregard and contempt for human rights have resulted in barbarous acts, which have outraged the conscience of mankind, the advent of a world in which human beings shall enjoy freedom of speech and belief and freedom from fear and want has been proclaimed as the highest aspiration of the common people. . . ." Much of the Declaration would make perfect sense to some of the million-plus immigrants from around the globe who came to the United States seeking these freedoms and, by some strange symmetry, ended up in Queens.

Other Fun Activities
CLOUD 9 CRUISES. 321-0013, by appt. only.

Surprise your honey or best buddy with a chartered cruise on a small luxury yacht leaving from the World's Fair Marina. Cocktails or a meal are served by staff dressed in formal attire, so you can relax and enjoy the view. After a couple martinis, you'll really be on cloud nine. In operation for over twenty years, the same company organizes cruises from Manhattan's midtown sky port and the 79th St. Boat Basin.

☺ Cultural Festivals and Special Events
If you like street fairs, Chinese New Year, Halloween parades, and the like, you'll love the special festivals held at Flushing Meadows—Corona Park. For instance, an annual highlight is the weekend-long Hong Kong Dragon Boat Festival starting the second weekend in August. Imagine a large lake with competing teams of over one hundred narrow boats, forty feet long and made of teak. In-

ternational and U.S. teams of rowers move furiously to the beat of on-board drummers. The boats are decorated like dragons, with colorfully painted hulls, a wooden dragon head on the bow, and a dragon tail at the stern. Day-long live entertainment includes Chinese music ensembles, demonstrations of kung fu and other martial arts, world music, Chinese drummers, and folk dances. You can watch demonstrations of traditional crafts such as calligraphy, rice-doll and kite making, see a dumpling-eating contest, or snack on the special festival treat, zongzi (also called jung), a steamed rice dumpling wrapped with bamboo or lotus leaves for strength and health (www.hkdbf-ny.org).

The Chosok Festival is the Korean equivalent to the American Thanksgiving, celebrated with food, dance, and traditional cultural entertainment. The two-week-long summer Latino Cultural Festival (www.latinofestival.org) brings in performers from Spanish-speaking countries; advance booking is necessary. The Colombian Independence Day Festival, with a roster of live performances, is hugely popular and attended by thousands.

Other events include Peruvian and Ecuadorian festivals, a dog show, and the summertime Queens Museum of Art **PASSPORT FRIDAYS**, offering free outdoor flicks, dance, and concerts (see listing, pp. 129–30).

☛ **TIP: Festivals and Events in the Park (selected list).** For information on these and other special events, see www.discoverqueens.info, watch local newspaper listings, or call the City hotline (311), or the park administration at 750-6561. All festivals are held in the area to the left of the Theatre in the Park unless otherwise noted. Dates subject to change.

May: Cinco de Mayo; Buddhist Children's Fun Day; It's My Park Day; and Seniors Day in the Park.

June: Children's Festival.

July: Colombian Independence Day; Passport Fridays, free outdoor movies, dance, and concerts (at Queens Museum); Peruvian Festival; and the Latino Culture Festival.

August: Hong Kong Dragon Boat Festival (on Meadow Lake); Passport Fridays (at Queens Museum); and the U.S. Open Tennis Championships (USTA Billie Jean King National Tennis Center).

September: Korean Harvest and Folklore Festival; Junta Hispana Festival; and the U.S. Open Tennis Championships (Tennis Center).

October: Queensboro Kennel Club Dog Show; and Halloween.

MEADOW LAKE. 760-6567.

The largest freshwater lake in New York City, this eighty-four-acre man-made lake is used for fishing and boating. There are playgrounds and picnic sites, as well as a model airplane field nearby. You can take sailing lessons here, too, from the American Small Craft Association (contact 699-1951).

☺ **POOL AND ICE SKATING RINK.** Enter from College Point Blvd. off Avery Ave. (near Van Wyck Expwy)., 271-1996. Hours to be announced.

On the easternmost side of the park, a new Olympic-sized indoor pool and NHL regulation-sized skating rink is scheduled to open in 2007, replacing the sixty-year-old World's Fair ice skating rink. Glass panels will allow natural light into the entire pool area. The building's shape and design allude to the 1939–40 and 1964–65 World's Fair pavilions and also include a "floating canopy" and tension wires holding up the roof. The $55 million complex includes features to enable the physically disabled to swim and play sled-hockey.

☺ **PLAYGROUNDS.** 271-1996 or the New York City information line 311.

There's nothing more frustrating that schlepping a child around a big park in search of a playground. Flushing Meadows–Corona Park is huge, so parents are advised to check a map and pick your playground accordingly.

Albert H. Mauro Playground: Park Dr. East and 73rd Terrace.
Buzz Vollmer Playground: Path bet. Passarelle Building and Fountain of Planets.
Jurassic Playground: West side of Meadow Lake and Grand Central Pkwy.
Lawrence Playground: College Pt. Blvd., near Botanical Garden.
Playground for All Children: 111th St. and Saultell and 56 Aves. (handicapped accessible equipment).
Triassic Playground: Jewel Ave. and Van Wyck Expwy.
World's Fair Playground: 62nd Dr. and Grand Central Pkwy. Service Rd.

WORLD'S FAIR MARINA. 478-0480. Open May-Oct.

Built as part of the huge construction for the World's Fairs, the marina leads out into Flushing Bay. Both small yachts and houseboats are moored here. There's a banquet hall and the Grand Bay Marina Restaurant (898-3663), as well. No matter where you are, you see planes taking off and landing at LaGuardia Airport nearby.

☞ **TIP: Queens' Parks Information.** Queens has more parkland than any of New York City's other boroughs. Included throughout this book are many interesting Queens parks. Information can be obtained at 286-2900 or the New York City information line 311.

11

Forest Hills, Kew Gardens, Kew Gardens Hills, and Rego Park

COUNTRY-IN-THE-CITY SUBURBS

Students of architecture and urban planning should not miss a trip to this part of Queens, home to classic New York City country-in-the-city communities. Plus, these neighborhoods share a wonderful urban amenity in Forest Park, a three-hundred-acre public park that alone is cause enough to visit.

Kew Gardens and Forest Hills are contiguous middle- and upper-middle-class neighborhoods. They both look ardently British. (It wouldn't be surprising if, together, they account for the largest stock of Tudor-style houses this side of the Thames River.) Visitors can hike through lush residential areas, full of old trees and beautifully tended gardens, and explore some good restaurants and several substantial shopping districts here. In Kew Gardens you'll find municipal buildings, including the Borough President's offices. Rego Park was built in the 1920s, when business was brisk and apartment-style living popular, and today it is home to Russian Jews from the Central Asian area called Bukhara (in Uzbekistan).

History and trivia lovers will be tickled by local lore. For instance, Rego Park was built on land previously farmed by Chinese farmers growing vegetables for Manhattan's Chinatown. Teddy Roosevelt spoke at Forest Hills' Station Square, when he said conscientious objectors should go to war unarmed, and if they got shot, well, that served 'em right. Scratch the surface of these communities and there are stories galore.

PARKS, PUBLIC SPACES, AND PUBLIC WORKS

☺ **FOREST PARK.** Jackie Robinson Pkwy. and Myrtle Ave. at Park Lane and Forest Park Dr. (NOTE: Forest Park is divided by Woodhaven Blvd. and the Jackie Robinson Pkwy.) Call the New York City information line 311 or 235-4100. www.nycgovparks.org.

Forest Park is the third-largest park in Queens. According to the New York League of Conservation Voters, about 60 percent of the park is natural forest that "represents one of the last densely forested areas of mature oak in New York City."

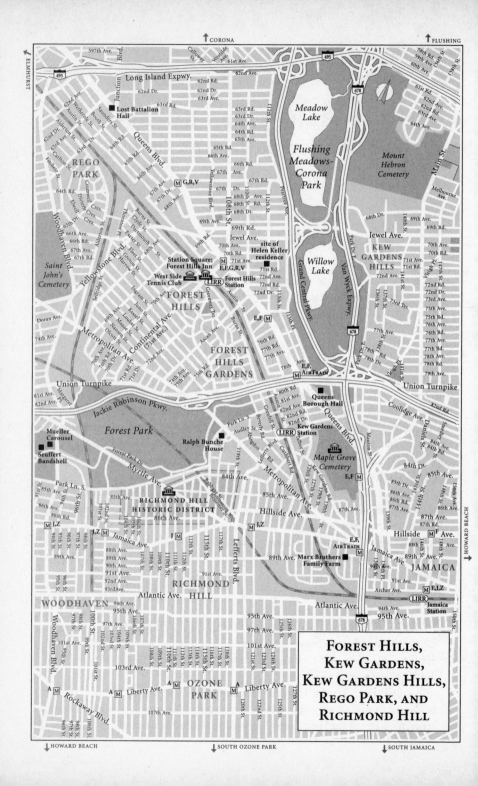

ELMHURST

597th Ave.
Calloway St.
Westside
61st Ave.
62nd Ave.

Long Island Expwy.
Junction Blvd.
62nd Rd.
62nd Dr.
63rd Rd.
62nd Dr.
62nd Dr.
63rd Ave.

■ Lost Battalion
Hall
63rd Rd.
63rd Rd.
63rd Dr.
64th Ave.
64th Rd.
65th Rd.

REGO
PARK
Queens Blvd.
108th St.
65th Ave.
66th Ave.
66th Rd.

Yellowstone Blvd.
67th Ave.
67th Ave.
67th Dr.
67th Dr.
68th Ave.
68th Ave.
68th Dr.
68th Dr.

M G,R,V

Saint
John's
Cemetery
69th Ave.
69th Rd.
Jewel Ave.
70th Ave.
70th Rd.
71st Rd.

Station Square;
Forest Hills Inn
West Side
Tennis Club
E,F,G,R,V
LIRR Forest Hills
Station

FOREST
HILLS

Metropolitan Ave.
Continental Ave. (71st Ave.)

Meadow
Lake

Flushing
Meadows-
Corona
Park

Willow
Lake

Mount
Hebron
Cemetery

Main St.

Melbourne
Ave.

Jewel Ave.
KEW
GARDENS
HILLS

site of
Helen Keller
residence
71st Ave.
72nd Ave.

E,F M

FOREST
HILLS
GARDENS

Aican St.
Burns St.
76th Rd.
77th St.
77th Rd.

78th Ave.
E,F
AirTrain

M

Union Turnpike

Jackie Robinson Pkwy.

Forest Park

Mueller
Carousel

Seuffert
Bandshell

M J,Z

Forest Park Dr.

Myrtle Ave.

Ralph Bunche
House

RICHMOND HILL
HISTORIC DISTRICT
86th Ave.

Jamaica Ave.

J,Z M

J M

RICHMOND

HILL

WOODHAVEN

Atlantic Ave.

OZONE
PARK

A M

Liberty Ave.

A M

Rockaway Blvd.

Woodhaven Blvd.

Park Ln. S.
84th St.

Hillside Ave.

Metropolitan Ave.

Queens Blvd.

Queens
Borough Hall

LIRR Kew Gardens
Station

Maple Grove
Cemetery

E,F M

Union Turnpike

Coolidge Ave.

84th Dr.

85th Dr.
86th Ave.
87th Ave.
87th Rd.

Hillside

E,F
AirTrain

Marx Brothers
Family Farm

Jamaica Ave.

JAMAICA

Archer Ave.

LIRR

M F Ave.

E,J,Z

Jamaica
Station

Liberty Ave.

Atlantic Ave.

95th Ave.

HOWARD BEACH

FOREST HILLS, KEW GARDENS, KEW GARDENS HILLS, REGO PARK, AND RICHMOND HILL

In addition to wandering through the gentle woods, there's a ton to do in Forest Park. Of interest to residents and visitors alike are the Spring Extravaganza and summer events at **SEUFFERT BANDSHELL** (Woodhaven Blvd. and Forest Park Dr., 235-0815) that range from Motown concerts, dancing, classic car shows, outdoor movies, and musicals.

You can ride a carousel horse or a real one here, too. **THE MUELLER CAROUSEL** (Woodhaven Blvd. at West Main Dr., 235-4100, open daily through summer; weekends in autumn and spring) is within walking distance of the bandshell. It's a classic, ornate wood carousel, built in 1902–10, with forty-nine beautifully painted horses, a few chariots, and a Wurlitzer organ. Now landmarked, it is one of only two such D.C. Mueller and Brothers Co. carousels still operating. You can also take a horseback ride in Forest Park along a four-mile bridle path on a trusty steed rented from one of two nearby riding schools. Both have pony rides for little kids, too. **LYNN'S RIDING SCHOOL** (88-03 70 Rd., bet. Metropolitan Ave. and Union Tnpk., 261-7679. Daily 9:00 a.m.–5:00 p.m.) or **D AND D STABLES** (88-11 70 Rd. off Metropolitan Ave., 263-3500. Daily 9:00 a.m.–5:00 p.m.) organize group trail rides for about $30 an hour, as well as more expensive private and semiprivate sessions.

FOREST PARK GOLF COURSE (101 Forest Park Dr., 296-0999. www.golfnyc.com.) is considered one of the best public golf courses in the city. It's an 18-hole, 6,000-yard course, and it's open year-round, weather permitting. The facilities include a clubhouse, rentals, lessons, and clinics. You can book tee times on-line.

You can also play tennis here, or entertain the kids at Victory Field. Don't miss the annual Halloween Walk, the Victorian Christmas, Nature Trails Day, and battle reenactments. It's fun to visit rustic Oak Ridge House in the southwest corner of the park, a century-old Dutch colonial revival house that was built by the old Forest Park Links golf course, that today serves as a community center and home of the Queens Council on the Arts.

For kids who'd rather grind than putt, there's a **SKATEBOARD PARK** (near the Greenhouse basketball courts on Woodhaven Blvd. just past Myrtle Ave., open mid-June to late September, Tu–Sa 3:00 p.m.–8:00 p.m.). Kids love the launch ramp, grind rail, quarter pipe, and more. However they have to wear the required gear: helmets and knee and elbow pads. Minors must wear wrist guards and have a signed release waiver. Playgrounds abound in all corners of the park, namely: Joseph Devoy Playground (Union Tnpk. and 71st Dr.); Dry Harbor Playground (80th St. and Myrtle Ave.); Giovannelli Playground (Freedom Dr. [102nd St.] and Park Lane So.); Greenhouse Playground (Myrtle Ave. and Woodhaven Blvd.); Jackson Pond Playground (108 St. and Myrtle Ave.); Mary Whalen Playground (79th St. and Park Lane So.); Sobelsohn Park (Union Tnpk. and Park Lane So.); Strack Memorial Pond (Forest Park Dr. off Woodhaven Blvd.).

☀ Insight

The "Garden Communities" of Queens

Queens prides itself on its "garden communities." It's a phrase one hears all the time, but what exactly is a garden community?

To understand the garden communities of Queens, roll back the clock to about 1900. The idea of a "suburb" as we know it today didn't yet exist. It was a time of great social change and urbanization. New York was growing rapidly as immigrants and farm workers sought work in new manufacturing industries in the city. By the early 1900s, 40 percent of the U.S. population was already concentrated in large towns or cities, compared with 3 percent only four decades before. Rampant poverty and filthy cramped living conditions in the urban slums, documented by photojournalist Jacob Riis, led to social unrest, strikes, and a fear of epidemics. Living conditions became a huge social issue, sometimes called "the housing problem." Earlier urban industrialists had simply built small towns for their workers, as William Steinway did for his piano factory workers in Astoria in the 1870s (see p. 34). By 1900, the problem was not just finding housing but preventing tuberculosis, labor problems, and social unrest.

"Healthy living" emerged as a catchphrase for design principles that are still valued today: ample space per person, fresh air circulating in the buildings, access to the outdoors, and a litter- and pollution-free environment. Ebenezer Howard, a British utopian socialist, is credited with being the father of the English Garden City movement, which promoted these principles in self-sustaining worker communities with cooperative ownership. Adapting some of these ideas, Forest Hills Gardens (see Bits of History, pp. 142–43), Sunnyside Gardens (see Bits of History pp. 269–70), and Jackson Heights (see Bits of History, p. 165) were each designed as a cooperative with common green spaces. However, most early-twentieth-century developments in Queens adopted only the "garden" part of Howard's vision. For instance, Kew Gardens and nearby Richmond Hill have lovely homes, winding streets, and gardens—but the communities don't share ownership of, and access to, common park space.

In the 1930s a dearth of decent, affordable housing again became a prominent social issue, and some of the ideas articulated by Ebenezer Howard were echoed in the development of worker co-ops in Sunnyside such as the Celtic Park Apartments (see p. 272) and Phipps Garden Apartments (see p. 272).

So if you're confused about what a "garden community" is, there's a reason. It could refer either to historic planned cooperative communities, or any residential area (and there are many in Queens) boasting easy access to the owner's private gardens.

Forest Hills

WHERE IT IS: Central Queens. Bounded by Queens Blvd. and the LIE to the north, Flushing Meadows–Corona Park to the east, Union Tnpk. to the south and Yellowstone Blvd. to the west.

HOW TO GET THERE BY SUBWAY: E and F to 71st/Continental Ave., 75th Ave. G, R, V to 67th Ave. By LIRR, go to Station Square (Austin St. and 71st Ave.).

WHAT'S NEARBY: Kew Gardens to the southeast, Kew Gardens Hills to the east, Flushing Meadows–Corona Park to the northeast, Forest Park to the southwest, and Rego Park to the northwest.

MAJOR SHOPPING/RESTAURANT STREETS: Austin St. and Queens Blvd., 71st Ave./Continental Ave. for general shopping, Metropolitan Ave. for antique shops.

SPECIAL CHARACTERISTICS: Tudor architecture, great shopping, and an eclectic mix of cultures.

ON NOT GETTING LOST: The street grid system is useful except in the northern part of Forest Hills, where you'll find many instances like this: "63rd Ave.," "63rd Rd.," or "63rd Dr." (NOTE: Avenues are the northernmost streets and drives the southernmost.) In Forest Hills Gardens there's a central circular street, Greenway, which has both north and south drives. Orient yourself to the Forest Hills Station, Austin St., and Queens Blvd.

CAR SERVICES: Four One's 441-1111 or 456-1111, Community 846-4500.

URBAN ECOLOGY: NOT ONE, BUT THREE FORESTS

One might say there are three "forests" in Forest Hills. The first is Forest Park, carved out in 1896, and encompassing, literally, a small forest. The second, the historic neighborhood of 1,500 Tudor-style homes in Forest Hills Gardens, an exclusive planned community (quite green, very suburban, but not at all forested), was created around 1901. The third is a virtual forest of apartment buildings that rose up around Queens Blvd. in the 1920s and thereafter. Together, these quite different urban ecosystems define Forest Hills.

If you've never been to Queens and aren't sure you can handle the uncertainty of not knowing where you are, start in Forest Hills. It's easily reached by LIRR or subway, and there are routes aplenty for biking, walking, shopping, and eating. Forest Hills seems so, well, mainstream American that it's no wonder Spider-Man's alter ego Peter Parker gave as his address an actual home here, on Ingram St.

THINGS TO SEE AND DO

A day trip to Forest Hills hardly counts as adventure travel, but as an old, established New York neighborhood it's worth seeing. You can shop the boutiques and chain stores on Austin Street or browse a handful of antique stores on Metropolitan Ave., or take the kids for a banana split at old-fashioned Eddie's Sweet Shop. For take-home food, head to Queens Blvd. for rugelah at Andre's Hungarian Bakery and fresh (and freezable) you-know-what at Knish-Nosh. If you think that New York City is all skyscrapers, a walk around Forest Hills Gardens, a manicured private residential community, will be a big eye-opener.

BITS OF HISTORY

Forest Hills Gardens, one of America's first model garden-in-the-city suburbs, was a social experiment in affordable housing. Under the direction of Mrs. Russell Sage, whose wealthy husband died in 1906, bestowing upon her a large fortune, the Russell Sage Foundation provided what we today might call seed money for what became the Forest Hills Gardens project. Its mission was to create improved housing that would be affordable for a wage earner, and that adhered to "higher standards and more efficient handling of land development and distribution, the application of collective or co-operative principles, and the science and art of town planning and good housing." They chose to site the project in Forest Hills, which had been created in 1904 when developer Cord Meyer bought 600 acres and began laying out streets. The area was pristine. Landscape designer Frederick Olmstead, Jr. (son of Frederick Olmstead who designed Central Park) and supervising architect Grosvenor Atterbury (who years later designed the American Wing of the Metropolitan Museum of Art) were selected as the design team for Forest Hills Gardens.

The master plan included a train station and town square, a common with a church, an inn for visitors, and winding streets. Smaller houses were built to resemble inns. Larger homes were set against common garden space of which homeowners could rent a small piece for gardening. Throughout, the style of the area is romantic neo-Tudor, with homey, rural touches. Forest Hills Gardens was meticulously planned, even down to the color of the houses and the distance between front doors and the street. Visually, Forest Hills Gardens works as a coherent, integrated whole.

Forest Hills Gardens failed as an experiment in affordable housing. The project ran into financial difficulties and local residents took over management, creating restrictive barriers to residency. Ironically, what was meant to be affordable housing became a bastion of upper-middle-class life. However, the experiment was a success in terms of design and livability, proven by the fact that a century later it remains a very beautiful, if expensive, private community. Originally mostly white and Protestant in population, today Forest Hills Gardens is more diverse.

The larger community of Forest Hills grew up a few years later, in response to the availability of transportation to Manhattan. In 1911 the opening of the Long Island Railroad at Forest Station enabled commuters to reach the city in half an hour. Within a decade there were several hundred homes built in the area. The population, mostly Jewish and Italian, soared to 18,000 by the 1930s as new subway lines arrived and high-rise apartments were built along Queens Blvd. In a classic spiral of urban development, new residents brought commercial life, which in turn stimulated more residential development. Today few single-family homes in the area remain outside of Forest Hills Gardens. The Indians, Iranians, and Israelis who live in Forest Hills tend to be middle- and upper-middle-class and well educated. Other recent immigrants who have settled here come from China, Colombia, Korea, Romania, Russia, Pakistan, and Poland.

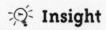 Insight

Tudor Tudor Everywhere: Why the Very Englishness of It All?

Q: Why is there so much neo-Tudor architecture in Queens? And so few brownstones?

A: Experts call this an invented English heritage. Brownstones built in the 1880s and 1890s, with their long, dark corridor insides, were seen as old-fashioned by 1910. A Tudor-style home was affirmation of middle-class or upper-class status in the early twentieth century. The invented English heritage was a way to establish a sense of tradition and stability when in fact rapid economic growth and urbanization were causing both social upheaval and opportunity. This was the era of Horatio Alger; paupers could become millionaires. Living in a Tudor-style home suggested that the occupant was educated, cultured, and entitled. The style remains popular today.

POINTS OF CULTURAL INTEREST

AQA GALLERY. 99-10 Metropolitan Ave. bet. 70th Ave. and 70th Rd., 520-9842. www.arts4u.org. Tu–Sa., 1:00 p.m.–6:00 p.m.

The Alliance of Queens Artists runs this gallery, offering a calendar of shows of local artists as well as classes in painting and drawing.

ARBOR CLOSE AND FOREST CLOSE. 75th Ave. to 76th Ave., near Austin St. to back of Queens Blvd.

You can walk along the streets of 1920s row houses to get an idea of Forest Hills in its early years.

🏛 FOREST HILLS INN. 1 Station Square bet. Dartmouth St. and 71st Ave., 896-5445. Tu–Th 5:00 p.m.–2:00 a.m., F 5:00 p.m.–4:00 a.m., Sa 7:00 p.m.–4:00 a.m.

Forest Hills Inn was built in the early 1900s as part of Forest Hills Gardens. Rooms were in demand particularly during the decades when throngs came to watch the tennis matches at the Forest Hills Stadium. Designed by Grosvenor Atterbury, who is responsible for much of the neo-Tudor-themed style for which Forest Hills is famous, the inn resembles buildings you might expect to see in the central squares of Europe, with an impressive tower and, in this case, a curious helmet-shaped dome. Although converted to an apartment building, to this day it remains the tallest building in Forest Hills Gardens.

FOREST HILLS JEWISH CENTER. 106-06 Queens Blvd., 263-7000. M–F 9:00 a.m.–4:00 p.m., F, Su 9:00 a.m.–noon. Call for hours of services.

This long-standing Conservative Jewish synagogue, affiliated with United Synagogue and the Jewish Theological Seminary, is at the heart of a vibrant Jewish community in this area of Queens. On-site is a small Judaica shop selling tasteful contemporary renditions of traditional Jewish religious books.

FOREST HILLS STADIUM. See West Side Tennis Club (pp. 145–46).

JEWISH HERITAGE LIBRARY AT CENTRAL QUEENS YMHA AND YWHA. 67-09 108th St. bet. 67th Rd. and 67th Ave., 268-5011. Hours vary with programs.

Probably one of the most extensive libraries in any Y in the nation, the Hevesi Jewish Heritage Library at the Central Queens YMHA and YWHA boasts a circulating collection of 15,000 volumes (in English, Hebrew, and Yiddish), and hundreds of videotapes, audiotapes, and compact discs. The library is open to the public for borrowing, free of charge. There's a free monthly film program, and lectures and workshops for adults and children.

REFORM TEMPLE OF FOREST HILLS AND ALSO SITE OF HELEN KELLER RESIDENCE. 71-11 112th St., near 71st Rd., 261-2900.

The Jewish Reform Temple of Forest Hills is a major religious and cultural center in Forest Hills. It's also built on the site of the home in which Helen Keller lived from 1917 to 1938 with her teacher Ann Sullivan and secretary Polly Thompson. A plaque at the front of the synagogue notes that "... conquering adversity, Helen Keller wrote, lectured and inspired others to succeed."

🏛 REMSEN FAMILY CEMETERY. 69-43 Trotting Course Lane at Metropolitan Ave. and Alderton St. Open to the public.

Landmarked in 1981, this tiny cemetery holds only eight graves, dating from 1790 to 1819.

STATION SQUARE. (Intersection of Continental Ave. and 71st Ave.), Burns St., Greenway Terrace, and Dartmouth St.

Are you in Westchester? Or Winchester? The Long Island Railroad station (Forest Hills Station) and elegant Station Square in Forest Hills were built in mock Tudor style as the gateway to Forest Hills Gardens. The train station is a symphony of arches, gables, and red tiles. (If the entire complex reminds you of a late nineteenth-century European town, that's exactly what it's supposed to do.) Many politicians have spoken here. Former President Teddy Roosevelt delivered a fiery speech about America's role in the world on July 4, 1917, as the United States was entering World War I, roaring that America is "not a boardinghouse and countinghouse for foreigners who hold allegiance to another nation."

TRYLON THEATER. 98-81 Queens Blvd. Not open to the public.

When the Trylon opened in 1939, it was timed to coincide with the opening of the 1939–40 World's Fair. It had an art deco marquee and entrance pavilion and also murals and tile work depicting the 1939 World's Fair and its symbols, the Trylon (an enormous spire) and the Perisphere (a huge ball-like sculpture). The building, which had fallen into disrepair, is being renovated by the Educational Center for Russian Jewry. Local preservationists complain that some of the original tiles and other architectural elements were not landmarked and so are being lost to posterity as the building gets recycled to new uses.

WEST SIDE TENNIS CLUB. 1 Tennis Pl., 268-2300. www.foresthillstennis.com.

Tennis fans know the legendary West Side Tennis Club as home of the U.S. Open for more than a half century. Everyone else knows it as Forest Hills Stadium, where Frank Sinatra, the Beatles, Jimi Hendrix, the Rolling Stones, the Who, Diana Ross, and the Boston Pops performed. This was where Bob Dylan was booed when he first played an electric guitar in public in 1965.

Today it's a private club, with thirty-nine courts and a fourteen-acre facility with a tennis stadium, swimming pool (in summers only), dining room, and historic clubhouse. It hosts U.S.T.A. Pro Circuit events, some of which are free to the public. A star-studded list of tennis talent including recent stars Jimmy Connors, John McEnroe, Vital Gerulitis, Billie Jean King, Virginia Wade, Chris Evert, Tracy Austin, and Martina Navratilova have played here.

The West Side Tennis Club was founded in 1892 by thirteen men who first rented ground on Manhattan's Central Park West, between 88th and 89th Streets, for three clay tennis courts. After moving from place to place in Manhattan, the growing club struck a deal for land owned by philanthropist Margaret Olivia Slocum Sage of the Russell Sage Foundation, which was developing nearby Forest Hills Gardens (see Bits of History pp. 142–43). The price was

$2,000 down payment and $75,000 mortgage. In 1914, the West Side Tennis Club opened as a world-class tennis center. Its proximity to Manhattan and superior facilities enticed the United States Lawn Tennis Association National Championship (the entity that became the U.S. Open) to move the prestigious tournaments away from the stuffy old Newport Casino in Rhode Island to Queens. When in the late 1970s the West Side Tennis Club could no longer accommodate growing consumer demand for tickets, the U.S.T.A. moved to Flushing Meadows–Corona Park.

SELF-GUIDED TOUR OF FOREST HILLS GARDENS

You can walk or drive this route to discover who lived in Forest Hills Gardens. Note that this is a private community and that parked cars will be booted, but you can park on nearby Austin St. and walk in. The streets in this area are winding; bring a map. (The tour below is excerpted with permission from "Self-Guided Walking Tour of Homes of Famous Forest Hills Gardens Residents," © Terrace Realty.)

Walking from Station Square up Greenway North: Trygve Lie lived at #123 from 1946 to 1953. He was the first secretary general of the United Nations, which first met in Flushing Meadows–Corona Park nearby. Photos show him hosting President Truman at this home in 1950. Fred Stone, a popular vaudeville actor and the first Broadway Scarecrow from the New York debut of the musical *The Wizard of Oz,* lived at #150 from 1926 to 1946. Mike Miranda lived at #167 from 1948 to 1974, during which time he got arrested at a Mafia meeting in the highly publicized 1957 Appalachian Conference raid.

Interestingly, on Greenway South are homes of people associated in some way with pioneering. The house at #275 was home to Lyman Beecher Stowe, grandson of Harriet Beecher Stowe, from 1914 to 1930. At #239 lived John Hogan, radio pioneer, developer of single-dial radio, and also star of the WQXR radio station. Residing at #234-236 from 1917 to 1962, Adolph Weinman designed the façade of New York City's Penn Station, the Liberty half dollar, and Mercury dime. At #105, it's said that bookie Frank Erickson, who lived here from 1928 to 1963, ran a gambling operation in the basement. Branch Rickey lived at #34 for three years, during which he made history by signing Jackie Robinson, the first African-American major league baseball player, in 1945. Geraldine Ferarro, first woman to run for vice-president of the United States, lived at #22 Deepdene Road from 1967 until 2002. New York's columnist Jimmy Breslin lived in #52 Deepdene Road from 1964 to 1982.

The records are unclear, but #8 Markwood Road may have been the home of Grosvenor Atterbury who designed many homes in the area, Forest Hills Inn, and Church-in-the-Gardens. Slightly off the beaten track, check out #6 Burns Street, where futurist Buckminster Fuller lived in 1949. He invented many things, including the geodesic dome that was featured in the World's

Fair 1965 and is today at the aviary at the Queens Zoo. For a quarter of a century, from 1928 to 1955, at #27 Wendover Road, Dale Carnegie was winning friends and influencing people. And #7 Middlemay Circle was where singer and actress Pia Zadora grew up.

Detour to Ingram St. to see where Spider-Man, aka Peter Parker, of comic book and movie fame, lived (fictionally) at #20, and also #56, where David Caruso, a TV actor who starred in *NYPD Blue,* grew up (1956–74). While you are in Forest Hills Gardens, visit the **CHURCH-IN-THE-GARDENS,** 15 Borage Place.

CAFÉS, BARS, AND RESTAURANTS

Cafés, Pizza, and Light Fare

DEE'S BRICK-OVEN PIZZA. 107-21 Metropolitan Ave. bet. Ascan Ave. and 74th Ave., 793-7553. Tu–Th noon–10:00 p.m., F–Sa noon–11:00 p.m., Su 2:00–10:00 p.m.

People travel for this brick-oven pizza, served in a white-tableclothed restaurant environment. You can design your own pizza with the usual toppings, or concoct your own recipe with great ingredients such as shiitake mushrooms, homemade pesto, or fresh sausages. For appetizers, you can get spanakopita, shrimp sautéed with garlic and wine, caponata, or crab cakes.

EDDIE'S SWEET SHOP. 105-29 Metropolitan Ave. at 72nd Rd., 520-8514, Tu–F 1:00–11:30 p.m., Sa–Su noon–11:30 p.m.

Eddie's retro decor, complete with peach-colored walls, tin ceiling, and counter, is original. You can sit at the old-fashioned soda fountain and sink into a bowl of whipped cream or an ice cream sundae with a cherry on the top. Kids will love the stuffed toys dangling from the chandeliers. How long has Eddie's Sweet Shop been in business? "Nobody knows," says one of the soda jerks, "but we think over ninety years." The hot fudge is sensational.

NICK'S PIZZA. 108-26 Ascan Ave. bet. Austin and Burns Sts., 263-1126. Su–Th 11:00 a.m.–9:30 p.m., F–Sa 11:00 a.m.–11:00 p.m.

It's hard to be the "best" in a city full of pizzerias, but Nick's has a loyal following who crave their thin-crusted brick-oven pies with fresh toppings. Snuggle into a booth with your honey, and you're set for a pizza-salad-beer dinner.

RALPH'S FAMOUS ITALIAN ICES. 73-04 Austin St. bet. Booth and Burns Sts., 263-8816. www.ralphsices.com. April–October. Daily 10:00 a.m.–10:00 p.m., Sa–Su til midnight.

New York in the summer wouldn't be the same without a plethora of Italian ice stands. Ralph's Famous takes its place as an outer-borough fave. Started about eighty years ago in Staten Island, Ralph's knows how to keep New Yorkers cool from April to October. Also at 264-21 Union Tnpk. bet. 264th and 265th Sts.

Bars

BARTINI'S. Forest Hills Inn, 1 Station Square bet. Dartmouth St. and 71st Ave., 896-5445. Tu–Th 5:00 p.m.–2:00 a.m., F 5:00 p.m.–4:00 a.m., Sa 7:00 p.m.–4:00 a.m.

Bartini's makes about six hundred different versions of the venerable cocktail. This friendly joint is like a trendy Manhattan lounge minus the cover charge and is busy on weekends. You'll find it tucked away in the basement of the historic Forest Hills Inn, now converted to condos. Ladies' night is every Thursday complete with a DJ. Free valet parking Friday and Saturday. (On second thought, after trying six hundred martinis, take a taxi.)

NETWORK CAFÉ. 108-02 72nd Ave. at Austin St., 263-5700. Daily 4:00 p.m.–11:00 p.m. Th, Sa, jazz.

This is the quintessential Forest Hills hangout. Stop by the lounge that attracts an easygoing, multicultural crowd.

Restaurants

5 BURRO CAFÉ. 72-05 Austin St. bet. 72nd Ave. and 72nd Rd., 544-2984. Daily noon–midnight.

This tiny joint's a-jumpin'. There's a friendly, noisy bar scene, with waiters racing around the long narrow space with big platters of Mexican food. Folks come for inexpensive but tasty fajitas, burritos, a mountainous salad with chicken, and salsa you can't stop eating. Popular on weekends, 5 Burro attracts an amiable crowd. (And ha, ha, their name is a pun). Entrées cost about $11 per person.

ALBERTO'S. 98-31 Metropolitan Ave. bet. Ascan Ave. and 74th Ave., 268-7860. Daily 11:00 a.m.–11:00 p.m.

Get in line. Alberto's is the kind of place frequented by locals who say, "I'm Italian, so I don't go to Italian restaurants." Well, they do come to Alberto's. Weekend reservations are recommended.

AUSTIN HOUSE. 72-04 Austin St. at 72nd Ave., 544-2276. Daily 7:00 a.m.–midnight.

The average age of Sunday brunch customers is well past Social Security eligibility, but heck, you are as old as you feel, right? This retro-1950s diner is the perfecto place to take that cranky older relative who makes frequent requests in regard to, say, ordering a burger. ("Hold the mayo, no garlic, toast that muffin a little better, will ya, darling? And you don't have fat-free milk?") At Austin House, they'll understand.

BANN THAI. 69-12 Austin St. bet. 67th Dr. and 68th Ave., 544-9999. Daily 11:30 am–11:00 p.m.

If you can judge a neighborhood by its Thai food, Forest Hills can hold its own against the Upper East Side. This restaurant is a bit pricier than others in Queens, but not as expensive as Manhattan.

CHO-SEN GARDEN. 64-43 108th St. bet. 64th Rd. and 65th Ave., 275-1300. Su–Th noon–10:00 p.m., Sa 6:00 p.m.–midnight.

This kosher Chinese restaurant called Cho-Sen Garden (as in, "chosen." Get it?) serves fusion cuisine—it even has a sushi bar—but most patrons come for the kosher more than the cuisine.

CORFU. 70-17 Austin St. near 70th St., 263-6263. Daily 11:00 a.m.–midnight.

More take-out than eat-in, this eatery is totally no-frills but sells Mediterranean souvlaki, chicken kebabs, and *befteki* (ground beef and herbs). It's good, and reasonably priced. The gyro plate comes with rice, Greek salad, veggie, tzatziki sauce, and pita for about $10.50.

JUST LIKE MOTHER'S. 110-60 Queens Blvd. bet. 73rd Rd. and Ascan Ave., 544-3294. Daily 7:30 a.m.–10:00 p.m.

Offering a taste of Poland in Queens, this aptly named restaurant serves breakfast, lunch, and dinner. Mother's big portions satisfy. So do the blintzes served with fresh fruit, bacon, and potato latkes with freshly grated onion. The borscht, schnitzel, and slaws hit the spot and the perogies are great!

MICKEY'S PLACE. 101-16 Queens Blvd. near 67th Rd., 897-9898. Daily 5:00 p.m.–10:30 p.m.

Mickey's Place has the best sushi in Queens. Oh, and the staff is just terrific. Please, just don't tell all those folks in Manhattan.

MOOD. 120-29 83rd Ave. off Lefferts Blvd. 849-6663. Daily, 11:00 a.m.–10:00 p.m. Sa–Su brunch noon–3:00 p.m.

Upscale Mood is a popular destination for sophisticated Forest Hills residents. Choose from a menu of artfully presented American nouvelle cuisine dishes ranging from the $13 broccoli rabe ravioli to a $25 filet mignon. Reservations are recommended.

NARITA SUSHI. 107-08 70th Rd. bet. Queens Blvd. and Austin St., 263-2999. M–Th noon–10:00 p.m., F–Sa noon–11:00 p.m., Su 1:00 p.m.–midnight.

One of the best sushi restaurants in the borough, Narita makes a delicious meal out of standards such as tuna and yellowtail sushi. Prices are reasonable.

Q, A THAI BISTRO. 108-25 Ascan Ave. bet. Austin and Burns Sts. 261-6599. Su–Th noon–10:30 p.m., F–Sa noon–11:30 p.m.

What makes this popular Forest Hills Thai restaurant a "bistro"? It's not the steamed dumplings with ginger dipping sauce. Or the crispy whole red snapper in red coconut curry sauce. It's not the chef, either, whose résumé includes the five-star Grand Sheraton in Bangkok. Nope, it's the cozy ambience that rates "bistro." Entrées in the $20 range.

FOREST HILLS TANGO MAMBO. 111-08 Queens Blvd. bet. 75th and 76th Aves. 520-6488. Daily 11:00 a.m.–midnight; floor show F–Sa 8:00 p.m. and 11:00 p.m., Su 8:00 p.m. No cover.

Try something different: Enjoy a tango floor show in an Argentinean restaurant. You can order moderately priced pasta or tasty Argentinean beef or chicken dishes here. On weekends there's a live tango show by professional dancers, followed by DJ music and dancing.

SHOPPING

ANTIQUE ROOM IN THE GARDENS. 105-22 Metropolitan Ave. bet. 72nd Rd. and 72nd Ave., 793-2384. Tu–Sa noon–6:00 p.m., Su noon–5:00 p.m.

You will find fine and costume jewelry, nineteenth- and twentieth-century furniture, silver items, chandeliers and lamps, and bric-a-brac here. The owner is helpful and often brings in new pieces, so let her know if you are seeking something special.

AUSTIN SHOES BUSTER BROWN. 71-25 Austin St. at 71st St., 544-6790. Daily 10:00 a.m.–6:00 p.m.

If the shoe fits wear it—and fit is what Austin Shoes is all about, for newborns and first walkers to orthopedic footwear. A throwback to the 1950s, when it first opened, this shop features Buster Browns, one of the nation's oldest children's shoe brands, launched more than one hundred years ago and named after a cartoon character. You'll find old-fashioned sturdy leather shoes here as well as sneakers.

BODY & SOLE BOUTIQUE. 105-20 Metropolitan Ave. at 72nd Rd., 575-3335. M 11:00 a.m.–6:00 p.m., Tu–Th 11:00 a.m.–7:00 p.m., F–Sa 11:00 a.m.–6:00 p.m.

Ladies, want something unique to wear to work or on a date? With new arrivals weekly, Body and Sole is just the place to go for trendy but tasteful dresses, suits, casual clothes—and, of course, shoes and accessories. In a borough that's got more national brand chain stores than boutiques, this is a welcome find. Moderate prices.

EMILIO'S SKI SHOP. 112-32 Queens Blvd. bet. 75th Ave. and 76th Rd., 554-0404. M, W–F 10:00 a.m.–8:00 p.m., Tu, Sa 10:00 a.m.–6:00 p.m., Su noon–5:00 p.m.

Both a store and a de facto clubhouse for skiers and snowboarders, Emilio's sells a wide range of ski equipment and also organizes group trips to local slopes like Hunter Mountain and southern Vermont destinations. In business since 1959, they carry all the big brands like North Face and Burton. You can buy or rent on a daily or seasonal basis.

GAMES WORKSHOP. 71-59 Austin St. at 67th Dr., 263-7574. M–F noon–9:00 p.m., Sa 10:00 a.m.–8:00 p.m., Su noon–6:00 p.m.

A fantasyland of warfare, with make-'em-yourself warrior figurines, this variation on a chain-store environment beckons kids, teens, and adults to while away time and money on games such as Fantasy Warhammer. Enthusiasts build and paint figurines from precut pieces, and set up opposing armies according to rule books that come with the boxed kit.

INSIDE. 71-21 Austin St. at 71st St., 275-3355. M–Sa 11:00 a.m.–8:00 p.m., Su noon–6:00 p.m.

This boutique specializes in jeans and tops that appeal to wealthy, hip women in the under-thirty generation. The $400 sweaters, Diesel and D&G gear is pricier than most of Austin Street's sensible middle-America stores such as Banana Republic, Sephora, Bolton's, and the Gap.

JACKLYN'S BOUTIQUE. 71-50 Austin St. near. 67th Dr., 544-4422. M–Sa 10:00 a.m.–7:00 p.m., Su noon–6:00 p.m.

Upscale, trendy clothing for the mature woman has kept the customers coming back for nearly twenty years. You'll find suits, dresses, and casual wear with lower prices than you'll find in Manhattan department stores plus personal service that's priceless.

INSTANT REPLAY. 67-50 Austin St. near 67th Ave., 544-3556. Tu–Sa 11:00 a.m.–7:00 p.m.

Wonderful vintage jewelry, furs, clothes—and more jewelry—is Marc Pine's specialty. In fact, he's got about 30,000 bangles, pins, necklaces, rings, earrings, and collectibles such as gold, diamonds, antique jewel-studded brooches—all organized into neatly labeled boxes. The shop has been here for about thirty years.

OZ BOUTIQUE. 70-09 Austin St. near 70th Ave., 544-1087. M–Sa 10:30 a.m.–8:00 p.m., Su noon–6:00 p.m.

This shop is jam-packed with the girliest, glitteriest, slinkiest special-occasion gear you can imagine: evening dresses, prom gowns, and accessories, including shoes, to match. Dresses average $400 but there are a wide variety of prices, with designers such as Gionni, BCBG, Pinera, and Dina Birelle (who reportedly designed costumes worn in *Desperate Housewives*).

☺ **PICCOLO MONDO.** 107-06 71st Rd. at Austin St., 261-6771. M–Sa 10:00 a.m.–8:00 p.m., Su 10:30 a.m.–6:00 p.m.

Dress 'em in only the best. It's hard to believe the labels in these cute outfits: dresses for children by Moschino, coats by Diesel, skirts by Versace. Boys' and girls' clothing from two months to sixteen years is sold here, at prices commensurate with the labels. For shoes to match, go a few stores down to **BLUE ELEPHANT** (107-21 71st Rd., 261-3222).

SARINA'S LINGERIE. 70-09 Austin St. bet. 67th Dr. and 68th Ave., 263-0461. Daily 10:00 a.m.–7:00 p.m.

Sarina's, an old-fashioned ladies' store, focuses on fit. If you want ooh-la-la black lace bras in enormous sizes, go across the street to the **MAGIC CORSETS AND LINGERIE** (70-10 Austin St., 261-6999) where the window display is likely to showcase a size 18 red garter belt. Both stores also specialize in mastectomy products. Sarina's alters strapless gowns.

SOLEIL. 71-43 Austin St. at 72nd Ave., 520-8419. M–Sa 10:00 a.m.–8:00 p.m., Su noon–6:00 p.m.

Soleil sells an eclectic mix of home furnishing items, including leather chairs, trunks, faux antiques, and tons of colorful trendy bric-a-brac such as vases, decorative dishes, and mirrors. A good place for a housewarming gift.

SPIN CITY CYCLE. 110-50 Queens Blvd. bet. 72nd Dr. and 73rd Rd., 793-8850. M–W 11:00 a.m.–7:00 p.m., Th 11:00 a.m.–8:00 p.m., F 11:00 a.m.–7:00 p.m., Sa 10:00 a.m.–6:00 p.m., Su 11:00 a.m.–5:00 p.m.

One of the borough's higher-end bike shops, Spin City is centrally located on Queens Blvd., where most of the wheels being spun are of the automobile variety. Get in tip-top shape riding one of these light high-tech bikes, made by major names such as Bianchi. You'll look great in an aerodynamic helmet, sweat-wicking bike jersey, skintight spandex leggings, special biking shoes, and sexy wraparound sunglasses.

☺ **THANK HEAVEN.** 72-18 Austin St. bet. 72nd Ave. and 72nd Rd., 575-2269. M–Sa 11:00 a.m.–6:00 p.m., Su 11:00 a.m.–5:00 p.m.

Those who remember the Maurice Chevalier song from the musical *Gigi* with the lyrics "Thank heaven for little girls, for little girls get bigger every day" will comprehend the sentiment behind this delightful children's clothing store. Its cutie-pie, expensive duds will make any indulgent grandma's heart sing.

Food Shops and Bakeries
ANDRE'S HUNGARIAN BAKERY. 100-28 Queens Blvd. bet. 67th Ave. and 67th Rd., 830-0266. Daily 8:00 a.m.–7:00 p.m.

This tiny Hungarian bakery has been around forever, it seems, and has perfected the recipe for to-die-for rugelach. Also try the strudels and anything with chocolate. A tad less rich than German pastries, these goodies will bring out your inner Hungarian.

CHEESE OF THE WORLD. 71-48 Austin St. bet. 71st Ave. and 72nd Rd., 263-1933. M–Sa 8:30 a.m.–6:00 p.m., Su 8:30 a.m.–3:00 p.m.

You can find a moderately priced selection of raw milk and fresh and aged cheeses here, along with their natural counterparts: olives, pickles, sausages, and cold cuts. This is a perfect place for one-stop shopping for a cocktail party or picnic.

KNISH-NOSH. 100-30 Queens Blvd. at 67th Rd., 897-5554. Su–Th 8:00 a.m.–9:00 p.m., F–Sa 8:00 a.m.–10:00 p.m.

There are sinfully delicious treats at this Jewish fast-food classic. The inch-and-a-half-high spinach knish is so stuffed you'll feel like Popeye. Or try the sweet potato, chopped liver, or potato knishes. There are also zucchini and potato pancakes to freeze at home. They ship. Other locations: Manhattan and Flushing Meadows–Corona Park.

☺ **PIU BELLO GELATO.** 70-09 Austin St. bet. 67th Dr. and 68th Ave., 268-4400. Su–Th 9:00 a.m.–1:00 a.m., F–Sa 9:00 a.m.–2:00 a.m.

Piu Bello Gelato is a casual café with salads, sandwiches, grilled panini, and daily soups. There's a children's menu, too, with "smiles fries" and more. But it's the gelatos, sorbettos, semifreddo, tartuffo, spumoni, plus baked specialties (made in Jamaica, Queens) that attract the crowds. This family business began in Milan in 1940.

WINE AND SPIRIT COMPANY. 72-09 Austin St. Blvd. bet. 72nd Rd. and 72nd Ave., 575-2700. M–Th 10:00 a.m.–9:00 p.m., F–Sa 10:00 a.m.–10:00 p.m.

You can pick up four or five bottles of wine and still get change for your $100 bill. There's friendly staff, a large selection of kosher wines to meet the needs of a large local Jewish population, and you can place special orders.

ENTERTAINMENT
CINEMART CINEMAS. 106-03 Metropolitan Ave. bet. 72nd Rd. and 72nd Ave., 261-2244.

Right across from fabulous Eddie's Sweet Shop, this renovated five-screen movie theater was first opened in 1927 as the Metropolis.

CONTINENTAL (ALSO KNOWN AS UA BRANDON CINEMA CENTER). 70-20 Austin St. bet. 70th Ave. and 70th Rd., (212) 777-FILM.

This cute old twin-screen theater on Austin St., dating from the 1950s, is a local favorite. Snuggled right in the center of things in Forest Hills, this conveniently situated theater shows first-run flicks. You can send the kids to a show while you shop, or make a day of it—shopping, dining, and taking in the latest film.

UA MIDWAY STADIUM 9. 108-22 Queens Blvd. bet. 71st Ave. and 71st Rd., (800) 326-3264.

This nine-screen multiplex offers the best of all worlds: a modern interior with the original 1942 exterior intact.

Kew Gardens and Kew Gardens Hills

WHERE IT IS: Central Queens. Kew Gardens is bounded in the north by the Jackie Robinson Pkwy. and Queens Blvd., east by Kew Gardens Rd., south by Myrtle Ave., and west by Forest Park. Kew Gardens Hills is bounded to the west by Flushing Meadows–Corona Park, to the east by Kissena Blvd., to the north by Jewel Ave., and to the south by Union Tpke. Despite similar-sounding names, Kew Gardens and Kew Gardens Hills are distinct areas.
HOW TO GET THERE BY SUBWAY: E and F to Union Turnpike/Kew Gardens.
HOW TO GET THERE BY LIRR: Austin St. and Lefferts Blvd.
WHAT'S NEARBY: Forest Hills, Forest Park, and Richmond Hill.
MAJOR SHOPPING/RESTAURANT STREETS: Queens Blvd., Lefferts Blvd., Metropolitan Ave., and Union Turnpike.
SPECIAL CHARACTERISTICS: Municipal offices and Tudor-style homes.
CAR SERVICES: Kew Gardens Car Service 846-5800, Four One's 441-1111, 456-1111, or 441-1111.

"CREW GARDENS"

Don't be surprised to see stewardesses dressed in dark work suits dragging rolling carts down tree-lined Lefferts Blvd. The largest airline carrier at JFK Airport, JetBlue, has established its headquarters in Kew Gardens. Many airline pilots and stewardesses live here, which is why it's jokingly called "Crew Gardens."

Kew Gardens is both residential and commercial. Arrayed along twelve-lane Queens Blvd. are a series of large office buildings and municipal offices, including the Borough President's office. Just a block away from the hurly-burly of Queens Blvd. is an exclusive residential area with homes worth close to a million dollars and little rows of shops and restaurants. Kew Gardens has long been racially integrated and has tended over the years to be a socially open-minded community.

THINGS TO SEE AND DO

Aside from municipal business, the best reason to go to Kew Gardens is to see an art flick at the Austin movie theater, which some people call Kew Gardens Cinema. It's interesting to walk by the Ralph Bunche House, a national historic landmark commemorating this African-American U.N. diplomat. It's also pleasant to stroll four or five blocks down the main shopping street in Kew Gardens, from Austin to Cuthbert along Lefferts Blvd. past Russian delis, hair salons, kosher bakeries, and a gourmet sandwich shop. On the side streets there are faux Tudor-style homes in quiet neighborhoods reminiscent of farther out on Long Island.

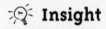

☼ Insight

Kew Gardens Hills

A visitor might understandably confuse Kew Gardens with Kew Gardens Hills. While the two neighborhoods share some history and a name, the latter is more residential, and can be found on the map to the northeast of Kew Gardens, on the opposite side of two major roads, Union Tnpk. and the Van Wyck Expwy.

Recently an Orthodox Jewish community has moved into upscale, residential Kew Gardens Hills, including many families from Manhattan's Upper West Side. On a Friday evening you may note a lot of activity around the numerous synagogues and yeshivas in the area. If you'd like to get a sense of what a traditional Jewish lifestyle is, you can sample kosher food at the Persian-run Colbeh Restaurant (p. 157), or go food shopping at a kosher butcher.

BITS OF HISTORY

Albon Mann, who developed nearby Richmond Hill, bought this land in the 1860s. The Richmond Hill Golf Course was first built, and Mann's sons, who inherited the property, developed it fifty years later into a residential community. The oldest homes date to about 1910, when a new rail station opened up in Kew Gardens. Apartment buildings were constructed in the 1920s. The Manns designed a range of housing types, from single-family homes to apartment buildings to mansions, in order to ensure a socioeconomic mix. They also invested in a country club, Forest Park, a church, and the local elementary school. You can still see the architectural consistency of the two-story buildings on the main street near the LIRR station, also built by the Manns. The area was named after the hometown of the British Royal Botanical Gardens at Kew, England.

The extension of the independent subway line in 1936 opened the entire area to rapid development. In the post–World War II era many German Jewish refugees moved here. Kew Gardens Hills, originally a farming area dubbed

Queens Valley, was developed into golf clubs in the 1920s and subsequently into a residential area in the 1930s and 1940s. After liberalization of the 1965 immigration laws, there was an influx of immigrants from China, Colombia, India, Iran, Israel, and Russia. In addition, Kew Gardens Hills includes an eclectic mix of Chinese, Koreans, South Asians, and African-Americans.

POINTS OF CULTURAL INTEREST

THE AUSTIN (AKA KEW GARDENS CINEMAS). 81-05 Lefferts Blvd. at Austin St., 441-9835.

Fans liken it to SoHo's Angelika. Built in the 1930s, this Kew Gardens movie theater has gone through various changes of identity, but today it's a classy fifteen-screen multiplex theater showing foreign, independent, and revival movies. Some of the original architectural art deco details have been kept in the lobby and in one small downstairs theater. Old-timers will remember this theater by a different name: the Austin. Expect lines on weekends, and don't confuse it with UA Brandon Cinema Center on Austin St.

POTTERS WHEEL. 120-33 83rd Ave. off Lefferts Blvd., 441-6614. www.potterswheelny.com. Su noon–7:00 p.m., M–Tu 10:30 a.m.–9:30 p.m., W 10:00 a.m.–10:30 p.m., Th 4:00 p.m.–10:30 p.m., F 10:00 a.m.–10:00 p.m.,

Come for lessons in throwing pots using a potters wheel or hand-building pottery. In existence for nearly twenty years, this comfortable, inviting studio in Kew Gardens has four ten-week semesters with classes from beginner to advanced for about $220 a session. You can also pick up unique pottery items, perfect for gifts, at bargain-basement prices. Courses for kids are available as well.

QUEENS BOROUGH HALL AND THE REDBIRD SUBWAY CAR. 120-55 Queens Blvd., 286-3000.

This is the home of the Queens Borough President and numerous municipal offices. Queens County Criminal Court is nearby at 125-01 Queens Blvd. Other municipal offices are in Jamaica.

The old subway car on the lawn is really an information booth. Old-timers (and movie buffs) may remember the red subway trains fondly nicknamed "Redbirds" that used to run on the #7 line between Flushing and Times Square. In service so long that these trains transported riders to the 1964–65 World's Fair, they were retired in 2001. Learning that the MTA planned to dump the old subway cars in the ocean to help stimulate the growth of a barrier reef in the Atlantic, the local *Queens Tribune* launched a save-the-subway-car campaign. One old red car, #9075, now resides at the corner of Borough Hall and will be retrofitted to serve as a tourist information center. What a deal: The MTA sold the subway car to the Borough President for $1.

🏛 **RALPH BUNCHE HOUSE.** 115-24 Grosvenor Lane. Private residence; not open to the public.

A National Historical Landmark, this 1927 Tudor-style residence was home to Nobel Peace Prize winner Dr. Ralph Bunche. A brilliant academic and diplomat, Bunche was instrumental in the negotiations in 1948 between the newly formed Israel and hostile neighboring Arab states. He subsequently spent a long career in the United Nations, culminating in fifteen years as undersecretary-general, the highest post ever held by an American. U.N. Secretary General U Thant described Bunche thus: "An international institution in his own right, transcending both nationality and race in a way that is achieved by very few." One of the nation's most prominent African-American diplomats, he lived here for more than thirty years.

RESTAURANTS

BAGEL OASIS. 183-12 Horace Harding Blvd. bet. Long Island Expwy. and 64th Ave., 359-9245. Daily 24 hours.

Since 1961, Bagel Oasis has been in the upper-crust of bageldom in the Big Apple (and arguably in the world, as New York must be the Kingdom of Bagels). This family business is dedicated to old-fashioned bagel making, hand-rolling dough made from basic ingredients (flour, malt, salt, yeast, and water), then boiling and baking the bagels. They wouldn't know a multisyllabic preservative if they saw one.

COLBEH RESTAURANT. 68-34 Main St., bet. 68th Rd. and 68th Dr., 268-8181. M–Th 10:00 a.m.–10:30 p.m., F until one hour before sundown, Su 10:00 a.m.–10:30 p.m.

Located in nearby Kew Gardens Hills, Colbeh stands out among a number of glatt kosher restaurants in the area for its Persian cuisine. Try excellent appetizers, chicken kebabs, rice dishes, and chopped tomato salad. Portions are ample, and the service is friendly, but there's no fancy decor. If you come with two or three people, try a combination platter. Note that no dairy dishes will be served here.

HOT BIALYS. 116-63 Queens Blvd. bet. 77th and 78th Aves., 544-0900. M–F 6:00 a.m.–6:30 p.m., Sa–Su 6:00 a.m.–4:00 p.m.

Forget that low-carb diet for a nibble of yeasty yummies at this local favorite. This Kew Gardens shop specializes in poppy. Although the bialys come out hot only once a day, at 8:00 a.m., they are delicious all day long.

INCA'S. 120-20 Queens Blvd., near Union Tnpk., 263-6767. Su–Th noon–11:00 p.m., F–Sa noon–1:00 a.m.

So you've been to Queens Borough Hall or one of the many nearby law offices and you're famished. Inca's, within walking distance of the government center in Kew Gardens, is a decent Peruvian restaurant with ceviche, grilled steaks, and good rice-based lamb and seafood dishes.

Rego Park

WHERE IT IS: Central Queens. Bounded to the north by the LIE and Queens Blvd., to the east by Yellowstone Blvd., to the west by Woodhaven Blvd., and to the south by the intersection of Yellowstone and Woodhaven Blvds.

HOW TO GET THERE BY SUBWAY: G, R, V to 63rd Drive/Rego Park and 67th Ave.

WHAT'S NEARBY: Corona to the north, Elmhurst to the northwest, Flushing Meadows–Corona Park to the east, Forest Hills to the southeast, Middle Village to the southwest.

MAJOR SHOPPING/RESTAURANT STREETS: 108th St. for Central Asian–Russian, Queens Blvd., 63rd Drive, 63rd Place, and Eliot Ave.

ON NOT GETTING LOST: The shops and restaurants listed in this chapter are largely on 108th St., which is to the north of Queens Blvd. and technically in Forest Hills. In general, Rego Park has many little streets with word names, not numbers, so it can be confusing, but it's a small area.

CAR SERVICES: Four One's, 441-1111, 456-1111.

ABOUT REGO PARK

Rego Park is an alphabet soup of nationalities, including Russians, Iranian and Israeli Jews, and smaller communities of Colombians, Indians, Koreans, and Romanians. If you hear people jokingly referring to the neighborhood as "Regostan," it's because thousands of Central Asian Jews, that is, immigrants from the Bukharan region (Uzbekistan) of Russia have settled here in the past decade. Although largely residential, there is also a large shopping plaza on Queens Blvd. and 63rd Dr. in Rego Park.

Many stores and restaurants along 108th St. in Rego Park close before sundown on Friday, remain closed on Saturday, and do not reopen until after sundown on Saturday, in celebration of the Jewish Sabbath.

THINGS TO SEE AND DO

Come to a different world. For a dining experience with live music, including some traditional Bukharan songs, check out the Vechemy Tashkent restaurant. Nearby you can have a Russian nightclub experience at Cheburechnaya. At Best European Deli it's hard to believe you're two blocks not from the Volga but from Queens Blvd. with its Sears and Old Navy stores. Just wandering around "Bukharan Broadway" at 108th St. you will feel transported as you explore unusual food stores, haggle over prices at the jewelry shops, and marvel at the extraordinary (and some might say gaudy) taste in home furnishings shops. Don't be surprised if, in the middle of a Sunday visit, you are passed by a parade of orthodox Jews in a holiday celebration, often accompanied by a truck with a horn atop blaring out Hassidic tunes.

BITS OF HISTORY

Rego Park has a colorful background. In the early twentieth century, Chinese immigrant farmers settled in Queens raising produce to sell in Manhattan's Chinatown. In the 1920s, the Real Good Construction Company, which apparently had a gift for marketing, promoted their real estate under the classy-sounding name of Rego Park, which blends the first two initials of its company name: REal GOod = Rego.

As with many New York neighborhoods, residential development followed fast on the heels of transportation. In 1928 the LIRR railroad station opened, the Long Island Expressway arrived in 1935, and the subway to Union Tnpk. opened in 1936. The first New York City World's Fair in 1939–40 stimulated further housing development.

POINTS OF CULTURAL INTEREST

LOST BATTALION HALL. 93-29 Queens Blvd. bet. 62nd and 63rd Aves., 263-1163. M–F 9:00 a.m.–10:00 p.m., Sa 10:00 a.m.–5:00 p.m.

It ain't a lost battle at Lost Battalion Hall, a popular recreation center that's used for free educational and athletic after-school programs, daily toddler activities, senior programs, adult and children's sports, and more. In 1902, New York City acquired this property through a donation from Frank deHass Simonson. In 1939, the WPA built this $100,000 building (complete with a firing range and drill hall) for the Veterans of Foreign Wars (VFW) and the American Legion. The original inhabitants occupied the building until 1962. In 1995 two historic murals were restored, and the firing range was converted into a fitness center. Today Lost Battalion Hall has computers, a boxing ring, karate classes, a gym, a preschool, and more. The VFW still has an upstairs office, but Lost Battalion is a major community center.

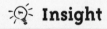 Insight

Jewish Life in Queens Meets the Silk Road

For decades, there has been a substantial Jewish population in this area. Synagogues in Forest Hills and Kew Gardens have represented all three branches of Judaism: reform, conservative, and orthodox. Recently about 40,000 Jewish immigrants from the Central Asian former Soviet republics of Uzbekistan, Tajikistan,

(continued)

and Kyrgyzstan have come to New York, many settling in the Forest Hills–Rego Park area. These are people whom, when describing the lives of their grandparents in Tashkent, may still refer to the rich and powerful Emir of Bukharan in tones of awe. Jews have lived in Central Asia for more than 2,000 years in communities along the famous Silk Road trade route, and have evolved unusual customs and cuisines, which they have brought to Queens.

RESTAURANTS, RUSSIAN CLUBS, AND DELIS IN REGO PARK

CHEBURECHNAYA. 92-09 63rd Dr., off Austin St., 897-9080. Su–Th 10:00 a.m.–1:00 a.m., F 10:00 a.m.–4:00 p.m., Sa after sundown–1:00 a.m.

Thankfully you don't have to go all the way to Bukhara to eat Bukharan cuisine. Order from a wide selection of grilled kebabs than you thought possible (nearly two dozen choices), cool it down with fresh Israeli salad, and put some meat on your bones with those great fries and unusual and delicious ethnic breads. The *chebureki,* a kind of thin-crusted fried turnover with a choice of fillings, is worth the trip.

REGISTAN. 65-37 99th St. bet. 65th Rd. and 66th Ave., 459-1638. M–Th 10:00 a.m.–10:00 p.m., F 10:00 a.m.–4:00 p.m., Sa after sundown–midnight, Su 11:00 a.m.–11:00 p.m.

This tiny ethnic eatery dishes up excellent, authentic Bukharan foods; it's worth a visit. You'll enjoy the garlic-laden carrot salad and warm *lepeshka* bread.

SALUT. 63-42 108th St. at 63rd Dr., 275-6860. Su–Th 11:00 a.m.–11:00 p.m., F 11:00 a.m.–5:00 p.m., Sa after sundown–11:00 p.m.

You'll find enormous portions of meats, dumplings and, of course, vodka at Salut, a Bukharan restaurant in what was formerly a Greek diner. Don't expect just a kebab here, prepare for a half a lamb on a swordlike skewer.

VECHEMY TASHKENT. 94-03B 63rd Dr. bet. Weatherstone and Booth, 275-5101, 896-2826. Su–Th 11:00 a.m.–midnight, F 11:00 a.m. until one hour before sundown, Sa after sundown–midnight.

This small restaurant, owned by the wife of a famous Bukharan traditional musician and named after the capital of Uzbekistan, serves excellent traditional food from Central Russia. You will get an Israeli salad, delicious breads, Bukhara pilaf, and lamb kebabs with rice and veggies. Don't miss the healthful green tea or the special *lagman* soup, a meal-in-a-bowl that combines homemade noodles, bits of beef, and tons of vegetables, all spiced with cilantro in a rich broth. There's live music most evenings.

SHOPPING ON "BUKHARAN BROADWAY" AT 108TH ST.

BEST EUROPEAN DELI. 93-07 63 Dr. at Wetherole St., 997-0501. Daily 9:00 a.m.–9:00 p.m.

Best European Deli sells foodstuffs from all over Russia, including caviar. Try the jams, cookies, smoked fish, pickles, herring, and prepared foods such as the carrot salad or baba ghanoush. Not on 108th St. but in Rego Park.

BORIS INTERNATIONAL MUSIC AND VIDEO. 64-49 108th St. bet. 64th Rd. and 65th Ave., 997-8237. M–F 11:00 a.m.–9:00 p.m., Sa 10:00 a.m.–8:00 p.m., Su noon–6:00 p.m.

A wide selection of Russian videos and music, including traditional classical music of the Bukharan Jewish community is sold here.

CARMEL MIDDLE EASTERN AND EUROPEAN FOODS. 64-27 108th St. bet. 64th Rd. and 65th Ave., 897-9296. Daily 9:00 a.m.–8:00 p.m.

The smell of roasted coffee wafts from the huge roaster at the front of this jam-packed deli. Carmel's customers seem content to stand in a line fifteen-deep on a Sunday afternoon. That's because there's excellent, inexpensive prepared foods, a wide range of freshly baked breads, and bulk displays of dried fruits, different flours, and so on in scoop-your-own-buckets. You can find Osem brand Israeli jams, pickles, crackers, and candies.

M&M AND SON, INC. (AKA MANYA AND MISHA EUROPEAN DELI). 64-46 108th St. bet. 64th Rd. and 65th Ave., 459-0180. Daily 8:00 a.m.–9:00 p.m.

Lots of smoked fish, Israeli imported jams, canned goods, fresh blinis, and a full deli counter, along with fresh bread called *lepeshka,* a fluffy, round, flat loaf about eight inches in diameter, are sold here. Signs are in both Russian and English.

NAGILA MARKET. 63-69 108th St. bet. 64th Ave. and 64th Rd., 268-2626. Su–Th 8:00 a.m.–9:00 p.m. F 8:00 a.m. until one hour before sundown, Sa after sundown–midnight.

Big open vats of spices, herbs, dried legumes, and dates rolled in almond shavings are sold at this slightly messy immigrant's food emporium, which also sells kosher Middle Eastern food to immigrants from Bukhara.

ROMANOFF GROCERY. 63-64 108th St. off 64th Ave., 897-3600. Daily 8:00 a.m.–10:00 p.m.

This Russian international supermarket is open daily and has a fabulous array of Eastern European and Middle Eastern imported foods, from breads to cheeses, condiments, sausages, and herbs and spices.

12

Jackson Heights

WHERE IT IS: Northwestern Queens. Bounded to the east by 94th St. and Junction Blvd., to the west by the BQE, to the north by Astoria Blvd., and to the south by Roosevelt Ave.

HOW TO GET THERE BY SUBWAY: #7 subway line to 74th St./Broadway, 82nd St./Jackson Heights. Also E, F, G, R and V to Roosevelt Ave./Jackson Heights.

WHAT'S NEARBY: Astoria to the northwest, Corona to the southeast, Elmhurst to the south, LaGuardia Airport to the north, and Woodside to the southwest.

MAJOR SHOPPING/RESTAURANT STREETS: 37th Ave., 82nd St., Roosevelt Ave., and Junction Blvd.

SPECIAL CHARACTERISTICS: South Asian stores and restaurants. Landmarked garden apartments. Ethnic diversity.

ON NOT GETTING LOST: The street grid in Jackson Heights is simple. Orient yourself to Roosevelt Ave. and Northern Blvd., and 74th St. and Junction Blvd.

CAR SERVICES: Central 335-4141/3116, Mexicana 446-8700.

AN INDIAN-LATINO FUSION

Talk about fusion. You can visit two parts of the world at once: India and Latin America. You can get great Indian food, buy frozen samosas to take home to your book club, wander through the gold jewelry and sari shops, and get your eyebrows threaded. Or in a parallel universe (two blocks away), you can try on Mexican cowboy boots and Colombian team soccer jerseys, practice your Spanish while munching fresh arepas from the corner stand, get the latest Latin music, and have a rib-sticking meal at an Argentinean beef restaurant. Top it off with your choice of a Bollywood movie or the latest Hollywood hit with big Spanish subtitles. All this, just three subway stops from Manhattan. Is it safe? Yes.

"Liveable" is the word to describe Jackson Heights. It wouldn't be surprising if Jackson Heights zoomed into prominence as one of New York's next "hot" neighborhoods. Jackson Heights feels like a village. The shopping districts are

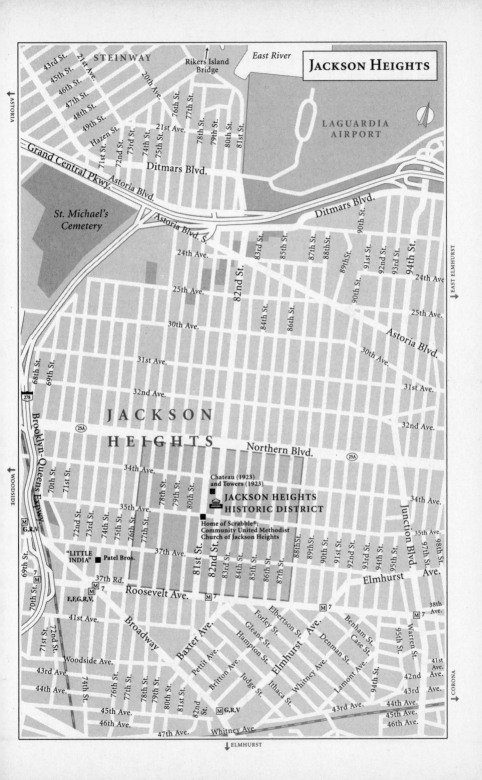

JACKSON HEIGHTS

STEINWAY

East River

→ Rikers Island Bridge

43rd St.
45th St.
46th St.
47th St.
48th St.
49th St.
21st Ave.
20th Ave.
76th St.
77th St.
78th St.
79th St.
80th St.
81st St.

← ASTORIA

Hazen St.
71st St.
72nd St.
73rd St.
74th St.
75th St.
21st Ave.

Grand Central Pkwy.

Astoria Blvd.

Ditmars Blvd.

Ditmars Blvd.

LAGUARDIA AIRPORT

St. Michael's Cemetery

Astoria Blvd. S.

24th Ave.

83rd St.
85th St.
87th St.
88th St.
89th St.
90th St.
91st St.
92nd St.
93rd St.
94th St.

→ EAST ELMHURST

24th Ave.

82nd St.

25th Ave.

30th Ave.

84th St.
86th St.

25th Ave.

Astoria Blvd.

30th Ave.

31st Ave.

30th Ave.

31st Ave.

32nd Ave.

JACKSON

68th St.
69th St.

278

Brooklyn-Queens Expwy.

32nd Ave.

HEIGHTS

25A

Northern Blvd.

32nd Ave.

25A

34th Ave.

70th St.
71st St.

Chateau (1923) and Towers (1923)

JACKSON HEIGHTS HISTORIC DISTRICT

34th Ave.

← WOODSIDE

35th Ave.

72nd St.
73rd St.
74th St.
75th St.
76th St.
77th St.
78th St.
79th St.
80th St.

M G,R,V

37th Ave.

81st St.
82nd St.
83rd St.
84th St.
85th St.
86th St.
87th St.
88th St.
89th St.
90th St.
91st St.
92nd St.
93rd St.
94th St.
95th St.

Home of Scrabble®; Community United Methodist Church of Jackson Heights

35th Ave.

96th St.

Junction Blvd.

35th Ave.

"LITTLE INDIA" ■ Patel Bros.

37th Rd.

M 7

Elmhurst

97th St.
98th St.

69th St.
70th St.

M 7

Roosevelt Ave.

M 7

M 7

38th Ave.

E,F,G,R,V,

41st Ave.

Broadway

Baxter Ave.

Pettit Ave.

Britton Ave.

Elbertson St.
Forley St.
Gleane St.
Hampton St.
Judge St.
Ithaca St.

Elmhurst Ave.

Whitney Ave.

Denman St.

Benham St.
Case St.
Lamont Ave.

94th St.
95th St.

Warren St.

M 7

→ CORONA

71st St.
72nd St.

43rd Ave.
44th Ave.

74th St.

Woodside Ave.

76th St.
77th St.
78th St.
79th St.
80th St.
81st St.
82nd St.

41st Ave. Ave.
42nd Ave.
43rd Ave.

45th Ave.
46th Ave.

M G,R,V

43rd Ave.
44th Ave.
45th Ave.
46th Ave.

47th Ave.

Whitney Ave.

↓ ELMHURST

concentrated. Numerous stores are mom-and-pops rather than anonymous chains. Many people live in one of the many apartment buildings within a four- or five-block walk to a post office, a school, food stores, restaurants, library, and subway. Jackson Heights has tree-lined streets, and many of the stately apartment buildings have front and back gardens. There's quick subway access to Manhattan on several lines (which is convenient if there's a problem on one line).

THINGS TO SEE AND DO

Jackson Heights is not a rich area, yet it's strikingly international. Many residents speak at least two languages. It's a food lover's dream, with lots of food stores and inexpensive restaurants serving authentic Peruvian, Indian, Thai, Bangladeshi, Brazilian, and Italian cuisine. A trip to Little India on 74th St. is considered the quintessential cool adventure to Queens for many folks from other boroughs. Walk just one block away from Little India—one small block!—onto Roosevelt Ave., and you've traveled to Colombia faster than any airplane could get you there. There's history, too. You can see where Scrabble was invented. Take a self-guided walking tour of Jackson Heights Historic District to see the garden-apartment communities that were all the rage in the 1920s—and still offer some of the best value-for-money real estate in town.

Little India on 74th St. appeals to the imagination (and stomachs) of many New Yorkers. The Jackson Diner, famous for their weekend buffet, is probably the best-known restaurant in Queens. After chowing down there or at nearby al-ternatives, you can visit Patel Brothers and select some treats to take home from a wall's worth of chutneys, frozen samosas, twenty-five-pound sacks of rice, and other specialty items at very low prices. Try to avoid shopping there when you are hungry, lest you find yourself with enough tamarind sauce to feed all of Tacoma. Across the street, Butala Emporium, an authentic lifestyle store, sells imported books written in Sanskrit, incense, and a range of calendars and eso-teric Hindu ritual objects. Up and down the block silk saris and *salwar kamiz* (tunic-like pantsuits) are on display at stores such as the International Saree Palace. Still on the same block, you will find ten or so extraordinary jewelry stores such as Sona Chaandi, crammed with traditional Indian gold chandelier earrings, bangles, rings, and elaborate, multitiered necklaces resembling breast-plates. You can catch a Bollywood flick around the corner at the Eagle Theatre, or if you don't have time, wander around the busy video rental shops to see rows of movies in Hindi and Urdu featuring Pooja Bhatts and other Bollywood stars you've never heard of. In a few concentrated blocks you can find an incredible little Indian and Pakistani world here, complete with astrologers, travel agents, photography stores, shops advertising the cheapest international phone service, and salons such as Gulzar Beauty Salon, where you can henna your hair or get your eyebrows threaded.

The Latino community in Jackson Heights hails from different countries and distinct cultures: Colombia, Brazil, Peru, Ecuador, Mexico, Argentina, and elsewhere. For visitors, this spells a bonanza of food and fun. Walking on bustling Roosevelt Ave. between 74th and 82nd Sts., under the rumbling elevated #7 subway line, you'll find Colombian, Ecuadorian, and Peruvian restaurants, travel agents, and outdoor food carts selling fresh tacos and *arepas*. Spanish is the primary language spoken here. It is a working-class community, and these folks know how to party. Peruse the posters for the popular nightclub Chibcha. A few blocks later you'll pass El Abuelo Golon Bailadero, a dance hall featuring Vallenatos, which is typical Colombian music. You can get international soccer jerseys at Soccer Fanatic, or buy inexpensive leather cowboy boots at Zapateria Mexico.

Typically, cafés and restaurants are busy until two or three in the morning on weekends. In the summer, families, including young children, are out late at night. One of the best-known chefs in Jackson Heights (thanks to a profile in *The New York Times*) is the Arepas Lady, an ex-judge from Colombia whose new job in the United States is as a street corner cook, doling out hot *arepas* to hungry club-hoppers starting at 1:00 a.m., weekends only.

After you absorb all this energy, drop into Cositas Ricas for a beer, coffee, or sustaining rice-and-beans-based meal for under $8. Or, head to 37th Ave. for a more middle-class Latino vibe. On the way pass Rudy Volcano, a Guatemalan import store. Check out Natives Restaurant for live shows and a busy restaurant scene. Don't miss Little Argentina on Northern Blvd., either. Go for huge portions of chicken at the exuberant, excellent Peruvian Pio Pio.

BITS OF HISTORY

Jackson Heights came into prominence as one of Queens' early planned garden communities. Over a dozen major apartment building complexes were built by the 1920s. These buildings are human-scaled, only four and five stories high. Those in the Jackson Heights Historic District were built around internal courtyards. The area has had a stable residential base for decades, and over the past forty years has become more densely populated and extremely diverse as immigrants continued to settle here after a relaxation in U.S. immigration laws in 1965. The area was named after a major thoroughfare, Jackson Ave., now called Northern Blvd.

POINTS OF CULTURAL INTEREST

GULZAR BEAUTY SALON. 74-01B Roosevelt Ave. bet. 74th and 75th Sts., 779-2800. Daily 10:00 a.m.–8:00 p.m.

Tattoos have become mainstream, but you can come here for a traditional mehndi tattoo and eyebrow threading.

☼ Insight

Indian Gold Jewelry Shops

Your jaw will drop in surprise the first time you walk down 74th St. past one, no two, no a dozen store windows shimmering with ornate gold jewelry: enormous pendant earrings, gold necklaces gracefully studded with diamonds and gems, two-inch-thick wrist bangles in tints of red, green, and blue, and other bangles made for ankles. Most exotic are the *panya,* the golden bracelets attached with a slender chain to finger rings, and the elaborate breastplate necklaces that look like something out of *The Arabian Nights* or Punjabi children's stories. All the jewelry is made of malleable 22-karat gold. Prices are calculated by the gram weight of the gold, but factor in gems and design, too. Many of the most modest necklace and earring sets, as of this writing, start at $1,000. However, you can find small earrings or rings in the $100 and up range.

The gold jewelry district relies on tourists—especially those shopping for a traditional Indian wedding. According to Indian custom, gold jewelry is the bridal gift of choice, given by the bride's own parents (and to a lesser extent, by her in-laws-to-be) as a form of insurance in the event the marriage doesn't work out. Women gossiping about their wedding gifts will not talk about what brand of this or that they received but boast of how much weight in gold they got, giving new meaning to the notion of being "worth your weight in gold." It is not uncommon to sell wedding jewelry for a trade-in for something new and different. (The jewelers melt it down and reuse it.) New York is one of the few centers of traditional Indian gold jewelry in the United States. As one customer put it, "South Asians come to Jackson Heights from all over—it's closer than going home to India."

Some shops sell mostly Indian traditional designs while others cater to more Western tastes. The main drag is 74th St. between Roosevelt and 37th Aves., with a few shops spilling over to nearby streets (37th Ave. between 74th and 73rd Sts., and 73rd St. between 37th Ave. and Roosevelt Ave.). Customers are expected to bargain; don't be shy. Also, hey, window-shopping is free! Check out **SONA CHAANDI** (37-14 74th St., 429-4653) and compare with the more traditional **KARA 22 JEWELERS OF LONDON** (37-50 74th St., 507-2288).

KALPANA CHAWLA WAY. 74th St. bet. Roosevelt and 37th Aves.

Kalpana Chawla was the first Indian-American spacewoman to work with NASA. She died along with six others in the tragic 2003 crash of space shuttle *Columbia.* In July 2004, the main commercial hub in Little India, the Indian-Pakistani-Bangladeshi community in Jackson Heights, was renamed in her honor.

PRIDE PARADE. www.queenspride.com.

For a festive, multicultural gay and lesbian celebration don't miss the annual Pride parade here, attended by as many as 40,000 people, from gorgeous drag queens on floats to city officials. Officially called the Queens Lesbian, Gay, Bisexual, and Transgender Pride Parade and Festival, it's organized by the Queens Rainbow Community Center and usually runs between 37th Ave., and 89th St., and finishes with a street festival on 75th St. and 37th Rd.

⋰⋱ Insight

Jackson Heights Is an International Tourist Destination

In certain circles, 74th St. is as well known as Madison Avenue. It surely ranks along with the U.S. Open and Shea Stadium as one of the most famous tourist destinations in Queens. People of South Asian descent—including physicians, professors, businessmen, and a spectrum of the middle and upper-middle class—from Nassau and Suffolk Counties, New Jersey, Connecticut, and even as far away as Michigan, Ohio, and Florida come to Jackson Heights to stock up spiritually and materially. That explains the extraordinary weekend traffic jams in Jackson Heights. It also explains how so many sari and gold jewelry stores could survive on one block.

PEOPLE, PLACES, AND THINGS OF HISTORICAL INTEREST

🏛 **HOME OF SCRABBLE.** Community United Methodist Church of Jackson Heights, 81-10 35th Ave. at 81st St., 446-0690.

Alfred M. Butts, who invented the game Scrabble, lived in Jackson Heights and was a member of the Community United Methodist Church. He tried out his game on parishioners here. You can see the oval plaque on the exterior of this building (in the middle of the block), a Historic Landmarks Preservation Center Cultural Medallion.

JACKSON HEIGHTS TOURS. Jackson Heights Beautification Group. 565-5344. www.jhbg.org. Sa–Su second weekend in June.

In mid-June, there's an annual celebration of historic Jackson Heights. The weekend-long festivities include such events as a slide lecture, vintage photo exhibit, self-guided tour of private interior gardens, escorted walking tours of the historic district, and more. It's a wonderful way to learn about Jackson Heights, the first planned garden and cooperative community in the United States. If you can't make it, get a copy of the book *Jackson Heights: A Garden in the City* by Daniel Karatzas.

☛ **TIP: Unusual Movie Theaters.** Jackson Heights has more than its fair share of historic movie theaters. Today one shows American movies with Spanish sub-titles, another shows Bollywood sizzlers, and a third shows porn. Call theaters for schedules.

EAGLE THEATRE. 73-07 37th Rd., off 74th St., 205-2800.

Bollywood flicks are shown in this renovated art deco theater, originally a 600-seat movie house called the Earle that, in a period of subsequent decline, was briefly a porn house. Catering to the local South Asian community, it has been renovated and renamed the Eagle. Make an afternoon of it—a flick and an informal dinner at a local Indian restaurant around the corner on 74th St.

JACKSON TRIPLEX. 40-31 82nd St. bet. Roosevelt and Baxter Aves., 779-2834 or 335-0242.

Lovers of historic movie theaters say it's "arguably the best 'cinema treasure' theater still operating in Queens." The original fixtures and architecture of the main 1,000-seat theater have been left intact. Built by the prolific theater architect Herbert J. Krapp, the Jackson is a 1920s-era theater that now serves as a triplex showing Hollywood hits with Spanish subtitles. The Jackson and the Boulevard Theater were both designed by the same architect. The Boulevard Theater is now in use by Natives Restaurant (see listing, p. 174).

POLK THEATER. 93-09 37th Ave. at 93rd St. 639-4081.

This musty old 1938 theater has seen better days—and, as it shows porn part-time, you'd better think twice about bringing your kids. That said, what's appealing are the fixtures and fittings of a period long gone. Unless someone has scooped up this place and renovated it since we went to press, you'll see a 1938 neon marquee, old ticket machines, and an old-fashioned ticket box. The candy concession looks like it's straight out of old black-and-white movies. Upstairs there's an old-fashioned phone booth with no phone in it. Visitors often say the Polk feels "suspended in time." It's called the Polk because 37th Ave. used to be called Polk Ave.

🚶 🏛 SELF-GUIDED TOUR OF HISTORIC JACKSON HEIGHTS

This is an approximately thirty-minute walking tour of some of the land-marked cooperative buildings built by the Queensborough Corporation in the early 1920s, which gave Jackson Heights the reputation as a community of garden apartments. The buildings have internal courtyards, often quite spacious, an amenity in stark contrast to the overcrowded conditions in many city dwellings in the early twentieth century. Look for: gardens in the back of the buildings, entrance vestibules that stand out from the buildings, details at the roofline, French doors with fanlights, slate roofs, and orange Spanish tiles.

Start at 82nd St. and 37th Ave. The corner Tudor-style building with English gables and lambs' head decorations, now occupied by a North Fork Bank, was the headquarters for the Queensboro Corporation, which developed all of historic Jackson Heights. On 82nd St. you will see stores built in the 1920s and 1930s by the Queensboro Corporation as part of its vision of an architecturally coherent Jackson Heights. This commercial street has handsome neo-Tudor commercial buildings on both sides of the street. Today, it's landmarked.

Moving to the residential areas, walk along 82nd St. bet. 37th and 35th Aves., where you can see 🏛 Plymouth and Willow Courts (1916). Walking to 81st St. and 35th Ave., you can see where Scrabble was first played and informally product-tested at the Community United Methodist Church. Note the plaque that honors local resident Alfred Butts, who invented the game. Charmingly, the street sign resembles a Scrabble game piece.

Walk down 82nd St. bet. 35th and 34th Aves., passing (on your right) the colonial-style buildings (1915). Note their tiny front gardens and no sign of fire escapes. Arriving at 34th Ave. bet. 80th and 81st Sts., you will see the famous 🏛 Chateau (1923) and 🏛 Towers (1924) coops. Local historian Daniel Karatzas writes, "The Chateau, with its sumptuous garden, slate mansard roofs, and elegant carved limestone entranceways was the epitome of Jackson Heights style when it opened in 1923." The Chateau and Towers stand opposite each other and occupy almost a full city block each, from 35th Ave. to Northern Blvd. You can't enter, but you can glimpse their gardens. The Towers has a fountain and a baldacchino (formal ornamental columns) at its center. The Chateau has extensive shrubbery and trees. Walk to 80th St. bet. 34th and 35th Aves. to view the interior garden of the Chateau.

Across the street is Elm Court (1922), modeled after dormitories at Harvard. As a last stop, take a good look as you go down 80th St. bet. 35th and 37th Aves. because the term "garden apartment" was apparently coined for these buildings, called the 🏛 Greystones (1917). Note the large front gardens, and interior gardens hidden behind their gray brick facades. Return to 37th Ave. and 82nd St. near the beginning of the tour. If you want to continue, check out the private homes (also part of the original 1920s Jackson Heights developments) on 86th and 87th Sts. bet. 37th and 34th Aves.

(NOTE: For the annual open house, see Jackson Heights Tours, p. 167.)

RIKER-LENT SMITH HOMESTEAD. 721-0508. www.lentrikersmithhomestead.com. By appointment only.

A private home today, this historic house dates, in its earliest incarnation, to 1654–56. There's a graveyard in the back with more than a hundred graves, some as old as the house. Born as a one-bedroom home by settler Abraham Riker, it's arguably the oldest dwelling in New York City that is still being used as a dwelling. Incredibly, while change has overcome most of New York City during the centuries, this house has had only three owners: the Riker-Lent family, William Gooth, and the Smiths, who bought the property in 1975 and have taken a huge interest in its history. For the whole story and some photos of the cemetery see the Web site.

RESTAURANTS, CAFÉS, AND BARS

ARUNEE THAI. 37-68 79th St. bet. 37th and Roosevelt Aves., 205-5559. M–F 11:00 a.m.–10:30 p.m., Sa–Su noon–11:00 p.m.; lunch special noon–3:45 p.m.

One of the best Thai restaurants in the borough, you can get inexpensive meals at award-winning Arunee Thai. Try a hot *goong pra ram* (shrimp with green curry, eggplant, and basil), *ba me moo dang* (egg noodles with roast pork), or for vegetarians, *pad prik khing* (Thai curry with green beans) with some jasmine rice, and you'll be happy you made the trip. Entrées under $9. Cash only.

ASHOKA. 74-14 37th Ave. near 74th St., 898-5088. Daily 11:30 a.m.–10:30 p.m.

One of several Indian restaurants where you can get a buffet selection, Ashoka has all the classic dishes, from tandoori chicken to curries, condiments, and those wonderful breads. There's a vegetarian selection, too. The dinner buffet costs under $10.

CABAÑA. 86-07 Northern Blvd. bet. 86th and 87th Sts., 426-5977. Daily 1:00 p.m.–11:00 p.m.

The culinary curious will appreciate interesting combos at this Argentine-Italian restaurant, born of the marriage of the Argentine romance with beef and the Italian passion for pasta. The dimly lit, brick-walled restaurant offers a quiet, upscale alternative in a neighborhood with lots of noisy, crowded eateries. Food mavens have been known to melt over the Dominican *chicharrones de pollo* (fried chicken dish) here. Those with a hollow leg or large appetite might try the *parillada*, a sizzling-hot mixed grill entrée that costs about $32. Ask for salmon and coconut rice if it's not on the menu. Soft music and drinks make for a quiet date especially early on a weekend evening. NOTE: There are two restaurants by the same name, run by the same owner; the other is at 95-51 Roosevelt Ave.

CAVALIER RESTAURANT. 85-19 37th Ave. at 85th St. 458-7474 M–F 11:00 a.m.–1:00 a.m. Sa–Su brunch costs $12, noon–3:00 p.m., 5:00 p.m.–11:00 p.m.

Cavalier promises diners a quick trip to the past—specifically, to the mid-twentieth century. If you long for the security of a good pot-roast-and-potatoes restaurant, from an era before anybody ever heard the word "globalization," this cosy, old-fashioned restaurant is for you. Special entrées run about $13.

CHIBCHA RESTAURANT AND NIGHTCLUB. 79-05 Roosevelt Ave. at 79th St., 429-9033. F–Su cover charge $16–$20, Su–W 4:00 p.m.–4:00 a.m., Sa–Su 9:00 p.m.–4:00 a.m.

This Colombian restaurant-nightclub has live entertainment on most nights. Come and enjoy salsa and merengue and the latest Latin dance crazes. It's been around for years, and keeps drawing friendly local crowds. Dinner runs about $35 per person. Check www.elchibcha.com to find out who's performing.

COSITAS RICAS. 79-19 Roosevelt Ave. at 79th St., 478-1500. Su–Th 6:00 a.m.–2:00 a.m., F–Sa 6:00 a.m.–4:00 a.m.

Sopas del dia, arepas rellenas, caprichitos ricos, entremeses de mariscos, and *rico pollo* are on the menu at this always busy, always upbeat Colombian restaurant. It's a combination of bakery, sit-down restaurant, take-out joint, and bar. The place is always hopping, and the food's the main reason. (Although the cute waitresses in sprayed-on white jeans and head kerchiefs might be another.) Daily soups, Latin specialties, generous portions, and meals that fuel you for hours are priced under $10, with the numerous steak dishes priced a bit higher.

DELHI PALACE. 37-33 74th St. off 37th Ave. and Roosevelt Ave., 507-0666. Su–Th 11:30 a.m.–10:00 p.m., F–Sa 11:30 a.m.–10:45 p.m.

You can get Indian fast food, Indian take-out, and ingredients for a home-cooked meal. For a sit-down meal you can expect good quality and lots of northern and southern specialties. It's also the perfect place for that take-out samosa, costing about 50¢ apiece.

DIMPLE. 35-68 73rd St. near 37th Ave., 458-8144 M–Su 11:00 a.m.–9:00 p.m.

This is a vegetarian's delight! This unassuming Bombay take-out, eat-in joint serves up dahl, roti, naan, *pakoras, raita,* and other favorites at prices that are as modest as the decor. It's a good place for people-watching, and cheap, too; cash only. There's another in Manhattan.

DOSA DINER. 35-66 73rd St. at 37th Ave., 205-2218. Daily 10:00 a.m.–8:30 p.m.

Dosa Diner cooks up spicy vegetarian foods South Indian style. It's a modest restaurant, located next to a halal grocery and another vegetarian Indian eatery. It's not easy to find a truly vegetarian restaurant in New York, and this is one of several in Jackson Heights.

FAMOUS PIZZA. 75-12 37th Ave. bet. 75th and 76th Sts., 205-5000. Daily 11:00 a.m.–10:00 p.m.

If you like novelty foods, try the Indo-Pak pizza here. It comes slathered in curried sautéed onions and decorated with thinly sliced green chili peppers. Other standards include pasta dishes, souvlaki, and pizza with eighteen kinds of otherwise pedestrian toppings. Across the street you can check into the cyber café and wow all your friends with tales about the latest fusion 'za you've just tried. (There's another location in Elmhurst at 83-07 Broadway, 271-3000.)

FIESTA MEXICANA. 75-02 Roosevelt Ave. at 75th St., 505-9090. Daily 11:00 a.m.–10:00 p.m.

Fiesta Mexicana is decked out in traditional Mexican decor, and you can grab some Mexican food to get energized for a walk around Jackson Heights. Equally important, if you are meeting friends for an outing, this restaurant is located right near the Jackson Ave. subway station.

> ☛ **TIP: Gay Bars.** Jackson Heights is known as a gay-friendly area, with a popular annual Pride parade and bars such as **THE MUSIC BOX** (40-08 74th St. at Broadway, 457-5306); **FRIEND'S TAVERN** (78-11 Roosevelt Ave., 397-7256), and **ATLANTIS 2010** (76-19 Roosevelt Ave., 457-3939) catering to this crowd.

HORNADO ECUATORIANO. 76-18 Roosevelt Ave., bet. 76th and 77th Sts., 205-7357. Daily 11:00 a.m.–11:00 p.m.

Yellow tablecloths perk up this little restaurant, known for its roast pork and *platos tipicos* or typical Ecuadorian dishes, such as *bandera, hornado,* and *morcilla.* There's another a few blocks away at 81-10 Roosevelt Ave., 651-6162.

INTI RAYMI. 86-14 37th Ave., near 86th St., 424-8968. M–Th 1:00 p.m.–11:00 p.m., F–Sa 10:00 a.m.– midnight, Su 10:00 a.m.–11:00 p.m.

It might be hard to find a seat here—ever since *The Wall Street Journal* cited this as one of five restaurants recommended for fans of the U.S. Open. Still, if you love Peruvian food (*papas rellenas,* ceviche, barbecued meats), this cute joint with big portions is a good bet. Just make sure you call ahead if you're hoping to score a seat during late August or early September.

☺ **JACKSON DINER.** 37-47 74th St. bet. Roosevelt Ave. and 37th Ave., 672-1232. Daily 11:30 a.m.–10:00 p.m.

Probably the best known of Queens eateries, this big, hangarlike eatery is famous for its sizable Sunday buffet, entertaining Hindi soap operas playing on large TV sets hanging from the wall, and a curious sense of decor. The crowd is an eclectic mix of Indians, food-centric Brooklynites, Queens natives, and visitors who've heard those three magic words that are often used to describe this place: good, plentiful—and cheap. Expect to find Northern Indian staples: mulligatawny soup, tandoori chicken, delicious naan, murgh masala (curried chicken), puris, and flavored rice. It's not necessarily the best Indian food in Queens, but it's the best known. Despite its name, rest assured this is not a diner at all.

KABAB KING PALACE. 74-15 37 Rd. at 73rd St., 205-8800. Daily 24 hours.

Kebab King has great grilled meats. Cheap and totally lacking in ambience, this is the perfect chow-down for your inner carnivore. Skip the buffet, order from the menu—in other words, seek freshness. Don't confuse this place with the **KEBAB KING** (37th Road and 73rd St.); not only are the names similar but the street numbers are confusing.

KABABISH RESTAURANT. 70-64 Broadway, 565-5131. Daily 11:00 a.m.–11:00 p.m.

Packed with locals, Kababish offers cheap, flavorful BBQ and curries. There's good halal Pakistani food here, with charcoal grilled beef and chicken kebabs, *chapli*, beef, and lamb *tikka*. Try the special *haleem* (beef with five kinds of lentils) and spicy chicken *koffa*. Don't come with a first date you're trying to impress; the decor doesn't go beyond tables and chairs. But the people-watching is good, and it's near the subway. Most entrées are under $6. Another location is nearby at 37-66 74th St.

LA PORTENA RESTAURANT Y PARRILLADA. 74-25 37th Ave. bet. 74th and 75th Sts., 458-8111. Daily 11:00 a.m.–11:00 p.m.

With a menu that marries pasta and beef, this intimate restaurant located near Little India is a favorite of Argentines. Try the gaucho beef or chicken pie for starters, a *carreras* soup of vegetables, chicken, and rice, and the mixed grill, which includes pork and blood sausage, skirt steak, short ribs, sweetbreads, and tripe. There are also pastas and an excellent watercress salad. They serve large portions, and entrees run about $20 per person.

☺ **MAHARAJA SWEETS AND SNACKS.** 73-10 37th Ave., 505-2680. Daily 10:00 a.m.–10:00 p.m.

This is a sleeper, so hurry before the lines go around the block. A terrific place for Indian chat dishes: *begara baigan* (sweet and chutney yogurt, mint, and red onions), *chat papri* (sweet and sour chutney, chana, yogurt, and onions), and *bhel puri* (mixed puffed rice topped with chutney and red onions). You can also get homemade samosas and a variety of tasty snacks such as masala chickpeas. There's a huge assortment of vegetarian entrées and Indian sweets along the front counter; many are made with cheese and come in psychedelic pink and orange colors.

MESON ASTURIAS. 40-12 83rd St., near Roosevelt Ave., 446-9154. M–Th noon–midnight, F–Sa noon–1:30 a.m., Su noon–11:00 p.m.

Meson Asturias, or is that *Astoria's*? No, it's Asturias, Spain, a region that's home of the prince of Asturias, the son of the king and queen of Spain. This attractive white-stuccoed restaurant serves the foods of its namesake, a rustic coastal province near Galicia. Try the pungent blue cheese, tapas, and grilled chorizo sausage. Asturias is on the coast and Meson Asturias prepares good seafood dishes, too. There's live guitar music on Thursdays and Sundays, and live flamenco dancing on Saturdays. Meson Asturias lives with the shadow of an un-invited infamy. In 1992, Manuel de Dios, a well-regarded Cuban journalist and antidrug-crusading former editor of *El Diario-La Prensa*, was dining with friends when he was killed, silencing his vivid reports about the Cali Colombian drug-trafficking cartel. The Manuel de Dios Triangle at 83rd St. and Roosevelt Ave. nearby memorializes that tragedy.

NATIVES RESTAURANT THEATER BAR. 82-22 Northern Blvd. at 82nd St. Restaurant, 335-0780. Theater, 335-4319. M—W 7:00 a.m.–midnight, F–Su 24 hours.

Come to this popular bar and restaurant serving Colombian and South American foods for a terrific, filling breakfast or for a late-night Saturday night snack. In business for more than twenty years, Natives is one of the most happening places in Jackson Heights with entertainment on the week-ends, when it's open twenty-four hours a day. There's also an interesting story behind the building. What's Natives today was originally a 1926 theater that once booked vaudeville shows and Broadway musicals. Natives' owners, Colombian immigrants, renovated the historic playhouse and transformed the old lobby and entrance into a bar and restaurant. Upstairs there's gallery space and a 400-seat stadium-style theater. Call for schedule of performances and reservations.

PIEDAD'S AREPAS (AKA AREPAS LADY). At the corner of Roosevelt Ave. and 79th St., 355-0780. F and Sa only; from midnight (more or less) until the dough runs out.

Nobody except the locals took much notice of this Colombian lady selling *arepas* (cornmeal pancakes) on a corner underneath the elevated subway tracks in Jackson Heights. That is, until *The New York Times* ran an article in 2004 about her and other street corner cooks. Now, if you mention the Arepas Lady in Queens, well, it seems that just about every *Times* reader in the city knows who you're talking about. Still, it's picturesque. Piedad, with her cart, arrives around midnight on Friday and Saturday evenings, and right there on the street pro-duces pitch-perfect *arepas,* a versatile staple of Colombian cuisine, topped or wrapped with such favorites as cheese, ham, and veggies. They are so good, so authentically suggestive of home, that happy partygoers spilling out of local dance halls and clubs line up to refuel after a night of dancing. According to the *Times,* Maria Piedad Cano, herself an immigrant, long ago and far away led a surprisingly different life: She was a judge.

☺ **PIO PIO.** 84-13 Northern Blvd. bet. 84th and 85th Sts., 426-1010. Daily 11:00 a.m.–11:00 p.m.

Pio Pio's chicken is out of this world, and you won't believe the portions. If you're from Manhattan, you also won't believe the low prices. It's loud, friendly, and you're likely to hear a lot of "Happy Birthday" sung on weekends (this is a favorite birthday party place). Relax with a sangria and a *Tyrannosaurus rex*–sized platter of Peruvian rotisserie-style chicken and sauce. Sometimes there's a line, and reservations are recommended. Pio Pio is a huge local success story. There are other locations in Rego Park (62-30 Woodhaven Blvd., 458-0606), Manhattan, and the Bronx.

RANCHO JUBILEE. 23-04 94th St., near 23rd Ave., 335-1700. Daily 11:00 a.m.–2:00 a.m.

If you're stuck at LaGuardia, take a little trip to the Dominican Republic via this large thatched-roof eatery right across the highway. (To be fair, it's really in East Elmhurst, not Jackson Heights.) You can relax over a piña colada at one of four cocktail bars, shake your bootie to a DJ in the lounge (dancing Th–Su nights), cheer on your favorite team on the big-screen TV, and if you time it right even listen to a Mexican mariachi band. Try the ceviche, plantain fries, and pineapple sweet and sour chicken.

RICE AVENUE. 72-19 Roosevelt Ave. bet. 72nd and 73rd Sts., 803-9001. Su–Th 11:30 a.m.–11:00 p.m., F–Sa 11:30 a.m.–11:30 p.m.

Rice's sleek decor suggests a Chelsea sensibility, but the prices are from Bangkok. Try the mango sticky rice, red curry, and duck salad. If you aren't too hungry, choose from the menu of small dishes including curry puffs, or fried tofu with spicy plum sauce.

TAQUERIA COATZINGO. 76-05 Roosevelt Ave. at 76th St., 424-1977. Daily 9:00 a.m.–6:00 a.m.

The ambience (including the moose head on the wall and decorator arches) is almost embarrassingly touristy Mexican, but the Puebla-style cuisine is home-cooked and tasty. You can't beat the chicken soup made with chunks of fresh corn on the cob in the winter. Try the chicken enchiladas with green sauce or chocolate molé. Entrées cost about $9.

ZABB QUEENS. 72-18 Roosevelt Ave. bet. 72nd and 73rd Sts., 426-7992. Daily 11:30 a.m.–2:00 a.m.

You'll find a different range of tastes at this well-reviewed Thai restaurant, with less coconut milk, more fermented and salty dishes, and lots of chili, all commonly found in the Issan region whence the owner hails. Favorites are the papaya salad and minced salad dishes called *labbs*.

SHOPPING

Latino Shops

EL INDIO AMAZONICO. 86-26 Roosevelt Ave. bet. 86th and 87th Sts., 779-9390. Daily 10:00 a.m.–8:00 p.m.

Who could resist this astonishing *botanica*, with its life-size statue of a scary Amazon Indian in the window, alongside Buddhas and astrology charts, incense, amulets, and garish statues? Step inside into a world of beliefs and rites, trinkets and services aimed at the market of local Colombian and other Latino immigrants. Here they'll read your palm, your tarot cards, or even your *caracoles,* or shells, using a special folk technique. You can learn your destiny, understand why your lover split, find out who is shooting you the evil eye, and then get back at the sucker. Be prepared to converse in Spanish.

MONIQUE FINE JEWELRY. 32-60 82nd St. bet. Northern Blvd. and 32nd St., 426-5559. M–Sa 10:30 a.m.–7:00 p.m., Su 11:00 a.m.–5:00 p.m.

The Tiffany of Jackson Heights is what they call Monique's. Well, maybe not quite, but this slick, popular little shop on busy 82nd St. has a good selection of necklaces, rings, earrings, bracelets, and watches at reasonable prices.

MUSIC-MEX. 80-12 Roosevelt Ave. at 80th St., 533-6900. M–F 10:00 a.m.–8:00 p.m., Sa–Su noon–6:00 p.m.

CDs and DVDs from Mexico and Latin America are the specialty here. Most of the music is imported and therefore not inexpensive, and includes folk music such as ranchero, *nortena, grupera,* and *sondera.* You can also find salsa, merengue, *guajiro,* and occasionally Latino rock.

NIVEL MUSICAL. 76-12 Roosevelt Ave. at 76th St. www.nivelmusical.com. M–F 10:00 a.m.–8:00 p.m., Sa–Su noon–6:00 p.m.

Check this Web site if you want to know what's going on citywide in the world of Latin contemporary music, film, and concerts. It's the on-line version of an equally great Latino music shop, specializing in Latin crossover rock. The friendly proprietor will answer questions and according to one satisfied customer, will "make suggestions based on other Latin artists you like, play anything in the shop for you, and exchange CDs without a hassle if it turns out you don't go for something."

SOCCER FANATIC. 84-28 Roosevelt Ave. off 84th St., 779-8570. M–Sa 10:30 a.m.–8:30 p.m., Su 11:00 a.m.–6:00 p.m.

"El Partido Empieza Aqui" the sign reads. That translates as, "the game begins here." Truly, soccer players and fans will find a full range of equipment here, including affordable soccer jerseys that will make your suburban friends drool.

You can get jerseys from Italy, Brazil, Mexico, Costa Rica, Argentina, and so on. It's on a strip with tons of good Latino restaurants, near the 82nd St. shopping drag, and just ten blocks from the 74th Ave. Indian restaurants and shops.

ZAPATERIA MEXICO. 88-07 Roosevelt Ave. near 88th St., 899-1742. Daily 10:00 a.m.–8:00 p.m.

Did you know that Mexicans invented the cowboy? They did, and if that's not reason enough to check out the wide selection of imported Mexican leather cowboy boots, then the prices should be. Boots are about $140. And if you get in the swing of things, pick up a Mexican ranchero shirt, sombreros, and belts. There's a sister store in Sunset Park, Brooklyn.

South Asian Shops

BUTALA EMPORIUM. 37-46 74th St. bet. Roosevelt and 37th Aves., 899-5590. www.butalaemporium.com. Daily 10:00 a.m.–8:30 p.m.

Butula is a cultural lifestyle store for a community that takes its traditional texts, religious rituals, and ancient music seriously. You will find the basics of imported Indian culture here: incense and small altars for home rituals, religious paintings, statues, musical instruments like sitars and tablas, imported South Asian magazines and newspapers, Hindu calendars and posters, rice cooking pots, carved wooden furniture, and even a row of imported beauty supplies. Butula sells an impressive number of books in English, mostly classics such as Ramayana, Mahabharata, and the Upanishads, and works by cultural icons Mahatma Gandhi and Tagore along with tomes on aryuvedic medicine, yoga, and Sanskrit.

INTERNATIONAL SAREE PALACE. 37-07 74th St. bet. Roosevelt Ave. and 37th Ave., 426-2700. Daily 10:00 a.m.–8:30 p.m.

There are fifteen shops within a two-block area specializing in saris. Classic New York black be damned. Here's a sea of color: blue mixed with emerald green, decorated with gold thread and amber-colored baubles. You can buy fabric from the bolt, or buy an off-the-rack (or custom order) sari or *salwar kamiz,* a tunic and pant outfit. Prices range from $35 for polyester prints to hundreds of dollars for silks decorated with embroidery or jewels. Accessories are cheap: bangles, chandelier earrings, and jeweled slippers for under $15. The saris are six or seven feet in length and forty-five inches in width; if you're handy, you can use these exuberant fabrics for other things, such as tablecloths, pillows, curtains, bed canopies, and heck, maybe belly dancing in the boudoir.

☛ **TIP: Seasonal Sales on Saris.** Sari prices are slashed by 20 to 50 percent during sale time in the late autumn during the Hindu festival of Diwali, and for Pakistani shopkeepers, during the Eid holiday at the end of Ramadan. Also, there are minor differences among stores in terms of fabric quality and price range. Shop around. There's **KARISHMA FASHION** across the street, **NEENA SARI PALACE** (37-23 74th St., 651-1500), **BOMBAY BAZAAR** (37th Ave. at 75th St.), **LITTLE INDIA EMPIRE** (70-01 37th Ave., 565-6872), and **AMIT FABRICS** (75-04 37th Ave., 426-7885).

MOONLITE INTERNATIONAL. 73-15 Broadway, corner of 73rd St., 803-0800. Daily 11:00 a.m.–7:00 p.m.

What's a Rodeo Drive L.A.–type store doing in the middle of a busy Jackson Heights street intersection, selling thousand-dollar Breitling watches? It's a destination shop dealing in top-of-the-line fine Swiss watches and diamond rings! Good prices.

MUSIC HOUSE OF NY. 72-31 37th Ave. at 73rd St., 424-3600. M–Sa 10:00 a.m.–9:00 p.m., Su 11:00 a.m.–8:30 p.m.

Around the corner from the sari shops, Indian restaurants, and gold jewelry stores of 74th Ave. is another small strip catering to the Indian and Pakistani customer. Among the thousands of recordings here, you can choose artists who are Bengali, Gujarati, or Tamil. What to try: Hindi film music, meditation music, Indian classical, or patriotic music from the days of the struggles for independence? The latest Bollywood star's DVD or a smash hit of classical Indian dance? Also try **PUNJAB MUSIC** (37-13 74th Ave., 429-5555).

SAM AND RAJ. 37-08 74th St. bet. Roosevelt Ave. and 37th Ave. 651-6969. Daily 10:00 a.m.–7:00 p.m.

Sam and Raj is an electronics store. From the outside it doesn't look much different from other such shops selling waffle irons, electric coffeepots, radios, and such. But it's a local institution, a hub where, if you are a member of the South Asian community you can, for instance, buy tickets to the annual film and dance festivals, learn about community goings-on, and plug in to a large informal network of contacts.

SONA CHAANDI. 37-14 74th St., 429-4653.

One of more than a dozen gold jewelry stores in Jackson Heights, specializing in expensive, more contemporary designs. Compare more traditional **KARA 22 JEWELERS OF LONDON** (37-50 74th St., 507-2288). See "Indian Gold Jewelry Shops" (p. 166).

☛ **TIP: 37th Ave. Shopping Strip for Gals, 37th Ave. bet. 79th and 81st Sts.** This is a good strip for women with a girlie swish. Most stores are open daily 10:00 a.m.–8:00 p.m.

☺ **KIM'S STATIONERY.** 80-14 37th Ave., off 80th St., 899-8672. Daily 10:00 a.m.–8:00 p.m.

For the younger set, this is Little Kitty world. There are about 2,000 branded (and frequently pink) children's items in the Miss Kitty line: pencils, umbrellas, stationery items, you name it. A bored older sib can just go across the street to D'lishus clothing boutique and peruse the trendy teen clothes.

MADE IN BRAZIL. 81-09 37th Ave., off 81st St., 429-3413. Daily noon–midnight.

Walk in dumpy, walk out a sex pistol. Great, affordable underwear, camisoles, tops, jeans, and jewelry imported from Brazil, much by the manufacturer Scala, can be found here.

NEWMAN GIFTS. 78-03 37th Ave. at 78th St., 429-3413. M–Sa 9:30 a.m.–6:30 p.m., Su 11:00 a.m–5:00 p.m.

If you'd like to spend a small fortune on an exquisitely kitschy porcelain doll or doggie from some alternative universe inhabited by little ladies wearing lace gloves and having tea parties, come to Newman's. Kids love this shop's windows.

PRIMA DONNA. 80-27 37th Ave., off 80th St., 507-6552. Daily 10:00 a.m.–8:00 p.m.

There's an entire wall full of earrings under $10, fashionable belts, flashy rings, handbags, shawls, shoes, glittery plastic hair clips, and necklaces for under $15. This is a great place for holiday gifts and accessories to add zip to your wardrobe without breaking the bank. (Other locations are in Corona at 37-64 Junction Blvd., 396-7604, and Astoria at 29-24 Ditmars Blvd., 274-2131.)

RUDY VOLCANO. 79-07 37th Ave., 651-7100. Daily 10:00 a.m.–10:00 p.m.

To find that ethnic poncho, or unique candelabra, peruse this Guatemalan-import store that carries jewelry, clothing, ceramics, religious figures, original textiles, and articles made of leather.

Specialty and Ethnic Food Shops

DESPAÑA BRAND FOOD. 86-17 Northern Blvd., off 86th St., 779-4791. www.despanabrandfoods.com. M–F 7:00 a.m.–5:00 p.m., Sa 9:00 a.m.–4:00 p.m.

These foods are out of this world, literally. On October 29, 1998, astronaut Pedro Duque took some Despaña brand chorizos from Despaña with him on the space shuttle *Discovery*. If he'd had more space he might have also brought along some of their imported cheeses from Spain, or peppers, baby eels, or Serrano hams. You can order by phone or e-mail and they will ship via UPS—but only to terrestrial destinations, please.

GREENMARKET AT TRAVERS PARK. 34th Ave. bet. 77th and 78th Sts. (212) 788-7476. July–Nov, Su 8:00 a.m.–3:00 p.m.

Come to this greenmarket on Sundays, from May to November. Look for the "rugelach guy" selling baked goods, and also the usual cornucopia of fresh fruits and veggies. Greenmarket is a program of the New York City Council on the Environment.

☺ **PATEL BROS.** 37-07 74th St. bet. 37th Ave. and 37th Rd., 898-3445. www.patelbrothersusa.com. M–Sa 9:30 a.m.–9:00 p.m., Su 9:30 a.m.–8:30 p.m.

Your jaw will drop the first time you walk the aisles at Patel's, which ranks a place in the Food Hall of Fame for authentic ethnic groceries. Patel's is food shopping heaven for Indian, Bangladeshi, and Pakistani ingredients. The motto of this family-owned business is "Serving Since 1974 Bringing Motherland Closer" and on weekends, the place is packed with people making the pilgrimage from all over the tristate area to stock up on the tastes of motherland India. You'll find huge bunches of cilantro and enormous bags of raisins, coconut, poppy seeds, and aromatic herbs and spices like cardamom, bay leaves, mango powder, fenugreek leaves, various chilies, and saffron. There are sweets, household items, utensils, health and beauty products, and teas, as well as *puja* items such as incenses that are used in religious rituals.

Under no circumstances overlook the rice aisle! The twenty- and forty-pound bags of rice piled four feet high resembles a fortified castle wall. The variety in both brands and prices bears witness to a subtle hierarchy of quality beyond simple categories like white or brown, short or long grain. Be prepared for a weekend parking crunch. You can visit satellite locations in Bellerose at 251-0 Hillside Ave. at 251st St., 470-1356, or Flushing at 42-79C Main St. bet. Blossom and Cherry Aves., 321-9847.

Bakeries

BUZZANCA'S BAKERY. 37-49 90th St. bet. Roosevelt and 37th Aves., 429-4323. M–F 6:00 a.m.–8:00 p.m., Sa 6:00 a.m.–6:00 p.m.

Beloved by locals, Buzzanca's Bakery, now in its second generation, sells good traditional Italian baked goods, like braided thick-crusted breads with soft insides, and tons of delicious Italian cookies.

LA NUEVA RIOPLATENSE, 86-10A 37th Ave. bet. 86th and 87th. Sts., 507-2339. Daily 7:00 a.m.–9:00 p.m.

"The best Colombian bakery in Queens," exclaims a prominent Colombian jazz musician. And he should know—he travels here weekly to get his store of *pan de yuca* (bread made of yuca flour), *pan de bono, almojabana, sacramentos* (elephant ears pastries), and other specialities. They have a wide selection of sandwiches and empanadas made of flaky shells with a variety of fillings. Petit fours and cakes fill nearly a wall of refrigerators. They also sell *yerba mate,* a tea-like drink favored by Argentineans and Uruguayans. For coffee, try the light and foamy (regular) or a stronger and foamier (*cortadito* or "little cut one"). If you need a whole roast pig for Christmas, they cater.

PANO FINO. 85-01 Northern Blvd., corner 85th St., 205-5596. Daily 24 hours.

Sabor Latino, indeed! Try the *chorros* (deep-fried dough), round breads filled with cheese and guava paste, and sweet elephant ears. If you come with, say, friends from Venezuela, the little imported cups of *dulce de leche* and condensed milk will transport them back to their childhood. Don't miss the fig pastry. If you're taking food home for a snack, pop across the street to the supermarket and pick up imported cheeses such as *Quesito Colombiano,* or the Dominican *Queso de Freir.*

13

Greater Jamaica, Including Jamaica Estates and St. Albans

WHERE IT IS: Southeastern Queens. Jamaica is bounded by Grand Central Parkway to the north, South Jamaica and JFK Airport to the south, Hollis lies to the east, Rosedale and Laurelton to the southeast, and the Van Wyck Expressway to the west.

HOW TO GET THERE BY SUBWAY/LIRR: By subway, E to Jamaica/Van Wyck, Sutphin Blvd. /Archer Ave., Jamaica Center (Parsons Blvd. and Archer Ave.) Or, F to Sutphin Blvd., Parsons Blvd., 169th St., and 179th Street/Jamaica. By LIRR to Sutphin Blvd. and Archer Ave.

WHAT'S NEARBY: Jamaica Estates to the northeast, Kew Gardens to the west, St. Albans to the southeast, and Richmond Hill to the southwest.

MAJOR SHOPPING/RESTAURANT STREETS: Jamaica Ave., for about one mile east of Sutphin; Sutphin Ave.

SPECIAL CHARACTERISTICS: Afro-Caribbean immigrants and cultural institutions; historic sites dating to pre-Revolutionary era.

ON NOT GETTING LOST: Jamaica is an important transfer point linking the city with Long Island. It is a hub where you can transfer among LIRR, the New York City transit system, and AirTrain/JFK to the airport.

Make sure you know what neighborhood you're going to as there are several with the word "Jamaica" in their names. Jamaica is working to middle class, has lots of businesses as well as homes, and is largely African-American. Jamaica Estates is exclusively residential and expensive. Southside Queens doesn't exist at all on a map, although that's what hip-hop star 50 Cent (Curtis Jackson) calls his hometown; it's officially South Jamaica.

CAR SERVICES: Unity 297-2222, Delta 525-3500.

NEW TERRITORY FOR THE URBAN EXPLORER

A lot of people have been to Jamaica repeatedly, but have never seen it once. That's because millions of people take the LIRR to the Hamptons or AirTrain

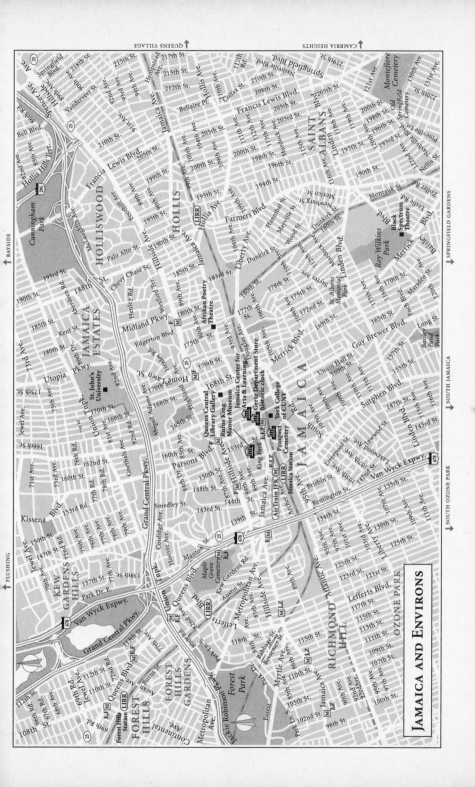

JAMAICA AND ENVIRONS

to JFK, and, as the conductors say, "switch at Jamaica." Underground, Jamaica
is just a train station. Aboveground, Jamaica and nearby neighborhoods offer
rich territory for the urban explorer. Southwestern Queens is home to the borough's largest community of African-Americans and others from the African
diaspora. Immigrants living in the area come from Guyana, El Salvador, Haiti,
China, India, Colombia, Jamaica, the Philippines, the Dominican Republic,
and Pakistan. In downtown Jamaica, posters advertise concerts, community
events, language lessons in Swahili, jazz, and poetry slams. There are African
import stores, mosques, free Sunday concerts, and a pedestrian mall geared to
hip-hop fashions. In what we are taking the liberty of calling the greater Jamaica area, you can find quiet residential neighborhoods like Hollis and Addesleigh Park, not to mention Jamaica Estates, a wealthy enclave where Donald
Trump grew up.

THINGS TO SEE AND DO

The Jamaica Center for Arts and Learning and local Cultural Collaborative
Jamaica both offer classes and organize programs and community events. The
Afrikan Poetry Theater has musical, dance, and art performances. York College,
part of CUNY and St. John's, has public programs, lectures, and concerts. The
main branch of the Queens Public Library has a gallery, concerts, a new Children's Library Discovery Center, and historical resources. Shoppers can make a
beeline for the sneakers, urban health and beauty products, and hip-hop fashion
and jewelry at the Pedestrian Mall at 165th St. See the Jamaica Self-Guided Tour
for sites on the National Register of Historic Places, too.

BITS OF HISTORY

Jamaica, along with Elmhurst and Flushing, is one of the oldest villages in the
borough of Queens. English colonialists from Hempstead, who were granted
land by Governor Peter Stuyvesant, settled here in about 1655. Jamaica was designated the county seat in 1683. During the Revolutionary War, the Tories occupied the area. By the mid-1850s, Jamaica was a prestigious address. Rufus King,
one of the founding fathers of the United States, lived here, as did his son, who
was elected governor of New York State (1856). The extension of the LIRR
(1836) into Jamaica was a stimulus to economic and residential development in
much of southern Queens.

In the early twentieth century, Jamaica Ave. between Sutphin Blvd. and 168th
St. was a bustling middle-class shopping strip. Loew's Valencia Theatre, a grand,
ornate showpiece that opened in 1929, accommodated thirty-five hundred
moviegoers! Instead of going to Manhattan to shop, people would go to Jamaica. It boasted the Gertz department store and Macy's, too. America's first

supermarket, King Kullen (named after its founder, Michael C. Cullen) opened here.

Many middle-class residents moved to Nassau County in the post–World War II era, following the lure of suburbia. By 1980 Jamaica had become largely African-American and Latino. In the last decade the area's economy improved with new construction and the arrival of York College, new municipal buildings, and AirTrain. Jamaica retains some of its original identity as a municipal center insofar as there are two courts located here, Queens County Family Court (89-14 Parsons Blvd.) and Queens County Surrogate's Court (88-11 Sutphin Blvd.).

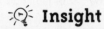 **Insight**

About Jamaica's Name

Because there's a West Indian population living here today, including Jamaicans, some people assume that this Queens neighborhood was named after the Caribbean island or vice versa. Not so, although apparently both names were derived from Indian words. This Jamaica was first called Rusdorf by the Dutch, and later, Jameco, a Native American word that was Anglicized to Jamaica and adopted for the entire southeast portion of Queens in 1680.

PARKS, PUBLIC SPACES, AND PUBLIC WORKS

BAISLEY POND PARK. No. Conduit Ave. at Baisley Blvd. So. Call New York City hotline 311. www.nycgov parks.org.

This one hundred-acre park, alongside Baisley Pond, has the usual facilities: tennis, basketball, and handball courts, a running track, an athletic field, and more. The pond has big lily pads and you can see many species of wildlife including snapping turtles, musk turtles, bullfrogs, dragonflies, Canadian geese, cormorants, and mockingbirds.

The American mastodon (*Mammut americanum*), a kind of a four-ton hairy elephant with large tusks, was apparently drawn to this area, too, some 10,000 years ago. Park workers dredging the bottom of Baisley Pond in the 1890s found remains of a mastodon buried in the sediment. Note the sculpture of a mastodon in Sutphin Playground in Baisley Pond Park.

CRICKET FIELD AT ST. ALBANS MEMORIAL PARK. Bounded by Merrick Blvd., Linden Blvd., and Sayres Ave. Call New York City hotline 311. www.nycgovparks.org.

Cricket, anyone? This state-of-the-art public cricket field in St. Albans is the second to be built in the entire United States. (There was so much cricket already being played in this park that finally the authorities decided to make it official.) The new field, to be completed summer 2007, will have a clay pitch (the surface off which the pitched ball is bounced). You can watch two kinds of games, softball cricket, which doesn't require a clay pitch and is played mainly by the Indian and Pakistani population, and hardball cricket, which is played competitively in the Caribbean, England, and Australia. Admission's free!

JAMAICA BAY WILDLIFE REFUGE. See listing, pp. 258–59.

☺ 🏛 **KING PARK.** 150-03 Jamaica Ave. bet. 150th and 153rd Sts.

Enjoy the well-kept lawns, benches, Victorian pergola (once used for band concerts), and shaded areas of this eleven-acre park located on one of Jamaica's main shopping streets. It's big enough for kids who want to run and play. Both King Manor (pp. 192–93) and King Park are listed on the National Register of Historic Places.

ROY WILKINS PARK. Bounded by Merrick Blvd. and Baisley Blvd. Call New York City hotline 311. www.nyc govparks.org.

Roy Wilkins Park in St. Albans was created in the early 1970s from the grounds of the abandoned St. Albans Naval Hospital. The park is where local kids play basketball, handball, and soccer. There's a large public pool at 119 St. and Merrick Blvd. The former hospital is now an active Veterans Administration facility.

POINTS OF CULTURAL INTEREST

African and African-American Culture

☺ **AFRIKAN POETRY THEATRE, INC. (APT).** 176-03 Jamaica Ave. at 176th St., 523-3312. www.afrikapoetrytheatre.com. Call for hours of events.

Established in the mid-1970s the Afrikan Poetry Theatre is, in their own words, "a pivotal player in the restoration of African peoples history and humanity." The vibrant cultural center offers Afro-centric musical instruction, drama, film, journalism classes for teens, karate, instruction in French and Swahili, and East African dance classes, and hosts community meetings on issues such as hunger in Africa. Visitors can attend or join in at readings, open mikes, poetry slams, and publishing workshops. See Web site for information on Calabash Drummers, a West African drum and dance ensemble, Kwanzaa presentations, and tours to Africa.

AMERICAN ROOTS ART GALLERY. 193-17 Linden Blvd. at 193rd St., 712-4141. 10:00 a.m.–3:00 p.m., but call first.

A framer and art dealer in St. Albans for more than twenty-five years, owner David Hodge's gallery's collection of prints and sculptures shows the work of African-American artists, including NFL-player-turned-artist Ernie Barnes, sculptor Tina Allen, and painter Brenda Joysmith.

BLACK AMERICAN HERITAGE FOUNDATION MUSIC HISTORY ARCHIVE. York College Library, 94-20 Guy Brewer Blvd., 262-2644. Call for appointment.

A small but important collection of artifacts of the numerous notable African-American musicians and composers of southeastern Queens has been stowed for posterity here. It includes musical compositions, memorabilia, videos, records, instruments—some donated by living musicians, including Wilbur "Buck" Clayton, Al Sears, Brook Benton, and Irving Burgie. It also includes rare recordings by Duke Ellington. Clarence L. Irving, a local resident who is founder and chair of the Black American Heritage Foundation, helped organize the housing of the collection at the York College of the City of New York in 1989.

☺ **BLACK SPECTRUM THEATRE.** Roy Wilkins Park, 177th St. and Baisley Blvd. bet. 119th Rd. and 20th Ave., 723-1800. www.blackspectrum.com. Tu–W 10:00 a.m.–6:00 p.m., Th, F 10:00 a.m.–4:00 p.m. Fee varies with event.

If you come to the three cutting-edge performances in this four hundred-seat state-of-the-art theater in St. Albans, you'll find them provocative, funny, relevant—and cheaper than Off Broadway theater. Their shows have won praise from some of the toughest critics in town. Don't miss the annual Women of Color Theatre & Film Festival, launched in 1999.

Much more than just a performance space, Black Spectrum Theatre is a creative center, a community leader, and a theater company. Born in 1970, its mission is to create "theater, films, and videos examining issues of concern to the African-American community, particularly African-American youth." This professional theater company, a training ground for new and emerging playwrights and actors, is targeted to the local African-American, Caribbean-American, and Latino audiences, but everyone is welcome. Among those associated with the organization are Obie-winning actor Arthur French, a founding member of the Negro Ensemble Company, and Bob Law, host of the syndicated radio show *Night Talk*. Over the years, guest celebrities have included Roy Ayers, Roberta Flack, Jon Dinizulu Lucien, Angela Bofill, Lonnie Liston Smith, Bobbi Humphrey, and Dick Gregory.

GREATER ALLEN CATHEDRAL OF NEW YORK. 111-54 Merrick Blvd., 206-4600. Services are open to the public. Su 6:30 a.m., 8:30 a.m., 11:15 a.m.

With a flock of 15,000, this powerhouse church has perhaps the largest congregation in the state of New York. The $23 million cathedral was built in 1997. The Rev. Floyd H. Flake has been senior pastor since 1976. Flake, who served in the U.S. House of Representatives for eleven years (1986–97), helped obtain financial and government support for community programs that include housing for senior citizens, a school, a medical clinic and drug counseling program, a neighborhood preservation and development corporation, and television and radio shows. The African Methodist Episcopal Church (AME) claims to be the second-largest private-sector employer in Queens, after JFK Airport.

The model for this range of activities is the historic Free African Society, founded by two former slaves Absalom Jones and Richard Allen. The latter was one of the founders of the African Methodist Episcopal Church, after whom the Allen Cathedral is named. Jones and Allen purchased their own freedom and advanced the idea that the path to advancement was black-run community institutions.

☀ Insight

Hip-Hop and Jazz in Jamaica

Hip-hop stars such as 50 Cent, LL Cool J, Run-DMC, and Ja Rule came from this area (including Hollis and South Jamaica). So did the clothing line Fubu. Russell Simmons, co-owner and founder of the rap label Def Jam Records, credited with launching rap onto the national music scene, grew up here, too. Jazz greats who once lived here are Count Basie, Fats Waller, Billie Holiday, Bessie Smith, Fes Williams, James P. Johnson, Charlie Mingus, Sidney Bechet, and Cootie Williams. Trumpeter Buck Clayton still lives here.

JAMAICA CENTER FOR ARTS AND LEARNING (JCAL). 161-04 Jamaica Ave., 658-7400, www.jcal.org. M, F 9:00 a.m.–6:00 p.m., Tu–Th 9:00 a.m.–7:00 p.m., Sa 10:00 a.m.–4:00 p.m.

JCAL is an important all-purpose community center with tons of programs, including arts workshops and concerts. In operation since 1972, its arts facilities include several painting studios, dance studios, a ceramics studio, a 1,600-square-foot gallery, music room, and a ninety-nine-seat proscenium theater. JCAL holds workshops on African dance, samba/Afro-Brazilian dance, and hip-hop dance. The elegant 1925 building was built as the Office of the Register and is listed on the National Register of Historic Places.

OTHER POINTS OF CONTEMPORARY INTEREST

AIRTRAIN JFK. www.panynj.gov/airtrain.

Tired of expensive taxis to JFK? Take the AirTrain. This eight-mile-long light-rail system opened in 2003 (on the centennial anniversary of the Wright Brothers' first flight) and links JFK to the New York City subway system. There are three places to pick it up: Jamaica Station (E, J, Z subways and LIRR), at Sutphin Blvd.–Archer Ave. (E, J, Z subways), or Howard Beach (A subway). Service from Penn Station in Manhattan to JFK's terminals takes forty-five minutes to an hour and costs $5 each way, which is a good deal considering that the car ride from midtown Manhattan to JFK can take as much as two hours during rush hour. AirTrain runs every eight minutes or so, and it goes to all the airline terminals at JFK.

BLUE PAINTED PLACES OF HINDU GURU SRI CHINMOY. Not open to the public.

The light-blue-painted homes of Hindu guru Sri Chinmoy followers dot the neighborhoods of Jamaica Hills and Briarwood, with many found on Normal Street. The group owns and manages several local stores and vegetarian restaurants. As signs of spiritual devotion his mostly American followers pursue ultra-marathons and other tests of endurance. Annam Brahma Ashrita Furman, the guru's most famous follower, claims the record for having broken the most records in the *Guinness Book of World Records*—fourteen, as of 2005—including the record for the greatest distance walked by a person continuously balancing a milk bottle on his head. He also holds the record for fastest pogo-stick ascent of Canada's CN Tower—fifty-seven minutes and fifty-one seconds.

FILIPINO AMERICAN HUMAN SERVICES, INC. (FAHSI). 185-14 Hillside Ave. at 185th St., 883-1295. M–F 9:00 a.m.–6:00 p.m.

Jamaica is the epicenter of New York's Filipino community, the fourth-largest Asian American group in New York City, numbering about 60,000 according to the 2000 census. FAHSI helps Filipina women—many of whom find first jobs as babysitters, house cleaners, and maids—get a leg up on life by teaching them computer and job skills. Visitors can attend programs of Filipino folk dance as well as hip-hop by the award-winning Youth Performing Arts Ensemble, and the admission-free annual Light a Parol (Christmas lantern), a program with cultural performances, food, singing, a silent auction, and Filipino holiday market.

IMAM AL-KHOEI ISLAMIC CENTER. 89-89 Van Wyck Expressway at 90th Ave., 297-6520. Daily dawn–sunset. Call for appointment; limited access for women.

What many drivers on the Van Wyck Expressway think is a blue-domed mosque is not technically a mosque, but the Al-Khoei Islamic Center, the spiritual home for the Shia sect of Islam in the tristate region. The center has a prayer hall where worshipers come from throughout the city and as far away as Rochester for weekly and special holiday services. Al-Khoei is part of the London-based Imam Al-Khoei Benevolent Foundation. The congregation includes Shia Muslims who've emigrated from across the Mideast, East Africa, South Asia, and Guyana, as well as Latino and American converts to Islam. The center offers Islamic education from prekindergarten through twelfth grade, to approximately two hundred children. Visitors might be interested in visiting the library with its religious tomes in English, Arabic, Farsi, Urdu, and Spanish.

JAMAICA ARTS & MUSIC SUMMER FESTIVAL (JAMS). Cultural Collaborative Jamaica, 161-04 Jamaica Ave., 526-3217, www.go2ccj.net.

Sponsored by the Cultural Collaborative Jamaica, this summer festival organizes events and free concerts in local parks. The collaborative seeks to maximize participation by Jamaica's diverse communities in the cultural arts.

JOSEPH ADDABBO FEDERAL OFFICE BUILDING. 88-11 Sutphin Blvd., 520-3116. M–F 9:00 a.m.–5:00 p.m.

This building houses Queens' civil courts. In the lobby you will often see exhibits of Queens-based artists, many from Long Island City.

☺ **QUEENS CENTRAL LIBRARY GALLERY.** 89-11 Merrick Blvd. bet. 89th and 90th Aves., 990-0700, www.queenslibrary.org. M–F 10:00 a.m.–9:00 p.m., Sa 10:00 a.m.–5:30 p.m. Sa-Su Sept.–June, noon–5:00 p.m. Special hours for youth division, film and video, and Long Island division.

This is the central branch of a vast library system. In addition to books, visitors can enjoy free Sunday Concerts at Central, which are midday concerts with a multicultural twist. Performers might be South Asian, Spanish, Hebrew, Celtic, Latino, Russian, African, or Afro-Caribbean—just for starters. (Sept.–June, Sun 2:00 p.m.) A 2,500-square-foot gallery mounts exhibitions, too.

The Children's Library Discovery Center (scheduled to open in 2007) will be a marvelous place to bring children. The two-story, 14,000-square-foot children's library will have museum-quality interactive exhibits for children age three to twelve, focusing on math, science, engineering, and technology. A giant globe will provide a focus for learning about geography, history, and world cultures.

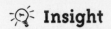 **Insight**

Libraries Can Reach Out

The Queens Borough Public Library—the second-largest public library in the United States in terms of size of collections—has embraced the immigrant population of the borough. There are books, periodicals, CDs, and videos available in foreign languages. Even when you call for information, the tape recording gives five language options: English, Spanish, Russian, Korean, and Chinese. The library will mail any new immigrant living in Queens books and other materials in Chinese, French, Greek, Italian, Korean, Russian, or Spanish. The selection includes romances, computer books, cookbooks, biographies, best-sellers, martial arts novels, parenting books, and more. In 1997 the Queens Borough Public Library and the Shanghai Library of China (the largest public library in China) signed a four-year agreement enabling the exchange of library materials, exhibitions, personnel, and Internet-accessible information.

ST. JOHN'S UNIVERSITY. 8000 Utopia Pkwy. in Jamaica Estates. 888-990-6161. www.stjohns.edu.

St. John's is located in an upscale area called Jamaica Estates. This private coed Roman Catholic University founded over a century ago by the Vincentian Community has several campuses in the New York area, plus a location in Rome. Among its prestigious alumni are former New York governors Hugh L. Carey and Mario M. Cuomo, New York City Police Commissioner Raymond W. Kelly, and Ron Silver, Tony Award–winning actor. A diverse student body comes from forty-four states and 130 countries. Offerings include an undergraduate school, numerous academic centers, and graduate schools of education, business, pharmacy, and law among others.

If you are on campus, visit **SUN YAT-SEN HALL** with its yellow pagoda with a gilt roof adorned with carvings. Inside is the **DR. M. T. GEOFFREY YEH ART GALLERY,** a permanent collection of six hundred pieces of Chinese art. (990-7476, www.university-gallery.com. Tu–Thu 10:00 a.m.–5:00 p.m., F 10:00 a.m.–3:00 p.m., Sa noon–5:00 p.m.). St. John's, of course, has famous basketball and other sports teams.

YORK COLLEGE OF CUNY. 94-20 Guy R. Brewer Blvd., 262-2000. www.york.cuny.edu.

York College, a senior college of the City University of New York (CUNY) offers a baccalaureate degree in majors ranging from liberal arts and sciences to career programs in aviation, business, and education. Interestingly, the U.S. FDA has offices on campus. This is the only CUNY senior college offering majors in gerontology, biotechnology, and a BS/MS degree in occupational therapy. A diverse student body of 6,000 includes African-American, Caribbean, Latino, and South Asian backgrounds.

Visitors can attend shows, generally free, of performing arts, chamber music, and other special events. The free Jazz Forum series are workshop-style events where participants view a performance and then play with the artists. On campus a special collection, the Black American Heritage Foundation Music History Archive, focuses on local musicians. (See listing, p. 187.)

PEOPLE, PLACES, AND THINGS OF HISTORICAL INTEREST

COUNT BASIE'S RESIDENCE. 174-27 Adelaide Lane at 175th St. Not open to the public.

This was the home of Count Basie from the late 1940s through the late 1960s. Imagine him and neighbor Fats Waller jamming the afternoon away!

🏛 GERTZ DEPARTMENT STORE HISTORIC CLOCK. Jamaica Ave. and 160th St.

Gertz was one of the main department stores of old Jamaica that attracted throngs of shoppers. This old sidewalk clock marks the spot where the store was. Using big sidewalk clocks to draw attention to a store was a form of twentieth-century advertising. There's another at 30-78 Steinway St. in Astoria.

🏛 GRACE EPISCOPAL CHURCH AND CEMETERY. 155-15 Jamaica Ave. at 155th St. and Parsons Blvd., 291-0555.

This 1862 church, with a cherry-red door and a historic graveyard in the front and backyards, sits amidst the swirl of shoppers and pedestrians along Jamaica Ave. It's a slender building, designed in English Gothic style with a tall spire. The church was built on the site of a 1702 mission by settlers in a Dutch colony who belonged to the "English Society for the Propagation of the Gospel in Foreign Parts." The church is listed on the National Register of Historic Places. The chancel (1901) and Tudor Revival parish house (1912) were added later.

Wander among the gravestones and you will recognize the names of old New York: Rufus King, after whom the King Mansion down the street is named, is here along with Charles King, president of Columbia University, whose grave has been marked by the university.

☺ 🏛 RUFUS KING MANOR MUSEUM AND PARK. King Park, 150-03 Jamaica Ave. bet. 150th and 153rd Sts., 206-0545. www.kingmanor.org/Home.asp. Museum open March through December, Th–F noon–2:00 p.m., Sa–Su noon–5:00 p.m. Tours in Spanish provided on weekends. Admission is $5 adults, $3 seniors and students, free for children sixteen and under.

King Manor is a National Historic Landmark. It was the home of Rufus King, one of the signers of the Constitution, who lived here intermittently from 1806 until his death in 1827. King was an abolitionist, outspoken in his opposition to the 1820 Missouri Compromise, which allowed slavery to continue outside the original thirteen states. He sat in the Continental Congress (1784–86), and served as a U.S. Senator (1789–95), and Minister to Great Britain (1796–1803). He was also the Federalist Party's vice-presidential nominee (1804 and 1808) and presidential candidate (1816). There are special programs and activities for both children and adults. This is not to be confused with Kingsland Homestead Museum.

GRAVE OF LUBAVITCHER REBBE IN MONTEFIORE CEMETERY. Bounded by 130th Ave., Springfield and Francis Lewis Blvds.

Montefiore is a well-known Jewish cemetery. It's also become a place of pilgrimage for the Lubavitchers, a Hassidic sect of orthodox Jews who are fervently devoted to the Lubavitcher Rebbe, Rabbi Menachem Schneerson, who is buried here. On special occasions, thousands of his followers may visit his grave.

🏛 PROSPECT CEMETERY. 159th St. at Beaver Road.

Landmarked in 1977, this was the first public graveyard in Queens, established in the 1650s shortly after British subjects settled the area. About forty graves date as far back as 1668. The early graves belonged to paupers. However, the status of the cemetery improved over time, proven by the fact that one of the later graves belongs to Egbert Benson (1746–1833), a U.S. Court of Appeals judge. The cemetery is listed on the National Register of Historic Places and has the graves of prominent New York families such as the Merricks, Sutphins, and Van Wycks. The chapel is undergoing restoration.

🚶 SELF-GUIDED TOUR: JAMAICA SITES ON THE NATIONAL REGISTER OF HISTORIC PLACES

This half-mile route starts at the landmarked 🏛 King Manor at 150th St. and Jamaica Ave. (see pp. 192–93). All of the sites listed are on the National Register of Historic Places. After visiting King Manor, walk south on 150th St. (that is, away from King Manor) and turn left on Beaver Pl. to see 🏛 Prospect Cemetery, 159th St. at Beaver Rd. It was the earliest public cemetery in Queens. Returning to Jamaica Ave., pass the 🏛 First Reformed Church, 153 Jamaica Ave., a redbrick Romanesque Revival with notable arches, built 1858–59, renovated 1901. Next door is the 🏛 Grace Episcopal Church Complex (155-15 Jamaica Ave.). (See p. 192.) On the same side of the street, note the 🏛 Jamaica Savings Bank (161-02 Jamaica Ave.), a gorgeous and highly decorative Beaux-Arts building built in 1897–98. It is now sadly empty, but it is rumored to have been purchased recently and may be renovated. In front of it is a landmarked 🏛 Sidewalk Clock, 161-11 Jamaica Ave., manufactured about 1900. Next door is the 🏛 Jamaica Arts Center (formerly the Jamaica Register Bldg.) at 161-04 Jamaica Ave. bet. 161 and 162nd Sts., an old English-style club in Italian Renaissance style, built about 1898. Continuing, you will pass

(continued)

🏛 J. Kurtz and Sons Store Building (162-24 Jamaica Ave.). It is in the art deco style and was built in 1931. This six-story store, which in its heyday sold modern design furniture, has been called "one of the finest examples of art deco architecture in Queens."

Somewhat farther afield are two more sites near each other. 🏛 La Casita (Polyform Bra Co., Roxanne Swimsuit Co., 90-33 160th St.), is a commercial building circa 1907 that made bras and bathing suits. It was remodeled about 1936 as a nightclub. Four blocks up 160th St. is St. Monica's Church, 94-20 160th St., a Romanesque Revival structure built 1856–57.

🏛 **LOEW'S VALENCIA THEATRE** (AKA TABERNACLE OF PRAYER FOR ALL PEOPLE INC. PRAYER TOWER). 165-11 Jamaica Ave. at 165th St. and Merrick Blvd., 297-5511. Services F 8:00 p.m., Su 11:30 a.m., and 7:30 p.m.

It's hard not to stare the first time you see this outrageously baroque terracotta facade. It's an old 3,554-seat movie house. When it opened in the disastrous stock-market year of 1929, the Valencia was the first of five so-called Wonder Theaters built by the New York–based Loew's chain of movie theaters. Each had organs, fancy bathrooms, ornate ceilings, extravagant wall murals, and elaborate staircases. The Valencia operated as a movie theater for fifty years. Today this building houses a church.

NORTH FORK BANK. Corner of Jamaica and Sutphin Aves.

Walking down Jamaica Ave., you're likely to stumble on a number of beautiful art deco buildings. This old bank building, with the words "for the encouragement of thrift" inscribed on the outside, features an enormous mural inside called *View of Jamaica Village*, depicting rural Queens over a hundred years ago, by Earl Purdy.

RESTAURANTS AND CAFÉS

There are many small restaurants in this area, mostly West Indian or Guyanese. The food is simple and tastes home-cooked. There are also a smattering of Italian, Latino, fast food, and bagel shops.

JEAN'S CARIBBEAN-AMERICAN RESTAURANT. 188-36 Linden Blvd. at Farmers Blvd., 525-3069. Daily 7:00 a.m.–11:00 p.m.

Several Caribbean and Jamaican restaurants have opened their doors in St. Albans, but Jean's outshines them all. The ambience is clean and pleasant, but it's the oxtail gravy, roti stuffed with chicken, jerk chicken, or stewed chicken that keeps the regulars coming back. Main courses come with a side salad, plantains, and rice and peas (aka white rice and red beans). Jean's also serves a full American diner menu with eggs, grits, and burgers.

RIDDICK'S CATERING RESTAURANT. 198-18 Linden Blvd. at 198th St., 276-4108. Daily 6:00 a.m.–11:00 p.m.

The barbecued ribs alone are worth a visit, and the chicken and waffles are a specialty. It's impossible to walk out of this Southern-food diner not stuffed. The big meals of the day are breakfast and dinner, and the generous portions mean you can skip lunch.

PROPER CAFÉ. 217-01 Linden Blvd. at 217th St., 341-2233. Daily 6:00 p.m.–4:00 a.m., kitchen 8:00 p.m.–3:00 a.m.

More nightclub than café, Proper has earned a reputation since opening in 1985 as the classiest place to party and meet on Linden Blvd. Tuesday and Sunday are karaoke nights, when some of the best and worst talent in the extended neighborhood vies for the approval of a lively crowd. Comedy night on Tuesdays and jazz on Wednesday ramp up to weekend dancing when a dressed-up thirty- and forty-something crowd grooves to R&B. It's located in Cambria Hts., across Springfield Blvd. from St. Albans, and there's a cover charge certain nights.

SYBIL'S GUYANESE BAKERY. 159-12 Hillside Ave. at 160th St., 297-2359. M–Sa 7:00 a.m.–11:00 p.m.

This West Indian (Guyanese) bakery makes the best sweet coconut bread, cheese rolls, and coconut rolls called salaras. Try the cane juice, ginger beer, and mauby as well. There's a small eat-in here; it's a smaller version of the highly regarded Brooklyn institution by the same name.

SHOPPING: FOOD, CLOTHING, AND STUFF

GERTZ PLAZA MALL. Jamaica Ave. and 160th St. M–Sa 10:30–a.m.–7:00 p.m., Su noon–6:00 p.m.

The old department store has given way to a large indoor mall–style retail smorgasbord of different shops selling inexpensive clothing, shoes, and accessories.

☺ **JAMAICA COLISEUM MALL.** 89-02 165th St. at the corner of Jamaica Ave. M–Sa 11:00 a.m.–7:00 p.m., Su noon–6:00 p.m.

Bling! Walk down the central stairwell and you descend into a 2,500-square-foot subterranean jewelry universe. The entire basement floor is occupied by one-stop shopping for thug-style accessorizing: thick gold-chain necklaces and bracelets, four-inch gold pendants shaped as crosses, African faces, and dollar signs, walnut-sized sparkly gold rings for men, and drop-dead flashy watches, including spinners studded with either diamonds or zirconium, plus dog tags, name belts, and cuff links. Display cases stuffed with thousands of pieces of glittering gold and silver are staffed by tough-looking Chinese and Eastern European men. There's trendy urban gear in this mini-mall such as baseball hats and sneakers at **MOE'S SNEAKER SPOT** (739-1578), wigs at **KIM'S HUMAN HAIR** (291-5535), and everywhere, glittery skintight clothes for women.

COOKIE'S DEPARTMENT STORE. 166-21 Jamaica Ave. at 166th St., 291-7700. M–Sa 9:00 a.m.–7:30 p.m., Su 10:00 a.m.–6:00 p.m.

Cookie's is a great place to go for low-priced children's wear, basic underwear, and school uniforms.

GREENMARKET IN JAMAICA. 90-04 160th St. off Jamaica Ave. April–November, F–Sa 7:00 a.m.–4:00 p.m. (212) 788-7476.

The Jamaica Farmer's Market opens in late April, selling flowers and plants. Fruits and vegetables become available as the season progresses.

KLINGBEIL SHOE LABS. 145-01 Jamaica Ave. bet 145 and 146 Sts., 297-6864. M–F 8:00 a.m.–noon, 1:00 p.m.–4:00 p.m., Sa 8:00 a.m.–noon.

Klingbeil Shoe Labs crafts custom leather boots for figure skaters costing $500 (without the blades). They also make boots for roller skaters and ice hockey skates. Many competitive skaters, including gold medalist Sarah Hughes, have trekked here for the best fit in town. Sitting at his desk, with rows of antique boots and Dutch clogs, piles of professional skating magazines scattered around, the elderly Mr. Klingbeil has a twinkle in his eye, reminding visitors of a kindly Swiss watchmaker. Personal service is the key here.

TOUBA CLOTHES AND TAILORING. Jamaica Coliseum Mall, 89-02 165th St., 658-3875. M–Sa 11:00 a.m.–7:00 p.m., Su noon–6:00 p.m.

A few Senegalese men sit in a tiny booth inside this mall, sewing while you watch. They make gorgeous wedding gowns, dresses, children's clothing, and special orders with imported African fabrics. They also machine-sew elaborate embroidery with gold and silver thread on the colorful imported clothing.

NEARBY NEIGHBORHOODS

JAMAICA ESTATES (bounded to the east by 188th St., to the west by Homelawn Ave., to the north by Union Tnpk., and to the south by Hillside Ave.) is an exclusive residential area, zoned for single-family homes only. Jamaica Estates is one of the most expensive areas of Queens. It is home to St. John's University (see p. 191) and where Donald Trump grew up. If you're shopping for youngsters, visit **MALAWI** (187-22 Union Tnpk. bet. 187th and 188th Sts., 454-9699. M–S 10:00 a.m.–6:00 p.m., Su noon–5:00 p.m.), one of the borough's hippest boutiques, specializing in colorful toys, clothing, jewelry, and handbags for teens.

ST. ALBANS (bounded to the east by Springfield Blvd., to the west by Farmers Blvd., to the north by Hollis Ave., and to the south by Merrick Blvd.) is home to middle-class African-American families and increasing numbers of upwardly mobile Caribbean Americans and a smattering of African immigrants as well. The major shopping drag is Linden Blvd. St. Albans is accessible by the LIRR, which stops at Linden Blvd. and Montauk St. although service is limited; check the schedules.

Named after a famous British village, St. Albans is an important center of black middle-class life in Queens. The **ADDISLEIGH PARK** section, just west of the LIRR station, is the pinnacle of southeastern Queens suburbia. Beautiful Tudor-style homes built in the 1920s are set back on wide lots. The neighborhood's unusual crisscrossing one-way streets protect its quiet oasis, St. Albans Park. Older homes (Victorians and row houses) are also found in another middle-class and largely black area nearby, Hollis, developed by Frederick W. Dunton in the 1880s.

Visitor highlights include the Black Spectrum Theatre (see p. 187) based in Roy Wilkins Park, a nonprofit professional theater company. You can see the homes of jazz legends Thomas "Fats" Waller (173-19 Sayres Ave.), Mercer Ellington (113-02 175th St.), Lena Horne (112-45 178th St.), and Roy Eldridge (194-119 109th Ave.) among others. For food you can chow down at Riddick's Catering Restaurant (see p. 195), or Jean's Caribbean-American Restaurant (see p. 194). And, for free spectator sports, there are cricket matches in the park! (See pp. 185–86.)

14

Long Island City

WHERE IT IS: Northwest Queens. Bounded to the north and west by the East River, to the south by Newtown Creek, and to the east by 49th St. and New Calvary Cemetery.

HOW TO GET THERE BY SUBWAY: There are eight subway lines. #7 to Vernon Blvd. /Jackson Ave., Hunter's Point Ave., 45th Road/Courthouse Square, Queensboro Plaza. F to 21st St. /Queensbridge and 23rd St. /Ely Ave., Queens Plaza. E and V to 21st St. /Van Alst, Court Square, Queens Plaza, 36th St. N and W to Queensboro Plaza, 39th Ave. /Beebe Ave., 36th St. /Washington Ave., Broadway. R and V to Queens Plaza, 36th St.

HOW TO GET THERE BY LIRR: Limited service only at Borden Ave. and 2nd St., and Hunter's Point and Skillman Aves.

OTHER WAYS TO GET THERE: New York Waterway ferry from Manhattan at 34th St. and Wall St.

WHAT'S NEARBY: Astoria to the north, Sunnyside to the southeast, Woodside to the east, midtown Manhattan to the west, and Greenpoint, Brooklyn, to the south.

MAJOR SHOPPING/RESTAURANT STREETS: Vernon Blvd., Jackson Ave., and Queens Plaza.

SPECIAL CHARACTERISTICS: Artists, museums, and art galleries.

ON NOT GETTING LOST: This is an old neighborhood, and distances between sites can be far. Check the map if you're walking. Also note that the E and V line stop at a station called 23rd and Ely. You will not find Ely St. on any street map, however, as it no longer exists. Also, Queens Plaza, Queensbridge, and Queensboro Plaza may sound similar but are different subway stations. Hunter's Point is the old section of town but it is not otherwise marked. Orient yourself to the Manhattan skyline, overhead subway, and Citicorp Bldg.

CAR SERVICES: Skyline 482-8585, Yes 539-7777, 274-4153, or 777-1234.

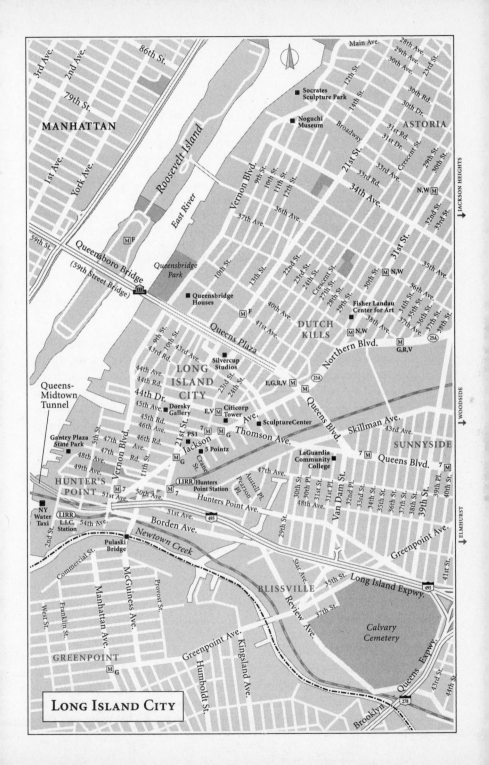

LONG ISLAND CITY

⚡ **Insight**

The City That Isn't

Let's get it straight! Long Island City is *not* a city. And it's *not* in Nassau or Suffolk Counties, which comprise Long Island, either. (Geographically speaking, purists could consider this area [and all of Queens and Brooklyn] part of Long Island, but politically speaking, Long Island City has been part and parcel of New York City for more than a century.)

If Long Island City is not in Long Island, then where the heck is it, anyway? If you cab down the FDR Drive, it's where that big PEPSI sign is when you look across the East River from the East 50s or 60s. If you're heading home from a Mets game on the #7 subway, it's where that outrageous-looking, graffiti-covered building is. If you've ever idly wondered where you'd land if a tornado plopped you down on the non-Manhattan side of the Queensboro Bridge, it's Long Island City.

AN ART EPICENTER

Long Island City is gritty. It was built for trucks, machines, and manufacturing, unlike human-scaled residential Astoria nearby where you're likely to see senior citizens, teenagers, and even the occasional grape arbor. Lacking in street trees and (except in the parks) general greenery, Long Island City is unforgivingly hot in New York's blazing summers. In the winter the wind whips off the East River and howls down broad, empty side streets. For a century, Long Island City was so industrial one could barely have called it a "neighborhood."

Yet in the past decade or so, Long Island City has been morphing into LIC, a hot spot of artists and art institutions. Just one subway stop from Grand Central Terminal, LIC boasts an East River waterfront that stretches for two miles with views of the United Nations, the Empire State Building, and the Chrysler Building. More important, there are five major arts institutions here, thousands of working artists, and many art studios.

THINGS TO SEE AND DO

P.S. 1 is one of New York's best-respected museums of avant-garde art, and an affiliate of the Museum of Modern Art. The Noguchi Museum is a marvelously calm indoor/outdoor museum, created from the studio where sculptor Isamu Noguchi worked in his later years. SculptureCenter shows large-scale cutting-edge works, some created specifically for its unusual factory-turned-gallery space created by Maya Lin. Socrates Sculpture Park's outdoor waterfront exhibit space and public park is the site for festivals, outdoor movies, artist residencies, and sculpture exhibitions. The Fisher Landau Center for Art has made available for public viewing a private collection of over 1,000 works by major artists from 1960 to the present. Dorsky Gallery, a nonprofit exhibition space, produces four independently curated exhibitions a year. Many arts organizations are members of the Long Island City Cultural Alliance, which produces an on-line culture map and quarterly program guide (see pp. 210–11).

Long Island City is so spread out that it's impossible to see all the art venues in a single day. Compared to Williamsburg or DUMBO, cafés and bars are still few and far between. The best approach is to divide and conquer. Here are three recommended itineraries, though of course you can make your own. Check the Web sites for exhibition information and travel directions.

 THREE ART ITINERARIES

1. SculptureCenter, P.S. 1, and Dorsky Gallery. These three venues are close enough to walk from one to another. If you are hungry, snack in the P.S. 1 cafeteria (although it's pricey), or finish with a fresh crêpe at Café Henri near Vernon Blvd. Visit nearby shops such as Subdivision. You could also fit in forty minutes for our Hunter's Point Historic District Walking Tour.

2. Noguchi Museum and Socrates Sculpture Park. It's wise (but not essential) to visit both in good weather, if possible, as the former has a sculpture garden and the latter is a sculpture garden. Check the schedule of the Socrates Sculpture Park in summer for festivals or films. Both are hefty walks from the nearest subways. About a mile away, Astoria's eateries are accessible by car.

3. Fisher Landau and the Museum of the Moving Image. These are very different kinds of museums, a healthy half-mile walk from each other. Fisher Landau is contemporary, austere, and high-end; the Museum of the Moving Image in Astoria is filled with interactive exhibits and, of course, movies. There are several restaurants within walking distance of the Museum of the Moving Image.

What to Do, Other Than Art

Year-round you can play tennis at Tennisport and enjoy incredible views. In summer it's fun to see an outdoor film at the Socrates Sculpture Park and attend a Friday night Warm Up at P.S. 1. Or, take the Water Taxi across from Manhattan and relax in a faux beach setting with a drink and elk burger at Harry's LIC at Water Taxi Beach. Tournesol and Café Henri please the palate as well as Manhattan's best and at lower prices. Nearby, Manducati's old-fashioned Italian restaurant has fans citywide. Any time of year, you can enjoy an excellent meal at a Vernon Blvd. restaurant for less than Manhattan prices and get tickets to a performance art piece or dance at the Chocolate Factory. Whatever you do, try to visit LIC at night. When the lights go on at night, you've got one of the best cityscape views in the city, of the United Nations, the Citicorp, Empire State, and Chrysler buildings, and all of midtown Manhattan. For no admission fee whatsoever (other than a subway fare) you can take a romantic walk along the waterfront and ogle the views. When you just can't get to the beach, hop the subway and join other sunbathers at Gantry Plaza State Park, where you can daydream while watching East River boat traffic.

BITS OF HISTORY

Long Island City was an independent municipal entity in the 1800s. Back then, it subsumed Ravenswood, Dutch Kills, Hunter's Point, Astoria, Steinway, and a handful of other neighborhoods. You can see vestiges of the early communities in buildings that date between 1850 and 1900 in the Hunter's Point historic district (see pp. 216–17). Long Island City joined New York City in 1898, dissolving its municipal independence. When the Queensboro Bridge opened in 1909, followed by the opening of the IRT subway six years later, the population swelled and many industries located there. The list of companies reads like an early history of New York manufacturing. However, industry flagged after World War II as manufacturing moved out of the city. Some large factories and warehouses were vacant for decades, until "discovered" by pioneering artists seeking space, great light, views, and cheap rents. P.S. 1 was the first major art institution to gain public recognition, establishing LIC as a place to go see art.

PARKS, PUBLIC SPACES, AND PUBLIC WORKS

Parks and Waterfront
☺ **GANTRY PLAZA STATE PARK.** 474 48th Ave. at the East River, 786-6385, or call New York City information line 311. www.nycgovparks.org. Open daily year-round. No pets.

Come for a picnic or a tan. Come for free summer concerts, or to watch the Fourth of July fireworks over the East River. This award-winning park transformed two giant defunct railroad "thingees," called gantries, and four piers into a postindustrial waterfront experience. From the park you get big-sky, zilliondollar views of the Empire State Building and the United Nations. Recreational facilities include seating, playgrounds, handball courts, and a fishing pier with its own cleaning table. Part of the New York State Park system since 1998, Gantry Plaza State Park is proof positive that Queens waterfront redevelopment can indeed work. (NOTE: The park is not named for Sinclair Lewis's book *Elmer Gantry*. A gantry is a giant metal frame spanning the railroad tracks that were once used to load and unload rail-car floats and barges.)

LIC COMMUNITY BOATHOUSE. Anable Pier, Hallets Cove on East River at 44th Dr., 786-8388. www.licboathouse.org. Contact for schedule and directions by car, subway, and kayak.

Paddlers and other water lovers will find this an incredible opportunity. Long Island Community Boathouse offers recreational paddling programs and free boat tours. You can also arrange for canoe and kayak rides in protected coves. It is run by volunteers with an interest in opening up both New York Harbor and the Queens waterfront for environmentally friendly community use.

☺ **MURRAY PLAYGROUND.** 21st St. bet. 45th Ave. and 45th Rd. Dog run at 21st St. and 45th Rd.

If you schlep little kids to the museums in LIC, you can bring them here afterward for an outdoor break. They can swing on the swings or play basketball while you gaze at the Empire State Building and Chrysler Building across the East River. If Fido comes along, the dog run is at 21st St. and 45th Rd. on the southeastern part of the park.

☺ **NEW YORK WATER TAXI.** 2 Borden Ave., near the Tennis Center, at the East River, (212) 742-1969. www.nywatertaxi.com. Multiday passes are available. M–F 6:45 a.m.–10:00 a.m., 3:45 p.m.–7:00 p.m. every forty-five minutes; weekends Apr.–Oct. $5.50 each way. Call or check Web site as schedules do change.

You can take the New York Water Taxi to Long Island City from Manhattan's 34th St. or Wall Street piers, or Brooklyn's DUMBO at Fulton Ferry. The yellow catamarans decorated with black-and-white checks offer comfy seats, views, and a small café/bar. If you miss the boat you can always nip into the Waterfront Crab House (see p. 219) for a drink. TIP: The New York Water Taxi docks about a mile from P.S. 1 and there is no cab stand; be prepared to hike or call a local car service. The Long Island City stop is called Hunter's Point, the historic name for this area.

NEWTOWN CREEK AND NEWTOWN CREEK ALLIANCE. 875-5200. www.newtowncreek.org.

Newtown Creek should be Long Island City's own glorious little canal. Instead it is bright green in places, a stagnant three-and-a-half-mile stretch that serves as a natural boundary (and mutual headache) for Brooklyn and Queens. It was used in the 1800s to ferry agricultural products from Long Island and Queens farms to the growing metropolis. As the city's economy shifted to manufacturing, a host of industrial firms—oil refineries based in Greenpoint, fertilizer, rope works, shipyards, glue companies, and others—polluted the waterway. Some of the pollution is of more recent vintage. In late 2005, a lawsuit was filed against three oil companies by Greenpoint, Brooklyn, residents over ill-health effects of a tank explosion that left a fifty-five-acre underground oil spill that today is a U.S. Superfund site. Visitors should heed the NO SMOKING signs.

Community activists such as the nonprofit entity Newtown Creek Alliance are working toward a cleanup here and along the entire Long Island City water-front. The City Parks Foundation (www.cityparksfoundation.org) is undertak-ing projects that link these areas that line the East River in northwestern Queens. Watch for special events, environmental cleanup, and developing plans for a continuous waterfront greenway.

Bridges and Tunnels

PULASKI BRIDGE. 50th Ave. in Queens or at McGuiness Ave. and Freeman St. in Greenpoint, Brooklyn.

This six-lane drawbridge over Newtown Creek might well be called the Hip-ster Bridge (it connects LIC and Greenpoint, Brooklyn) or the Halfway Bridge (it's Mile 13 in the New York City Marathon). It's named after Polish freedom fighter Casimir Pulaski (1747–79) who was recruited by Benjamin Franklin to help the colonies in the war against the British. "I came here," Pulaski wrote to General Washington, "where freedom is being defended, to serve it, and to live and die for it." Patriot or mercenary, die he did at the Battle of Savannah in 1779. (See also Kosciuszko Bridge, below.)

KOSCIUSZKO BRIDGE. Brooklyn-Queens Expwy. from Morgan Avenue in Brooklyn leading to the Long Is-land Expressway (LIE) cutoff in Queens.

If the Kosciuszko Bridge, connecting Brooklyn and Queens, always seems congested, that's because 170,000 vehicles a day cross this one-mile segment of the Brooklyn-Queens Expressway (BQE). The bridge was built in the 1930s, and named after Thaddeus Kosciuszko, a Polish engineer born in 1746 who offered his services to the American colonies, became a friend of General Washington's, and ultimately became chief engineer of West Point. One of the bridge towers is adorned with eagles: one Polish and one American.

QUEENS MIDTOWN TUNNEL. On Queens side: Long Island Expressway (Route 495) or 11th and 21st Sts. In Manhattan: 34th St. bet. 1st and 2nd Aves. and 36 St. near 2nd Ave.

Built in 1940, the Queens-Midtown Tunnel is a two-tube tunnel running un-der the East River. It connects Manhattan's East Side to Long Island City. When the traffic flows, it can be wondrously fast. When it doesn't, grab an aspirin for that headache, and try not to breathe the fumes. The tunnel was built in 1940 by the New York City Tunnel Authority and was designed by Ole Singstad, who was also chief engineer of the Holland Tunnel. TRIVIA: Once a year in mid-March after midnight the Ringling Bros. Barnum and Bailey circus animals march through the Queens Midtown Tunnel to make a grand entrance to New York City, eventually arriving at Madison Square Garden.

🏛 **QUEENSBORO BRIDGE (AKA 59TH ST. BRIDGE).** Queens: Between 11th St. and Bridge Plaza No. and Bridge Plaza So. Manhattan: On 2nd Ave. bet. 59 and 60th Sts. in Manhattan. Cyclist entrance is at Queens Plaza and Crescent St.

This gorgeous 1909 cantilevered structure helped transform Queens, making accessible huge tracts of land for urban/suburban living. Modeled on the Pont Mirabeau in Paris, it was designed by architect Henry Hornbostel and engineer Gustav Lindenthal. In its early days the bridge had six lanes for motor vehicles, four pairs of trolley tracks, two elevated subway lines, and lanes for pedestrians and bicyclists. The trolley was discontinued in 1957. The Queensboro Bridge is listed on the National Register of Historic Places and today has ten lanes, with biking and walking pathways on the North Outer Roadway. A multidecade rehab project is slated for completion by 2009.

The views are stupendous heading into Manhattan. Various writers, photographers, and filmmakers have immortalized it. In *The Great Gatsby*, F. Scott Fitzgerald wrote, "The city seen from the Queensboro Bridge is always the city seen for the first time, in its first wild promise of all the mystery and beauty in the world." The Queensboro Bridge makes an appearance in movies like *Spider-Man* and *The Interpreter*. Simon and Garfunkel's smash hit "Feelin' Groovy" was also called "The 59th St. Bridge Song."

Oh, and to avoid confusion, be aware that this bridge goes by two names. Queens residents tend to call it the 59th St. Bridge, but officially it's the Queensboro Bridge.

POINTS OF CULTURAL INTEREST

Museums and Major Galleries

In LIC art tends to be mostly made and shown, rather than bought and sold. Unlike SoHo and Chelsea, there are few commercial galleries here. The convergence of so many nonprofit museums and galleries alongside many artists' studios makes for a lower-key environment.

DORSKY GALLERY CURATORIAL PROGRAMS. 11-03 45th Ave., near 11th St., 937-6317. www.dorsky.org. W–Su 11:00 a.m.–6:00 p.m.

A nonprofit exhibition space, Dorsky Galleries produces four independently curated exhibitions a year. The rotating curators who select the artwork are an eclectic lot including, for instance, art historians, artists, and museum-based curators, which ensures a fresh perspective. In operation since 2001, Dorsky has been an important participant in the growing arts community in Long Island City.

FISHER LANDAU CENTER FOR ART. 38-27 30th St., 937-0727. www.flcart.org. Th–M, noon–5:00 p.m. Visitors can obtain a free LICCA culture map of Long Island City by phone.

The cool, calm, and modern Fisher Landau Center for Art is one of New York's best-kept museum treasures. That's because when it first opened in 1991 it stashed a private collection and has been open to the public only since 2003. It is a 25,000-square-foot exhibition and study facility. The core of the 1,100-work collection spans from 1960 to the present. It contains key works by artists who have shaped the most significant art of the last forty years, including Jenny Holzer, Jasper Johns, Donald Judd, Robert Rauschenberg, Ed Ruscha, Kiki Smith, and Cy Twombly, to cite a few. This building was previously a parachute harness factory, and was renovated by Max Gordon, the architect of London's Saatchi Gallery, together with designer Bill Katz. Behind all of this wondrous gift to the public is philanthropist Emily Fisher and her husband, Sheldon Landau.

GARTH CLARK GALLERY. 45-46 21st St. bet. 45th Rd. and 46th Ave., 706-2491. www.garthclark.com. By appointment only.

In 2001 ceramics specialist Garth Clark opened his gallery in Long Island City, in addition to the Garth Clark Gallery in midtown Manhattan. The gallery claims to sell more contemporary ceramic art on the New York resale market than Christies, Sotheby's, and Phillips combined. Among the over three dozen well-known ceramicists represented by this gallery are Akio Takamori, Kurt Weiser, and Sir Anthony Caro, perhaps Britain's greatest living sculptor. The LIC gallery shows are dedicated to experimental works.

☺ **NOGUCHI MUSEUM.** 9-01 33rd Rd. bet. 9th and 10th Sts., 204-7088. www.noguchi.org. W–F 10:00 a.m.–5:00 p.m., Sa–Su 11:00 a.m.–6:00 p.m. Suggested contribution: $5 for adults; $2.50 for seniors and students. Check the Web site about weekend shuttle-bus service to and from Manhattan.

Peaceful is the word harried New Yorkers often use to describe the Noguchi Museum. And so it is. Japanese-American sculptor Isamu Noguchi worked from 1975 until his death in 1988 in this converted photo-engraving plant. Today the entire space is a sculpture garden dedicated to his work. About 240 of Noguchi's pieces—including stone, metal, and wood pieces, models for gardens, dance sets, and his Akari Light sculptures—are set both indoors and in a small outdoor garden punctuated with huge granite and basalt pieces. Everyone, it seems, falls in love with a different piece of sculpture, but few depart unmoved. Come for an hour or two, or for Second Sundays talks and concerts. Don't miss the recently renovated education center, café, and shop. The Noguchi Museum is a true urban oasis.

P.S. 1. CONTEMPORARY ART CENTER. 22-25 Jackson Ave. at 46th Ave. 784-2084. www.ps1.org. Th–M noon–6:00 p.m. Suggested contribution: $5 for adults; $2 for seniors and students. Free for MoMA members and MoMA admission ticket holders. (The MoMA ticket must be presented at P.S. 1 within thirty days of date on ticket; not valid for Warm Up.)

Wickedly inventive, an invitation to imagination, P.S. 1 is a captivating place. It's a museum, but its mission, in a sense, is to break the mold of what you expect to find in a "museum." P.S. 1 was Public School #1 from 1893 until 1963. Except for artwork everywhere and the bustle of a bright, artsy young staff, the building still looks and feels like a one-hundred-year-old school, complete with long narrow hallways. The museum's curators use every part of it as exhibit space, including the hot water pipes, institutional stairs, and even the downstairs boiler room with a dirt floor. Some semipermanent pieces were designed specifically for the space, such as the silhouettes by William Kentridge in the stairwells, but in general, exhibits change three or four times a year. Wandering from room to room—each one a different environment—visitors may find themselves bemused, amused, and challenged by the unconventional experience.

WARMUP (July–Sept. Sa 3:00 p.m.–9:00 p.m. $8 admission) is P.S. 1's critically acclaimed annual summer music festival series. A young, artsy, single crowd that comes from Queens, Brooklyn, and downtown Manhattan crams into P.S. 1's large outdoor courtyard for live DJ music, dancing, and socializing. On display are installations designed by winners of the Young Architects Program, who've created their vision of an "urban beach" in the courtyard.

Started in 1971 by Alana Heiss, P.S. 1 today is an affiliate of the Museum of Modern Art. P.S. 1 served as MoMA's home-away-from-home for several years when MoMA's 53rd St. building was undergoing renovation and expansion. Recognized internationally as well as in the United States as a leader in the alternative space movement, P.S. 1 was also a pioneer in the transformation of Long Island City from a dreary manufacturing area to a vibrant cultural center.

P.S. 1's **DAP** bookstore is the best art bookstore in Queens. LeRosier Café serves coffee and light lunches, and, of course, is also used as an opportunity to display art. Gallery talks led by artists whose work are on exhibit come free with the price of admission. P.S. 1 operates www.wps1.org, the world's first Internet art radio station, sponsored by Bloomberg L.P., as well as the Clocktower Gallery in Lower Manhattan.

SCULPTURECENTER. 44-19 Purves St., off Jackson Ave., 361-1750. www.sculpture-center.org. Th–M, 11:00 a.m.–6:00 p.m. New shows in Jan., May, and Sept. Admission is free with a suggested donation.

Founded in 1928, the nonprofit SculptureCenter has a reputation for showing edgy, often large sculptural pieces, sometimes specifically created to fit within its unusual 6,000-square-foot indoor/outdoor exhibition space. It mounts three cutting-edge exhibits every four months, drawing on emerging and established, national and international artists. Having relocated from the stodgier environs of Manhattan's Upper East Side in 2000, today SculptureCenter is housed in a former trolley repair building reconfigured into an exhibition space. The renovation was designed by Maya Lin, whose Vietnam War Memorial in Washington, D.C., and other work have won international acclaim. SculptureCenter also has an artist in residence program and image library. Check the Web site for a calendar of artists' talks, lectures, and screenings.

☺ **SOCRATES SCULPTURE PARK.** 32-01 Vernon Blvd. at Broadway. 956-1819. www.socratessculpture park.org, Daily 10:00 a.m.–sunset.

It's scruffy and industrial. Socrates Sculpture Park is four and a half acres spotted with iconoclastic contemporary sculptural works. Previously an illegal waterfront junkyard, reclaimed as an internationally renowned outdoor museum, Socrates is well situated for eye-popping views of Manhattan. You can attend concerts, outdoor theater, a springtime kite festive, summer solstice and Halloween celebrations, and bring the kids for children's classes, all in a unique outdoor setting. Summer outdoor movies here are one of the Big Apple's best free events.

Socrates Sculpture Park was created by one of the urban pioneers who forged "something out of nothing" in LIC, made beauty where there had been just a landfill beast. What you see today is a labor of love by a coalition of artists and community members under the leadership of artist Mark di Suvero. They reconfigured this space as open studio and exhibition space combined with public access to a waterfront park, in the belief "that reclamation, revitalization, and creative expression are essential to our urban environment." Socrates Sculpture Park offers artist residencies.

☛ **TIP: Traveler's Advisory.** It's a long and unpretty hike from the other cultural institutions and the nearest subway, the N. If you can, travel by car.

☀ Insight

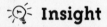

Old Factories and Warehouses Become Hip Art Spaces

Long Island City has one foot in the past and one in the future. Many of its large old industrial buildings are being adapted and reused for art studios, galleries, and museums. P.S. 1 was brilliantly created from a lumbering old school building. The giant Silvercup bakery plant has been recycled into a world-class television and movie production studio, where stars like Dustin Hoffman have worked. As it expands, the company continues to transform old industrial buildings into studios. Socrates Sculpture Park offers the public both art and green space created from a waterside dump site. The Noguchi Museum was originally a photo-engraving plant. And so on.

Officials estimate that there are about 2,000 artists in the Long Island City area. Among those who live and work in Long Island City, there's a neighborliness, a touch of urban pioneering spirit. Sometimes in the summer you hear loud music coming from the window of a warehouse on a lonesome street, a sure sign of a loft party going on. The restaurants and cafés are as chummy as a Vermont ski hut in a blizzard.

Other LIC Art Spaces and Performance Venues

ARTISTS STUDIO BUILDINGS. Not open to the public.

If your image of an artist is of a lonely Van Gogh painting away in splendid isolation, that's not necessarily what's happening in Long Island City. While of course some artists work alone, many entire buildings have been retrofitted into studio spaces accommodating not two or three, but twenty or thirty art studios for people working in a wide range of media. The public is welcome to visit some studios during the twice yearly Open Studio events organized by **LONG IS-LAND CITY ARTISTS, INC.**, 784-2935. www.licartists.org.

Within just a couple of blocks of each other, **JUVENAL REIS STUDIOS** (43-01 22nd St., 784-5530, www.juvenalreis.com) is an umbrella for about thirty artists' studios. Nearby, **WILLS ART DECO BUILDING** (43-01 21st St., 706-0370) houses several dozen artist's studios as well. **INDEPENDENT STUDIOS** (10-26 46th Ave., 729-8001) is an artist's collective started in 1978. Also, numerous organizations exist to support artists, such as **THE SPACE** (42-16 West St., corner of Queens Plaza So. and Jackson Ave., www.licweb.com/thespace) and **LOCAL PROJECT** (see p. 210). The latter offers open-to-the-public films and events.

CENTER FOR HOLOGRAPHIC ARTS. 45-10 Court Square, near Jackson and Thomson Aves., 784-5065, www.holocenter.org. By appointment; see Web site for special events.

Started in 1998, the Center for the Holographic Arts promotes the development of the art of holography, sponsoring an artist-in-residence program, small exhibitions, and talks.

CHOCOLATE FACTORY. 5-49 49th Ave., off Vernon Blvd., 482-7069. www.chocolatefactorytheater.org. Hours depend on performance schedule.

Located in an old factory building previously used for the manufacture of paints, and subsequently chocolates, this quirky performance space provides rough-hewn, moody environments for a range of contemporary dance, theater, music, and exhibits. Popular with Williamsburg and other hipsters, it's attracting increasing attention from the art mainstream.

5 POINTZ. 46-23 Crane St. at Davis and Jackson Ave, across the street from P.S. 1. 592-9700 (x 306). www.5ptz.com. Open mornings and afternoons during the week and on weekends. Occasional events on the weekend.

Riders of the #7 subway line are all too familiar with the once abandoned industrial building that stands on Jackson Ave. in Long Island City. Almost every inch of its exterior walls has been covered in bright tags, murals, and designs. It's exuberant. It's outrageous. It's an unofficial landmark. Inside, there are about forty studio artists from all over the world on five floors, doing sculpture, mixed media, installation, textile arts, fine jewelry, prints, and more, from the most classical styles to cutting-edge work. Inside the building there's more graffiti in the stairwells. You can see a short video clip of the graffiti on the Web site.

The project was originally known as the Phun Factory, and it evolved from an effort to stop defacement of buildings, which led to the idea that graffiti artists could be channeled into working on permitted spaces.

LOCAL PROJECT. 21-36 44th Rd., 433-2779. www.localproject.org. Call for hours.

Founded in 2003, this nonprofit organization is dedicated to building a community for area artists involved in video, photography, music, and visual art and helping new and emerging artists find professional networks. There's an international flair here; many of the people involved are from various countries in Latin America. Visitors can attend period film series on Sunday afternoons where local work is shown.

MATERIALS FOR THE ARTS. 33-00 Northern Blvd. at 33rd St., 729-3001. www.mfta.org. Not open to public, only nonprofit entities.

Materials for the Arts' mission is retrieval and recycling. It takes materials that are one person's junk—plywood, paints, furniture, props, wiring, whatever—for recycling to nonprofit arts organizations like museums, community theaters, and school-based art programs. On their Most Wanted List are office chairs, new computers and computer equipment, video and projection equipment, wallpaper and home decorating supplies, and, well, stuff. Donors range from Queens-based Kaufman Astoria and Silvercup Studios to multinationals like AT&T. Offering something to everyone, it is supported by the city departments of education, culture, and sanitation.

LONG ISLAND CITY ARTISTS (LICA). 37-06 36th St. near 37th Ave., 784-2935. www.licartists.org. Call for hours.

This fifteen-year-old nonprofit organization works to assist local artists. If you want to see what local artists are working on, be sure to attend their public art events, including annual Open Studio events representing the work of many sculptors, painters, photographers, and other artists. LICA also has a large slide registry for member artists living in Queens.

LONG ISLAND CITY CULTURAL ALLIANCE AND CULTURE MAP (LICCA). www.licarts .org. See their Web site for contact info.

This cultural umbrella organization includes major museums and nonprofit galleries in LIC, plus a few organizations from other neighborhoods. Members include the Dorsky Gallery Curatorial Programs, the Fisher Landau Center for Art, Museum for African Art, Museum of the Moving Image, the Noguchi Museum, P.S. 1 Contemporary Art Center, SculptureCenter, Socrates Sculpture Park, and Thalia Spanish Theatre. LICCA publishes a quarterly guide to arts and culture in Long Island City that is distributed citywide. During their Summer in LongIsCity each organization offers special programs, including music, multimedia performances, artist-led tours, and art workshops. See their Web site for a downloadable culture map, or call the Fisher Landau Center for Art at 937-0727 to have one mailed to you. You can also order a groovy T-shirt with "Long Island City" written in old-fashioned script lettering from them.

☛ **TIP: Alphabet Soup.** Don't get confused between two similar-sounding art organizations in Long Island City. One is LICCA, the Long Island City Cultural Alliance (www.licarts.org). The other is LICA, Long Island City Artists, Inc. (www.licartists.org). The former has as members some leading museums and a handful of major nonprofit arts organizations based in Queens (though not all of them). The latter represents individual artists and organizes Studio Tours.

NY DESIGNS. 45-50 30th St. at 45th Ave., 482-5960. www.lagcc.cuny.edu/lgincubator. Call for gallery hours, as shows vary.

Don't miss the shows at the NY Designs' curated gallery. Nonprofit NY Designs, under the umbrella of LaGuardia Community College, has transformed a 25,000-square-foot space in the humongous old Sunshine Biscuit Factory into a state-of-the-art design center. It serves as an incubator for about two dozen small specialty design firms working in product design, industrial design, fashion design, graphic design, interior design, architecture, lighting design, set design, jewelry, and craft. Participants get a great package: business consulting, office space, private studio spaces, conference rooms, and access to 9,000 square feet of workshops with equipment for metal and woodwork, mold and cast jewelry, and design packaging, as well as a paint shop. If you're interested, you can take a course here, too, for instance in Guerilla Marketing for Professional Designers. The curated shows exhibit some of the design products being created by participating firms.

OPEN STUDIO TOUR. (See Long Island City Artists, p. 210.)

PHUN PHACTORY. (See 5 Pointz, pp. 209–10.)

SILVERCUP STUDIOS. 42-22 22nd St. at the base of the Queensboro Bridge, 361-6188. No public tours.

Everybody knows it takes a lot of dough to make hit movies. In 1983, the Sunas family, a father-and-two-sons trio, recycled the former flour silo room of the Silvercup Bakery into film studios. It's since expanded to 400,000 square feet of production facilities, the largest independent film and television production facility in the northeastern United States. The old bakery-turned-studio is marked by the huge 1952 Silvercup sign visible from Manhattan and the Queensboro Bridge. The name Silvercup has long been associated with entertainment. If you were a kid in the 1950s or 1960s and listened to the Lone Ranger on radio, you may remember the commercial sponsor: It was Silvercup Bread.

The roster of feature films completed here is huge. It includes *When Harry Met Sally, Godfather III,* and *Romancing the Stone.* Nicole Kidman (in *Birth*) and Robert DeNiro (in *Hide and Seek*) have filmed here. Just about everyone in America has seen TV shows filmed at Silvercup Studios. *The Sopranos* and *Sex and the City* were filmed here. The ABC comedy *Hope and Faith* was filmed here. So were CBS's *Now and Again, Welcome to New York, The Education of Max Bickford,* and *Queens Supreme. Sopranos'* fans may recognize the set for some episodes at the nearby **PUNTA DURA RESTAURANT** (4115 34th Ave. bet. 41st-42nd Sts. in Astoria, 721-2137), which displays Tony Soprano's picture outside.

An expansion to a third studio site, Silvercup Studios West, has been mapped out by British architect Lord Richard Rogers, designer of the Centre Pompidou in Paris. This project will transform six acres on Vernon Blvd. into film studios, offices, apartments, shops, and a cultural organization. The new site encompasses the landmark New York Architectural Terra Cotta Company building (see listing, p. 217).

In 2005 Silvercup built an environmentally friendly "green roof" atop the bakery building, a contribution to cleaning up the air in LIC.

WOMEN'S STUDIO CENTER. 21-25 44 Ave. at 21st St., 361-5649. womenstudiocenter.org. M–F 1 p.m.–9 p.m., or by appointment.

The Women's Center provides a nurturing environment for professional or aspiring writers and artists, who can rent studio space, hear published authors speak, draw from live models, attend drawing workshops, and get some practical tips on the business side of art. Participants are men and women of all ages. Women's Studio Center is invitingly nestled in a restored warehouse with eighteen-foot ceilings and glass block windows.

Other Points of Cultural Interest
BREWSTER BUILDING. 27th St. and Queens Plaza.

Now officially the Bridge Plaza Tech Center, this huge 1911 building in Queens Plaza has been renovated by the Metropolitan Life Insurance Company. It once housed the manufacturing plant for Brewster carriages, the high-end, horse-drawn carriage of the early twentieth century before the age of the automobile. Cole Porter included a line about them in his song "You're the Tops" from the 1934 musical *Anything Goes.*

BROADWAY'S BACKSTAGE PRODUCTION AREA. Borden Ave. and Vernon Blvd. Not open to the public.

With its warehouses, convenient access to Manhattan, and creative talent, LIC is home to many companies that provide behind-the-scenes necessities for Broadway and Off-Broadway theater productions. **KRYPTON NEON** (34-43 Vernon Blvd. at 34th St., 728-4450) produces high-tech neon signs that have appeared in films, television shows, and also in Broadway shows from *Spamalot* to *La Cage Aux Folles* to *The Producers.*

Companies on Borden Ave. (bet. 5th and 2nd Sts.) rent theatrical draperies and rigging equipment for Broadway shows and various other performing arts companies. **ALCONE** (5-49 49th Ave., off Vernon Blvd., 361-8373) is housed in an elegant old building built by the Mutual Hardware Company. Inside, Alcone is a manufacturer of theatrical makeup. With the expansion of both Silvercup and nearby Kaufman Astoria Studios in Astoria, film production facilities have moved here, too.

CITICORP TOWER. Court Square, near Jackson and Thomson Aves., M–F 8:00 a.m.–6:00 p.m.

In 1989 when the head of Citicorp cut the ribbon on this modern fifty-story building designed by Skidmore, Owings & Merrill, it was cleverly hailed as the tallest structure between New York and Boston. (Manhattan's taller skyscrapers are to the south.) The Citicorp Tower mirrors Citicorp's world headquarters across the East River on 53rd St. In the lobby level you'll find an unusually spiffy New York City public library, food court, and small shops geared to serve the 3,000-plus people who work here. The lobby doubles as an art gallery area where local artists' works are sometimes on display.

HAGSTROM MAP COMPANY, INC. 36-36 33rd St., (800) 432-6277. Not open to the public.

How fitting that a premier mapmaker is headquartered in a borough as geographically confusing as Queens.

☺ **LAGUARDIA COMMUNITY COLLEGE (CUNY).** 31-10 Thomson Ave. at 31st St., 482-7200. www.lagcc.cuny.edu.

LaGuardia calls itself the World's Community College for good reason. Students hail from 150 countries and represent the very face of a multicultural, diverse society. LaGuardia offers thirty-one degree and three certificate programs; many students go on to four-year colleges. It has the lowest college tuition in the City University of New York system. LaGuardia Community College is based in a 1930s building that was originally the Equitable Bag Company factory. This is an example of the adaptive reuse of many old manufacturing plants located in the heart of LIC that have been renovated and adapted for reuse in the information age.

Visitors might be interested to know of some innovative programs here, including a school for cab drivers ("charm school for cabbies," as a news report dubbed it), interpreter education for the deaf, and a new program called **NY DESIGNS** (see p. 211). You can attend shows at **LAGUARDIA PERFORMING ARTS CENTER** (ticket office 482-5151), which is known as *the* place in Queens for children's theater. Bring the kids for family matinees of theater, dance, and music with performances by groups such as the Paper Bag Players and the Nai-Ni Chen Dance Company. Adult evening shows include films and an impressive Jazz Jam series. Tickets start at $12 and it's located close to Manhattan and subway lines.

History buffs may enjoy the free exhibit on the history of New York City. History buffs may enjoy the free exhibit on the history of New York City. The college also keeps a collection of documents relating to the Mayors of New York City called the **LAGUARDIA AND WAGNER ARCHIVES** www.laguardiawagnerarchive.lagcc .cuny.edu (482-5065), as well as those of the piano maker Steinway.

MING PAO NEWS. 43-31 33rd St. at 43rd Ave., 786-2888. Not open to public.

Printed daily, this Chinese newspaper covers the Chinese-American community and international news focusing on Hong Kong, Taiwan, and Mainland China. Papers are distributed in nearby Flushing and elsewhere.

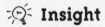 **Insight**

☺ Pepsi Sign and Other Rooftop Signs

Part of the industrial charm of LIC is its rooftop signage. The 120-foot-long original Pepsi sign visible from Manhattan was constructed during the 1930s. The Pepsi plant is long gone but the sign, rebuilt in 1994, remains as a testimony to Long Island City's industrial past. (Note that the Pepsi sign is geared to the Manhattan viewer. From the Queens side, you read it backwards.) The Silvercup sign dates from 1952 (see p. 211–12). And the IDCNY sign sits atop the old Sunshine Biscuit factory, one of Long Island City's best-known brands. Sunshine Biscuit's ten-story 1921 building today is occupied by LaGuardia College.

QUEENSBRIDGE HOUSES AND PARK. Bet. Vernon Blvd. and the East River.

Queensbridge was one of the first and is still one of the largest public housing projects in the United States. It started as a dream of decency, built to help those left destitute by the Great Depression. It opened in 1939 with more than 3,000 units available only to people whose income fell beneath a certain level. It's so large that it has its own subway stop on the F train called "21st St. Queensbridge."

In the 1980s it was infamously plagued with drugs, thugs, and guns. Queensbridge Houses has produced numerous rap artists: Marlon "Marley Marl" and MC Shan, Roxanne Shanté, Nas, Mobb Deep, and Capone-N-Noreaga are among the stars. If you hear a reference to "the Bridge" in a rap song by Queens-born artists and it's got nothing to do with water, they're likely referring to Queensbridge Houses. A 2005 documentary called *Queensbridge: The Other Side,* by longtime resident Selena M. Blake, showed the positive side of the project, in terms of honest working-class families looking out for one another. Nearby, Queensbridge Park is a forty-acre park running between Queensboro

Plaza and 40th Ave., and between Vernon Blvd. and the East River. The area near the Queensbridge Houses public housing complex is heavily used by residents.

QUEENS PLAZA. 21st St. at Queens side of Queensboro Bridge.

You may wish to avoid this area at night. When New York's Mayor Giuliani oversaw the cleanup of Times Square in the late 1990s, some strip joints and related businesses of the flesh just moved across one bridge or another. Felons released from nearby Rikers Island are discharged in the area in the early dawn hours. Although part of the area near the MetLife building has been renamed MetLife Plaza, it's not a tourist destination.

☺ **SUBWAY ART.** www.nycsubway.org/perl/artwork.

MTA Arts for Transit, which selects artists through a formal competitive process, has mounted two different works in the LIC area. The first is in the corridors connecting the G subway at Long Island City Court Square with the E and V line at 23rd/Ely; Elizabeth Murray used glass mosaic murals to depict whimsical boots striding over the city skyline. The second is at 33rd St. /Rawson St. and was created by Korean-born Yumi Heo as an A-to-Z of Queens in stained glass. See if you can find *A* for Aqueduct racetrack, *B* for Botanical Gardens, and *D* for Dragon Boats. In addition there are large panels depicting the Redbirds subway cars, Queens children, and the Queensboro Bridge. (See the rest of the A-to-Z mural in Sunnyside stations at both 40th St. /Lowery and 46th St. /Bliss.)

TENNISPORT. 51-24 2nd St. at Borden Ave., 392-1880. www.tennisport.com.

Enjoy sixteen indoor and eight outdoor courts, a restaurant, massage facilities, and the works. Courts are open to nonmembers during the workweek. You can also reserve ahead for a Fourth of July barbecue with great cityscape views.

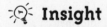 Insight

The Future: High-Rises with Mid-Manhattan Views

As we go to press, it's hard to find a place to live in LIC; the old housing stock is small. Because LIC originally developed as an industrial center, there are only a handful of row houses and older apartment buildings. Nevertheless, Long Island City is ideally suited to become a successful business district due to its location, just east of midtown Manhattan, and service by eight subway lines and an interstate highway. In 2001, a thirty-seven-block area was rezoned to allow up to 15 million square feet of commercial development and additional residential development.

The impact of the rezoning has already been felt at the residential level. You can't miss the forty-two-story luxury apartment **CITYLIGHTS AT QUEENS LAND-**

(continued)

ING (4-74 48th Ave. at 5th St., 786-2034). Built in 1997 in a New York real-estate boom period, most of its 500-plus co-ops have views of the Manhattan skyline. An old
Eagle Electric building on Thomson Ave. is being turned into residential lofts.
Queens West will include fifteen residential buildings, four commercial office
buildings, and 225,000 square feet of retail space. A new waterfront complex
called East Coast is promising over 3,000 units where the old Pepsi bottling plant
once stood. The first building will be thirty-one floors, designed by the world-
renowned Arquitectonica. Of course, dozens of industrial buildings have been
converted into artists' lofts as well.

Discussions have been held about ways to reduce traffic congestion, improve
the streetscapes, and create a better environment for pedestrians and cyclists who
want to reach offices, retail outlets, and cultural institutions in the area.

PEOPLE, PLACES, AND THINGS OF HISTORICAL INTEREST

GREATER ASTORIA HISTORICAL SOCIETY. Quinn Memorial Bldg., 35-20 Broadway, 4th floor, 278-
0700. www.astorialic.org. Sa noon–4:00 p.m. Research by appointment only.

A Queens virgin could be forgiven for asking the obvious: If Astoria is one
place, and Long Island City another, then why is the Greater Astoria Historical
Society located in Long Island City? When Long Island City was an actual city
(before Queens joined New York City in 1898), it was comprised of numerous
areas—Astoria, Steinway, Dutch Kills, Ravenswood, Hunter's Point, and Sunnyside. Astoria evolved as a distinct neighborhood. Today the historical society
covers topics of interest to a large swath of the borough. Be sure to check their
regular schedule of field trips, walking tours, slide presentations, and guest lectures. Contact them if you want to organize a group tour of the Steinway piano
factory, or learn about the history of transportation in New York.

The archives hold an unusual collection of historical artifacts, official maps,
and old atlases. There's also material assembled by Rev. Oliver Chapin, who was
a pastor for many decades on Roosevelt Island and collected information relating to the growth of prisons, hospitals, poorhouses, and asylums. The Greater
Astoria Historical Society is one of numerous local historical societies in
Queens.

🏛 **HUNTER'S POINT HISTORIC DISTRICT.** 45th Ave. bet. 21st and 23rd Sts.

Listed on the National Register of Historic Places, Hunter's Point historic district dates to the period between 1850 and 1900. The area was also known as
Dominie's Hook and Bennett's Point.

For a view of the historic row houses, see the Hunter's Point Historic District
Walking Tour, p. 217. Also in the area are the historic Engine Company 258 (10-
40 47th Ave.), 108th Police Precinct (5-47 50th Ave.), and St. Mary's Roman
Catholic Church (10-08 49th Ave.). A full description of the row houses, apart-

ment buildings, and institutions is available from the Queens Historical Society, which awarded the area their Queensmark designation.

🏛 🚶 HUNTER'S POINT HISTORIC DISTRICT WALKING TOUR

Give yourself a treat. Take a walk on 45th Ave., a Victorian-era street lined with redbrick row houses (a rarity in Queens), built when Hunter's Point was part of independent Long Island City.

Walk down 45th Ave. bet. 21st and 22nd Sts. Note the informative Landmarks Preservation Society sign in front of 21-40 45th Ave. Also look at #21–49, #51, and #53 45th Ave., all row houses typical of the late 1870s to 1880s, built with details such as a stone arch, stained glass, half-moon upper windows, iron railings, stoops, and elegant cornices. To see earlier wooden row houses, walk down Vernon Blvd. to 46th Rd. to see a grouping of row houses: #10–48, #50, and #52 46th Rd.

🏛 **NEW YORK ARCHITECTURAL TERRA COTTA COMPANY.** 42-10 Vernon Blvd. bet. Queens Plaza and 43rd Ave. Not open to the public.

New York was plagued by terrible fires throughout the nineteenth century. The New York Architectural Terra Cotta Company was one of New York's first successful manufacturers of fireproof architectural terra cotta. The use of fireproof terra cotta in building construction became popular, for both practical and ornamental purposes, from the late 1800s until the 1930s. To see how it was used decoratively, see the historic apartment building in Jackson Heights at 11-31 47th Rd. Silvercup Studios has announced plans to convert this landmark 1892 building (see pp. 211–12).

🏛 **LIC COURTHOUSE/NY STATE SUPREME COURT, 11TH JUDICIAL DISTRICT.** 25-10 Court Square at Jackson Ave. and Thomson Ave.

Long Island City became the seat of Queens County in 1870, before Queens joined New York City in 1898. The original 1877 courthouse burned down and was replaced with this fabulous 1908 Renaissance Revival Beaux Arts building. Picturesque enough to be in the movies, it is home to New York State Supreme Court.

OLD SWINGLINE FACTORY. 33rd St. and Queens Blvd., (212) 708-9400. Not open to the public.

The old Swingline Factory housed the MoMA administrative staff that kept things together when the Museum of Modern Art relocated to Queens while their Manhattan digs were undergoing renovation. Redubbed "The Factory," it is now used by MoMA for storage and research. It was originally used to make staplers and related products, another example of an adaptive reuse of an old manufacturing facility to a new service sector life. (See P.S. 1, pp. 206–7.)

P.S. 1. See listing, pp. 206–7.

SILVERCUP STUDIOS. See listing, pp. 211–12.

📖 **U.S. POST OFFICE.** 46-02 2nd St. bet. 46th Ave. and 46th Rd.

Built right before the big Wall Street crash of 1929, this old post office is one of the more elegant relics of industrial Long Island City. It occupies the width of a full city block. Note the old marble staircase, brass railing, and fabulous restored white-and-blue deco ceiling. It is listed on the National Register of Historic Places.

RESTAURANTS, CAFÉS, AND BARS

Restaurants

BELLA VIA. 46-76 Vernon Blvd. at 48th Ave., 361-7510. M–Sa noon–10:30 p.m., Su 3:00 p.m.–10:30 p.m.

Bella Via is beloved for its coal-fired, brick-oven pizza pies. The pizzas go beyond the standards to include the Bella Via (with sausage, broccoli raab, and mozzarella), quattro formaggi, and a killer focaccia with *bresaola* and arugula. Classier than a by-the-slice pizzeria, this beige-and-brick restaurant also has good pastas and classic Italian soups (*gagioli,* minestrone, and *stracciatella*). Also nearby is **MANETTA** (10-76 Jackson Ave. at 11th St., 786-6171. M–F 11:30 a.m.–10:00 p.m., Sa 4:00 p.m.–10:00 p.m.), which serves pizzas, plus a full Italian menu of chicken, fish, homemade pasta, and sandwiches.

MANDUCATIS. 13-27 Jackson Ave. at 47th Ave., 729-4602. M–F noon–3:00 p.m. and 5:00 p.m.–10:00 p.m., Sa 5:00 p.m.–10:00 p.m., Su 2:30 p.m.–8:00 p.m.

An Italian classic. Manducatis makes comfort food and keeps 'em coming back with a stage set–worthy, homey ambience that's too relaxing to resist. At lunch try a basic hero sandwich; at dinnertime you can order simply prepared substantial entrées such as fresh fish or roast baby pig. If you don't see exactly what you want, ask and they will cook it to order. The wine selection is surprisingly good at less-than-Manhattan prices. A meal costs about $40 per person.

RIVERVIEW RESTAURANT. 2-01 50th Ave. at 2nd St., 392-5000. Tu–Th 11:30 a.m.–3:00 a.m., F–Su 11:30 a.m.–4:00 a.m.

This large, perfect-for-a-special-occasion restaurant sparkles with zillion-dollar views of the Empire State and Chrysler buildings, not to mention the United Nations. The menu is eclectic American—steaks, salmon, plenty of salads—the decor is plush; and the prices are Manhattan. It's across from Gantry

Plaza State Park, near the new fancy Riverview and Avalon high-rises, on LIC's rapidly gentrifying waterfront.

TOURNESOL. 50-12 Vernon Blvd. at 50th Ave., 472-4355. Tu–F 11:30 a.m.–3:00 p.m., Tu–Sa 5:30 p.m.–11:00 p.m., Su 5:00 p.m.–10:00 p.m. Sa–Su brunch 11:30 a.m.–3:30 p.m.

Friendlier than most French restaurants, classy but comfortable, artsy Tournesol hits the spot both on style and substance. The menu is inventive French food. Try, for instance, a melt-in-your-mouth rabbit prepared with mushroom sauce, or poached salmon served on a bed of ratatouille lasagna. Save room for the chocolate mousse. It's so near Manhattan that you'll barely have time on the #7 subway to read your newspaper. All told, dinner runs about $40 per person. Reservations recommended.

TUK TUK. 49-06 Vernon Blvd., off 49th Ave., 472-5598. Su–Th, 11:30 a.m.–10:00 p.m., F, Sa 11:30 a.m.–10:30 p.m.

One of the first Smith Street, Brooklyn, transplants to Queens, Tuk Tuk is known for its *tom yum* soup, *khao* soy (crisp noodles served in a yellow curry with veggies), hot green chili, and even Thai ice cream. Opened in 2005 on Vernon Blvd., Tuk Tuk draws crowds—and rave reviews—for a hipster ambience and cheap, fiery, plentiful Thai food. What's a tuk tuk? It's a Thai version of a New York yellow cab.

WATER'S EDGE. 44th Drive and the East River at Vernon Blvd., 482-0033. Tu–Su 11:00 a.m.–11:00 p.m.

Water's Edge is so Manhattan you have to wonder if it got lost and ended up in Queens by mistake. The setting is lavish. The menu's a delight: artichoke hearts and chanterelles, Virginia crab bisque, Chilean sea bass with oven-dried tomatoes, or grilled sturgeon with sorrel-whipped potatoes and chanterelle mushrooms. As a cool perk, you get a free boat ride back and forth from Queens to the 34th St. Pier in Manhattan; schedules vary but generally run on the hour. Plus there's romantic al fresco dining in good weather. A full meal costs about $60. Reservations required.

WATERFRONT CRAB HOUSE. 2-03 Borden Ave. bet. 2nd and 5th Sts., 729-4862. Su–T noon–10:00 p.m., W–Th noon–11:00 p.m., F–Sa noon–midnight.

When you arrive by New York Water Taxi from Manhattan to this historic 1881 hotel-turned-restaurant, you feel like you've been transported a few hundred miles away. There's an inviting bar, kitschy decorations hanging from the rafters, live music, and a friendly waitstaff. Before the 1909 opening of the Queensboro Bridge, back when the only way to Queens was by ferryboat, people docked at Borden Ave. and ate and drank at this establishment. Past visiting dignitaries included Theodore Roosevelt. More recently, Dustin Hoffman, Maureen O'Hara, Paul Newman, and Ed Asner have been here, thanks to the proximity of both the New York Water Taxi pier and Kaufman Astoria Studios, where many stars have worked.

Cafés

CAFE HENRI. 1010 50th Ave. at Vernon Blvd., 383-9315. Daily 8:00 a.m.–midnight.

Stop in at this simple café for a well-prepared crêpe and fresh fruit, or smoked salmon with basil crème sauce, for the reasonable price (with a salad) of under $10.

COMMUNITEA. 47-02 Vernon Blvd. bet. 47th Rd. and 47th Ave., 729-7708. M–F 7:00 a.m.–8:00 p.m., Sa 9:00 a.m.–8:00 p.m., Su 10:00 a.m.–5:00 p.m.

Communitea is more than a coffee/teahouse. Sure, they sell a large variety of loose-leaf teas, hearty café-style food (try the curry chicken–salad sandwich and pesto chicken panino). There's also free Internet access, live music at least once a month, customer-run book and knitting clubs that meet here, and free access to a local message board called Neighbornodes. Check out the fliers about local goings-on.

HARRY'S LIC AT WATER TAXI BEACH. 2nd St. and Borden Ave., 855-2879. www.watertaxibeach.com. Th–F 4:00 p.m.–midnight, Sa–Su noon–midnight, Memorial Day–Columbus Day. Call to check hours.

What a hoot. Set up near the Water Taxi dock at a little faux beach this seasonal outdoor-only joint grills up your favorites: elk burgers and fish tacos. It's a camp version of an old beach shack. Indeed, they even imported sand from the Jersey Shore. Have a drink; enjoy the views. The ebullient characters who brought Schnack's irresistible miniburgers to Brooklyn opened the eponymous Harry's on LIC in 2005, and we hope they become a permanent fixture.

Bars

BROOKS 1890 RESTAURANT. 24-28 Jackson Ave., 937-1890. M–F 11:30 a.m.–8:00 p.m.

As if you hadn't already guessed, Brooks was founded in 1890, and the real reason to go is because the bar still has some Victorian fixtures and fittings. It's one of New York's oldest restaurants continuously in operation, and a favorite of office workers from the Citicorp complex across the street.

DOMINIE'S HOEK. 48-17 Vernon Blvd. bet. 48th and 49th Aves., 706-6531. Su–Th 11:00 a.m.–2:00 a.m.; F–Sa 1:00 a.m.–4:00 a.m.

Nestled into a cozy space on the far end of Vernon Blvd., Dominie's Hoek is the place to meet local residents. It is a low-key place with old tin ceilings, bar food, and occasional live music.

L.I.C. BAR. 45-58 Vernon Blvd. at 46th Ave., 786-5400. www.licbar.com. M–W 4:00 p.m.–2:00 a.m., Th–F 4:00 p.m.–4:00 a.m., Sa 1:00 p.m.–4:00 a.m., Su 1:00 p.m.–2:00 a.m.

This handsome bar with a tin ceiling and enclosed backyard draws locals with live music. Inside, enjoy a decent snack and an even better selection of single malt scotch. Outside, you can soak up stellar views of the Queensboro Bridge and Manhattan. Hipster pundits and Queens boosters often lay it on thick about the up-and-comingness of Vernon Blvd., but if you're expecting gentrification here, as of this writing L.I.C. Bar sits across from a truck lot and auto repair joint.

LOUNGE 47. 48-10 Vernon Blvd. bet. 47th Ave. and 47th Rd., 937-2044. M–Th noon–1:00 a.m., F noon–2:00 a.m., Sa 4:00 p.m.–2:00 a.m., Su brunch noon–4:00 p.m., open til midnight.

Decked out in retro seventies-style befitting its still ungentrified setting, Lounge 47 is a local favorite. Go with a friend and slouch into a couch and enjoy the ever-so-not-Manhattan vibe. Pluses include an interesting enough menu and moderately priced drinks, outdoor seating, and views of New York City Marathon runners every November. It's located (where else?) at the intersection of 47th and 47th.

MADE IN BRAZIL. 35-48 31st St. bet. 35th and 36th Aves., 707-0536. Daily noon–midnight.

Who'd ever have thought that buried in Queens is a vibrant Brazilian community? Made in Brazil is just one of several Queens bars and restaurants immersed in surround-sound Brazilian culture. Come and enjoy music, dancing, watching late-night soccer on satellite TV, mixed American-Brazilian snacks, and late-night energy. You can sip a caipirinha, learn the latest dance craze from Rio, and have a good time.

SHOPPING

Specialty Food and Wine Shops

GREENMARKET IN LONG ISLAND CITY. 48th Ave. bet. 5th St. and Vernon Blvd., (212) 788-7476. July–Nov, Sa 8:00 a.m.–2:00 p.m.

Enjoy a farmer's market here every Saturday with fresh local produce.

NEW YORK WINE WAREHOUSE. 8-05 43rd Ave. bet. Vernon Blvd. and 9th St., one block south of 59th St. Bridge, 784-8776. Sa 9:00 a.m.–2:30 p.m., M–F 9:00 a.m.–6:00 p.m.

"We sell the best for less" says the owner, Geoffrey Troy. New York Wine Warehouse partners with the auction house Christie's and specializes in French burgundies and Bordeaux wines. Professionals from top to bottom, they don't even ship the stuff unless the weather outside is not too hot or not too cold.

PARAMOUNT CAVIAR. 318-15 24th St. bet. 38th and 39th Aves., 786-7747. www.paramountcaviar.com. M–F 10:00 a.m.–4:30 p.m., sometimes open Sa in Dec.

Calm your caviar cravings at Paramount, which supplies some of New York City's best restaurants with top-of-the-line Iranian, Chinese, American, and even Uruguayan caviar, rare truffles, and smoked fish. A two-ounce jar of Iranian caviar costs $350 as of this writing. Order on-line. Gift certificates range from $50 to $2,000.

VINE WINE. 12-09 Jackson Ave., 433-2611. M–Sa noon–10:00 p.m., Su noon–midnight.

Take your pick from a good selection of whites and reds at moderate prices at this quintessential LIC shop with the punny name. It's informal, tasteful, and best of all, you can hang out and get lots of free information about LIC, too.

Interesting Neighborhood Shops

Vernon Blvd. is where you'll find most shops and restaurants. Nearby Jackson Ave. offers less interesting shopping, though that may change as more residential apartments are built and occupied.

ART-O-MAT L.I.C. 46-46 Vernon Blvd. at 47th Rd. Call for hours.

Opened in 2005, Art-O-Mat L.I.C. sells artisan-made objects as well as artist books and locally produced music CDs. There's also a small gallery with interesting shows. For instance, when Art-O-Mat L.I.C. opened there was an exhibit by former *Life* magazine photographer Tony Vaccaro, a longtime Hunter's Point resident, of images he'd taken of Georgia O'Keeffe at her New Mexico home.

CELTIC ARTS. 24-15 Jackson Ave. at 45th Rd., 482-7624. M–F 9:00 a.m.–6:00 p.m., Sa 11:00 a.m.–4:00 p.m.

This is likely the only shop in Queens to have an alternate address in Roscommon, Ireland. You can find reproduction Irish county maps along with jewelry, sweaters, lap blankets, and imported Irish packaged foods. If your family name is Irish, you can also purchase a special plaque with the surname written in English and Gaelic, its meaning, history, coat of arms, and motto.

DIEGO SALAZAR, INC. 21-25 44th Ave. at 21st St., 937-9077. By appointment only.

Diego Salazar, Inc., sells museum-quality antique frames and fine-quality replica frames. Their collection of European and American frames ranges from contemporary to the sixteenth century. The average cost for an antique frame for a painting is usually $10,000 to $40,000. Clients include the Metropolitan Museum of Art, the National Gallery of Art, and the Museum of Modern Art. The company does frame restoration and appraisals as well.

JUST THINGS. 47-28 Vernon Blvd. bet. 47th Rd. and 48th Ave., 786-3675. W—Sa noon—5:00 p.m.

A pack rat's delight, this old-fashioned, secondhand everything store, aptly named "Just Things," has an eclectic selection of stuff at bargain basement prices. You can find old LPs, jewelry, clothing, dishes, shoes, utensils, kitchenware, toys, paintings, bric-a-brac, you name it.

MUSEUM SHOPS

Each of the museums in this area has a gift shop. Most sell posters, books, postcards, and interesting objects. See listings for Fisher Landau Center for Art (see pp. 205–6), the Noguchi Museum (see p. 206), and P.S. 1 (see pp. 206–7).

NEXT LEVEL FLORAL DESIGN. 47-30 Vernon Blvd. near 47th Ave., 937-1155. M—F 8:00 a.m.—6:00 p.m.

So you live in a converted warehouse building with views of an industrial bridge and the Manhattan skyline, in an area with more trucks than trees. What do you need? A bit of nature. Next Level sells large potted plants and small trees fit for large lofts and even supplied leafy props for *The Sopranos,* filmed at nearby Silvercup Studios.

☺ **PURPLE PUMPKIN.** 47-14 Vernon Blvd. bet 47th Rd. and 47th Ave., 784-7300. M, W, F 10:00 a.m.—7:00 p.m., Th 10:00 a.m.—9:00 p.m., Sa 10:00 a.m.—5:00 p.m. Open Su during major holidays.

A pioneer on Vernon Blvd., Purple Pumpkin sells toys, children's books, and greeting cards. Stop in for a gift and a chat with the knowledgeable local owners.

RO GALLERY. 47-15 36th St. at 47th Ave., 937-0901. By appointment only.

Combo on-line art store, gallery, and dealer, this twenty-five-year-old business has 10,000 square feet of limited editions, original paintings, photography, and sculpture. You can trade in old artwork or get appraisals for a $150 service fee.

SEITO TRADING, INC. 52-15 11th St.; enter at 53rd Ave. under Pulaski Bridge, (877) 876-3388. M—F 9:00 a.m.—5:00 p.m.

This small retail store sells such Japanese imports as iron kettles called *tetsubin,* sake cups inscribed with Japanese poetry, sushi sets, and skirts made of kimono fabric. For that special someone who has everything, pick up a uniform for the at-home sushi chef. Big cloth posters, called noren, feature fierce sumo wrestlers.

SLOVAK-CZECH VARIETIES. 10-59 Jackson Ave. bet. 50th and 51st Aves., 752-2093. M—F 11:30 a.m.—7:30 p.m., Sa 11:00 a.m.—5:00 p.m.

Carved wooden toys, Slovac ceramics, Bohemian crystal, and other curios from Prague and the Czech and Slovak region are sold here.

SUBDIVISION. 48-18 Vernon Blvd. bet. 48th and 49th Aves., 482-1899. M–Sa noon–8:00 p.m., Su noon–6:00 p.m.

You can find edgy, interesting clothing for women and men, jewelry, hand-bags, stationery, and even shoes for hipsters here. Subdivision sells works by in-dependent designers who make just a few of each thing. There are small art shows here, too, about every two months.

✎ ESSAY

Long Island City: No Longer Uncharted Territory

by Alana Heiss, Founder and Director of P.S. 1.
(AUTHOR'S NOTE: P.S. 1 today is an affiliate of the Museum of Modern Art. Three decades ago, P.S. 1 was also a pioneering art institution in Long Island City, founded by Alana Heiss. It has been an anchor of the transformation of the community. "MoMA QNS" was the name given to the temporary residence of the Museum of Modern Art in Queens for two years from 2002-4.

During the ribbon-cutting ceremony officially opening MoMA QNS, the Museum of Modern Art's temporary exhibition space during the two-year renovation and expansion of its Manhattan facilities, trustee Ronald Lauder made a confession. Standing inside a renovated staple factory not far from a string of Irish pubs, he admitted to not knowing the first thing about Queens and acknowledged that he would have never managed to reach QNS without the aid of a driver. Up next, Governor George Pataki risked a bit of improv. "Now I know what to give the man who has everything," he announced and handed Ronald Lauder a MetroCard.

This candid moment in an otherwise predictably stiff ceremony speaks volumes about Queens and how it is perceived from both inside and out. Though just minutes from midtown by subway, Queens remains uncharted territory to much of the New York art world. Those who do brave the bridges and tunnels to get here, however, find an environment that is fresh, loose, and intoxicatingly off the radar. MoMA's temporary stay in Queens only drew attention to what many of us already knew: that Queens—in particular, Long Island City—is a laboratory for the arts, a busy playground where the usual rules of supervision have been suspended.

P.S. 1 Contemporary Art Center, the museum founded in 1976 in the Romanesque shell of Long Island City's first public school, has in many ways shaped and responded to the trajectory of the Queens art scene. For gallery-goers, a trip to Queens once belonged on the same order of art safari as Robert Smithson's *Spiral Jetty*. The arcane and contradictory system of street numbers never helped matters, and the interiors of P.S. 1 were commensurately difficult to navigate. Propped up in parts by a structural timber system reminiscent of archaeological digs and connected by a disorderly network of stairwells and walkways, P.S. 1

was mysterious, guarded, even sinister, but it rewarded the intrepid with fortu-itous discoveries: site-specific artworks tucked into crevices, hanging off a ceil-ing, or lurking behind the boiler.

In 1997, P.S. 1 started a three-year renovation that turned the entire building into exhibition areas, gaining 30 to 40 percent more gallery space. This renova-tion aptly corresponded to the real-estate transformation taking place in Queens and citywide. Just as P.S. 1 expanded by rebuilding its insides, so too has New York grown, even as the city limits haven't budged. In nearly every instance, ex-pansion of the cultural life of the city into new neighborhoods beyond Manhat-tan has been led by artists in search of cheap rents, good light, and room to play. When P.S. 1 and MoMA embarked on a massive survey of new artwork being done around the city (resulting in an exhibition called Greater New York 2005), we dis-covered a surprising number of participating artists who had settled in Long Is-land City, Astoria, and Sunnyside.

Queens has become home to many arts institutions dedicated to experimen-tation and exploration. To name just a few, The SculptureCenter, which in 2002 relocated from Manhattan to a former trolley repair shop, constantly pushes at and contorts the definition of sculpture. Flux Factory mischievously reworks the standard conventions of curated exhibitions, poetry readings, and even tea par-ties. In Flushing, the Queens Museum showcases an appealing mixture of inter-national and local, contemporary and historic—a fitting complement to the diversity and energy of the borough.

MoMA QNS has come and gone, and MoMA probably will not budge from 53rd Street in our lifetimes. Meanwhile, the raw spaces and demographic up-heavals of Queens continue to provide the room and inspiration for fresh and ex-citing work.

15

Richmond Hill

WHERE IT IS: Southern Queens. Bounded to north by Myrtle and Hillside Aves., east by the Van Wyck Expwy, and south by Linden Blvd.
HOW TO GET THERE BY SUBWAY: J and Z lines to 104–102th Sts., 111th St., and 121st St.
HOW TO GET THERE BY LIRR: Service to the Richmond Hill Sta. has been discontinued; nearest LIRR stop is Forest Hills.
WHAT'S NEARBY: Kew Gardens, Jamaica.
MAJOR SHOPPING/RESTAURANT STREETS: Ethnic shops on Liberty Ave. General shopping along Jamaica and Atlantic Aves.
ON NOT GETTING LOST: Orient yourself to Liberty Ave., Hillside Ave., Lefferts Blvd., and the Van Wyck Expwy.
CAR SERVICES: Kew Gardens Car Service 846-5800, Fanny 641-4444.

AIR OF FALLEN SPLENDOR

They call it, proudly, Queens' best-kept secret. Scenes from the movie *Goodfellas* were filmed here, and there's often a film crew in the area. That's because tiny Richmond Hill today has the romantic air of tarnished, if not quite fallen, splendor. You certainly see this in the ornate 1929 RKO Keith's Theater, which is astonishingly intact on the inside despite being used as a bingo hall for more than forty years. The Richmond Hill Historical Society says it is "one of the first planned communities, whereas land was purchased, streets were planned, and sidewalks were laid out and trees planted to line the streets." But the area is only partly protected from development by landmark status. Less than one in four of the 1,000 Victorian homes built by the founding fathers of Richmond Hill are legally protected from the wrecker's ball.

There are wonderful characters and stories associated with Richmond Hill. An old, now-defunct drinking establishment called Triangle Hofbrau (now a medical office) in its heyday was a favorite haunt of Babe Ruth who, they say, ate

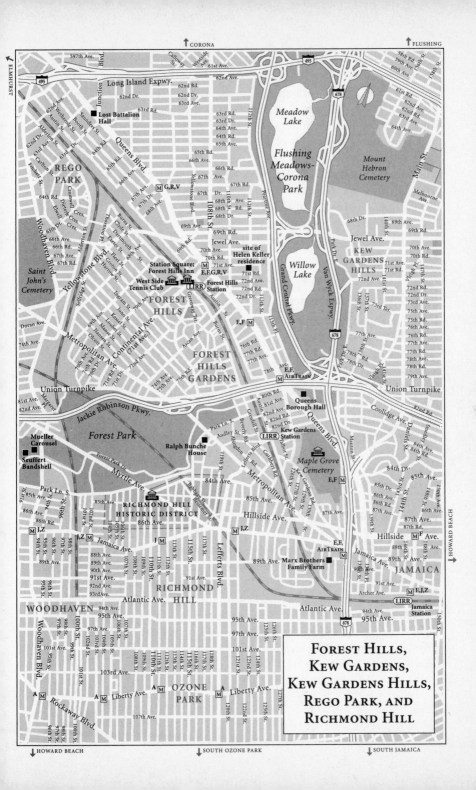

← ELMHURST

597th Ave.
Long Island Expwy.
495
61st Ave.
62nd Rd.
62nd Dr.
63rd Rd.

62nd Ave.
62nd Wetherole St. Austin St. Booth St. Saunders St.
Lost Battalion Hall
63rd Rd.

62nd Dr.
63rd Dr.

62nd Ave.

63rd Rd.
63rd Dr.
64th Rd.
64th Ave.

63rd Ave.

Meadow Lake

678

61st Rd.
62nd Ave.
62nd Rd.
63rd Ave.
64th Ave.

Flushing Meadows-Corona Park

58th Rd. 59th Ave. 130th St.
60th Ave.

Main St.

62nd Dr.
62nd Cr.
63rd Dr.
Carlton Cr. Flushed Cr.
Queens Blvd.
64th Rd.
65th Rd.
66th Ave.

REGO PARK

65th Dr. Dierdre Cres. Elwell Cres. Cromwell Cres.
64th Rd.

65th Ave.
66th Ave.
67th Ave.

M G,R,V

67th Rd.
67th Dr.
68th Dr.

Yellowstone Blvd.
108th St.

67th Ave.
67th Dr.
68th St.
68th Ave.
68th Dr.

69th Ave.

110th St.
112th St.

Pearson St.

Mount Hebron Cemetery

Melbourne Ave.

Saint John's Cemetery

Woodhaven Blvd.
65th Pl.
66th Rd.
66th Ave.
67th Rd.
67th Ave.

Selfridge St. Burns St. Clyde St. Dartmouth St. Exeter St. Fleet St. Groton St. Harrow St.
Thornton Pl.

69th Rd.

68th Dr.

69th Rd.
Jewel Ave.

70th Ave.
70th Rd.

site of Helen Keller residence

68th Dr.
100th St.

69th Ave.
69th Rd.

70th Ave.
70th Rd.

KEW GARDENS HILLS

136th St.
137th St.
141st St.
144th St. Wright Ave.

71st Ave.
71st Rd.

Doran Ave.
74th Ave.

Ingram St.
69th Ave. Loubet St. Kessel St. Manse St. Olcott St.

Continental Ave. (71st Ave.)

Station Square; Forest Hills Inn
West Side Tennis Club

M
E,F,G,R,V
LIRR
Forest Hills Station

71st Ave.
71st Rd.
72nd Ave.
72nd Rd.
72nd Dr.

113th St.

Grand Central Pkwy.
Willow Lake

Van Wyck Expwy.

72nd Rd.
72nd Dr.
73rd Ave.

75th Ave.
75th Rd.
76th Ave.
76th Rd.

FOREST HILLS

70th Rd. 70th Ave.
71st Dr. 72nd St.

74th St.
75th St.
75th Ave.

Ascan Ave.

76th Rd.
77th Rd.
77th Ave.

115th Pl.

E,F M

73rd Ter.
77th Ave.
77th Rd.
78th Ave.

Metropolitan Ave.

Margaret

81st Ave.
82nd Ave.

Union Turnpike

FOREST HILLS GARDENS

Burns St.

78th Ave.
78th Rd.
79th Ave.

78th St.

E,F
AirTrain

M

678

77th Ave.

Union Turnpike

Jackie Robinson Pkwy.

80th Rd.
81st Ave.
82nd Rd.

Austin St.
Grenfell St. Beverly Rd. Audley St. Abingdon Rd.
Park Ln. S.

Queens Borough Hall

Coolidge Ave. Daniels St.

82nd Rd.
84th Ave.
84th Rd.

Speaker Rd.

Manton St.

Forest Park

Mueller Carousel

Seuffert Bandshell

Forest Park Dr.

Myrtle Ave.

Ralph Bunche House

118th St.

Lefferts Blvd.
Cuthbert Rd.

82nd Dr.
LIRR
Kew Gardens Station

Queens Blvd.

Kew Gardens Rd. 125th St. 127th St. 128th St.

Maple Grove Cemetery

E,F M

84th Dr.

85th Dr.
86th Rd.
86th Ave.
87th Rd.

134th St.
139th St.
144th St.

84th Ave.

85th Ave.

86th Ave.
87th Ave.

Park Ln. S.
85th Ave.
96th St.
86th Ave.

M J,Z

RICHMOND HILL HISTORIC DISTRICT
86th Ave.

Babbage Reserve Ave.

84th Ave.

85th Ave.

Hillside Ave.

87th Ave.

Hillside
M F Ave.
87th Rd.

↓ HOWARD BEACH

36th St. 97th St. 94th St.
87th Ave.
88th Ave.
89th Ave.

J
M

101st St. 102nd St. 103rd St. 104th St. 105th St. 106th St. 108th St. 109th St. 110th St. 111th St. 112th St. 113th St. 115th St. 117th St.

J M
Jamaica Ave.

M J,Z

89th Ave.
90th Ave.
91st Ave.
92nd Ave.
93rd Ave.

Metropolitan Ave.

89th Ave.
Marx Brothers Family Farm

E,F
AirTrain
M

139th St.

88th Ave.
89th Ave.
90th Ave.

Jamaica Ave.
91st Ave.

JAMAICA

WOODHAVEN

94th Ave.
95th Ave.
97th Ave.

96th St. 95th St. 94th St.

Atlantic Ave.

RICHMOND HILL

Lefferts Blvd.
91st Ave.

Atlantic Ave.

91st Ave.
Archer Ave.

M E,J,Z

LIRR
Jamaica Station

168th St.

Woodhaven Blvd.
100th St. 98th St.
95th Ave.
97th Ave.

97th Ave.
101st Ave.

106th St. 107th St.
104th St. 103rd St. 102nd St.
101st Ave.
103rd Ave.

108th St. 109th St. 110th St. 111th St. 113th St. 115th St. 116th St. 118th St.

125th St. 124th St. 123rd St. 121st St. 120th St.
95th Ave.

678

94th Ave.
95th Ave.

97th St. 96th St. 95th St.
Rockaway Blvd.
101st Ave.

A M

OZONE PARK

A M
Liberty Ave.

A M
Liberty Ave.

127th St.

99th St. 98th St.
107th Ave.

120th St. 122nd St.

FOREST HILLS, KEW GARDENS, KEW GARDENS HILLS, REGO PARK, AND RICHMOND HILL

fried eels and ice cream there, and Mae West (who lived at 89-05 88th Street in nearby Woodhaven from 1914 to 1928, according to newspapers of the day) often got thrown out for rambunctious behavior. Triangle Hofbrau is also where composer Ernest Ball is said to have written the song, "When Irish Eyes Are Smiling." Jacob Riis, the muckraking journalist and social reformer, friend of Teddy Roosevelt, and author of *How the Other Half Lives* (and the man after whom Rockaway's Jacob Riis Park is named), lived in the area and his wife is buried in the local cemetery. The Marx brothers' mother helped them evade the draft in Richmond Hill, too. And beat generation writer Jack Kerouac, author of *On the Road,* lived at 133-01 Cross Bay Blvd. in Ozone Park from 1943 to 1950, and then moved with his mother to 94-21 134th Street in Richmond Hill, where he lived until 1955. Kerouac published a series of poems called *Richmond Hill Blues.*

THINGS TO SEE AND DO
If you want to see what's left of historic Richmond Hill, you'd better hustle. Top of the list: Don't miss the extraordinary Jahn's Ice Cream Parlor. Or across the street, the Carnegie-built library with a WPA mural depicting the splendors of suburban life. There's the landmarked Maple Grove Cemetery and P.S. 66. Our Richmond Hill Historic District: Self-Guided Tour gives you a peek into a late Victorian middle-class community.

Nearby the new Atlas Park Mall is an upscale mall with a weekend Greenmarket, movie theater, and special community events.

BITS OF HISTORY
Albon Platt Man developed Richmond Hill and was Richmond Hill's first village president in 1885. His son Alrick H. Man developed nearby Kew Gardens. This area was possibly named after Edward Richmond, a noted landscape architect who helped design the neighborhood, or named after a popular Thames River resort near London. Richmond Hill joined Greater New York City in 1898, but still today retains a small-town feel. The area enjoyed a middle-class stability until World War II. Following the 1965 changes in immigration laws, an influx of Latin Americans changed the local demographics. By the 1980s, there was a large population of Guyanese immigrants, as well as immigrants from the Dominican Republic, Colombia, Ecuador, India, and Jamaica. Toward Liberty Ave., a large Sikh temple is being erected.

PEOPLE, PLACES, AND THINGS OF HISTORICAL INTEREST

🏛 **CHURCH OF THE RESURRECTION.** 85-09 118th St. bet. Hillside and 85th Aves., 847-2649. W noon and 6:00 p.m., Su 10:00 a.m.

This Queen Anne Tudor Revival landmark church was the first to be erected in Richmond Hill. It was founded in 1874 as a mission of the already established Grace Church of Jamaica. Jacob Riis was a parishioner here. The stained glass windows are dedicated to his wife, who is buried in Maple Grove Cemetery. Note the parish house on the corner.

🏛 **MAPLE GROVE CEMETERY.** Bounded by Van Wyck Expwy. on the east, 83rd Ave. on the north, Kew Gardens Rd. on the west, and 86th Rd. and 87th Ave. on the south., 847-2649.

Maple Grove dates back to 1875. It is typical of a rural cemetery that provided a secluded, naturalistic final resting place for the deceased. Among others, the wife of social reformer Jacob Riis is buried there. This cemetery is on the National Register of Historic Places as a prime example of a historic rural cemetery set in an urbanizing context. Maple Grove was sufficiently appealing as a final resting place that a small train line was built in Richmond Hill to service mourners. Tours and information are available from the Richmond Historical Society (see below), which has offices on the second floor of a funeral home.

MARX BROTHERS FAMILY FARM. 134th St. near 89th Ave. No tours.

The Marx Brothers lived here during World War I and the 1920s, when they were adults. Chico was born in 1888, Harpo in 1890, Groucho in 1892, and Gummo in 1901. As the story goes, their mother was trying to keep her four draft-age boys out of the draft and owned a house both here and in Little Neck that had a farm. Needing the boys to work the "farm" was an excuse to not have them sent off to war (because they farmed the land, they were exempt!). Note the plaque by the Central Queens Historical Society. Teddy Roosevelt made a fiery speech not far from here about draft evasion (see Forest Hills Station Square, p. 145).

🏛 **P.S. 66: THE OXFORD SCHOOL.** 85-11 102nd St.

A large Romanesque-style institution with a notable bell tower, P.S. 66 was built in 1898 and is a New York City landmark.

🏛 **RICHMOND HILL REPUBLICAN CLUB.** 118-15 Hillside Ave. Closed for renovation.

Built at the turn of the twentieth century, the Richmond Hill Republican Club is a fabulous institutional structure, centrally located in the historic district. Years of neglect have left it in sorry condition. However, it has recently been landmarked by New York City, and there are hopes that it will be rehabilitated. Stay tuned.

RICHMOND HILL HISTORICAL SOCIETY AND MUSEUM. 86-25 Lefferts Blvd., 847-7878. www.richmondhillhistory.org.

The Richmond Hill Historical Society occupies the second floor of a 1905 Victorian mansion (actually a funeral home that's in a Victorian mansion). Come for one of their marvelous tours of the area—especially the Spirits Alive cemetery tour at the end of September—and to see a few display cases jam-packed with historical memorabilia from Richmond Hill and Kew Gardens. Call for updates on efforts to obtain historic district status for Richmond Hill and house tours.

🚶 🏛 RICHMOND HILL HISTORIC DISTRICT: SELF-GUIDED TOUR

The historic district includes the area encompassed by 104th St. and Park Lane South, 84th Ave. to 118th St., 118th St. to Jamaica Ave., and roughly along 86th Ave. to Park Lane So., plus several additional blocks of 109–111th Sts. between 86th and Jamaica Aves. to 104th St.

For a self-guided walk of part of the area, begin at the corner of Jamaica Ave. and Lefferts Blvd. Walk north on Lefferts Blvd., passing the 1. 🏛 Republican Club (see pp. 229–30) and the 2. Richmond Hill Library (see p. 231) and, if open, go inside to view the *Story of Richmond Hill* mural. Cross Hillside Ave., turn left, and continue on 118th St. to 85th Ave., passing the 3. 🏛 Church of the Resurrection, the first church built in Richmond Hill dating to 1874 (see p. 229). Turn left on 85th Ave., and walk as far as Myrtle Ave. At 4. 85-14 111th St., corner of Myrtle, note the outstanding Victorian home, then backtrack to 5. historic 110th St. to see more blocks filled with Victorian homes, characterized by big front gardens, gables and dormers, shingled roofs, stained-glass windows, woodwork, and elegant porches. (Inside there are mahogany railings, elaborate fireplaces, and servants' quarters.) Continue to 86th Ave., noting the Victorian home on the corner. Make a right until you reach 102nd St. to complete the tour. To continue, follow the path of the elevated LIRR train, around 114th St. and 85th Ave., going toward Myrtle Ave.

RKO KEITH'S THEATER. 117-03 Hillside Ave. bet. Jamaica and Myrtle Aves.

Another buried treasure. The marquee outside this 1929 theater has been restored, but inside it's been a flea market and bingo hall since the 1960s. Remarkably, the balcony and ceiling are still gorgeous. Eminently restorable, this RKO theater is a white elephant. What a pity. Why isn't more of Queens landmarked? (Don't confuse this with RKO Keith's in Flushing.)

THE STORY OF RICHMOND HILL MURAL. Queens Public Library, Richmond Hill Branch. 118-14 Hillside Ave., 849-7150. M 1:00 p.m.–8:00 p.m., Tu 1:00 p.m.–6:00 p.m., W and F 10:00 a.m.–6:00 p.m., Th 10:00 a.m.–8:00 p.m., Su noon–5:00 p.m.

The 1936 WPA mural by Richard Evergood in this library is called *The Story of Richmond Hill.* One panel depicts the suffering laborers in terrible conditions. A second panel shows a train with the letters "LIRR" painted on it and businessmen (the architect, the realtor, and the founder of Richmond Hill, the developer) signing papers. The third panel shows workers happily dancing outside in a healthy suburban setting. Note the sign next to the mural saying, "We have books in English, French, Spanish, German, Hindi, Lithuanian, Russian, Urdu, and Punjabi." The library itself is historic, one of three in Queens financed by Andrew Carnegie. Jacob Riis was one of its first trustees.

TRIANGLE HOFBRAU. 117-13 Jamaica Ave. bet. Jamaica and Myrtle Aves. Not open to the public.

Originally Doyle's Hotel in 1864, the Triangle Hofbrau is still standing—but just barely. It was once a German-style beer hall and restaurant, a hot spot conveniently located near the train station and stables where people kept their carriages to drive home after a trip from the city. There are a lot of colorful stories associated with this old wayhouse. It is now located under the elevated train tracks, a stone's throw from the equally decrepit RKO Keith's Theater.

POINTS OF CONTEMPORARY CULTURAL INTEREST

PHAGWAH PARADE. For exact dates, check Rajkumari Cultural Center. See below.

Each March or early April the Indo-Caribbean community (originally from Guyana and Trinidad) in New York hits the streets of Richmond Hill with hijinks, celebrating Phagwah, a springtime Hindu holiday parade known as the Festival of Colors. And colorful it is. You'll see celebrants splashing colored dust and dye on one another as the parade snakes down Liberty Ave., their stereo systems blaring Bollywood hits and Indo-Caribbean music. It ends in Smokey Oval Park (25th St. at Atlantic Ave.) where revelers keep warm by swaying (and spraying more color) to more music and enjoying traditional dance performances. In the Indian diaspora the festival is called Phagwah but elsewhere is known as Holi.

RAJKUMARI CULTURAL CENTER. 83-84 116th St. bet. Curzon Rd. and 84th Ave., 805-8068. rajkumari center@aol.com.

This is a nonprofit organization in operation since 1966. Unlike other social service entities, this group is dedicated to the arts and culture of Indo-Caribbean communities that evolved during the nineteenth and early twentieth century when workers were brought forcibly by the British from the Indian subcontinent to work as indentured laborers on colonial plantations in the Caribbean islands, like Trinidad and Jamaica, and the South American mainland countries Guyana and Suriname. The cultural forms that evolved as a result are unique. Indo-Caribbeans are the largest ethnic communities in Trinidad and Suriname and a majority of the population of Guyana. Many people of this ethnic background have emigrated to the United States, settling in Queens. This organization conducts after-school classes, workshops, and seminars, culminating in annual musical dance-drama productions.

SIKH CULTURAL SOCIETY. 95-30 118th St. at 95th Ave., 846-9144. Daily dawn to evening. Limited access for women.

The Sikh Cultural Society of New York is building the largest *gurdwara,* or Sikh house of worship, on the East Coast. The new building will replace one that burned to the ground in 2002. The number of men in New York who are Sikhs, recognizable by their distinctive turbans, has been estimated as 150,000. Thousands come on the weekends and for special holidays. Visitors are welcome as long as you abide by temple rules, which include the covering of the head and the removal of shoes.

RESTAURANTS AND CAFÉS

DARBARS HALAL CHICKEN, INC. 12609 Liberty Ave., 529-4900. Daily 11:00 a.m.–11:00 p.m.

Zabihah is the Arabic word for "slaughtered," and to be halal, or religiously acceptable, meat and poultry must be prepared according to specific Islamic laws. Some menus combine *zabihah* and ordinary meats, but Darbars serves only the former. Try the fried chicken and spicy cheese steak.

PUNJABI KEBAB HOUSE. 91-52 Lefferts Blvd. at Atlantic Ave., 846-2800. Daily 11:00 a.m.–midnight.

Want to stuff your face for lunch? You won't be disappointed at this northern Indian kebab house that serves a better-than-expected buffet at lunchtime. Located near a Sikh temple, you'll find the full complement of curries, tandooris, spicy stews, condiments, and, of course, kebabs.

SINGH'S ROTI SHOP. 131-18 Liberty Ave. bet. 131st and 132nd St., 323-5990. Su–Th 6:00 a.m.–midnight, F 6:00 a.m.–2:00 a.m., Sa 6:00 a.m.–4:00 a.m.

So you're delayed at JFK or on the Van Wyck Expwy. waiting endlessly for an accident to be cleared, and your tummy is rumbling. Have an adventure. Nip over to Liberty Ave. where you'll find a little Guyanese and South Asian community. Try Singh's Roti Shop for West Indian roti and conch stew—spicy, flavorful, and really inexpensive. From Kennedy, get off at the Liberty Ave. exit from the Van Wyck Expwy.

TANDOORI HUT. 119-04 94th Ave. bet. Lefferts Blvd. and 120th St., 850-8919. Daily noon–midnight.

There's so little ambience it's almost antiambience here. But who cares when the chicken tikka and other tandoori items are baked in clay ovens according to ancient techniques? Go for the fiery vindaloo or *calmer biryani*. Fusion fans can try eclectic Indian-Chinese combos. It's located near the hindu temple and offers a full menu of halal foods.

JAHN'S ICE CREAM PARLOR & RESTAURANT. 117-03 Hillside Ave. bet. Jamaica and Myrtle Aves., 847-2800. M–Th 11:30 a.m.–10:00 p.m., Sa 11:30 a.m.–11:00 p.m., Su 11:00 a.m.–10:00 p.m.

Come for the romance of the past—but do so soon, as nobody knows how much longer Jahn's will survive. Old-timers still schlep their kids to this old-fashioned ice cream parlor for a family-sized ice cream sundae called the Kitchen Sink. One of a chain first opened in 1897, this one dates to 1929. The interior decor is intact, complete with an original nickelodeon, an enormous ornate syrup dispenser, red leather booths, elaborate wood paneling, old-fashioned gaslight fixtures, and even high school names carved into the wood. Jahn's isn't land-marked but it should be. Today, Russian immigrants run it. Next door is the old RKO Keith's Theater. (Don't confuse this place with Jahn's Diner at 81-04 37th Ave., Jackson Heights, once owned by the same family.)

SHOPPING

RUBIE'S COSTUME COMPANY. 1 Rubie Plaza, 120-08 Jamaica Ave. bet. 120th and 121st Sts., 846-1008. www.rubies.com. M–F 10:00 a.m.–6:00 p.m.

Rubie's has been working magic for Halloween and masquerade parties for decades. Whatever costumes you want, they have it in a neat little prepackaged set: mermaids, magicians, cops, princesses, frogs, presidents du jour, and a sorcerer's inventory of makeup and masks. Specialty costumes can be rented. If you've ever wondered what happened to homemade Halloween costumes, the answer might be Rubie's. In the 1950s, World War II veteran Willie Beige and his wife, Tillie, started a candy store in nearby Woodhaven. They started carrying a line of gags and then became Rubie's Fun House. By the early 1970s, they were mass-producing costumes for the Halloween industry. In 1990 they licensed *Star*

Trek; a decade later, Warner Brothers. Today Rubie's reportedly employs 2,000 workers worldwide.

Also Nearby

ATLAS PARK MALL. Cooper Ave. at 80th St., (212) 788-7476. www.theshopsatatlaspark.com. Greenmarket from July—Nov. Sa 8:00 a.m.—3:00 p.m.

As we go to press, this big upscale mall has just opened with dozens of stores, restaurants, offices, a Saturday greenmarket, and the new Regal Cinemas.

SCHMIDT'S CONFECTIONERY. 94-15 Jamaica Ave. bet. Woodhaven Blvd. and 95 St., 846-9326. M—Sa 11:00 a.m.—6:00 p.m.

In business for over eighty years, Schmidt's in nearby Woodhaven has been making their own chocolates filled with various creams, raisins, fruits, nuts, crackers, and even the humble marshmallow.

 ESSAY

I Thought I Was African-American

by Christina Alcalay
This young fashion designer's parents came to Queens from Vietnam in 1982 when she was three.

For the longest time I thought I was African-American. It was quite simple for me—I felt I was like everyone I knew. I was no exact race; I identified with my friends, who just happened to be African-American. At twelve years of age, to my surprise, I realized I was not. Growing up, I never saw anyone who looked like me, except my parents, in the four-block radius that was my world in Richmond Hill. It was a predominately African-American neighborhood. The first time I realized I wasn't African-American was when I stepped into junior high school and saw a little boy who looked like me and I said, "Oh my God, where did he come from?" Subsequently, I went through a whole period of my life in which all I wanted to do was to find people who looked like me. My best friend in junior high school was Korean; she lived in Ozone Park. Her parents owned a dry-cleaning shop. We ate wonderful Korean food together and giggled about boys. Her name was Christine, a name I identified with because it was close to my own. We shared a continent: Asia. In the two years in junior high school, I learned the ins and outs of the Korean culture. I saw how different Christine was from me. We became friendly because of our similarities, but became lifelong friends because of our *many* differences.

Growing up in Richmond Hill was amazing. I ate roti and curry chicken before I discovered the hamburger or hot dog. I watched Bollywood films with my friends and savored many Indian dishes. Slowly I realized that the neighborhood that I thought was Indian was actually West Indian. It could easily be called the

Little West Indies now. I watched the Phagwah celebration, their festival of color, where people were showered with food coloring and white powder. The streets during the festival of Phagwah were like a [Jackson] Pollock-inspired painting with people who looked like they were dipped into flour and sprayed with paint. It was a feast for my imaginative mind. I danced to reggae and had lamb curry with people who had come from beautiful colorful islands. That was why for so long, I thought I was one of them. In a way I am, because this was how I grew up, with a lot of flavor. We all grew up together. Nothing looks odd to me as an adult. The diversity, it's wonderful. I can't imagine coming here from Vietnam and not growing up like that.

16

Ridgewood

WHERE IT IS: Western Queens. Bounded to the north by Metropolitan Ave., to the east by LIRR tracks, to the south by Central Ave., and to the west by Flushing Ave.

HOW TO GET THERE BY SUBWAY: M to Fresh Pond Road, Forest Ave. and Seneca Ave. stations. Connection at Myrtle/Wyckoff to the L train.

WHAT'S NEARBY: Middle Village (as well as various neighborhoods not covered in this book) and Bushwick, Brooklyn.

MAJOR SHOPPING/RESTAURANT STREETS: Fresh Pond Rd., Myrtle Ave.

SPECIAL CHARACTERISTICS: Landmarks and Eastern European foods.

ON NOT GETTING LOST: Orient yourself to Metropolitan Ave. in the north (it runs east-west), Fresh Pond Rd. (it runs north-south from Maspeth to Myrtle Ave.), Forest Ave. (also north-south), and Myrtle Ave. in the south (it runs east-west).

CAR SERVICES: Four One's 456-1111, Lindy's 326-3333 or 456-1111.

THE BIGGEST HISTORIC DISTRICT IN THE UNITED STATES

Nestled near the Brooklyn-Queens border, Ridgewood looks as it did ninety years ago, at least in some parts. You'll find no Starbucks, no Internet cafés, no Thai fusion restaurants, and no big box stores or high-rises (yet). What you will find in Ridgewood is simply amazing, all the more so because nobody seems to trumpet the fact: its 2,980 landmarked buildings, listed on the National Register of Historic Places. Ridgewood is the largest historical district in New York and in the entire nation.

Ridgewood is known for its very early-twentieth-century row housing. Thousands of homes were built with yellow Kreischer brick, made in Staten Island, lending the area a brightness that's quite distinct from brownstones or redbrick homes. Stockholm St. is paved with these bricks, too, earning it the nickname "yellow brick road." Although Ridgewood's historic district is vast—actually, it

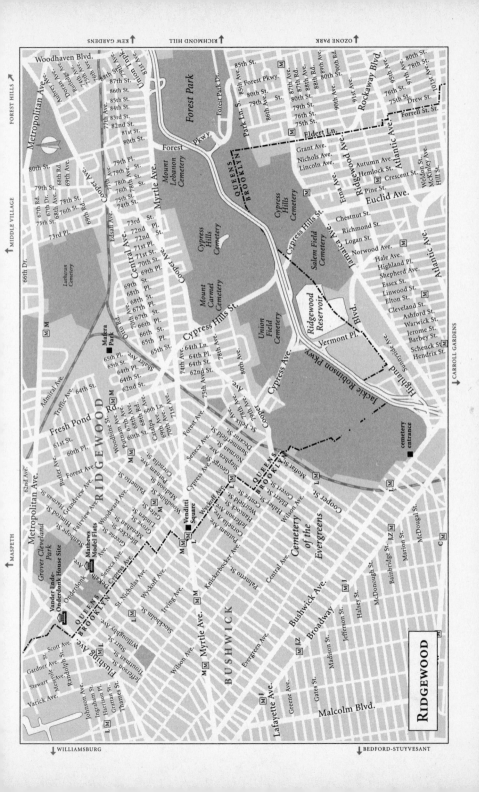

Woodhaven Blvd.

Metropolitan Ave.

Forest Park

85th St.
Forest Pkwy.
Park Ln. S.
80th St.
79th St.
76th St.
75th St.

Rockaway Blvd.
80th St.
78th St.
97th St.
95th St.
76th St.
Drew St.
75th St.
Forrell St. St.

87th Ave.
87th Rd.
88th Ave.
88th Rd.
89th Ave.
90th St.
91st Ave.

Eldert Ln.
Grant Ave.
Nichols Ave.
Lincoln Ave.

Autumn Ave.
Hemlock St.
Crescent St.
Pine St.

Weldon St.
McKinley Ave.
Hill St.

Atlantic Ave.
Ridgewood Ave.
Etna Ave.

QUEENS
BROOKLYN

Cypress Hills Cemetery

Euclid Ave.

Forest Pkwy.

Mount Lebanon Cemetery

Forest Park

Chestnut St.
Richmond St.
Logan St.
Norwood Ave.
Hale Ave.
Highland Pl.
Shepherd Ave.
Essex St.
Linwood St.
Elton St.
Cleveland St.
Ashford St.
Warwick St.
Jerome St.
Barbey St.
Schenck St.
Hendrix St.

Jamaica Ave.

Cypress Hills Cemetery

Salem Field Cemetery

Mount Carmel Cemetery

Cypress Hills St.

Ridgewood Reservoir.

Union Field Cemetery

Vermont Pl.

Highland Blvd.

Sunnyside Ave.

← CARROLL GARDENS

Fresh Pond Rd.

RIDGEWOOD

Mount Olivet Cemetery

Lutheran Cemetery

Madura Park

Grover Cleveland Park

Vander Ende-
Onderdonk House Site

Mathews Model Flats

Venditti Square

QUEENS
BROOKLYN

BUSHWICK

Cemetery of the Evergreens

Cooper Ave.

Jackie Robinson Pkwy.

cemetery entrance

Cypress Ave.

Myrtle Ave.

Bushwick Ave.

Broadway

Malcolm Blvd.

RIDGEWOOD

is comprised of seventeen individual historic districts—experts say it covers only 60 percent of the total number of yellow brick houses and model flats built here between 1900 and the early 1920s.

You'll find an Eastern European enclave (Poles, Romanians, Slovaks) and German Americans with retail shops along Fresh Pond Rd. There's a large Latino and smaller Italian community around Myrtle Ave. Of course, it wouldn't be twenty-first-century Queens without a smattering of Chinese and Koreans, Dominicans, and Ecuadorians living here, too. If you enjoy the interplay between an orderly old New York and the mumbo jumbo of today's world, take a day trip to Ridgewood.

THINGS TO SEE AND DO

The main reason to visit Ridgewood is real estate, either to see the architecture or look for a historic home that would be thrice the price in Manhattan. You can get the feel of the historic district quickly, just by strolling down one block of the Mathews Model Flats, popular early-twentieth-century attached houses. Or you can follow our Walk Through Historic Ridgewood (pp. 242–43).

Myrtle Ave., from Gates Ave. to Fresh Pond Road, is bustling. You'll pass Bank of America and Banco Popular, ice cream shops, groceries, and hundreds of shops selling the stuff of everyday American life. You may even catch the corner preacher saving lives in Spanish at the intersection of Knickerbocker and Myrtle, under the M train.

Fresh Pond Road is a quiet, clean shopping street lined with over a dozen Polish bakeries, restaurants, and delis. Note the community bulletin boards busy with handwritten signs seeking (or offering) jobs, rides, housing, and announcing cultural events and religious festivals. Nip into any bar and you are likely to find cigarette-smoking men intently watching a satellite TV broadcast of a European soccer match. On side streets, many homes fly American flags. At Kreden's Restaurant you can savor Polish cookery in a traditional setting. Or, take home loaves of hearty bread, homemade sausages, and imported cherry jam from Jantar Delicatesy.

Hobbyists and grade-school-age children will find a lot to buy at Nagengast True Value Hardware, a pre-electronics era hobby shop that sells electric trains, boxed model sets, and various do-it-yourself projects. Vintage clothing shoppers and bargain hunters must not miss the classic Domsey's. Birdwatchers might enjoy a visit to Highland Park. Pop music enthusiasts might be interested to know that the *original* Mr. Bojangles is buried in the Cemetery of the Evergreens.

☞ **TIP: Traveler's Advisory: A Word on the L and M Subways.** The only subway to go directly to Ridgewood is the M line, which comes infrequently and meanders through Queens, Brooklyn, Lower Manhattan, and back to Brooklyn

again. A better bet for Manhattan-bound visitors is the L train at Myrtle/Wyck-
off, in Ridgewood. In general, it's best to drive, and street parking is easy to
find.

BITS OF HISTORY

Ridgewood was settled originally by Mespachtes Indians, and later, land here was
farmed by the Dutch in the 1600s and 1700s. It was named by British settlers in the
early 1700s for its elevated, forested terrain, then renamed Evergreen in the 1880s
because another community in Long Island claimed the name Ridgewood. It re-
turned to its original name after joining New York City in 1898. Development of
the area began in earnest with the arrival of the horse car line in the 1850s, followed by elevated rapid transit in 1879. The early 1900s were formative, when
much of Ridgewood as you see it today was built. In the decade prior to World War
I a housing boom ensued; among the developers were Paul Stier and Gustave X.
Mathews, who built entire streets of attached homes. The area became a middle-
class German enclave. Many residents worked in local knitting mills and breweries. After World War II there was an influx of Gottscheers, German-Hungarians,
Romanians, Italians, and Slovenes. There's been a recent increase in Polish immigrants from Europe but also from Brooklyn, where once-Polish Greenpoint has
experienced a spillover of gentrification from Williamsburg, causing housing
prices to soar, so Greenpoint residents are now moving to Ridgewood.

Ridgewood is landmarked today, but about sixty years ago it was considered
just a rural "Queens extension" of Bushwick, which was then a well-respected,
wealthy German enclave in the borough of Brooklyn. Indeed, Ridgewood was so
married to Bushwick then that it was sometimes called Ridgewood-Bushwick.
Describing both communities in one breath, the authoritative 1939 WPA Guide
to the City of New York called them "old-fashioned and respectable" German-
American communities, and sketched Ridgewood thus: "Comfortable brownstones with neat stoops and polished brass."

The twin neighborhoods had quite different fates after World War II. As
Bushwick's population became increasingly poor, old mansions and turn-of-
the-twentieth-century institutional buildings were neglected, torn down, or
changed beyond recognition. Today the word "Bushwick" is likely to be associated with headline news of crimes committed there, or stories of arty young urban pioneers escaping Williamsburg's pricey rents.

In contrast, Ridgewood always retained a German, and later Eastern European, population, largely working and lower middle class but not impoverished.
Ridgewood's housing stock, albeit more modest than some of Bushwick's, was
maintained. In the late 1970s, Ridgewood divorced itself from inner-city Bushwick, obtaining a different zip code that established it as part of Queens, not
Brooklyn. In 1983, many little patches of Ridgewood were designated historic

districts. Still, New Yorkers are more likely to know there's a Ridgewood, New Jersey, than a Ridgewood, Queens.

PARKS, PUBLIC SPACES, AND PUBLIC WORKS

CEMETERY OF THE EVERGREENS. Entrance at 1629 Bushwick Ave. on the Queens–Brooklyn border, 455-5300. Walking tours May–October.

Among several landmarks in the nonsectarian Cemetery of the Evergreens is the Triangle Shirtwaist Factory Fire Memorial, commemorating the victims of one of New York's most notorious labor accidents in which 150 immigrant workers died, mostly women, leading to significant workplace labor reforms.

Among the famous individuals interred here are Lester W. Young, who played saxophone for Benny Goodman, Count Basie, and Billie Holiday (1909–59; grave #11418 Redemption), and Bill "Bojangles" Robinson, a black vaudeville dancer immortalized in the song "Mr. Bojangles" (1877–1949; lot #1 Redemption). Also here are John Bunny, the first comic star of the American screen (1863–1915; lot #407 Lake Side), and Winsor McCay, cartoonist and pioneering animator (1869–1934; lot #64 The Lawn). Landscape architect Calvert Vaux designed some parts of the Cemetery of the Evergreens. Other cemeteries in the area include Knollwood Park, Mt. Judah, Beth-El, Machpelah Mt. Carmel, Mt. Neboh, and Hungarian cemeteries.

☺ **HIGHLAND PARK.** Bounded by Highland Blvd., Jamaica Ave., Jackie Robinson Pkwy. Call New York City information line 311 or www.nycgovparks.org.

Snug by the Brooklyn border, this 140-acre park has basketball, tennis, playgrounds, and special seasonal events for children. It's near the Ridgewood Reservoir, which was recently decommissioned and is being turned into parkland. Highland Park is on the Atlantic Flyway and is a good site for bird-watching.

☺ **MAFERA PARK (FARMERS OVAL).** 65 Pl. and Catalpa Ave. at 68th Ave. Call New York City information line 311 or www.nycgovparks.org.

This five-acre park has a long history in the neighborhood. For decades it was known as Farmers Oval, then Ridgewood Park, and Glen Ridge Park. From it you can see the Long Island Railroad freight tracks (there are no passenger stops in this neighborhood). It has a roller rink with sideboards and bleachers as well as baseball, basketball, and handball courts.

☺ **METROPOLITAN OVAL.** 60-58 60th St (Maspeth), 417-4455.

The Metropolitan Oval is New York City's oldest soccer field in continuous use. Built in 1925 by German and Hungarian immigrants, it fell into serous disrepair, although it has remained in use as the venue for intense soccer games among more recent immigrants from South America.

But once again they call it the best soccer field in the city, thanks to a last-minute fiscal rescue by the U.S. Soccer Foundation, several corporations, and the New York City Department of Parks and Recreation. Still owned by the German-Hungarian Metro Soccer Club, the Oval now boasts a state-of-the-art durable synthetic soccer field with good lighting, new equipment, and even a concession area. The beneficiaries are the more than 2,000 kids ages 6 to 17 who play soccer each week.

RIDGEWOOD RESERVOIR. South of Jackie Robinson Parkway, straddling the border of Brooklyn and Queens. Call New York City information line 311. www.nycgovparks.org.

Originally built on a cornfield, the long-defunct Ridgewood Reservoir is being rejuvenated as a fifty-acre public park. From certain vantage points, you can see the Empire State Building in the distance. Ground was broken for the Ridgewood Reservoir in 1856 on the site of Snediker's Cornfield. Water was first raised into the reservoir in 1858 by two large pumps each with a capacity of 14 million gallons per day. (There's still a street named Force Tube Ave. on the Brooklyn, or south, side of Highland Park, named for the high-pressure water mains that once ran under the street.) By 1868 the reservoir held 154,400,000 gallons, which was enough for the City of Brooklyn. (Today, New York City consumes seven times that much water daily.) Used only as a back-up supply for Brooklyn and Queens since the 1960s, the complex was idle for over a decade until being turned into a public park.

JUNIPER VALLEY PARK. Bounded by Dry Harbor Rd., Juniper Blvd., and Lutheran Ave., Middle Village.

This fifty-five-acre park with fields for recreation, baseball, and tennis courts is the perfect place to enjoy a few hours of rural bliss. When you're done contemplating nature, stop in at Fortunata's for a slice of pizza.

POINTS OF CULTURAL INTEREST

GERMAN-AMERICAN SCHOOL. 70-01 Fresh Pond Rd. at 70th Ave., 456-8706. Call for class schedule.

A living testimony to Ridgewood's German-American immigrant roots, this school was founded in 1892 "with the purpose of cultivating German language and culture in the United States." Children as young as six can start learning German by drawing and singing; older students and adults study grammar and German literature. Other locations are in Manhattan and Long Island.

🏛 **GREATER RIDGEWOOD HISTORICAL SOCIETY. ONDERDONK HOUSE.** 1820 Flushing Ave., 456-1776. www.ridgewoodhistorical.org. W, Sa noon—4:00 p.m., and by appointment. Admission is $2, free for children.

The Greater Ridgewood Historical Society offers guided house tours, lectures with slides about local historical sites, films, genealogy workshops, and special Dutch celebrations such as St. Nicholas Day. It is one of a half-dozen local historical societies in Queens. See Onderdonk House, p. 243.

VENDITTI SQUARE. Corner Myrtle Ave. and St. Nicholas Ave.

This little park, marked by a prominent street clock and a nondescript diner, is a good central meeting place for visitors. It also marks the spot where, in 1986, a thirty-four-year-old police officer, Anthony J. Venditti, who was part of a Joint Organized Crime Strike Force surveillance unit assigned to the Genovese organized crime family, was killed in a shootout with mobsters at the Castillo Diner. A chef from the diner who'd witnessed the crime and testified was found dead several years later, with a pile of dead fish nearby. ("Dead fish" in mob-speak apparently warns informants of their fate: that they will end up in the river, sleeping with the fish.) News reports said that witnesses described how local Italian social clubs had been the site of illegal betting and numbers operations.

POINTS OF HISTORICAL AND ARCHITECTURAL INTEREST

EVERGREEN KNITTING FACTORY. Now Fleur Des Lis Caterers, 870 Cypress Ave., near Jefferson Ave.

According to the Web site Forgotten NY, this was apparently the site of the Evergreen Knitting Factory, back when Ridgewood was called Evergreen and knitting and breweries were big local industries. The building here today is new.

 MATHEWS MODEL FLATS. Stockholm St. bet. Onderdonk and Woodward Aves. (house #s 1862–68, 1870–74, 1867–93).

Mathews Model Flats were a huge hit in their day. Essentially three-story row houses, they were designed by Gusatav Mathews to have a bit of individual flair. They are faced in multicolored brick, some with arched windows on the third floor. These homes were recognized by New York City's Tenement House Department as so progressive in their conception that they were shown at the 1915 Panama-Pacific Exposition in San Francisco. Mathews Model Flats are scattered throughout the city, but there are whole streets of them in Ridgewood.

RIDGEWOOD NATIONAL BANK. Corner Myrtle and Cypress Aves.

It's a Rite Aid drugstore today, but one look at this ornate building with brass friezes inlaid in the doorways and a vintage clock, and you know it was designed as something grander than a drugstore. Paul Steir and other prominent businessmen formed Ridgewood National Bank in 1909. This was their building, erected in the 1920s, a concrete statement of success.

🚶 A WALK THROUGH HISTORIC RIDGEWOOD

If you want to get a general sense of what kind of houses were landmarked in Ridgewood, walk down Stockholm St. bet. Onderdonk and Woodward Aves. and look at houses numbered 1862–68, 1870–74, 1867–93. These classic row

houses by Mathews Model Flats, built for both function and a sense of indi-
viduality, are in the Stockholm-DeKalb-Hart Historic District (bounded by
Stockholm St., DeKalb Ave., and Hart St. bet. Onderdonk and Woodward
Aves.).

For a more detailed look-see, we've selected a handful of the mini–historic
districts in Ridgewood below. All feature a range of early-twentieth-century
homes built over a series of years in different styles. We suggest you take a
map and plot yourself a route, including a stop for a snack on Fresh Pond
Road.

🏛 Madison-Putnam-60th Pl. Historic District (bounded by Woodbine
St., 60th Pl., and 67th and Forest Aves.) is lined with row houses built from
1905 to 1921. The 🏛 Cornelia-Putnam Historic District (bounded by Jefferson St. and Putnam Ave., and Wyckoff and Myrtle Aves.) displays a range
of Renaissance and Romanesque Revival row houses and tenements, built
from 1907 to 1922. The 🏛 75th Ave.-61st St. Historic District (bounded by
St. Felix Ave., 60th Lane, and 60th and 62nd Sts.) has row houses from 1910
to 1925.

If you want to see more, explore the blocks around Cypress Ave. for fine
examples of homes and institutions built from 1902 until the beginning of
World War I. Specifically, the 🏛 Cypress Ave. East Historic District (defined
by Linden and Cornelia Sts., and Seneca and St. Nicholas Aves.) has classic
Romanesque and Renaissance Revival tenements built from 1900 to 1914.
Nearby, you can see row houses and tenements dating from 1888 to 1906.
Public School 81 (1902) at 559 Cypress Ave. is considered a fine example of
Georgian Revival style. Check out the rows along Bleecker and Menahan Sts.
across from the school, recognized as some of the best examples of model
flats of that era. Nearby you can also see Gothic Revival St. John's Ridgewood
United Methodist Church (1905–10). The 🏛 Central Ridgewood Historic Dis-
trict (bounded by Fresh Pond Rd. and Putnam, 68th, Forest, Catalpa, Onderdonk, and 71st Aves.) includes the marvelous Gothic Revival Covenant
Lutheran Church.

For detailed information on the history and architectural styles, as well as
the boundaries of all mini historic districts, contact the Greater Ridgewood
Historical Society (see p. 241).

☺ 🏛 **ONDERDONK HOUSE.** 1820 Flushing Ave., 456-1776. www.ridgewoodhistorical.org. W, Sa
noon–4:00 p.m., and by appointment. Admission is $2, free for children.

This landmark Dutch colonial farmhouse, originally built around 1709 and
restored to museum-quality by the Greater Ridgewood Historical Society, is one
of a few early-eighteenth-century structures extant in New York City. Inside you
can see artifacts of daily life in the colonial era, including clay pipes and ceramic
beer bottle tops. Occasional festivals, such as the traditional June Strawberry
Festival, are fun for children. It is the home of the Greater Ridgewood Historical
Society (p. 241). It's located in a light industrial area; it's best to drive.

ROMAN CATHOLIC CHURCH OF ST. ALOYSIUS AND RECTORY. 382 Onderdonk Ave. at Stockholm St.

This Catholic Church is noted for two 165-foot-high towers. It was built in 1907, when the neighborhood first really began to develop and attract new residents. The older building around the corner was built as a convent in 1817.

STIER PLACE. Bet. Putnam Ave. and 67th and 68th Aves.

To see why Ridgewood is considered so charming, take a gander down dead-end Stier Place, a small street lined with beautiful rounded buildings built between 1908 and 1914. It is named after Paul Stier, a German immigrant who built over seven hundred homes in Ridgewood. At Stier and Putnam Ave., note the building with the engraved "Ridgewood Democratic Club" above the doorway. This was originally Stier's home. Also nearby, check out tiny Kleupfel Court, where there are two private homes down an alleyway.

RESTAURANTS

BONA RESTAURANT. 71-24 Fresh Pond Rd. bet. Myrtle Ave. and 71st Ave., 386-4400. Daily noon—10:00 p.m.

Tiny redbricked Bona is an unpretentious and clean Polish eatery. Pick from among a variety of hearty vegetable, sauerkraut, or beef tripe soups, priced at $2.50. Or pay a buck extra and you can get classic fruit soup or red borsht with meat. There are seven different kinds of blintzes, pierogies with meat, sweet cheese, or fruit, and specials like stuffed meat loaf or pork chop with plums that will fill you up.

EXCLUSIVE ROSA PIZZA. 62-65 Fresh Pond Rd. near Bleeker St., 497-7672. Daily 10:30 a.m.—10:00 p.m.

This looks like any old pizzeria, but the Sicilian pizza tastes like the best in Queens. That's why some people will travel half an hour to get there.

KREDEN'S RESTAURANT. 66-36 Fresh Pond Rd. at Woodbine St., 628-5214. Tu—Su noon—10:00 p.m.

Kreden's Restaurant is named after a classy Warsaw eatery, and the New York version is appropriately old-world elegant down to the white lace tablecloths over dark wood tables. The European-style menu offers classics such as stuffed smoked salmon, varieties of herring, potato babka, and whole grilled fish. Don't miss the potato pancakes or side order of dumplings. You can order ahead for take-out.

ZUM STAMMTISCH. 69-46 Myrtle Ave. at Cooper Ave., 386-3014. Su—Th noon—10:00 p.m., F—Sa noon—11:00 p.m.

This two-generation family restaurant in nearby Glendale harks back to a time when there were many German immigrants in this part of Queens. With decor reminiscent of a Bavarian inn (complete with a large moose head on the wall), you are in for a trip down memory lane spiced with sausages, schnitzels, and strudel. Try the *kieler* rollmops (rolled pickled herring stuffed with mushrooms), goulash soup, and sauerbraten. The restaurant's name is derived from "tisch" meaning table, and "stamm" meaning family, roughly translated as "family table."

SHOPPING

Specialty and Ethnic Food Shops

JANTAR DELI. 66-66 Fresh Pond Rd. bet Madison St. and Putnam Ave., 326-5454. Daily 6:30 a.m.–9:30 p.m.

Home-cooking just like Mama's (well, if Mama came from Poland) explains why locals wait patiently in lines six people deep for chicken schnitzel, pork cutlets, and a half dozen kinds of slaws. Jantar Deli is spanking clean, well-stocked, modestly priced, and often the busiest of many delis along this street.

MORSCHERS PORK STORE. 58-46 Catalpa Ave., 821-1040. Daily 8:00 a.m.–7:30 p.m.

In need of pumpkin seed oil? Try Morschers, known for meats and German gourmet foods. Started in 1957, this two-generation family business has married high-tech meat processing with old-fashioned German sausage making. The display case is overflowing with delicious-looking smoked meats, salami, cold cuts, bratwurst, and many other varieties of sausages. Buy some German cookies or Polish pickles for a nosh while waiting at the Forest Ave. stop for the M train home, because wait you will. Nearby are two other long-standing specialty butchers, **FOREST PORK STORE** (66-39 Forest Ave., 497-2853), and **KARL EHMER** (several locations including 635 Fresh Pond Rd., 456-8100, www.karlehmer.com. M–W 8:00 a.m.–5:00 p.m., Th–F 8:00 a.m.–7:30 p.m., Sa 7:00 a.m.–6:00 p.m.).

STAROWIEJSKI DELI. 66-51 Fresh Pond Rd. bet. Woodbine and Madison Sts., 456-1558. M–F 9:00 a.m.–9:00 p.m., Sa 9:00 a.m.–8:00 p.m., Su 9:00 a.m.–6:00 p.m.

The handwritten signs posted in Polish on the community bulletin board outside this deli are a clue that Starowiejski serves as an informal neighborhood hub. Inside, you can purchase interesting imported or just-like-home products, from huge hearty loaves of bread and unusual jams to special cheeses, and, of course, sausages galore. They even sell Polish mayonnaise.

Other Interesting Neighborhood Shops

DOMSEY EXPRESS. 16-09 Palmetto St., at the corner of Wyckoff and Myrtle Aves., 386-7661. M–F 9:00 a.m.–6:00 p.m., Sa 10:00 a.m.–7:00 p.m., Su 11:00 a.m.–5:00 p.m. Other locations in Brooklyn.

Domsey is one of the Big Apple's premier sources of cheap vintage clothing. The masses of secondhand clothing often boast brand names, with some designer pieces mixed in. Come when you are in the mood to dig for gold.

EURO ESSENCE COSMETICA. 68-06 Fresh Pond Rd. at 68th Ave., 386-0806. M–F 11:00 a.m.–8:00 p.m., Sa 10:00 a.m.–7:00 p.m., Su 2:00 p.m.–4:00 p.m.

Adventuresome beauties will find an extensive line of imported Polish cosmetics, herbal treatments, cleansers, and hair products here, along with perfumes.

☺ **NAGENGAST TRUE VALUE HARDWARE.** 68-02 Fresh Pond Rd. at 68th Ave., 821-0958. M–F 9:00 a.m.–6:30 p.m., Sa 9:00 a.m.–6:00 p.m., Su 10:00 a.m.–3:00 p.m.

Nagengast Hardware is an old-fashioned hobby and toy shop from the days before cable TV, portable game players, and iPods. Known among mail-order hobbyists as a source for Trix model trains and accessories, it was started in 1947 by the late Thomas Nagengast, and retains an unmistakable mid-twentieth-century simplicity. Great for kids of all ages.

ALSO NEARBY

FORTUNATA'S. 65-26 Metropolitan Ave., off 65th St., 456-4786. M–F 9:00 a.m.–10:00 p.m., Sa–Su 10:00 a.m.–11:00 p.m.

There's a Little Italy in Middle Village, which is where you'll find Fortunata's terrific pizzeria. Napolitano and Sicilian slices come with all the regular New York toppings. There's also a limited menu tempting you with pasta, chicken, and seafood classics like shrimp parmiagana.

IAVARONE BROTHERS. 75-12 Metropolitan Ave. at 75th St., 326-0510. M–Th, Sa 8:00 a.m.–6:00 p.m., F 8:00 a.m.–6:30 p.m., Su 9:00 a.m.–2:00 p.m.

All-in-one butcher, deli, and specialty shop, Iavarone Brothers in nearby Middle Village is the kind of place where you can buy fresh sausage and braciole (rolled beef) from the meat counter in the back, then choose your homemade mozzarella from the deli counter, and select fresh locally baked loaves and homemade chicken soup from the two small aisles.

✐ ESSAY

QUEENS DESERVES MORE DESIGNATED LANDMARKS

by Jim Driscoll, President, Queens Historical Society.

Numerous historical societies in Queens have attempted to obtain landmark status for buildings in order to preserve them for posterity. There's a high level of frustration among these experts as they watch old structures get torn down or get irrevocably changed.

In October of 2005, the New York City Council blocked the Landmarks Commission from designating the modern 1968 Jamaica Savings Bank building at 89-01 Queens Boulevard in Elmhurst as a New York City Landmark building. As Yogi Berra said, "It's déjà vu all over again," because nearly ten years earlier the same group prevented the landmarking of another Jamaica Savings Bank building, a beautiful 1897 Beaux Arts building in downtown Jamaica.

Because of politics, Queens has barely fifty individual landmarks to Manhattan's more than 1,000. Many deserving sites in Queens—cemeteries, homes, churches, neighborhoods, some dating from as far back as the 1700s—therefore go unrecognized. Walk through Richmond Hill and look at the beautiful late-nineteenth-century Victorian homes and you'll ask yourself why this early suburban community hasn't been declared a New York City historic district. Visit nearby Kew Gardens, another suburban-style community, which grew up around a 1910 Long Island Railroad Station, and you'll ask yourself the same question. There are also a number of individual sites that cry out for landmarking, such as the Bowne Street Church in Flushing or P.S. 34 in Queens Village or the New York State building in Flushing Meadows—Corona Park.

There have been some victories in recent years. The Hill section of Douglaston has recently been declared a historic district and so have the homes on Stockholm Street in Ridgewood. There are now six historic districts in Queens, including Jackson Heights, one of the first garden apartment communities. But so much more needs to be done. Unless our historic treasures are protected, it will soon be too late, as more and more of these Queens landmarks are being bulldozed.

17

The Rockaways and Howard Beach

WHERE IT IS: Southernmost Queens, on a peninsula bounded to the north by Rockaway Inlet, to the east by Nassau County, and to the south and west by the Atlantic Ocean.

HOW TO GET THERE BY SUBWAY: A subway to Beach 105th St./Seaside or Rockaway Park/Beach 116th St.

WHAT'S NEARBY: Atlantic Ocean to the south, Jamaica Bay to the north, Long Island to the east, and Brooklyn to the west.

MAJOR SHOPPING/RESTAURANT STREETS: None.

SPECIAL CHARACTERISTICS: Beach, Atlantic Ocean, Jamaica Bay, and National Parkland.

ON NOT GETTING LOST: It's hard to get lost here, because the island is simply long and narrow. However, if you are traveling by public transport, bring a large dose of patience.

CAR SERVICES: Belle Rock 634-8282, Cross Bay 641-7070, Martin's 634-1200, Surf 327-4444.

BEACHES, BOARDWALK, AND BUNGALOWS

Here at the very outer reaches of New York City, Queens boasts broad sandy Atlantic Ocean beaches that are in every way equal to the famed beaches of the Hamptons and Montauk. Rockaway Beach has a seven-mile boardwalk that's longer than even the famous Atlantic City boardwalk. There's a wildlife preserve here, a decommissioned fort, and even a tiny museum.

It's well worth a full- or half-day trip to explore the Rockaways, especially in warmer weather when you can include an expedition to the beach or a meal overlooking the water. But where, exactly, to go? There's a reason this area is plural, as in the Rockaways. Rockaway Peninsula is about a ten-mile-long spit of sand, facing the Atlantic Ocean on one side, and Jamaica Bay and Rockaway Inlet on the other. It is comprised of a series of small, quite distinct communities:

THE ROCKAWAYS, JAMAICA BAY, HOWARD BEACH, & JFK AIRPORT

* Private with limited public access

ATLANTIC OCEAN

Breezy Point, Neponsit, Belle Harbor, Rockaway Park, Arverne, and Far Rockaway. What's what, who's who, and where are they anyway?

☛ **TIP: Bending the Map.** We've included Howard Beach in this chapter. It's not on Rockaway Peninsula, of course, but it shares Jamaica Bay with the communities of the Rockaways. Our apologies to those whose feathers may be ruffled.

THINGS TO SEE AND DO: FOUR ITINERARIES

For a getaway, you can save some money and instead of going to an overnight bed-and-breakfast in Connecticut, take the train to the Rockaways (or drive) and spend a day off just looking around. Pick up a copy of *The Wave* newspaper for local flavor.

🚶 ITINERARY #1 (SUMMER):

Subway riders can take the A train to Broad Channel, then switch to the shuttle to get to 116th St. (if you stay on the A train it will take you to Far Rockaway). Bring your beach gear. Walk around 116th, poke into the Surf Shop, check out the architecture walk on 117th St. (and eat your heart out that you didn't buy one of those apartments before the real estate boom hit here). Enjoy the beach. Or hop a bus to 129th St. to Plum Tomato for a hearty Italian meal.

🚶 ITINERARY #2:

If you have a car, trek out to Arverne to see the evolution of an entire neighborhood from scratch. On your way home, stop for a swim at 116th St.

🚶 ITINERARY #3:

Drive to Fort Tilden to bird-watch, fish, or see the old fort. You can use the beach, but not to swim (no lifeguards). Or, go for the day to Jacob Riis Park beach, with full public amenities. Contact the Post Theater to see if there's a good concert or play.

🚶 **I**TINERARY #4:

Contact Jamaica Bay Wildlife Reserve for a schedule of public events and tours, and pick your favorite outing. It's cheaper than going to the country, and the wildlife is fabulous. Take a peek at Broad Channel, too.

☞ **TIP: Do Not Swim Without Lifeguards.** Every year there are reports of off-hours drownings due to sudden dropoffs and riptides at the Rockaway Beaches when people venture into the water off-hours. This beach may look the same as Coney Island and Jones Beach, but the water can be more dangerous. Swim only when lifeguards are on duty.

BITS OF HISTORY

This spit of land at the southern end of Queens was initially settled by the Canarsie tribe, but was sold to the Dutch by the Mohegan tribe along with most of Long Island in 1639. During the 1600s Dutch settlers established a community on the island and began harvesting oysters, clams, shrimp, and fish. In the late seventeenth century, much of the land was sold to Richard Cornell, who settled here. (You can still see the Cornell Family Cemetery.) Fort Tilden was built as part of an outer harbor defense strategy during the War of 1812. Development of this waterfront area, including railroad transportation, occurred a half century later than in Brooklyn's Coney Island, which enjoys the same broad sand beaches and Atlantic Ocean frontage. In 1864 a ferry from Canarsie in Brooklyn to Rockaway Peninsula was the first public transportation available.

Old photos of the area show marvelous hotels in the Rockaways. Records indicate that many prominent people visited here: Henry Wadsworth Longfellow and Washington Irving visited the mid-nineteenth-century Marine Pavilion Hotel in Far Rockaway. In the late nineteenth century, three railroad lines were built to the end of the borough. The owners of the LIRR acquired a wide swath of waterfront property and designated it for private use in a fashionable development that was successful. New York City politicos used to hobnob on fancy Hog Island, gorgeously situated off the Rockaway shore. In Rockaway Beach, they built boardwalks, bungalows, boulevards, and hotels. Rockaway Beach Amusement Park (which opened in 1901) stayed in business for more than a half century. The nearby bungalows remained for decades.

Proximity to both the Atlantic Ocean and Jamaica Bay has offered ample opportunity for colorful goings-on, including, it is said, a brisk trade in whiskey and other bootleg items carried on by Irish Americans in the basements of homes, particularly in the inaccessible community of Broad Channel. The local history is fascinating and has been pieced together in part by a local newspaper, *The Wave.* The small Rockaway Museum may be of interest to history buffs.

OVERVIEW OF EIGHT AREAS IN THE ROCKAWAYS

By car you can see a lot of Rockaway Peninsula (pop. 115,000) in one day, assuming of course that you don't spend hours at the beach or paddling on Jamaica Bay. From west to east, nine distinct areas, some public, some not, are described below. So, choose the community you might want to explore; if you rely on public transportation from Manhattan, your choices will be limited and you should plan to spend considerable time getting here and back. Places that appear in bold below are described in more detail later in the chapter.

1. Breezy Point

On the westernmost tip of Rockaway Peninsula, Breezy Point is the first community you come to if you arrive by way of the Marine Parkway Bridge. The residential community is sited on an enviable location, on a spit of land surrounded by water on three sides. For decades it was a simple blue-collar and mostly Irish bungalow colony, with many families of firemen, teachers, and policemen. When the land was about to be sold for the construction of high-rise housing in the 1960s local residents got together and formed a cooperative community instead. Today the community consists of about 3,000 homes, from large elegant waterfront homes to modest bungalows. A small year-round population swells to more than 12,000 in the summer. The original Irish community has been diluted but the area lacks the diversity that characterizes the rest of the borough.

Most of Breezy Point is a private community. The private Breezy Point Security Force may request to see your ID at any time. Technically, however, anyone with a fishing permit (obtained at nearby Fort Tilden) has the right to traverse the private community's road to get to Breezy Point Tip, which is land owned by Uncle Sam.

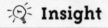 **Insight**

A Shifting Shoreline

According to the U.S. Geological Survey, "Had you planned a visit to Breezy Point before the Civil War you would have been in for a surprise. It did not exist! All the land west of the vicinity of **Jacob Riis Park** has formed within a little more than a century. This is largely because of the construction of a groin field to protect the beaches at Fort Tilden, and the placement of the Breezy Point jetty to prevent the filling of Rockaway Inlet. The sand has been contributed naturally by the westward longshore drift along the south shore of Long Island, particularly the Rockaway barrier island and sources offshore."

2. Fort Tilden, Gateway National Recreation Area, and Jacob Riis Park

Also on the western point of the peninsula, **Fort Tilden** began as an outer harbor defense post during the War of 1812. The site was expanded following the Spanish American War. Fort Tilden was host to a battery of Nike nuclear missiles in the 1950s. The fort was decommissioned and added to the land trust that, along with Jamaica Bay and other areas, became part of the **Gateway National Recreation Area** in 1972. Today you can fish and bird-watch or enjoy local cultural activities such as the **Post Theater** at Fort Tilden and shows at **Rockaway Center for the Arts (ROCA)** at Fort Tilden. **Jacob Riis Park,** a huge and recently renovated public beach facility, was initiated under the New Deal era of federally sponsored public works projects. Opened in 1936, it is one of New York's great resources.

3. Neponsit and Belle Harbor

Moving eastward, two small upper-middle-class residential communities evolved. Started in the early 1900s, Neponsit and Belle Harbor differed from other parts of the Rockaways in that they were built for year-round living and zoned only for residential use. There are beachfront properties with driveways that fit two cars (a rarity in New York) and brazen McMansions built on 30 × 100-foot parcels of land. Larger homes and winterized beach cottages from the 1930s are interspersed in some areas. Every block differs; you'll find yourself wanting to peek down the next block to see what's there. New Yorkers and tourists alike are often struck by how distant culturally and geographically this feels from, say, Times Square. You can use the beaches but no public or street parking is allowed May to September and there are no public facilities for miles. Cyclists might park at Riis Park and bike here. For food, coffee, and local color, go to the shops on Beach 129th Street.

4. Rockaway Park

About midway down the peninsula is Rockaway Park, developed in the post–Civil War period as a seaside resort. Several grand hotels, including the Hotel Imperial, were built (and later burned, as they were constructed of wood), and for decades developers tried to lure visitors by advertising ocean-side relief from stifling Manhattan summers. Starting in the 1880s, the Long Island Railroad linked the area to the outside world. Small colonies of unheated summer bungalows attracted vacationers. By the turn of the century, Rockaway Beach Amusement Park opened, surviving until 1985. Today there are efforts to revitalize the area. For instance, luxury apartments have been built at Belle Shores Condos (168 Beach 101st St. at Shore Front Pkwy.).

5. Rockaway Beach at 116th St.

Here's a public beach, accessible by the A subway line to 116th St. On the four commercial blocks along 116th St. approaching the beach and boardwalk, the old buildings are no more than two or three stories high. Sea breezes are unobstructed. The fabulously ramshackle 1860s Hotel Lawrence (condemned and missing the *w*) sits next door to the Baxter Hotel, a single-room-occupancy hotel that is now home primarily to recipients of welfare. As of this writing there are no chain stores, not even a Starbucks. Instead, you'll see Rockaway Surf Snacks, Ciro's Italian Pizza, Grants Hardware, and Ocean Wave Bagels. Some of the best beachfront real estate is taken up by institutions such as the Park Nursing Home and Park Inn. Woody Allen's 1987 movie *Radio Days* was set here, and perfectly captured the ambience. Things may be changing, however. One high-rise has already been built and the area may be subject to gentrification. There's been a recent surge in new housing development east of Beach 125th St.

☼ Insight

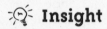

RIP Hog Island: Gone Forever

Hog Island was a popular resort in the 1890s, a favorite destination off Rockaway Beach where Tammany Hall's political elite partied, plotted, and (pardon the pun) lived high on the hog. Then a humongous storm blew in on August 23, 1893, totally eradicating the small barrier island—and everything on it. The storm was infamous in its era; newspaper accounts describe flooding in Central Park and the destruction of many homes and boats. Hog Island was long forgotten until the early 1990s, when some geology students on a field trip noticed unusual debris on Rockaway Beach. The shards turned out to be broken bits and pieces of century-old household items—whiskey bottles, teapots, and a hurricane lamp—dating to the demise of Hog Island. The story of Hog Island's fate resurfaced after Hurricane Katrina flooded New Orleans and the Gulf Coast in 2005.

6. Jamaica Bay and Broad Channel

Jamaica Bay Wildlife Refuge is more than 9,000 acres of protected marsh and wetland area. The National Park Service offers wonderful (and mostly free) programs.

Broad Channel is the name of a community that occupies the only inhabited island in Jamaica Bay, called Big Egg Marsh. Prior to European settlement, the Jameco and Canarsie Native Americans frequented this area. One of the most idiosyncratic communities in Queens, the less-than-accessible Broad Channel is a blue-collar bastion where houses on stilts line the shore, and everyone knows everyone else's brother-in-law. A fairly insular community with a rich lore of rumrunners in the Prohibition area, it's worth a visit. Broad Channel is north of Rockaway Peninsula. At its northernmost tip, it is close to the **Jamaica Bay Wildlife Refuge.** Broad Channel is accessible by the A train but it may be faster to drive over the **Cross Bay Veterans Memorial Bridge.**

☞ **TIP: Forever Wild Wildlife Preserves.** http://nycgovparks.org/sub_about/ parks_divisions/nrg/forever_wild/foreverwild_home.html.

The New York City Department of Parks and Recreation has a project to identify and protect the most ecologically valuable lands within the five boroughs, called the Forever Wild Program. Jamaica Bay is one.

7. Arverne

Instant communities have popped up all over the United States, like in the exurbs of Ohio and Texas, but in New York it's unusual. At the far end of Rockaway Beach, a community of twenty-three hundred homes, including single-family, double-family, and condo units, is to be completed before the end of the decade. This nearly 130-acre planned community is going up along what's been called "the nation's largest piece of vacant oceanfront land within city limits." It is the end of the line, literally the last stop on the snoozy A train. As envisioned by developers Benjamin-Beechwood, Inc., in addition to homes, a large YMCA, stores, a renovated subway station, marina, local parks, a school, and day-care facilities will also be built.

In the late 1880s and early 1900s, Arverne was one gem in a necklace of popular Atlantic Ocean resort communities in the Rockaways. There were bungalows, hotels, and restaurants here. But after World War II, white flight to the suburbs, and the advent of cheap air travel enabling people to vacation elsewhere ushered in decades of neglect. Many bungalows and old buildings were razed in the 1960s. The area was declared ripe for urban renewal that never quite happened. Wild dogs took up residence on the beachside. City officials and investors have eyed this swath of beachfront real estate for a long time, but earlier proposals, including one for a Japanese-style indoor, year-round ski resort, never took hold. Finally, the local community board took the pulse of local residents to discover what they'd like in their own backyard, and the resulting new Arverne mirrors the modest hopes of the middle class: affordable housing, a supermarket, nearby schools, and public transportation to work. The first several dozen units were priced for affordability, with single-family homes selling in the $400,000–500,000 range. The first families took up residence in 2005.

8. Far Rockaway

At the far eastern part of New York City, just on the border with Nassau County, Far Rockaway became a seaside resort in the pre–Civil War era and remained so until the end of World War II. In the 1960s and 1970s the area went into decline and many mansions were turned into nursing homes. Immigrants from Jamaica and Guyana have settled here. Today there's a large elderly population and a lower-income community.

9. Howard Beach

Howard Beach is *not* on the Rockaway Peninsula, but for the sake of convenience, we're including it here, partly because you can get there on the same A train that takes you to the Rockaways. This small, neatly laid out community has a certain quaint 1950s quality once you get off Cross Bay Blvd. It was founded in the 1890s by William J. Howard, a manufacturer of leather gloves. As the story goes, Howard built a goat farm here (to obtain skins for his gloves). He also dredged land and developed over 500 acres by World War I. The local railroad station and post office took on the name Howard Beach by 1916. Mostly Italian and Jewish, this noticeably flat area has some waterfront and several good Italian eateries. Unfortunately it is also well known as the site of several violent racial incidents.

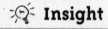 **Insight**

The Future: Will the Rockaways Become the Hamptons?

The Rockaways' natural assets—surf and sand, bay and ocean, beachside property just an hour's subway ride away from Lincoln Center—are obvious. Although many long-time residents are wed to the status quo, ambitious developers imagine a different future here. They envision a gentrified area with upscale boutiques, condos, restaurants, and cultural life. If artists often pave the way for such developments, then the early uptick of gentrification may already be happening, as historic 1920s-era bungalows are being snapped up and old Victorians renovated in Rockaway Park. Real estate prices have jumped in certain areas such as Beach 116th and 125th Sts. Long known as "the poor man's beach," the Rockaways might be the next big wave in New York's real estate boom.

PARKS, BEACHES, NATURE PRESERVES, AND PUBLIC WORKS

☺ Beaches

ROCKAWAY BEACH (AND SURFING BEACH). Beach 1st St. in Far Rockaway to Beach 149th St. in Neponsit, 318-4000. Memorial–Labor Day, 10:00 a.m.–6:00 p.m.

This is a huge expanse of beach, a 7.5-mile stretch that's all public. It's gorgeous. The boardwalk runs from Beach 9th St. on the eastern end of the peninsula to Beach 126th St. At Beach 86th St. there's an outdoor shower on the boardwalk and public rest rooms. A Surfers-Only Beach (between the jetties between Beach 87th and Beach 91st Sts.) was created in 2005 as the first ever legally surfable beach in the city.

🏛 **JACOB RIIS PARK.** Bet. Beach 149th and Beach 169th Sts. along the Atlantic Ocean front, 318-4300, or call New York City information line 311 or www.nycgovparks.org. Open, with lifeguards, from Memorial Day to Labor Day 10:00 a.m.–6:00 p.m.; otherwise 6:00 a.m.–midnight daily. Beach access is free. Parking is $4. Public transportation involves taking a subway and then a bus.

One full mile of broad sandy ocean beach, rolling waves, and landmark bathhouses make this one of the most remarkable destinations in New York City. There's no overestimating the power of that moment when, having fled the scorching New York pavement, you arrive at this wide expanse of sand spreading majestically before you. There are also places for pitch and putt golf, handball, basketball, a playground and picnic areas, as well as a small food concession stand. NOTE: The surf can be tricky and due to riptides it's advised not to swim unless lifeguards are present.

Festivals include the free New York Kite Festival in August and concerts, produced by the Rockaway Music and Arts Council, in September. The Park Service and various historic organizations occasionally run tours of historic Jacob Riis Park.

Jacob Riis Park is part of Gateway National Recreation Center as is contiguous Fort Tilden. Riis Park (1932–37) has been designated a historic district. This park is known among lovers of architecture for its classic 1930s-era Deco buildings, broad boardwalk, historic sidewalk clock, and other features. The huge bathhouses in particular convey a readiness to respectfully serve throngs of citizens. Only one bathhouse has been renovated; another stands ghostlike waiting for resuscitation. The park is named after journalist and social reformer Jacob Riis, who lived in Richmond Hill, Queens. (See p. 228.)

Bridges

CROSS BAY VETERANS MEMORIAL BRIDGE. Rockaway Beach Blvd. at Cross Bay Parkway (Beach 93rd St.).

This 1939 bridge is four miles east of the Marine Parkway Bridge. It connects the seaside communities of the Rockaway Peninsula to the Jamaica Wildlife Refuge, Broad Channel, Howard Beach, and the rest of Queens, as well as both the Belt and Southern State Parkways. As of this writing, there's a $2.25 toll.

MARINE PARKWAY–GIL HODGES BRIDGE. Beach Channel Dr. to South End of Flatbush Ave., Brooklyn.

This pleasant bridge with water views connects Brooklyn to Queens at Rockaway Peninsula. It's also a popular spot for fishing and a route for cyclists (but beware, the dedicated bike/pedestrian lane is tight). When it was built, the bridge's vertical lift span was the longest in the world. Gil Hodges was a Brooklyn Dodgers first baseman and Mets manager. As of this writing, there's a $2.25 toll.

Nature Preserves

☺ **GATEWAY NATIONAL RECREATIONAL PARK.** 318-4340.

Gateway National Recreational Park is a 26,000-acre recreation area located in the heart of the New York metropolitan area. The park extends through three New York City boroughs and into northern New Jersey.

In Queens, Gateway National Park includes Jamaica Bay Wildlife Refuge, Jacob Riis Park, Fort Tilden, West Beach, and the Breezy Point Tip, all south of Jamaica Bay on the western end of the Rockaway Peninsula.

Located north of Jamaica Bay in Howard Beach are the two recent additions to the district, Frank Charles Park and Hamilton Beach, both of which are managed for traditional recreational uses.

JAMAICA BAY WILDLIFE REFUGE. Gateway National Recreation Area, bordered by the Rockaway Peninsula to the South, Brooklyn to the West, and Queens to the East, 318-4340. www.nature.nps.gov/jbi/BPD.htm. Visitor center, Open daily 8:30 a.m.–5:00 p.m. Trails open by permit only.

Where in a city of 8 million can you find undeveloped natural terrain with a total area nearly equal to that of Manhattan? Here! You can walk the nature trails, bird-watch, and hike.

Jamaica Bay is twenty square miles of water between Brooklyn and Queens, sheltered from the Atlantic Ocean by Rockaway Peninsula. It is an 18,000-acre wetland estuary, containing numerous islands separated by a labyrinth of waterways, meadowlands, and water. Jamaica Bay is home to more than 325 species of birds, fifty species of butterflies, and one hundred species of fish. It's a favorite stop on the Atlantic Flyway, a migratory route of Northern American birds.

Jamaica Bay Wildlife Refuge is a protected area that encompasses 9,155 acres, with diverse habitats including salt marshes, several fresh and brackish water ponds, upland field and woods, and an open expanse of bay and islands. The National Park Service calls this "one of the most important urban wildlife refuges in the United States."

They also offer wonderful (and mostly free) programs such as introduction to canoeing, sailing, fly-fishing, and surf casting. You can don waders and use a seine net. You can take walking and bike tours of Rockaway Peninsula, tours of ecologically fragile environments, tours to identify local wildflowers, bird- and butterfly-watching trips, and a historic tour dedicated to learning about social reformer Jacob Riis after whom nearby Riis Park is named. See the Web site for lectures, environmental tours, and special events.

The refuge was initially managed by the New York City Parks Department. In 1951, Parks Commissioner Robert Moses, after consultation with the U.S. Fish and Wildlife Service, ordered the creation of two large freshwater ponds, today known as the East Pond (100 acres) and the West Pond (45 acres). In 1972, the refuge was transferred to the National Park Service as part of Gateway National Recreation Area.

☺ **JAMAICA BAY ENVIRONMENTAL TOURS BY THE AMERICAN LITTORAL SOCIETY.** 318-9344. www.alsnyc.org.

This organization is dedicated to the environmental integrity of Jamaica Bay and nearby marine environments. Contact them for their schedule of field trips. For instance, every autumn they organize a coastal cleanup and spring and autumn sunset tours of Jamaica Bay, costing $35 per person.

Other Wildlife Preserves
http://nycgovparks.org/sub_about/parks_divisions/nrg/forever_wild/foreverwild_home.html.

On Rockaway Beach the Arverne Shorebird Preserve is home to breeding piping plovers, and every summer an area between Beach 44th and Beach 57th Sts. is cordoned off to limit disturbance to these rare birds. The Dubos Point Wildlife Sanctuary protects the large salt marsh on the north shore of the Rockaway peninsula east of Rockaway Point. Idlewild Park Preserve is located northeast of John F. Kennedy International Airport, and is bounded by Rockaway Blvd., Springfield Blvd., and 149th Ave., and has woodland, wetland, meadow, and dune-scrub areas. All are nature preserves protected by the Forever Wild program of the New York City Department of Parks.

Other

☺ **ROCKAWAY SKATE PARK.** Shore Front Parkway at Beach 91st St., just off the boardwalk, 318-4000, New York City information line 311 or www.nycgovparks.org. April to mid/late Oct.(weather permitting) M–F 1:45 p.m.–4:45 p.m., Sa–Su 10:00 a.m.–5:00 p.m. Separate times for BMX bikes.

Ten ramps and four grinding rails attract the wild and brave of the young skateboard crowd at this new facility, opened in 2004. Required gear includes helmets and knee and elbow pads. Youth under eighteen must also wear wrist guards and parental release waivers are required.

POINTS OF CULTURAL INTEREST

THE A TRAIN

Like the #7 train, the A takes you places you wouldn't expect to find in New York City, if all you knew was Manhattan. Heading into the Rockaways, it passes Aqueduct Racetrack and rattles through a swampy area where you can still see shacks on stilts. You can get off and explore Howard Beach, and then hop back on the train across Jamaica Bay and into the Rockaways.

BEACH CHANNEL MARINA. 59-14 Beach Channel Dr. in Jamaica Bay's Sommerville Basin, 945-4500. Daily mid-April to mid-Oct.

Mostly used by locals, for many of whom a boat is a second home during the spring, summer, and fall months, this marina has a large number of slips and offers winter storage (outdoors).

CITY COLLEGE CAMPUS. 90-01 Beach Channel Dr., off 90th St. near Cross Bay Memorial Bridge.

The old Beach Channel Drive courthouse will be the location of the first City University facility in the Rockaways. Plans are being formulated as we go to press to upgrade the 1932 courthouse, which closed in 1962.

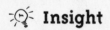 **Insight**

Famous Rockaway References.

What do *Moby-Dick* and the Ramones have in common? Both mention the Rockaways. The Ramones' 1970s hit song was called "Rockaway Beach," of course, and in the first chapter of *Moby-Dick,* written in 1851, Herman Melville wrote, "Were Niagara but a cataract of sand, would you travel your thousand miles to see it? Why did the poor poet of Tennessee, upon suddenly receiving two handfuls of silver, deliberate whether to buy him a coat, which he sadly needed, or invest his money in a pedestrian trip to Rockaway Beach?"

☺ 🏛 **FORT TILDEN.** Rockaway Beach Blvd. directly west of Marine Parkway Bridge, 318-4300. NOTE: Stop at the Visitor Center before parking or walking on the beach or the trails through the old fortifications. Certain access restrictions are applied, especially during shorebird nesting season and summer beach season.

Fort Tilden is a National Historic District. Since 1972, this 317-acre parcel of land has also been a part of Gateway National Park. It was built as part of an outer harbor defense strategy during the War of 1812 and expanded during the Spanish American War in 1898. In the 1950s, Fort Tilden was home to Nike missiles. Today it is decommissioned and there are private beach areas and places for fishing (permits are sold here; bring your own rod) and bird-watching; no swimming allowed.

Just two minutes away from the Marine Park Bridge, you feel as if you've stumbled into a ghost town. It's every bit as exciting as that as you enter a long driveway onto what feels like (because it is) an abandoned military base. The silence of the area—far from New York's addictive diet of fire truck sirens, honking cabs, screeching trains—is eloquent. Where else in the city does it seem perfectly normal to stand around and chew the fat about fishing with park rangers wearing Smokey the Bear uniforms?

Visitors can attend a theater performance at the **Post Theater** (Building T4, 850-2450). From summer through December you can see classics such as *My Fair Lady* or *Arsenic and Old Lace* performed by the Rockaway Theater Company, formed in 1997. The shows are held in an old base building that was renovated into a theater, thanks to a partnership with Gateway National Recreation Area. (Audience applause, please, for recent installation of heating and air-conditioning!) Tickets cost from $12 for seniors and kids at matinees, up to $20 full price, and parking is free.

On weekends you can also visit the **Rockaway Center for the Arts (ROCA)** (Sa noon–5:00 p.m., Su 1:00 p.m.–4:00 p.m., 474-0861), which shows work by the local artist community. Or, you can enjoy the Summer Sunset Picnic Concert Series, with ragtime, klezmer, or groups such as Kenny Vance and the Planotones. The Rockaway Music and Arts Council organize outdoor performances, rain or shine. There's an art show called Art Splash in September.

For family or funky group outings, you can rent one of the buildings on the premises and have a picnic, use some of the outdoor space (not gorgeously manicured, but outdoors nonetheless), and use the beach (but remember, there's no swimming). Oh, and please don't go to Bayside looking for Fort Tilden; that's Fort Totten.

OCEAN GRANDE CONDOS. 137 Beach 116th St. at Rockaway Beach Blvd. and Atlantic Ocean boardwalk, 634-6300. M–F 9:00 a.m.–5:00 p.m.

A harbinger of changes to come? Or unwelcome gentrification of a laid-back beach town? Politics aside, all can agree that the arrival of the ninety-two upscale oceanfront condos, complete with a twenty-four-hour doorman and on-site fitness center, represents a new development on otherwise sleepy Beach 116th St.

THE WAVE. 88-08 Rockaway Beach Blvd. 634-4000. www.rockawave.com.

If you don't read *The Wave,* you won't know what's going on in the Rockaways. The local newspaper, founded in 1893, acts as a force of nature here: a combo vox populi, cultural critic, and focal point of political activism. The historic Wave Building, as it's called, also houses a crafts shop.

PEOPLE, PLACES, AND THINGS OF HISTORICAL INTEREST

BUNGALOWS FROM THE 1920S. Beach 17th–Beach 26th Sts. in Far Rockaway bet. Seagirt Blvd. and the boardwalk.

Take a gander down these streets to see why the local residents think that these 1920s-era bungalows, built by Richard Bainbridge, should be landmarked. Design styles range from brick English Tudor to stucco Spanish revival. All have porches and overhanging eaves. The lanes leading from the bungalows to the beach afford public access to the beach. Efforts are being made to have the bungalows listed on the National Register of Historic Places. For some of the best-preserved bungalows, see Beach 24th and Beach 25th Sts. Currently priced at around a quarter of a million dollars, these one-and-a-half-story cottages are in demand by a new market comprised of artists, writers, and musicians, who come not only in the summer but year-round.

CORNELL FAMILY CEMETERY. Caffrey Ave. at New Haven Ave. adjacent to 1457 Gateway Blvd.

This tiny historic family cemetery, landmarked in 1970, holds more than two dozen graves dating from 1693 to 1820, and includes graves of some of the area's earliest colonial settlers. Volunteer preservationists have worked on cleanup of the site for over a decade.

FIRST PRESBYTERIAN RUSSELL SAGE MEMORIAL CHURCH. 1324 Beach 12th St. at Central Ave., 327-2440.

If you're a fan of Tiffany stained glass, do come visit this church. In memory of millionaire Russell Sage (as in, the benefactor of the Russell Sage Foundation and College), his widow Mrs. Sage built this church. She first hired the best church architect of the day, Ralph Adam Cram, designer of St. John the Divine Cathedral in Manhattan, and then hired Louis Comfort Tiffany to design this grand window. For more on Mrs. Sage, see Bits of History, p. 142.

IRISH BARS. 112-08 Rockaway Beach Blvd., 474-9564

Every neighborhood's got what seems like a lot more of something than other places. What does the long narrow slip of land in the Rockaways have more of than other neighborhoods? Beaches, of course, and old-fashioned, not particularly gentrified bars with Irish names, a living testimony to the Irish heritage here. They have names such as Connolly's and Healy's and Paddy K's Tavern.

ROCKAWAY MUSEUM. 88-08 Rockaway Beach Blvd.

In 1995 a group of local residents and artists banded together and formed this informal museum that's housed in the building owned by the area's local newspaper, *The Wave.* You'll see a bit of the boardwalk from the famous amusement park Rockaway Playland, a collection of bottles called Time in a Bottle, and more memorabilia. The organization is concerned with preserving Rockaway's colorful history, photographs, and artifacts.

WOODY GUTHRIE RESIDENCE. 159-13 85th St. Not open to the public.

Woody died in Howard Beach in 1967. He was the songbird of social justice, this balladeer of the poor in America. Associated with the folk music movement of the 1960s, he was famous for the song "This Land Is Your Land, This Land Is My Land."

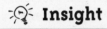 **Insight**

Two 2001 Memorials

This area of New York, home to many firemen and policemen, was terribly hard hit by the 9/11 disaster. Seventy residents of Rockaway died as a result of the attack on the Twin Towers that day. Two months and a day later, a plane crashed in Belle Harbor, in an unrelated tragedy that was the second deadliest aviation accident in American history. Two memorials honor those lost in these events.

TRIBUTE PARK. (Beach Channel Dr. and Jamaica Bay, 634-1300.) Honoring those who perished on September 11, 2001, a memorial park is planned for a site on the bay side of 116th St. The Belle Harbor Rockaway Tribute Park will feature a twelve-foot dome of faceted glass. A separate Firefighter's Tribute will list the names of over 340 firefighters lost that day.

FLIGHT 587 MEMORIAL. (Beach 116th St., near the entrance to the Atlantic Ocean beach.) At 9:16 a.m. on November 12, 2001, American Airlines Flight 587 crashed in Belle Harbor shortly after it took off from JFK en route to Santo Domingo. All passengers and crew perished, along with five people on the ground. The event created a profound loss for families in the United States, the Dominican Republic, France, Haiti, Israel, Taiwan, and the United Kingdom—and particularly for two New York City neighborhoods, Washington Heights and Belle Harbor. A memorial is being planned for this site.

RESTAURANTS AND CAFÉS

BELLE HARBOR STEAKS AND SEAFOOD. 268 Beach 116th St. at Rockaway Beach Blvd., 318-5100. M–Th 11:00 a.m.–9:00 p.m., F–Sa 11:00 a.m.–11:00 p.m.

Belle Harbor brings a touch of class to the area. There's a full bar and the fresh seafood is artfully served.

GINO'S PIZZA. 1038 Beach 20th St. bet. Mott and Cornaga Aves., 471-6825. Daily 11:00 a.m.–10:30 p.m.

You get good honest Italian food here. There's pizza in the front and table service with simple Italian fare in the back.

KENNEDY'S ON THE BAY. 406 Bayside, off Beach 210th St. at Rockaway Pt. Blvd. (Breezy Point) 945-0202. Lunch M–Sa 11:30 a.m.–3:00 p.m.; dinner M–Th 5:00 p.m.–10:00 p.m., F–Sa 5:00 p.m.–11:00 p.m., Su 4:00 p.m.–10:00 p.m., brunch Su 11:30 a.m.–2:00 p.m. Reservations recommended.

Located on a sandy beachfront with views of the distant Empire State Building, and Coney Island housing projects across the water, Kennedy's is a neighborhood bar and restaurant located in the gated community of Breezy Point. There's golf club plaid wallpaper, iceberg lettuce with Roquefort dressing, Muzak in the background, and an American flag in the bar. For the warmest reception, come with a local; otherwise, the security precautions may introduce a chill even on the balmiest evening. When you park in their lot (there's no place else you can park), you will receive a four-hour parking ticket that reads, "Beach use prohibited. Violators will be arrested. Fraudulent use will be prosecuted. . . . Display permit on the windshield or whenever requested by the Breezy Point Security Corps."

LA VILLA PIZZERIA. 82-07 153rd Ave. bet. 81st–83rd Sts. (Howard Beach), 641-8259. Daily 11:00 a.m.–10:30 p.m.

Enormous portions of tasty Italian basics can be found at this Howard Beach restaurant. Try the pizza cooked in wood-fired ovens, broccoli rabe, eggplant involtini, enormous salads, a dynamite antipasto plate, excellent pastas—hey, what more could you ask for? (Note that it's across Jamaica Bay from the Rockaway beaches.)

LENNY'S CLAM BAR AND RESTAURANT, 161-03 CROSS BAY BLVD. (Howard Beach) bet. 161 and 162 Aves., 845-5100. Su–Th 11:00 a.m.–2:00 a.m., F–Sa 11:00 a.m.–4:00 a.m.

Lenny's is a Howard Beach classic Italian seafood joint with good shellfish, and if you ask locals they'll say it's one of the places that defines their neighborhood. (Note that it's across Jamaica Bay from the Rockaway beaches.)

PLUM TOMATO. 420 Beach 129th St. bet. Cronston and Newport Aves., 474-1775. M–Th 11:00 a.m.–10:00 p.m., F–Sa 11:00 a.m.–11:00 p.m.

This family-owned pizzeria on a cute, one-block shopping strip has something for everyone: old-fashioned thin-crusted pizzas, panini, pastas, hearty bowls of hot soup, and a satisfying cappuccino to top it off.

SANDBAR CAFÉ. 122 Beach 116th St. at Rockaway Beach Blvd., 474-1055. Daily May–Sept. 9:00 a.m.–9:00 p.m.; closed in winter.

Fried shrimp and clams are sold on the boardwalk here, in an airy space that tries to evoke the Greek island of Mykonos with a funky nostalgic wall mural. But you are in Queens, not the Cyclades, so indulge in 100 percent American fare: ice cream, frozen custard, ices, hot dogs, beer, and onion rings.

THE WHARF. 416 Beach 116th St. (behind the gas station), Rockaway Beach Blvd., 474-8807. Su–Th 10:00 a.m.–midnight, F–Sa 11:00 a.m.–4:00 a.m.

A local hangout, the Wharf is the kind of beach joint tucked away on a nondescript corner that serves drinks and chicken in a basket. There are magnificent views of the far-off Manhattan skyline, and romantic sunsets, too. Speaking of local color, in fine weather sailors dock here for a bite. Pinch yourself: Is this really the Big Apple?

SHOPPING, ENTERTAINMENT, AND OTHER STUFF

AQUEDUCT RACE TRACK. 110-00 Rockaway Blvd. bet. Cross Bay Blvd. and 114th Pl., 641-4700. www.nyra.com/aqueduct. Late Oct.–early May W–Su 12:30 p.m.–4:10 p.m., gates open at 11:00 a.m.

Opened in 1894, Aqueduct Race Track is the last of the race tracks within the boundaries of the city. It was named after the Ridgewood Reservoir, which was the first large water system in the area (see p. 241). In 2007, it is expected that 4,500 video slot machines are going to open here.

CAKELINE. 220 Beach 132nd St. bet. Newport Ave. and Rockaway Beach Blvd., 634-5063. Not a retail store; by appointment only.

Written up by numerous national magazines, baker Cynthia Peithman produces gorgeously decorated, lusciously tasty, and memorable cakes here, but there's no retail shop.

CAPT. MIKE'S MARINA (AKA THE ANGLER). 158-35 Cross Bay Blvd. bet. 158th and 159th Aves., 659-8181. Late Mar.–early Dec. Daily 8:00 a.m.–noon and 1:00 p.m.–5:00 p.m.

You can charter a half-day fishing boat here, rent tackle, and generally pretend you are in Maine. To give a flavor of the place, Friday and Saturday evenings you have the special treat of fishing with live eels. Captain Ken and Tony are prone to comments such as, "See you reel soon."

CEDAR LANE STABLES. Tudor Park at No. Conduit Ave. bet. 80th and 88th Sts. (Howard Beach), 925-0777. www.federationofblackcowboys.com. By appointment only.

The horse stable used by the Federation of Black Cowboys is located in Howard Beach. The Federation of Black Cowboys aims to keep alive the legacy of America's forgotten black cowboys. They are likely to be found here at the stables, practicing bull riding, bucking horse riding, bull dogging, and calf roping for events such as the Black World Championship Rodeo.

ROCKAWAY BEACH SURF SHOP. 177 Beach 116th St., a block from the boardwalk, 474-1936. May–Oct. 10:00 a.m.–6:00 p.m.

This shop has been here for eons, selling all the necessities of daily life for those driven to catch the next wave and the one after that and after that. It's a laid-back place with modest prices and lots of local color, just a block from the boardwalk and beach.

18

Sunnyside and Woodside

Sunnyside and Woodside are two contiguous neighborhoods in northwestern Queens, which share some history as early-twentieth-century enclaves of Irish immigrants. They also share the #7 train and proximity to Calvary Cemetery and Queens Blvd. It's easy to visit both within a few hours.

Sunnyside

WHERE IT IS: Northwestern Queens. Bounded to the north by Sunnyside Yards, to the east by Calvary Cemetery and 51st St., to the south by the Long Island Expwy., and to the west by Van Dam St.

HOW TO GET THERE BY SUBWAY: #7 to 40th St. (Lowery St.), 46th St. (Bliss St.).

WHAT'S NEARBY: Astoria to the north, Long Island City to the west, Woodside to the east.

MAJOR SHOPPING/RESTAURANT STREETS: Queens Blvd., Greenpoint Ave., and 46th St.

SPECIAL CHARACTERISTICS: Diverse cultures and historic planned housing.

ON NOT GETTING LOST: It's hard to get lost in Sunnyside as it's small and the street grid is neatly laid out. Sunnyside Yards is a large old rail yard, and fairly desolate. Orient yourself to Sunnyside Gardens, Queens Blvd., and Roosevelt Ave.

CAR SERVICES: Caprice 424-4410 or 424-9300, Sunnyside 507-2600, Deborah 956-4007, 803-1920.

A SCRAMBLE OF CULTURES AND CO-OPS

In many ways a typical Queens neighborhood, Sunnyside is a largely residential area that would be considered astonishingly diverse by some standards. There's a vibrant scramble of Irish Americans, young Irish immigrants, Koreans, Colombians, Turks, and Eastern Europeans, as well as American-born residents. One

SUNNYSIDE & WOODSIDE

JACKSON HEIGHTS

71st St.
70th St.
64th St.
62nd St.
61st St.
60th St.
58th St.
56th St.
55th St.
54th St.

Brooklyn-Queens Expwy.

Northern Blvd.

70th St.
69th St.
68th St.
67th St.
65th Pl.
65th St.
64th St.
63rd St.
62nd St.
61st St.
60th St.
59th St.
58th St.
57th St.
56th St.
55th St.

G.,R,V

34th Ave.

37th Ave.
38th Ave.

Divya Dham

WOODSIDE

Woodside Station

Woodside Ave.

Vaux Rd.

Trimble Rd.

(LIRR)

7

M

39th St.

69th St.
68th St.
67th St.
66th St.
65th St.
65th Pl.
65th St.
64th St.
63rd St.
61st St.
60th St.

49th Rd.
50th Ave.

Laurel Hill Blvd.

69th St.

68th St.
66th St.
65th Pl.
65th St.
64th St.
63rd St.
61st St.

Tyler Ave.
59th Rd.

52nd Ave.
52nd Rd.

41st Ave.
41st Dr.
43rd Ave.

St. Sebastian's Roman Catholic Church

55th St.
54th St.
53rd St.

Roosevelt Ave.

59th Pl.
59th St.
58th Ln.

58th St.

New Calvary Cemetery

49th St.

278

↑ ASTORIA

Broadway
Newtown Rd.

51st St.

Knickerbocker Laundry Company

Phipps Garden Apartments

34th Dr.
39th Dr.

Woodside Ave.

Windmuller Park (aka Doughboy Park)

52nd St.
51st St.
50th St.
49th St.

Barnett Ave.

39th St.

SUNNYSIDE GARDENS HISTORIC DISTRICT

Skillman Ave.

Queens Blvd.

7

M

47th Ave.

48th Ave.

50th St.

45th St.

Thalia Spanish Theater

49th St.
48th St.
47th St.
46th St.
45th St.
44th St.
43rd St.
42nd St.
41st St.
40th St.
39th Pl.
39th St.
38th St.
37th St.
36th St.
35th St.
34th St.
33rd St.
32nd Pl.
32nd St.

SUNNYSIDE

Museum for African Art

43rd Ave.

Greenpoint Ave.

39th St.

Calvary Cemetery

495

278

↓ MASPETH, RIDGEWOOD

36th Ave.
37th Ave.
38th Ave.

31st St.

G.,R,V

M

N,W

M

Skillman Ave.

Thomson Ave.

Van Dam St.

Hunters Point Ave.

Review Ave.

BLISSVILLE

31st Pl.
31st St.
30th Pl.
30th St.
29th St.

48th Ave.

47th Ave.

Austell Pl.

27th St.

Star Ave.

Borden Avenue Bridge

DUTCH KILLS

Queens Plaza

Queensboro Bridge

Jackson Ave.

22nd St.
23rd St.
24th St.
27th St.
28th St.
29th St.
Crescent St.
31st St.
40th Rd.

N,W
G.,R,V
7
M
F

finds within a half mile two major cultural institutions, the Thalia Spanish The-ater and the Museum for African Art, representing South America, Africa, and Europe. Locals are nonchalant about the global culture that's everywhere in Sun-nyside. To a visitor, it's truly surprising. Sunnyside is just a hop, skip, and a jump from Greenpoint and Williamsburg on one side, and Long Island City and Asto-ria on the other and so has recently been attracting artists and musicians, as well.

Those interested in urban living should visit three interesting housing exper-iments dating from before World War II. Celtic Apartments and Phipps Garden Apartments were both 1931 experiments in healthy, attractive affordable hous-ing, urgently needed in the years after the Great Depression of 1929. Sunnyside Gardens is listed on the National Register of Historic Places.

THINGS TO SEE AND DO

There's the Museum for African Art, which has a major exhibition every spring and fall. A walk around Sunnyside Gardens' winding pathways and common garden spaces is both pleasant and gives you food for thought about options other than living on the thirty-fourth floor of a high-rise, or a my-home-is-my-castle suburban arrangement. You can attend an excellent performance at the low-key, somewhat bohemian Thalia Spanish Theater, a venue for Latin and Spanish plays and dance. Jazz lovers will find like-minded souls at Bix Beider-becke's annual memorial concert. You can have a nice upscale meal at Bliss restaurant, or, along Queens Blvd., you have a choice of informal world cuisine, notably at Turkish Hemsin Restaurant, Indian-Chinese Tangra Asian Fusion, and the French bakery La Marjolaine.

BITS OF HISTORY

Once part of rural Long Island, the area was defined in the colonial era by large farms owned by a few wealthy families. Sunnyside's early commercial existence was as the site of a Civil War–era roadhouse called The Sunnyside. Its patrons were visitors to the newly established Catholic cemetery at Calvary and at the short-lived Fashion Race Track. The pace of life quickened and the appeal of the area grew with the opening of the Queensboro Bridge in 1909 and the construc-tion of Queens Boulevard, which ran directly through Sunnyside. The extension of the elevated train line in 1917 to this part of Queens led to rapid develop-ment. Sunnyside was settled by German, Irish, Czech, and Dutch. The Irish pres-ence grew with the immigrations of the early twentieth century.

Sunnyside experienced a growth in residential development after World War I. Many of the attached homes still occupied today were erected in the early 1920s. Sunnyside Gardens' 770-acre complex was built in 1924–28 by architects Clarence Stein, Henry Wright, and financier Alexander Bing, roughly following the ideas of the British utopian Ebenezer Howard (see p. 140). Sunnyside Gardens is recognized as a classic innovation; for instance, Paul Goldberger, writing as architecture critic for *The New York Times*, called it "the most important of all the metropolitan area's housing developments." What makes Sunnyside Gardens so special is the emphasis on building community through shared public space in an urban setting.

The neighborhood became known in the 1940s and 1950s as the "maternity ward of Greenwich Village" as writers, singers, and performers left their tiny apartments for more affordable, greener Sunnyside. After World War II, immigrants from Asia, Latin America, and Eastern Europe moved to the area.

PARKS, PUBLIC SPACES, AND PUBLIC WORKS
SUNNYSIDE ARCH. Queens Blvd. at 46th St.

Need a place to meet in Sunnyside? Under the Sunnyside Arch is the logical place, near the subway. This 1983 faux art deco arch is slowly undergoing refurbishment. Some love it; some hate it, but the arch seems here to stay. It originally had dozens of small lightbulbs, which proved difficult to maintain in operation. Nearby is an undistinguished commercial strip in need of a boost.

SUNNYSIDE YARDS. Between Skillman and Jackson Aves.

This large rail yard was created from swampland and laid out by the Pennsylvania Railroad in 1901. Sunnyside Yards opened in 1910 simultaneously with both Penn Station and a connecting tunnel under the East River.

☺ THOMAS NOONAN PLAYGROUND. 42nd St. bet. Greenpoint Ave. and 47th Aves.

This small park has a community vibe, some tables, and a play area. It's a fine place for a picnic.

POINTS OF CULTURAL INTEREST
BIX BEIDERBECKE'S LAST HOME AND MEMORIAL CONCERT. 43-30 46th St. bet. 43rd Ave. and Queens Blvd. http://bixbeiderbecke.com.

This is the home where jazz cornetist Bix Beiderbecke died in 1931 at the age of twenty-eight, after moving here from Astoria. There is a plaque in commemoration of Bix near the entrance to the building. Since 1999, Bix fans have held an annual Bix Vigil, a live music celebration of his memory on August 6th, the anniversary of his death, in the nearby courtyard of the All Saints' Episcopal Church. Bix's life was the basis for the 1950 movie *Young Man with a Horn* starring Kirk Douglas and Lauren Bacall.

FLUX FACTORY. 38-38 43rd St. bet. Northern Blvd. and 37th St., 707-3360. www.fluxfactory.org. Call for schedule of public events.

This old warehouse has been transformed into a performance space and working studio by an artists' collective. Flux Factory was first created in 1994 by undergraduates who built a collective living space in an old spice factory in Williamsburg, Brooklyn. Over time, as they describe it, their living room "evolved into a site for art events and performances of all kinds." Flux Factory is a nonprofit art community space with a computer center, darkroom, performance space, musical recording space, publishing equipment, Thursday night dinners, and a salon.

☺ **MUSEUM FOR AFRICAN ART.** 36-01 43rd Ave. at 36th St., upstairs, 784-7700. www.africanart.org. M, Th F 10:00 a.m.–5:00 p.m., Sa–Su 11:00 a.m.–6:00 p.m. Admission is $6 for adults; $3 for seniors, students and children; free for children under six. Free M, Th, F 10:00–11:00 a.m.

The Museum for African Art is dedicated to "the majesty and wonder of the rich, varied, and diverse cultures of Africa." Visitors can attend lectures, dance performances, and films as well as check out the excellent gift shop with many traditional African arts and crafts. The museum also organizes tours to Africa and runs educational programs.

☺ **THALIA SPANISH THEATER.** 41-17 Greenpoint Ave. bet. 41st and 42nd Sts., 729-3880. F–Sa 8:00 p.m., Su 4:00 p.m. Tickets $10–18; discounts for seniors and students.

Thalia Spanish Theater stands out as a gem even in New York's cultural jewel box. It's a professional theater founded in 1977 that's dedicated to showcasing Spanish and Latin American theater and dance. Plays are produced in English and Spanish on different days. Contemporary works shown under the direction of Spanish writer-producer Angel Gil Orrios include plays by writers such as Mexico's Carlos Fuentes and Spaniards Antonio Gala, Jaime Salom, and Jerónimo López Mozo. Summer visitors should check out the annual free Thalia al Aire Libre/Outdoors Festival.

TURKISH-AMERICAN MULTICULTURAL EDUCATIONAL FOUNDATION (TAMEF). 43-49 45th St., 482-8263. www.tamef.org. M–F 9:00 a.m.–5:00 p.m., and special events.

Sunnyside has a substantial Turkish population. With a focus on arts, customs, sports, cuisine, and history, this nonprofit cultural institute holds special events that are open to the public, including interfaith dialogues and celebration of special Turkish holidays such as Noah's Pudding. This is one example of many cultural organizations in the borough.

POINTS OF HISTORIC AND ARCHITECTURAL INTEREST

BORDEN AVENUE BRIDGE. Over Dutch Kills Creek, south of the Long Island Expwy. bet. 27th St. and Review Ave.

One of the few early 1900s retractile-type moveable bridges in the nation, this was built in 1908 and hasn't changed much since. Note the stucco operator's house with the original clay tile on the roof, four pairs of rails, and stone retaining wall. It's four blocks away from the Hunter's Point Bridge, which was opened in 1910 but was replaced in the 1980s.

CELTIC PARK APARTMENTS. From 48th Ave. to 50th Ave. bet. 42nd and 44th Sts.

This was the site of the old Irish-American Athletic Club, which was used heavily by Irish immigrants who settled in the area. The 750-unit apartment complex here today was built by the City and Suburban Homes Co. in 1931 as cooperative apartments. These buildings offered amenities—access to open space and sunshine, for instance—that were a big improvement for working-class families who were often stuck in crowded, dark flats with no gardens. You can still see the ornamental archways and central courtyards.

KNICKERBOCKER LAUNDRY COMPANY (now NEW YORK PRESBYTERIAN CHURCH). 423-23 37th Ave. bet. 43rd and 48th Sts.

The big 1932 Art Moderne Knickerbocker Laundry Company site was an informal landmark for many riders on the adjacent LIRR. Now it's been transformed into a new 2,500-seat New York Presbyterian Church, built for a Korean congregation. There's a three-story fiberglass structure perched atop the roof of the old building. Inside there are classrooms, a cafeteria, wedding chapel, and an angular, very modern sanctuary with slices of Manhattan skyline views. Three bridges and wide flights of steps connect the church to the parking lot below.

PHIPPS GARDEN APARTMENTS. 51-01 39th Ave. bet. 50th and 52nd Sts. (1931); 52-02 to 53-20 Barnett Ave. bet 50th and 52nd Sts., www.phippsny.org.

Note the beautifully landscaped garden apartments here with a two-block square center court surrounded by four-, five-, and six-story apartment buildings. Built in the Depression years, the first building in this extraordinary housing complex was opened in 1931 for working-class families, with another nearby opening in 1935. This complex was one in a series of early philanthropic experiments by one of America's captains of industry in the late 1800s, Henry Phipps, who with his business partner, Andrew Carnegie, had earned a fortune from the sale of Carnegie Steel Company, a precursor to U.S. Steel. Pittsburgh-based Phipps became involved in philanthropic efforts to prevent tuberculosis in his hometown. In 1905, with a $1 million gift, he founded a nonprofit entity called

Phipps Houses out of concern over slum conditions in New York City, which were a primary contributor to the spread of tuberculosis. The goal was to provide affordable and well-designed housing for blue-collar New Yorkers. Phipps Garden Apartments was one of many such developments. The structure of the organization was unusual; to prove that low-income housing could be commercially viable, a target profit of 4 percent was set, with the stipulation that profit was to be reinvested in new housing. The Phipps Houses Groups is still in operation as a nonprofit developer/owner of affordable housing. For more information, see their Web site.

🏛 **SUNNYSIDE GARDENS HISTORIC DISTRICT.** Queens Blvd., 43rd and 52nd Sts., and Baronet and Skillman Aves.; private residences; please be respectful and quiet.

NOTE: While you can walk through Sunnyside Gardens, the courtyards are private and not a public park.

One of the nation's first planned communities, Sunnyside Gardens was developed for low- and middle-income families by Architects Clarence Stein and Henry Wright, along with landscape architect Marjorie Cautley (one of the nation's first female architects) from 1924 to 1928. Singer Perry Como, actress Judy Holliday, and jazz man Bix Beiderbecke lived here, as did painter Raphael Soyer. Lewis Mumford, progressive social philosopher and advocate of humanizing the modern city, lived here, too. Today residents include young families, professionals, performers, and artists who work in Manhattan, alongside longtime elderly residents.

This sprawling complex of 1,200 modest garden apartments strikes a balance between private and public spaces. It consists of sixteen blocks (about seventy-seven acres) of attached redbrick, two-and-a-half-story homes, built for one, two, or three families. All enjoy small private backyards and are linked in the back by large swaths of shared common space, crisscrossed by convivial little pathways and punctuated by vines and luxuriant old trees. Visitors can walk around the perimeter of the buildings and enter through side paths to peek at the common yards and central courtyards.

Fences separate individual homes, and as you walk on narrow paths, you see common spaces on one side and twenty-foot-square patches of individual gardens on the other. Individuality flowers in both front and back gardens; one plot is scrupulously well kept; another woody, rustic, and overgrown; and a third strewn with colorful plastic toys. While varied, the homes are modest in size, reminiscent of a time when the consumer culture had not yet been born, and thrift was a way of life.

When the community was first built, Sunnyside Gardens residents were bound by a forty-year covenant to abide by community standards for use of outdoor spaces. When the covenant expired, some people encroached on common space and privatized their public spaces. Sunnyside Gardens is listed on the National Register of Historic Places.

BARS, CAFÉS, AND RESTAURANTS

BLISS. 45-20 Skillman Ave at 46th St., 729-0778.

Near Sunnyside Gardens, this elegant bistro-style restaurant offers a good wine list and a short menu of dishes such as house-cured salmon and home-made ravioli. It's the most sophisticated restaurant in Sunnyside and a welcome addition; a full dinner costs about $36.

BOOK CHONG DONG. 40-06 Queens Blvd. at 40th St., 706-0899. Daily 11:00 a.m.–midnight.

Tofu lovers, here's a find. Tucked away in a modest Korean restaurant in Sunnyside, you can finally find the answer to that perplexing modern question of how one can make tofu taste, well, like something. This restaurant has some answers. Try tofu with noodles, meats, and seafood as well as veggies. The menu is full of unusual words, so you can learn a new word for the day: *soondubu* (meaning, soft bean curd).

DAZIES. 39-41 Queens Blvd. bet. 39th Pl. and 40th St., 786-7013, www.daziesrestaurant.com. M 11:00 a.m.–10:00 p.m., Tu–W 11:30 a.m.–10:30 p.m., Th 11:30 a.m.–11:00 p.m., F 11:30 a.m.–11:30 p.m., Sa 11:30 a.m.–midnight, Su noon–10:30 p.m.

Dazie's serves Italian classics such as parmigianas, plus a smattering of seafood standards and salads. The service is friendly, and the food's not only good, but you'll feel like you've discovered a great little corner of New York City here. Entrées run $25 on average. Reservations recommended.

HEMSIN BAKERY AND RESTAURANT. 39-17 Queens Blvd. bet. 39th St. and 39th Pl., 937-1715. Daily 8:00 a.m.–11:00 p.m.

Not too far from the Noguchi Museum and Thalia Spanish Theater, Hemsin is a combo bakery-restaurant serving Turkish treats such as *acu ezme* (spicy mashed peppers), *hunkar begendi* (also known as Sultan's Delight, with lamb chunks on eggplant puree), and *ezogelin* (lentil) soup. The food is halal.

MAMA'S EMPANADAS. 42-18 Greenpoint Ave. bet. 42nd and 43rd Sts., 729-1301. Daily 8:00 a.m.–11:00 p.m.

You can get forty different flavors of Colombian-style empanadas (pastry stuffed with a filling, like a turnover) here: chicken, veggie, cheese, broccoli and cheese, sausage, rice and bean, ham and cheese, guava and cheese, caramel and cheese, sweet plantain and cheese, and egg and cheese. Other choices include *envueltos de maiz* (sweet corn patties), tamales (corn patties filled with veggies and meat or chicken), and the soup of the day. Reflecting Colombian tradition, the pastry is mostly made with cornmeal. About $1 to $50 each. (Other locations are in Jackson Heights [85-05 Northern Blvd., 505-9937] and Queens Center Mall [91-20 59th St., 729-1301]).

MANGAL. 46-20 Queens Blvd. at Greenpoint Ave., 706-0605. Daily 11:00 a.m.–11:00 p.m.

Mangal is an unpretentious spot serving authentic Turkish dishes, including kebabs and appetizer-sized vegetable dishes. All are fresh and tasty.

SIDETRACKS. 45-08 Queens Blvd. bet. 45th and 46th Sts., 786-3570. Daily noon–4:00 a.m. Jazz brunch Su.

Sidetracks attracts locals (Manhattanites might call them a real bridge-and-tunnel crowd) with DJs and dancing on the weekends, inexpensive drinks, and a turn-of-the-twentieth-century railroad decor. While you dine you can also place a bet on thoroughbred and harness racing here, noon–11:30 p.m.

TANGRA ASIAN FUSION CUISINE. 39-23 Queens Blvd. at 40th St., 786-8181. Su–Th 11:30 a.m.–10:00 p.m., F–Sa 11:30 a.m.–11:00 p.m.

This is a huge Chinese banquet hall with seating for over two hundred, serving a fusion menu that combines Chinese and Indian menu items. This restaurant just opened; stay tuned.

TAILOR'S HALL. 45-10 Queens Blvd. bet. 44th and 45th Sts., 706-1010. Daily noon–4:00 a.m.

Uncrowded, Irish, and a place for meeting people or having a romantic date, this Sunnyside bar has Irish waitstaff, live music, and fresh Guinness. Recommended for those who love a good Irish pub.

SHOPPING AND ENTERTAINMENT

LA MARJOLAINE. 50-17 Skillman Ave. off 51st St., 651-0495. Tu–F 7:00 a.m.–7:00 p.m., Sa 7:00 a.m.–6:00 p.m., Su 7:00 a.m.–5:00 p.m.

When in Sunnyside, do as the French do: Get your pastries from a pâtisserie and your bread from the boulangerie. Come to this lovely pâtisserie for delicious cheese danishes, croissants, and delicate tarts.

CENTER CINEMAS 5. 42-17 Queens Blvd. bet. 41st and 42nd Sts., 361-6869. Hours vary.

Take in an inexpensive first-run flick at this six-screen local movie theater, conveniently located on Queens Blvd. near the subway station. Originally opened back in 1942, local film historians fondly recall an old entrance sign that read, GOOD MOVIES, LIKE GOOD BOOKS, NEVER GROW OLD.

✐ **ESSAY**

Monday Musing: #7 Train

by Morgan Meis
Morgan Meis is a founder of Flux Factory, an artists' collective in Sunnyside. The following is an edited version of a piece that first appeared on the Internet, excerpted with the author's permission.

It's a rather long story as to why, but Stefany, my wife, my love, and I have just spent roughly twelve hours riding back and forth on the 7 train in Queens, New York. It's a trip from one world into another.

A few years ago John Rocker, a pitcher for the Atlanta Braves, hurled some attention the 7 train's way with notable comments to *Sports Illustrated*. He said of New York, "It's the most hectic, nerve-racking city. Imagine having to take the [number] 7 train to the ballpark, looking like you're [riding through] Beirut next to some kid with purple hair, next to some queer with AIDS, right next to some dude who just got out of jail for the fourth time, right next to some twenty-year-old mom with four kids. It's depressing."

Imagine.

The 7 train is great in a million ways but it really shows off after Hunter's Point when it gets to burst out of the tunnel and go aboveground. It's a cocky train. That probably comes from sitting around at Times Square and Grand Central. The 7 train knows the bright lights and the glamour. But that's not where it stays. The 7 train heads out to Queens and it has its heart there. After the blast across the East River the 7 train bounces and weaves through the massive warehouses of Long Island City like an ancient snake that has its own well-worn path.

Queens was made for people to live in, and they do. When the 7 train settles down on Queens Blvd. and works its way into Woodside and Jackson Heights, you can feel its gentle chugging on the old wooden tracks and you can hear a kind of metallic, mechanical confidence.

There is no greater definition of "everybody" than the 7 train. Try scanning your eye across the 7 train at anytime, any day, whenever you like it, and some struggling immigrant from Mexico or Bangladesh or Korea or Uzbekistan or Ecuador or Kenya or Romania has a kid on his lap and is stroking the kid's hair and saying in whatever language, "Go to sleep my sweet child, go to sleep my lovely child, I'm doing everything for us that I possibly can." If you ride the 7 train enough like I do you see that all the time. You might think you get blasé about it, but you don't. It makes some part of your chest cavity swell up dumb and sputtering and overdrawn. That might be one response to John Rocker types if it could be expressed more clearly.

You've got Indians and South Asians around the '60s and '70s and then it's dominated by Latinos in the blocks after that. It's not the same New York as other places here, and that doesn't mean it's either better or worse. Manhattan is an international place, but it brings all the world into its own orbit. Queens

(continued)

reverses that. And then boom, you're in the Far East. Korea, China, a touch of the Philippines, and throw in whatever else. The last stop, Main Street, Flushing, is just simply Asia, which kind of delights the mind to consider for a moment.

I hope all cities get smooshed up and tossed around like Queens did. I hope the 7 train isn't something just accidental that will get lost or forgotten. When the sun is sliding away to the west and you're standing on one of the sparse platforms of the 7 train, you see Queens like a weird urban plain at the foot of the Manhattan skyline. It's sweet and quiet but for the slow rumble of the subway cars doing their rounds day and night. It's as good as anything.

Woodside

WHERE IT IS: Northwestern Queens. Bounded to the north by St. Michael's Cemetery, to the east by 70th and 74th Sts., to the south by Calvary Cemetery, and to the west by 43rd and 50th Sts.

HOW TO GET THERE BY SUBWAY: #7 to 61st St./Woodside, 69th St. (Fisk Avenue). G, R, V to Northern Blvd./65th St.

HOW TO GET THERE BY LIRR: Station at Roosevelt Ave. and 61st St.

WHAT'S NEARBY: Astoria to the northwest, Elmhurst to the east, Jackson Heights to the northeast, Long Island City to the west.

MAJOR SHOPPING/RESTAURANT STREETS: Roosevelt Ave., Northern Blvd., Queens Blvd., and Woodside Ave.

SPECIAL CHARACTERISTICS: A touch of the Irish and diverse religious institutions representing world cultures.

ON NOT GETTING LOST: It's easy to get around Woodside; stay within eye or earshot of the elevated subway track, which follows Roosevelt Ave. Alternatively, orient to Northern Blvd. and the BQE.

CAR SERVICES: Caprice 424-4410 or 424-9300, Community 846-4500.

AIR TRAFFIC ABOVE, THE WORLD BELOW

Sitting in Woodside Plaza, a triangular patch of green under the noisy elevated train, you can stop, have a bite, and take in your surroundings. You'll see three or four pubs with names like Saints and Sinners, so at first blush you think, "Okay, Irish." Meanwhile, the phrase "air traffic" has a palpable and audible presence. Woodside is just a few miles away from LaGuardia's runways and so you hear the planes before you see them—the sound of raw power, of acceleration, of movement. A jet glides by every ninety seconds; five planes fly by before you can half-consume a coffee and donut. Flying so low, seemingly barely clearing the church tower, the planes look enormous and close. Then you might notice women in traditional Pakistani dress pushing strollers past the Emerald Isle Immigration Center. Up the block there's the Han Ah Reum Korean grocery store, Seh Moon Baptist Church, a tae kwan do studio, a Korean hair salon with signs in English offering "magic straight perm," and Long Chan, a huge market selling Chinese foods and live fish. In the sky, the incessant air traffic hums. Woodside makes the world seem like it's just landed, right at your park bench.

BITS OF HISTORY
In the seventeenth century, land here was owned by a British settler named Sackett, and through the American Revolution there are records that the British occupied the area. In the 1830s several rural mansions were built in the area. By the 1860s the village streets were laid out by Benjamin Hitchcock, a music publisher who played a role in the development of Corona, Ozone Park, and other areas of Queens. The arrival in 1865 of trolley lines and in 1917 of the elevated trains enabled decades of housing development and growth. Many Irish immigrants moved to the area, and their influence is still visible. In the 1980s Chinese, Korean, Colombian, and Dominican immigrants arrived.

Woodside's name may derive from its original wealth of trees. A more colorful explanation holds that a series of articles called "Letters from Woodside" were written for a Brooklyn newspaper by John Andrew Kelly, whose farm was called Woodside, and whose father had lived in the area since 1825.

THINGS TO SEE AND DO
Aside from checking out the historic graves in Calvary Cemetery, the best reason to come to Woodside is for a drink in a good Irish pub, an authentic meal in a Thai restaurant such as Sripraphai, and simply to walk through an area enjoying the benefits of global diversity. It's easy to combine a visit here with a trip to Jackson Heights or Sunnyside.

PARKS, PUBLIC SPACES, AND PUBLIC WORKS
CALVARY CEMETERY. 4902 Laurel Hill Blvd., roughly encompassing area bet. Queens Blvd. and 55th Ave., and 58th to 49th Sts. Also, the area bounded by the Long Island Expwy., Rte. 278, and Laurel Hill Blvd., 786-8002.

Calvary is the huge cemetery that you see on your left for about a mile-long stretch as you're driving on the BQE into Queens. Actually, it's also the cemetery on your right. Like Shakespeare's play within a play, Calvary is so big that there are cemeteries within cemeteries. Covering 365 acres and four separate areas, Calvary Cemetery is said to be the largest cemetery in the United States in terms of the number of graves. It was founded by St. Patrick's Cathedral in 1846 when New York City declared that no more land in Manhattan could be used for burials. It was initially used for poor Roman Catholics, mostly poor Irish immigrants and children from the Lower East Side. Now it's at capacity; in New York, Roman Catholic burials have been relocated to Staten Island. Mass is celebrated in the 1908 chapel.

The colonial Cumberson and Alsop family plots (the latter is a landmark) are within the original Old Calvary Cemetery that sits on 115 acres of farmland bought, in bits and pieces, by St. Patrick's Cathedral starting in the mid-1800s. A city-owned Calvary Veterans Park burial grounds opened in 1863 for soldiers who fought for the Union during the Civil War (1861–65) and died in New York hospitals. The 1892 gatehouse (at Greenpoint and Gale Aves.) is a Queen Anne–style entrance and one of Queens' great formal monuments, though it goes virtually unacknowledged.

The people buried here include Robert F. Wagner, Jr. (1910–91), Mayor of New York (1954–65); Lorenzo de Ponte (1749–1838), colleague of Wolfgang Amadeus Mozart, who wrote librettos for Mozart's *Marriage of Figaro, Don Giovanni* and *Così fan Tutte*; Claude McKay (1890–1948), 1920s African-American poet and author of *A Long Way Home*; Una O'Connor (1880–1959), star of *The Adventures of Robin Hood*; Patsy Kelly of *Rosemary's Baby* (1910–1981); Thomas "Three Fingers Brown" Lucchese, mafia chief (1899–1967); and several Hall of Fame baseball players.

The city has grown up around Calvary. Driving down 58th St. at night, you notice an enormous, theatrically lit crucifix on a hillside with a sign that says Calvary Cemetery, opposite Rite Aid, Staples, and Kentucky Fried Chicken.

WINDMULLER PARK (AKA DOUGHBOY PARK). Woodside Ave. bet. 54-56 Sts.

This vaguely European parklet has a sculpture that won an award from the American Federation of Arts in 1928. It's of a "doughboy" (a term used to refer to infantrymen) commemorating those killed in World War I. Perched here, above Roosevelt Ave., you can count the airplanes arriving and landing at LaGuardia, and watch the elevated subway train screech round the curve.

POINTS OF CULTURAL INTEREST

BLISSVILLE. Area north of Newtown Creek between Dutch Kills and Greenpoint Ave.

It's almost too droll to admit, but the area called Blissville in Queens has been partly overtaken and certainly overshadowed by Calvary Cemetery.

Blissville, named after landowner Neziah Bliss, was part of Long Island City. When the cemetery opened in 1848 many locals found employment at the cemetery or in monuments, hotels, and saloons near the cemetery. If this is Bliss, then . . .

DIVYA DHAM. 34-63 56th St. bet. Broadway and 37th Ave., 606-2315. Daily 6:15 a.m.–8:30 p.m. Visitors are welcome, but shoes off, please.

Once an electronics factory, this building is today a large, busy Hindu temple called Divya Dham, which means "heaven on earth" in Hindi. Like temples in India, there's even a cave for personal mediation (though in Woodside it's a manmade, not natural, one). Inside there is also a huge scale model of the Himalayas, showing the source of the Ganges River, which is considered sacred, along with a thousand or more lingam, a phalliclike sculpture representing Shiva and symbolizing creative energy.

Divya Dham was founded in 1993 by Swami Jagdishwaranand, who also founded the Geeta Temple in Elmhurst. When he died in December 2005, *The New York Times* obituary described how he had arranged for the transport, in person, of an "eternal flame" that traveled from India through Central Asia to Europe, across the English Channel to the United Kingdom, where it was taken on a ship to California, and finally transported by car to this temple in Woodside. Divya Dham is run by the India-based organization Bharat Sevashram Sangha.

MOZART MUSIC STUDIO. 56-20 Woodside Ave. at corner of 56th St., 429-6363. Hours based on lesson schedule.

There are more neighborhood music schools in Queens than you might expect. Some Asian immigrants have brought with them a culture that values musical training as an important aspect of a child's education. Mozart Music offers lessons in piano, guitar, wind instruments, and singing to a primarily Korean clientele.

ST. SEBASTIAN'S ROMAN CATHOLIC CHURCH. 58-02 Roosevelt Ave. corner of 58th St., 429-4442. Daily 9:00 a.m., noon (in Spanish); Sa 5:00 p.m., 6:00 p.m., Su 8:00 a.m., 10:30 a.m., 1:15 p.m., 6:00 p.m. (in English).

St. Sebastian's church complex with a nearby convent and school is a neighborhood anchor. Holiday services are held in Gaelic, Korean, Spanish, Tagalog, Italian, and English. It is the kind of place that Bill Clinton visits when he is stumping for fellow Democratic candidates, which he did in 1998.

An architectural note: In 1952 the church took over a nearby historic 2,000-seat Loew's movie theater that dated from 1926 (when it opened with a Buster

Keaton comedy). The church recently restored the domed-ceiling auditorium and forty marble columns.

SUBWAY ART. #7 subway line station at 61st St. and Roosevelt Ave.

Take a look at the railings made of hand-forged steel. They illustrate the history of both the New York City subway and the LIRR, which intersect at the Woodside Station. See if you can find the hidden letters spelling the word "Woodside" in the large murals of neighborhood scenes. The art, by Dimitri Gerakaris (1999) and John Cavanagh (1986), respectively, are permanent installations sponsored by the New York City MTA Arts for Transit program.

TOPAZ ARTS. 55-03 39th Ave. near 54th St., 505-0440. Daily 10:00 a.m.–9:00 p.m.

Topaz Arts has been called the premier dance rehearsal space in Queens. Outside it resembles an old garage. Inside the 2,500-square-foot warehouse has been turned into an arts center offering affordable space, technical support, and an audio/media studio.

WOODSIDE ON THE MOVE. 39-42 59th St. bet. 39th and Woodside Aves., 476-8449. M–F 9:00 a.m.–5:00 p.m.

Want to know what's going on in Woodside? Get in touch with Woodside on the Move, a neighborhood hub for street fairs, economic development, and multicultural activities.

PEOPLE, PLACES, AND THINGS OF HISTORICAL INTEREST
BOULEVARD GARDENS. 45th St. and 31st Ave.

Heralded in its day as "A New Idea in Apartment Housing," Boulevard Gardens was built in 1935 with financial assistance from the WPA. The ten six-story buildings, designed by T. H. Englehardt, have 960 units set in an open, parklike space with mature shade trees, attractive seating, and community playgrounds.

CHILD'S RESTAURANT (former). Corner of 60th St. and Queens Blvd. No longer serving food.

Precursors to today's fast food joints, Child's was a chain of hundreds of self-service restaurants started in 1889 by Samuel and William Child. They were spiffy inside with white tiled floors and marble countertops. Child's developed a decorative building style (today we'd call it branding) that included elaborate terra-cotta ornamentation, sometimes with seashells, wriggling fish, gargoyles, and sailing ships, but always with a seahorse motif. They are all over the city; there's another old Child's Restaurant building in Sunnyside at 43rd Ave. and 45th St.

MOORE-JACKSON CEMETERY. 24th Ave. and 31st Ave.

The earliest grave in this old landmarked cemetery predates the American Revolution. The Moores settled in the area in 1652, and later moved to Chelsea in Manhattan. Descendant Benjamin Moore was the Episcopal Bishop of New York and President of Columbia College. His son Clement Clark Moore, a scholar, made a lasting mark on American culture when he wrote for his children and subsequently published "'Twas the Night Before Christmas" in the 1820s. Overgrown for decades, this cemetery was discovered by workers in the 1930s and groomed by a volunteer gardener.

BARS, CAFÉS, AND RESTAURANTS

Bars

Woodside has a large Irish population, and you can enjoy a half dozen authentic Irish bars here. Several feature live music or DJs on weekends as well as satellite TV so you can see Irish football games in real time. *Home and Away,* a freebie publication that you can find in the Irish pubs lists where musicians are playing.

DONOVAN'S PUB. 57-24 Roosevelt Ave. at 58th St., 429-9339. Daily 11:30 a.m.–11:00 p.m. Cash only.

A throwback to Queens' Irish heritage, here's an old-school place to watch sports, hang out, and munch your way to nirvana on what many claim is New York's best burgers and fried onions. It's a decent, multigenerational, neighborhood sort of place with an Irish flair. Also 214-16 41st Ave. in Bayside, 423-5178.

KILMEGAN. 60-19 Roosevelt Ave. bet. 60th and 61st Sts., 803-9206. Daily 11:00 a.m.–4:00 a.m.

This is a sports bar known for its funky decor, where you'll find TV screens, little quiet corners for quiet conversation, and tables in the bar area.

O'NEILL'S RESTAURANT. 64-21 53rd Dr. bet. 64 Pl. and 65 Pl., 672-9696. Daily 7:00 a.m.–3:00 a.m. Valet parking.

Place bets, watch the Mets. O'Neill's upscale sports bar in nearby Maspeth has nine big-screen TVs carrying live racing, and wagering from all major tracks. The decor is brick and wood, the fare is standard American dishes such as chicken salad platter, blackened swordfish, and lobster in season. O'Neill's is a popular gathering place for the local Irish residents.

SAINTS AND SINNERS. 59-21 Roosevelt Ave. at 60th St., 396-3268. Daily 11:00 a.m.–4:00 a.m. Th after 9:00 p.m. ladies get two for one. Food is served M–F noon–10:00 p.m., Sa–Su 11:00 a.m.–10:00 p.m.; weekend brunch 11:00 a.m.–4:00 p.m.

Slainte! ("Cheers!" in Irish.) This well-kept, wood-paneled Irish pub invites a good time: laughs, a cool pint of Guinness, camaraderie, and storytelling. Whether you're Italian, Jewish, or Chinese, by the time you've had a few drinks here, you'll feel like you're Irish, too. Live bands play Th–Su and lunch and dinner are served in a back room; try Adam's Grill (sausages, bacon, pudding, lamb chop, eggs, and fries) and Croagh Patrick (calves' liver, bacon, onions, and potato).

SEAN OG'S TAVERN. 60-02 Woodside Ave. at 60th St., 899-3499. Daily 11:00 a.m.–4:00 a.m.

With its long, narrow bar, red-painted ceiling, and picture of William Butler Yeats on the wall, spending some time in this pub makes you feel like you're in Ireland. Irish bands play here frequently.

Restaurants and Cafés

EL NUEVO IZALCO RESTAURANT. 64-05 Roosevelt Ave. at 64th St., 533-8373. Su–Th noon–9:00 p.m., F–Sa noon–11:00 p.m.

This Salvadoran restaurant serves traditional dishes, such as *salpicón* salad, enchiladas, and refried beans, and your choice of green peppers and other vegetables stuffed with delicious combos of rice and cheese. Izalco, by the way, is a volcano in El Salvador.

EL SITIO. 68-28 Roosevelt Ave. bet. 68th and 69th Sts., 424-2369. Daily 10:00–midnight.

El Sitio is the best place in Queens for Cuban pressed sandwiches and really good, strong coffee. It may be illegal to go to Havana but you can get to El Sitio for the price of a subway fare.

GO HYANG JIP. 40-03 73rd St. at Roosevelt Ave., 507-8182. Tu–Su 11:00 a.m.–10:30 p.m. Cash only.

This modest Korean restaurant run by immigrant women serves up family-sized hot pots and home-cooked black goat soup, or *kimchi bi bim bop,* at about $15 for a main course. Be prepared to wait; after a good review in *The New York Times,* Go Hyang Jip got busy.

IHAWAN. 40-06 70th St. near Roosevelt Ave., 205-1480 M–Sa 11:00 a.m.–11:00 p.m., Su noon–9:00 p.m.

Ihawan is one of a handful of Filipino eateries in the mini-Manila area around 70th St. and Roosevelt Ave. You can enjoy cooked pork, including various exotic organs and body parts, like pig's feet. Not much English is spoken, so be prepared to point at what you want to order.

KHAO HOMM. 39-28 61st St. bet. Woodside and 39th Aves., 205-0080. Daily 11:45 a.m.–11:30 p.m.

The local Thai moms bring the kids at lunchtime and the Irish ex-pats get their curry here at night. Feast your eyes on the wall candy, photos of elaborate Thai foods and sweets. Then feast your tummy on the menu's Thai-style barbecue chicken, mock duck for vegetarians, and spicy frog's legs for the curious. The broad noodle dish called *pad kee mao* is outstanding. Prices are low.

LA FLOR BAKERY, CAFÉ, AND RESTAURANT. 53-02 Roosevelt Ave. bet. 53rd and 54th Sts., 426-8023. Daily 8:00 a.m.–10:00 p.m.

Who would have thought that Greenwich Village intersects Mexico City in Woodside, Queens? Serving traditional Mexican dishes in a cozy atmosphere, this combo bakery-café-restaurant draws a large clientele. You get delicious food at prices closer to those of Mexico City than Manhattan. La Flor sits in the shadow of the elevated #7 train, but its flower motif and shattered ceramic mug-and-saucer art, which covers nearly every free surface, brighten the *mezcla* of faces here, from old Jewish Sunnysiders to local Latino Woodsiders. A huge vegetable quesadilla and the La Flor, a sandwich of pork tenderloin and chipotle sauce, each run about $7. Order fresh holiday cakes and tarts or even a pumpkin cheesecake from the bakery.

SAPORI D'ISCHIA. 55-15 37th Ave. bet. 55th and 56th Sts., 446-1500. Tu–Sa 11:30 a.m.–3:30 p.m. and 5:30 p.m.–11:00 p.m., Su 2:00 p.m.–10:00 p.m.

You can get fresh pizza and Italian cuisine served in this cool old warehouse, and even better, there's opera every Thursday at 7:00 p.m. (reservations are necessary for parties of more than two). How romantic!

SHANE'S BAKERY AND CAFÉ. 39-61 61st St. at Roosevelt Ave., 424-9039. M–F 6:30 a.m.–8:00 p.m., Sa 7:00 a.m.–8:00 p.m., Su 8:00 a.m.–5:00 p.m.

This small café with room for about two dozen people serves old-world favorites like Cornish pastie, Scotch eggs, shepherd's pie, and bangers and mash. But the most compelling reason to nip into this tiny café is for the traditional Irish soda bread and scones—cranberry, blueberry, raisin, or plain. Is Shane Irish? You bet.

SRIPRAPHAI THAI RESTAURANT. 64-13 39th Ave. bet. 64th and 65th Sts., 899-9599. M–Tu, Th–Su 11:30 a.m.–10:00 p.m. Cash only. (Pronounced See Pra Pie.)

A smallish restaurant with a big fan club, Sripraphai produces consistently excellent Thai food. Among the faves are papaya salads, steamed chicken dumplings, fried pork, and crabmeat roll—and those are just the appetizers. The chicken soup is creamy, the sticky rice, which comes in individual baskets, is perfect, and the green curry is out of this world. If there are four of you, order only three entrées; portions are ample. TIP: "Moderately" hot is pretty fiery. Dinner runs about $14 per person, and it's fun to eat in the garden in summer.

SHOPPING

Specialty and Ethnic Food Shops in Woodside

6IST STREET DELI. 39-67 61st St. bet. Roosevelt and Woodside Aves., 457-3182. Su–Th 5:30 a.m.–10:30 p.m., F–Sa 5:30 a.m.–11:30 p.m.

What's remarkable about this little food store—and so typically multicultural Queens—is that it's run by an immigrant from India who caters to the local Irish clientele. That explains the imported Irish breads, Barry's teas, and Scotts Porage Oats. About the ever-popular Irish sausage and bacon, says owner Raj, "the Irish eat it for breakfast, lunch, and dinner, like we eat rice and curry." You can also find traditional black pudding here, a half-dozen kinds of oatmeal, Colleen brand candy, and even Impulse body spray, as well as two dozen newspapers imported from different areas of Ireland.

HAN AH REUM MARKET. 59-18 Woodside Ave. off 59th St., 446-5880. Daily 8:00 a.m.–10:00 p.m.

Need seaweed to make sushi? Sesame leaves to wrap around dishes? This shop sells it all. If you can't decipher the Korean labels, here's what's in some of those mysterious boxes and vacuum-sealed bags: plum tea, *kimchi*, a salted Korean cabbage dish, dried things other than shiitake mushrooms such as bell root and balloon flowers, dried sweet potato stem, and chestnuts. There are many kinds of dried fish, too: salted shrimp, spicy octopus, spicy pollack roe, seasoned octopus, and sea squirt, as well as salted cod and fish sausages. Dumplings in the refrigerated case include crab, shrimp, vegetable, beef, and kimchi. If seaweed is still all you want, you've got plenty of choices: teriyaki nori, roasted seaweed nori, or dried shredded seaweed.

OTTOMANELLI & SONS. 61-05 Woodside Ave. at 61st St., 651-5544. M–F 9:00 a.m.–5:00 p.m.

Ottomanelli & Sons is one of the best butchers in the Big Apple if you're seeking high-quality cuts or ready-to-cook items such as stuffed pork chops, gorgeous shish kebabs, and a ready-to-roast trussed turkey breast. Try the sauces, too: soy-lime-ginger, honey teriyaki, lemon basil, sweet-and-sour, and cherry sauce.

PHIL-AM FOODS. 40-03 70th St. Roosevelt Ave., 899-1797. M, T, Th–Su 9:00 a.m.–8:00 p.m., W 9:00 a.m.–2:00 p.m.

Phil-Am is a well-known supplier of Filipino prepared foods and groceries. Try the delicious Filipino version of the Spanish *longaniza*, a cured pork sausage; if you're squeamish, don't ask how it's made!

LU CHANG BAKERY. 56-05 Roosevelt Ave. corner of 56th St. M–Sa 7:00 a.m.–7:00 p.m., Su 11:00 a.m.–7:00 p.m.

While exploring Woodside, stop in for delicious steamed buns filled with mini-meatballs of chicken, pork, or rice; a festive green tea roll; halo-halo drinks made of cream and milk; and literally ten different kinds of bubble teas.

Other Interesting Neighborhood Shops

A QUILTER'S NOTION. 59-08 Woodside Ave. at 59th St., 424-4691. M–F 11:00 a.m.–6:00 p.m., Sa–Su 11:00 a.m.–6:00 p.m.

Jammed with gorgeous, moderately priced cotton fabrics, A Quilter's Notion offers a full menu of on-site bilingual sewing classes in such skills as dressmaking, quilting, knitting, and crocheting, both for kids and adults. Fabrics run about $8–10 a yard. This spacious fabric store is brand-new as we go to press.

GEMINI CUT GLASS. 55-02 37th Ave. at 55th St., 397-8200. M–F 8:00 a.m.–4:00 p.m.

Want a Louis XIV chandelier? An art deco sconce? Gemini custom-makes and restores chandeliers. They also design prototype chandeliers for brands such as Ralph Lauren and William Sonoma. Gemini's client list includes auctioneers Sotheby's and Christie's, the Russian Tea Room, and various Trump palaces. If you want to buy a fixture or repair your favorite antique fixture, Gemini has a collection of antique lights, including crystal prisms, arms, and column parts, with crystal chandelier parts dating to the 1930s.

LIBRERIA CALIMA BOOKS AND RECORDS. 56-15 Roosevelt Ave. at 56th St., 478-9820. Daily 11:00 a.m.–8:30 p.m.

A large and interesting collection of Spanish-language books by well-known contemporary novelists as well as translations of classics such as Plato and Sartre are sold here.

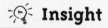 Insight

Globalization? Right on Your Block.

Everyone's talking about globalization, and, in a way, it's happening right here in Queens. Take an imaginary Saturday morning walk with, say, a resident of upscale Forest Hills. You emerge from the gym, waved good-bye from a Senegalese woman sitting at the desk. On the street, you pass some Mexican guys selling bagels, and go into a French bakery for a cup of coffee and pastry made by the baker who is of Indian ancestry, grew up in Uganda, and studied in France. A few stores down is the Chinese laundry where the woman speaks a few words of comfort Yiddish, as in "schlepping the shirts." Next door at the pizzeria, which is, of course, Italian, the waiter is from Bosnia. Adjacent, the big natural food stand is run by a Korean immigrant. You've barely walked one block, yet seen half the world.

What does it all mean? Economic development experts certify that immigration has revitalized many Queens neighborhoods, as new mom-and-pop businesses catering to different appetites open. For born-and-bred Americans, this spicy, complex yet appealing ethnic stew is about more than just money. It seems to add to the quality of life and enhance both tolerance and urbanity.

Queens, ladies and gentleman, has gone global.

19

The Airports: JFK and LaGuardia

THINGS TO DO AND PLACES TO GO NEAR NEW YORK'S AIRPORTS

Queens is home to two of New York City's three main airports, John F. Kennedy International Airport and LaGuardia Airport.

If you are traveling via either LaGuardia or JFK, and have time to kill while waiting for a connecting flight, why not have a little fun? There are numerous places to go for a good, inexpensive meal in nearby Queens neighborhoods, as well as a few restaurants where you can have a business meeting without bothering to cab into Manhattan. From JFK, you can even check your luggage, hop a cab, and spend a few hours at a big beautiful Atlantic Ocean beach, or take the kids to a working farm if you have a few hours between flights. If you're stuck at LaGuardia and are traveling light (there's no luggage storage there), you can go to Jackson Heights for Indian food, go to Astoria and pick up some Greek foods to bring along on your trip, nip into Flushing Meadows–Corona Park to see the one-of-a-kind Panorama of New York City, or go to Corona for a visit to the Louis Armstrong House. All of the above are viable, too, if you're a New Yorker returning home from a trip and want to detour for a meal or outing before reentering your real life.

The airports have a huge impact on Queens. JFK and LaGuardia airports were responsible for 328,000 jobs and more than $38 billion in New York State economic activity in 2004. Many airline staff live in the borough and JetBlue's headquarters is located in Kew Gardens. Of course, in certain parts of Queens, such as Woodside, you see and hear the airplanes all the time.

☞ **TIP: Traveler's Advisory: Transportation.** The fastest way to get from the airports to destinations *in Queens* is by car and cab (or radio car service). The cheapest is to use the New York City transit system. There's a combo subway-light rail service to JFK, but only buses to LaGuardia. (There's no direct subway or train connection.)

If you need transportation *between* JFK and LaGuardia airports there are several options, and all will take thirty to forty-five minutes. **NEW YORK AIRPORT SERVICE EXPRESS BUS** (875-8200). Costs about $12 and runs every thirty minutes, 7:30 a.m.–8:00 p.m.; allow forty-five minutes. A metered taxi ride will cost between $25–30, and take about a half hour. A private limousine or van is the most expensive option. You can find one through the Ground Transportation Information Counter in the Airport Baggage Claim Area. For transfer information to Newark Airport in New Jersey, see www .panynj.gov.

John F. Kennedy Airport (JFK)

WHERE IT IS: Southeastern Queens County, New York City, on Jamaica Bay.
HOW TO GET THERE: AirTrain. You can get to JFK in sixty to seventy-five minutes for a total of $7 (one way) by using AirTrain. To get to AirTrain, you must take either the LIRR or subway to Jamaica, Howard Beach, or the Sutphin Blvd.-Archer Ave. stop, where you can get on the AirTrain. Travel time is about an hour and a quarter from JFK to mid-Manhattan. AirTrain runs every four to eight minutes from 6:00 a.m.–11:00 p.m., and every twelve minutes from 11:00 p.m.–6:00 a.m. (See p. 189.) Directions to JFK by car are on the Web site (see below).
WHAT'S NEARBY: Howard Beach, Jamaica, Jamaica Bay, Ozone Park, Richmond Hill, the Rockaways (and Long Island).
NOTE: As in previous chapters, I list only nearby neighborhoods covered in this book.
FOR INFORMATION: 244-4444. www.panynj.gov/aviation/jfkframe.htm.

Kennedy Airport is *huge*. Just to quantify the vast size of this operation: In 2004 more than 320,000 planes moved in and out of JFK, carrying more than 37 million passengers, 1.8 million tons of air cargo, and nearly 90,000 tons of air mail.

The first commercial flights here began on July 1, 1948. Built on the site of the old Idlewild Golf Course, this airport was formally dedicated as New York International Airport in 1948. It was rededicated on December 24, 1963, as John F. Kennedy International Airport, one month and two days after the assassination of John F. Kennedy. 🏛 Terminal 5, also known as TWA Flight Center, is a landmark designed by architect Eero Saarinen. It opened in 1962 when air travel was just beginning to become affordable. Its design has been heralded as an expression of optimism in technology and an embrace of the age of air travel. It was among the first airports to introduce baggage carousels, satellite gates, and other features common today.

A $9 billion public-private redevelopment is resulting in new passenger terminals, more efficient roadway systems, and new parking garages. JetBlue, JFK's busiest carrier, is building a new twenty-six-gate terminal behind the existing landmark TWA building, scheduled to open in 2008–9. It will connect with Air-Train JFK. The new terminal will enable JetBlue to double its number of daily flights.

JFK is operated by the Port Authority of New York and New Jersey under a lease with the City of New York.

JFK PRACTICAL MATTERS

Overnight Baggage Check
There are two places in JFK where you can check your bags while you go explore Queens for a few hours or a full day. To access these storage places you need full photo ID (and passport if you are an international traveler), plus a ticket showing that you are en route to somewhere. Terminal 4 Arrivals, 751-4020, open 24 hours. Terminal 1 Arrivals, near Alitalia and Olympic Airlines, 751-2947, www.panynj.gov/aviation/jsbsfram.htm. 7:00 a.m.–11:00 p.m. Both cost $4.00–$16.00 per day depending on size.

Hotels for Same-day and Overnight
Airport area hotels may offer cheaper-than-Manhattan rates. If you want to freshen up, shower, nap or use a hotel gym, you can sometimes get a day-use rate (usually up to a third the price of an overnight rate), but these must be booked on a same-day or day-before arrival basis. For overnight stays, you will find accommodations booths at LaGuardia and JFK terminals 1, 4, and 7. These are affiliated with a Norwegian-based company called Hotel Express (www.hotelexpress.com). Or you can book ahead on-line with the same for rates with deep discounts off rack rates (up to 50 percent) but only with a $150 annual membership card.

TWENTY-EIGHT PLACES TO PLAY NEAR JFK
There are over two dozen nearby destinations that you can enjoy without hassling with traffic getting in and out of Manhattan. There are museums: the home of Louis Armstrong, P.S. 1 Contemporary Art Center, and a movie museum called the Museum of the Moving Image. You can play golf, ride a horse, bet on a horse, surf in the Atlantic Ocean, eat at an incredibly good ethnic restaurant, or just get out of that stale airport environment and go to the movies.

Each destination takes about ten to thirty minutes by cab and some are easily reached by public transportation. Getting back to the airport, you can take a subway or call a car that will generally arrive within ten minutes of your call. (Most of the destinations listed here will be able to call a local car service for you.) If you are on a tight schedule, then double the estimated cab times during rush hour, which is 7:00 a.m.–9:00 a.m. and 4:30 p.m.–6:30 p.m., or during inclement weather. A ten-mile cab ride in Queens may cost $15–25 depending on traffic.

KEY TO SYMBOLS

+ means a place is okay for a business meeting

* means a place is located in Jamaica, and can be reached by AirTrain, the fast rail service that runs from JFK to Jamaica ($5 each way; ten min.).

** means a place is located in Forest Hills or Jackson Heights, and can be reached by AirTrain to Jamaica and then a switch to the Long Island Railroad or a NYC subway, both from the Jamaica station.

SEVEN DIFFERENT ETHNIC CUISINES WORTH THE CAB FARE

There's no need to settle for standard chain food restaurants if you have a few hours between flights at JFK. Some of the following are good places for business meetings, too.

Get some Italian comfort food. For an informal meal, try pizza and Italian specialties at La Villa Pizzeria (see p. 264) or Lenny's Clam Bar (see p. 264). Both are in Howard Beach. Or, if you have time, go to Park Side Restaurant (p. 82), (11 miles; 25 min.) in Corona.

Have an authentic Indian meal at Jackson Diner (see p. 172) and explore Little India in Jackson Heights ** (10 miles; 25 min.)

Feed your inner carnivore at Argentinean La Portena Restaurant y Parrillada (see p. 173) in Jackson Heights ** + (10 miles; 25 min.).

Experiment with Korean cuisine at Kum Gang San (see p. 116) in Flushing + (11 miles; 20 min.).

Go for excellent Chinese food, in a setting that couldn't be more authentic: Chinatown in Flushing. For Szechuan see Spicy and Tasty (see p. 117), and for dim sum go to Gum Fung (p. 115), (11 miles; 20 min.).

Sample some of New York's best Thai cuisine at Sripraphai (see p. 284) in Woodside + (11 miles; 25 min.).

Relax and have a pint at one of New York's few remaining German beer gardens, which also has a restaurant at the Bohemian Hall & Beer Garden in Astoria (see p. 49) (12 miles; 25 min.).

SIX "ONLY IN NEW YORK" DESTINATIONS (THAT ARE REALLY "ONLY IN QUEENS")

Sure, the city's big-gun cultural institutions seem clustered in Manhattan, but because this is New York, even outlying cultural institutions are extraordinary. Quite a few are within reasonable driving distance from JFK.

Go to a Mets game at Shea Stadium (see p. 127) in Flushing Meadows–Corona Park (10 miles; 25 min.).

See the tennis greats at the USTA Billie Jean King National Tennis Center (see p. 127) in Flushing Meadows–Corona Park (10 miles; 25 min.).

Visit the Louis Armstrong House (see pp. 79–80) in Corona (11 miles; 25 min.).

See contemporary art at an affiliate of the Museum of Modern Art called P.S. 1 (see pp. 206–7) in Long Island City. In the same area, explore the Noguchi Museum (see p. 206) or Fisher Landau Center for Art (see pp. 205–6) (15 miles; 30 min.).

Get some real perspective in life by seeing the world's largest scale model of New York City. It's called the Panorama of the City of New York, and it's at the Queens Museum of Art (see pp. 129–30). While you're there, take your photo in front of a huge metal globe, the Unisphere, a relic of the 1964–65 World's Fair. All in Flushing Meadows–Corona Park (10 miles; 25 min.).

Bring a bouquet to the graves of some jazz greats. The grave of the original "Mr. Bojangles" is at the Cemetery of the Evergreens (see p. 240) in Ridgewood (14 miles; 30 min.). The graves of Louis Armstrong, Johnny Hodges, and Dizzy Gillespie are at Flushing Cemetery (see p. 108) in Flushing (10 miles; 25 min.).

FIVE OUTDOOR ADVENTURES THAT DON'T FEEL AT ALL LIKE NEW YORK CITY

The Big Apple is not all concrete and skyscrapers! Near JFK there are beaches and nature preserves, golf courses, and more.

Go on a nature walk in a national wildlife refuge at Jamaica Bay Wildlife Refuge (see pp. 258–59) in the Rockaways (9 miles; 20 min.).

Rent a horse for a ride through beautiful Forest Park (see pp. 137–39) in Forest Hills** (9 miles; 20 min.).

Go for a three-mile stroll or a run along an Atlantic Ocean boardwalk at

Rockaway Beach (see p. 257). (IMPORTANT: swim only when a lifeguard is on duty.) (12 miles; 25 min.)

Get a tan and body-surf at a classic Atlantic Ocean beach at Riis Park (see p. 257) in the Rockaways (12 miles; 25 min.).

Practice your golf swing and play 9- or even 18-holes at the public Forest Park Golf Course (see p. 139) in Forest Hills (9 miles; 20 min.).

FOUR MINITRIPS TO ENTERTAIN TRAVEL-TIRED KIDS

Nothing is as dreary as trying to entertain a child on a long layover in the airport. There's no need to struggle; there are lots of options for entertaining kids en route, without having to go into Manhattan.

Take younger kids to the Queens County Farm Museum (see pp. 73–74). It's a working farm with a museum, historic home, and petting zoo in Floral Park (10 miles; 20 min.).

Let them burn off some energy at Rockaway Skate Park (see p. 260) in Rockaway Park (12 miles; 25 min.).

Treat the kids to an old-fashioned ice cream sundae at Eddie's Sweet Shop (see p. 147) in Forest Hills (14 miles; 30 min.).

Take the family to the movies or a movie museum.

THREE MALLS WHERE YOU CAN SPEND TIME AND MONEY

If you want to shop while waiting for the next flight then you have some options in Queens, just a few of which are listed here. With 2.2 million residents, you can rest assured there are stores in the borough!

Check out Queens Center Mall (see p. 92) in East Elmhurst (3 miles; 10 min.).

Splurge at a new upscale mall called Shops at Atlas Park (see pg. 234) in Glendale (8 miles; 20 min.).

Visit a unique Chinatown mall (11 miles; 20 min.) at Flushing Mall (see p. 118) in Flushing.

TWO PLACES TO GO SEE A MOVIE

Queens has a long and prestigious history in the filmmaking business, so you can certainly go to a regular movie theater here, but if you can, visit the Museum of the Moving Image in Astoria** (see p. 37; 13 miles; 25 min.).

Take yourself and your significant other to an art flick at Austin Cinema (see p. 156) in Kew Gardens (12 miles; 20 min.).

THE AIRPORTS: JFK AND LAGUARDIA

ONE RACETRACK

Last but not least, while away some hours at Belmont Racing Track (though it's not really in Queens). Check out the weekend and holiday breakfast special when you can watch Thoroughbreds train in the morning (516) 488-6000 (9 miles; 20 min.).

LaGuardia Airport (LGA)

WHERE IT IS: Bordering on Flushing Bay and Bowery Bay.
HOW TO GET THERE: Car, taxi, shuttle, M60 bus (every half hour), and water shuttle.
WHAT'S NEARBY: Astoria, East Elmhurst, Flushing Meadows–Corona Park, Jackson Heights.
FOR INFORMATION: 533-3400. www.panynj.gov/aviation/lgaframe.htm or www.nyctourist.com.

Just eight miles from Manhattan, LaGuardia is one of two airports in Queens, and one of three major New York City area airports. It is comprised of a Central Terminal Building and three additional separate terminals (the U.S. Airways Terminal, the Delta Terminal, and the Delta Shuttle/Marine Air Terminal). Two buses connect the terminals. In 1947 the airport was named LaGuardia Airport, after New York City's Mayor Fiorello LaGuardia.

LAGUARDIA PRACTICAL MATTERS

As of this writing there is no luggage storage at LaGuardia. Passengers with multiple big suitcases may not be allowed on public transportation. Customer service reps are identified by red jackets. The Central Air Terminal has wireless Internet Service (WiFi) throughout the facility.

PLACES OF INTEREST AT THE AIRPORT

FIGS PIZZA. Terminal B, 446-7600. Daily 11:00 a.m.–8:00 p.m.

An oasis when you're stranded in an airport desert of fast food joints, Figs is a real restaurant serving both gourmet pizzas and a smattering of Italian dishes. This respite is part of a network owned by Todd English, a star chef. Bostonians know that Figs is a popular destination on Charles St. in Boston and in Wellesley, Massachusetts.

🏛 MARINE AIR TERMINAL

Built over sixty-five years ago as one of the numerous projects undertaken in conjunction with New York's World Fair of 1939–40, the Marine Air Terminal was designed to appeal to the upscale tastes of the few who could then afford to fly. The terminal was built for Pan American Airlines clipper ships—huge airplanes called flying boats—which made the transatlantic flights. The excitement of the early period of commercial transatlantic air travel is evident in the building; note, for instance, the outside terra-cotta decorative frieze with flying fish, and the 237-foot-long WPA mural in the rotunda simply called *Flight,* by abstract impressionist James D. Brooks (1942). The mural is the largest created under the WPA program. Today the Marine Air Terminal is used by commuter airlines, air taxis, private aircraft, Signature Flight Support, a fixed-base operator (FBO), and a private weather service.

EIGHTEEN PLACES TO PLAY NEAR LAGUARDIA

It's easy to get to Astoria, Flushing, or Jackson Heights from LaGuardia Airport. That means you can go to a museum, have a good ethnic meal, or, if you have time and the inclination, see a ball game, or even take a swim at Astoria Pool in the summer. A cab will cost less than $15 to any of these neighborhoods. Outbound travelers can easily return to the airport after visiting a venue in Queens. Those staying in the Big Apple can get a cab or catch a subway from any of these Queens neighborhoods to anywhere in Manhattan or the city.

You can easily get cabs at the airport, of course. It's smart to plan ahead about getting back to the airport, too. New York City yellow taxi cabs, commonplace in Manhattan, are not always cruising the streets in Queens. So you're better off calling a radio car service, which will arrive within ten to fifteen minutes of your call. You can also reach any of the listed LaGuardia destinations by the N60, Q33, or Q48 bus. Schedules do change, so double-check at www.panynj.gov/aviation/lgaframe.htm. Leave ample time to return to the airport if you have a scheduled flight. Whether going by car service, cab, or bus, beware of rush hour, between 7:00 a.m.–9:00 a.m., and 4:30 p.m.–6:30 p.m., which can double your travel time.

Each listing that follows indicates how far the destination is and how long it should take to drive one way in normal traffic. Cab fare one way will range from $10 to $15. See neighborhood chapters or the Subject Index for lists of car services for your return. (See Key to Symbols on p. 291.)

SIX PLACES NEAR LAGUARDIA WHERE YOU CAN GET GOOD FOOD

Once you get off the highways near LaGuardia Airport, you're in some wonderful New York City neighborhoods. And they're not far, either. Here are some places to grab a bite before or after a flight.

Imagine you're in Mykonos by feasting on Greek cuisine at Stamatis (see p. 43) in Astoria (1.5 miles; 10 min.).

Enjoy good, spicy Indian cuisine at Jackson Diner (see p. 172) in Jackson Heights (under 2 miles; 10 min.).

Indulge in some serious beef-eating at an Argentinean restaurant at La Portena Restaurant y Parrillada (see p. 173) in Jackson Heights + (2 miles; 10 min.).

Go to one of the city's best Thai restaurants at Sripraphai (see p. 284) in Woodside (2 miles; 10 min.).

Have some exceptional Italian food at Piccola Venezia + (see p. 47) and Trattoria L'Incontro (p. 48), both in Astoria (about 2 miles; 10 min.).

Lift your stein for a pint at the German beer garden and restaurant at the Bohemian Hall & Beer Garden (see p. 49) in Astoria. (2 miles; 12 min.).

FIVE PLACES TO GET ETHNIC TAKE-OUT YOU WON'T FIND IN OSHKOSH

Queens is the most diverse county in the United States, so there's really fresh, authentic food everywhere. Why settle for fast-food chains in the airport when you can get the real thing to take home, or take with you on your journey?

Grab some real New York bagels 24/7 at Bagel Oasis. Yes, that's in Queens! (see p. 157) (6 miles; 15 min.).

Store up on excellent Greek imported olives at Titan Foods (see p. 53) in Astoria (1.5 miles; 10 min.).

Sample honey-laden bakery goods at Middle Eastern Laziza Sweets (see p. 51) in Astoria (1.5 miles; 10 min.).

Buy a year's supply of mango chutney, twenty-five-pound-sacks of rice, and other Indian imported groceries at Patel (see p. 180) in Jackson Heights (under 2 miles; 10 min.).

Wander to your heart's content through the huge Hong Kong Supermarket (see p. 92) and Han Ah Reum Market (p. 118), both in Flushing (5 miles; 12 min.).

FOUR "ONLY IN QUEENS" DESTINATIONS THAT REALLY ARE WORTH THE TRIP

You're already in Queens, so make the most of it and visit some of the cultural institutions that you just can't see anywhere else. Here are several.

Go to a Mets game at Shea Stadium (see p. 127) in Flushing Meadows–Corona Park (10 miles; 25 min.). While you're there, visit the tennis greats at the USTA Billie Jean King National Tennis Center (see pp. 127–28) in Flushing Meadows–Corona Park (10 miles; 25 min.).

Visit the Louis Armstrong House (see pp. 79–80) in Corona (11 miles; 25 min.).

See contemporary art at an affiliate of the Museum of Modern Art called P.S. 1 (see pp. 206–7) in Long Island City. In the same area, explore the Noguchi Museum (see p. 206) or Fisher Landau Center for Art (see pp. 205–6), (15 miles; 30 min.).

Get some real perspective in life by seeing the world's largest scale model of New York City. It's called the Panorama of the City of New York, and it's at the Queens Museum of Art (see pp. 129–30). While you're there, take your photo in front of a huge metal globe, the Unisphere, a relic of the 1964–65 World's Fair. All in Flushing Meadows–Corona Park (10 miles; 25 min.).

THREE FUN PLACES TO RELAX BETWEEN FLIGHTS

One of the stressful aspects of air travel is unexpected delays. If you find yourself at LaGuardia with hours on your hands, here are some off-site ways to relax.

Visit a marvelous hands-on movie at Museum of Moving Image (p. 37) in Astoria** (2 miles; 10 min.).

Practice your golf swing and play 9 or even 18 holes at the public course at Kissena Park (see p. 99) (7 miles; 20 min.).

Do some laps and enjoy views at the Astoria Pool (see pp. 34–35). Note, however, there are no storage facilities and you must bring your own lock (2 miles; 10 min.).

☛ **TIP: Traveler's Advisory: Getting There.** You can drive or take a cab. But you can also get to the above by bus! You can take the M60 bus from all terminals to Astoria (see p. 31). (The M60 runs only once every thirty minutes.) The Q33 bus runs every twenty or so minutes from all terminals except the Marine Air Terminal to Jackson Heights (see p. 162), where there are Indian and Latino restaurants and shops. (From the Marine Air Terminal you can catch the Q47 to Jackson Heights.) The Q48 bus runs every fifteen minutes from all terminals and goes to Main St. in Flushing (see p. 95) where there are Asian restaurants and shops.

Also, on weekend afternoons, LaGuardia travelers who time it right can pick up the Culture Trolley from the LaGuardia Marriott (205 Ditmars Blvd.) and get a free ride to all the sights at Flushing Meadows–Corona Park and also into Jackson Heights (see p. 162).

In sum, there's no reason to moan and groan about sitting for hours in a New York City airport. Stuck with a delayed flight or overnight layover? Well, there are plenty of things to do outside the airports, right in Queens.

Tours

There are many different ways to see Queens, and we suspect that there will be more and more tours offered in the future. Check local listings for eating tours and seasonal festivals. Most of the tours listed below are described in the book (as indicated by "see p. xxx"); those that aren't are briefly described below.

ART, CULTURE, AND MUSIC TOURS

Art Tours

Culture Trolley (transportation to sites, no tour), Flushing Meadows–Corona Park (see p. 126).

Long Island City Cultural Alliance (see pp. 210–11).

Open Studio Tour, Long Island City, 784-2935, www.licartists.org (see pp. 211). An annual October event, with more than a dozen studios representing the work of many sculptors, painters, photographers, and more.

Music Tours

Queens Jazz Trail (see Flushing Council on Culture and the Arts, see p. 105).

Louis Armstrong House (see pp. 79–80).

HISTORICAL AND ARCHITECTURAL TOURS

Historical/Architectural Walking Tours Run by Organizations

Bayside Historical Society and Museum (see p. 64).

Fort Tilden, Fort Totten, U.S. Park Rangers (see p. 261 and pp. 60–61).

Greater Astoria Historical Society (see p. 216).

Jackson Heights Tours (Jackson Heights Beautification Group, see p. 167).

Jacob Riis Park, tours by U.S. Park Service (see p. 257).

Lawrence Family Cemetery (see p. 40).

Museum of the City of New York, (212) 534-1672, www.mcny.org.

Municipal Art Society, (212) 935-3960, www.mas.org. The Municipal Arts Society occasionally offers tours of Queens, focusing on architecture, public art, urban planning and design, and historic preservation. Destinations vary, but, for instance, in 2005 featured Jackson Heights and Gantry Plaza State Park.

Queens Historical Society (see p. 109).

Richmond Hill Historical Society and Museum (see p. 230).

Self-Guided Quick History/Architectural Tours, and Neighborhood Itineraries

Itineraries for Rockaways (see pp. 250–51).

Itinerary for Long Island City (see p. 201).

#7 Subway "National Historic Trail" (Obtain brochure *7: The International Express* from the Queens Borough President's Office, p. 156).

Old Astoria Village (see pp. 40–41).

Cemetery of the Evergreens (see p. 240).

Self-Guided Tour of Forest Hills Gardens (see pp. 146–47).

Self-Guided Tour of Flushing (see p. 110).

Self-Guided Tour of Historic Jackson Heights (see pp. 168–69).

Self-Guided Tour: Jamaica Sites on the National Register of Historic Places (see pp. 193–94).

Hunter's Point Historic District Walking Tour (see p. 217).

Self-Guided Tour: Richmond Hill Historic District (see p. 230).

A Walk Through Historic Ridgewood (see pp. 242–43).

One-Stop Tours of House Museums

Bowne House (see pp. 102–3).

Living Museum at Creedmoor Psychiatric Center (see p. 73).

Friends (Quaker) Meeting House (see p. 109).

Kingsland Homestead Museum, Louis Armstrong House (see pp. 103 and 79–80).

Lewis H. Latimer House and Museum (see p. 103).

Onderdonk House (see p. 243).

Poppenhusen Institute (see pp. 108–9).

Queens County Farm Museum (aka Colonial Farmhouse Restoration Society of Bellerose) (see pp. 73–74).

Rufus King Manor Museum and Park (see pp. 192–3).

Voelker Orth Museum, Bird Sanctuary, and Victorian Garden (see p. 104).

ECLECTIC TOURS

Big Apple Greeter (see p. 302).

Open House New York (OHNY) program, (917) 626-6869, event hotline (917) 583-2398. www.ohny.org. ONHY organizes weekends of free public access to exceptional sites, many normally closed to the public, as well as tours, talks, walks, performances, and family programs. A special Kids! program includes tours and design workshops, plus photography and drawing contests. In Queens 2005 sites included the East District 7 Annex Garage, Flushing Council on Culture and the Arts, Hindu Temple Society of America, Jacob Riis Park Bathhouse, and the Old Quaker Meeting House.

ENVIRONMENTAL TOURS

Alley Pond Environmental Center (see p. 69).

Jamaica Bay Environmental Tours by the American Littoral Society (see p. 259). This environmental organization is dedicated to the environmental integrity of Jamaica Bay and nearby marine environments. Contact them for a schedule of field trips, coastal cleanup, and a Jamaica Bay cruise. Sunset tours of Jamaica Bay twice per year in the spring and fall.

Jamaica Bay Wildlife Refuge, Gateway National Recreation Area, Rockaway (see pp. 258–59).

LIC Community Boathouse (see p. 203).

TOUR GUIDES FOR HIRE

There are many guides for hire in New York City, and the following lists just a few. The Tourism Department of the Queens Borough President's Office recommended most of the following; others are well-known and well-respected tour guides.

Lee Gelber, 626-7136, nydean@verizon.net.
Jeff Gottlieb, 896-4416.
Jack Eichenbaum, 961-8406, jaconet@aol.com.
Roy Fox, 523-0029.
Daniel Karatzas, 505-9220, Karatzas@verizon.net, Jackson Heights.
Historic New York Tours, (646) 298-8669.
Marc Preven, 575-8451, marc@newroticnewyorkcitytours.com.
Filomena Riviello, 278-3601, fofo58@yahoo.com.
Dmitri Sassov, (917) 804-8466, nyddt@yahoo.com.

SPECIAL OFFER FOR OUT-OF-TOWNERS: FREE PERSONAL COMPANION

Whether you're from New Jersey or New Zealand, you can get a free talk and walk with a Queens resident through a service offered by the New York City tourist office (go to www.bigapplegreeter.org). Called Big Apple Greeters, the volunteer-staffed program is for visitors from out of town staying for a minimum of two nights. The program is designed for informal groups of visitors of one to six people. Visitors who do not speak English will be provided a greeter who speaks their language, if available (thirty languages are represented). You can specify a neighborhood or some special interest (such as art or tennis), or just say, "Queens." (NOTE: These are not professional guides, but New York City residents who volunteer.) To arrange, please fill out a request form a month in advance.

Recommended Web Sites

The following is a short list of sites where you can find up-to-date and general information about Queens. We aren't listing blogs, because they come and go. Please find URLs for individual destinations such as museums in the neighborhood chapters, where they are listed.

FOR GENERAL INFORMATION

About.com, www.queens.about.com
Discover Queens, www.discoverqueens.info
Long Island City Business Development Corp., www.licbdc.org
Queens Borough President's Office, www.queensbp.org
Queens Borough President's Office Culture and Tourism Dept., www.queensbp.org
Queens Chamber of Commerce, www.queenschamber.org
Queens Public Library, www.queens.lib.ny.us

SELECTED LOCAL QUEENS NEWSPAPERS

Queens Courier, www.queenscourier.com
Queens Chronicle, www.zwire.com/site/new
Queens Gazette, www.qgazette.com
Queens Times Ledger, www.timesledger.com
Queens Tribune, www.queenstribune.com/news
The Wave, www.rockawave.com

ALSO: *Newsday,* www.newsday.com, and other daily and weekly New York City–area magazines list special events, etc.

Subject Index

Note: The principal page references to a subject are listed first in this index.

Tandoori Hut (Richmond Hill), 233
Tangra Masala (Elmhurst), 91
Indian/Pakistani (no beef in Indian; no pork
    in Pakistani)
  Ashoka (Jackson Heights), 170
  Delhi Palace (Jackson Heights), 171
  Dimple (Jackson Heights), 171
  Dosa Diner (Jackson Heights), 171
  Dosa Hutt (Flushing), 115
  Jackson Diner (Jackson Heights), 172
  Kababish Restaurant (Jackson Heights),
    173
  Kebab King (Jackson Heights), 173
  Maharaja Sweets and Snacks (Jackson
    Heights), 173
  Punjabi Kebab House (Richmond Hill),
    232
  Santoor Indian Restaurant (Floral Park),
    74
  Tandoori Hut (Richmond Hill), 233
  Tangra Asian Fusion Cuisine (Sunnyside),
    275
  Tangra Masala (Elmhurst), 91
International/Mixed
  Bistro 33 (Astoria), 46
  Restaurant Row (Flushing), 116
Italian
  Alberto's (Forest Hills), 148
  Bella Via (Long Island City), 218
  Dazies (Sunnyside), 274
  Fortunata's (Middle Village), 246
  Gino's Pizza (Far Rockaway), 264
  Il Toscano (Douglaston), 71
  La Villa Pizzeria (Howard Beach), 264
  Lemon Ice King of Corona (Corona), 82
  Lenny's Clam Bar and Restaurant
    (Howard Beach), 264
  Manducati's (Long Island City), 218
  Manetta (Long Island City), 218
  Nick's Pizza (Forest Hills), 147
  Papazzio Restaurant (Bayside), 66
  Park Side Restaurant (Corona), 82
  Piccola Venezia (Astoria), 47
  Plum Tomato (Rockaways), 265
  Ponticello (Astoria), 48
  Punta Dura (Astoria), 212
  Ralph's Famous Italian Ices (Forest Hills),
    147
  Sac's Place (Astoria), 48
  Sapori d'Ischia (Woodside), 284
  Tony's Pizzeria (Corona), 82
  Trattoria l'Incontro (Astoria), 48
Japanese
  Austin House (Forest Hills), 148
  Mickey's Place (Forest Hills), 149
  Minni's Shabu Shabu and Hibachi
    (Flushing), 116
  Narita Sushi (Forest Hills), 149
Korean
  Book Chong Dong (Sunnyside), 274
  Go Hyang Jip (Woodside), 283
  Kum Gang San Korean Restaurant
    (Flushing), 116

Kosher
  Ben's Kosher Deli of Bayside (Bayside), 65
  Cho-Sen Garden (Forest Hills), 149
  Colbeh Restaurant (Kew Gardens Hills),
    157
  Mazur's Market and Restaurant
    (Douglaston), 71
  Salut (Forest Hills), 160
  Vechemy Tashkent (Rego Park), 160
Malaysian
  Penang (Elmhurst), 90
  Sentosa (Flushing), 117
Mexican
  Fiesta Mexicana (Jackson Heights), 172
  5 Burro Café (Forest Hills), 148
  La Flor Bakery, Café and Restaurant
    (Woodside), 284
  Taqueria Coatzingo (Jackson Heights),
    175
Middle Eastern
  Eastern Nights (Astoria), 45
  Egyptian Coffee Shop (Astoria), 45
  Kabab King Palace (Jackson Heights), 173
  Mombar (Astoria), 45
  Sabry's (Astoria), 45
Peruvian
  Inca's (Kew Gardens), 157
  Inti Raymi (Jackson Heights), 172
  Pio Pio (Jackson Heights), 174
  Pollada De Laura (Corona), 82
Pizza
  Bella Via (Long Island City), 218
  Corona Pizza (Corona), 81
  Dee's Brick-Oven Pizza (Forest Hills), 147
  Exclusive Rosa Pizza (Ridgewood), 244
  Famous Pizza (Jackson Heights), 171
  Figs Pizza, LaGuardia, 294
  Gino's Pizza (Far Rockaway), 264
  Manetta (Long Island City), 218
  Nick's Pizza (Forest Hills), 147
  Rose and Joe's Italian Bakery (Astoria), 51
  Sac's Place (Astoria), 48
Polish
  Bona Restaurant (Ridgewood), 244
  Just Like Mother's (Forest Hills), 149
  Kreden's Restaurant (Ridgewood), 244
Salvadoran
  El Nuevo Izalco Restaurant (Woodside),
    283
Spanish
  Meson Asturias (Jackson Heights), 173
Thai
  Arunee Thai (Jackson Heights), 170
  Bann Thai (Forest Hills), 149
  Erawan (Bayside), 65
  Khao Homm (Woodside), 283–84
  Q, a Thai Bistro (Forest Hills), 150
  Rice Avenue (Jackson Heights), 175
  Sripraphai Thai Restaurant (Woodside),
    284
  Tuk Tuk (Long Island City), 219
  Ubol's Kitchen (Astoria), 49
  Zabb Queens (Jackson Heights), 175

Alphabetical Index

Note: The principal page references to a subject are listed first in this index.